New Approaches to Byzantine History and Culture

Series Editors
Florin Curta, University of Florida, Gainesville, FL, USA
Leonora Neville, University of Wisconsin Madison, Madison, WI, USA
Shaun Tougher, Cardiff University, Cardiff, UK

New Approaches to Byzantine History and Culture publishes high-quality scholarship on all aspects of Byzantine culture and society from the fourth to the fifteenth centuries, presenting fresh approaches to key aspects of Byzantine civilization and new studies of unexplored topics to a broad academic audience. The series is a venue for both methodologically innovative work and ground-breaking studies on new topics, seeking to engage medievalists beyond the narrow confines of Byzantine studies.

The core of the series is original scholarly monographs on various aspects of Byzantine culture or society, with a particular focus on books that foster the interdisciplinarity and methodological sophistication of Byzantine studies. The series editors are interested in works that combine textual and material sources, that make exemplary use of advanced methods for the analysis of those sources, and that bring theoretical practices of other fields, such as gender theory, subaltern studies, religious studies theory, anthropology, etc. to the study of Byzantine culture and society.

Aleksandar Jovanović

Michael Palaiologos and the Publics of the Byzantine Empire in Exile, c.1223–1259

palgrave
macmillan

Aleksandar Jovanović
University of the Fraser Valley
Abbotsford, BC, Canada

ISSN 2730-9363　　　　　　ISSN 2730-9371　(electronic)
New Approaches to Byzantine History and Culture
ISBN 978-3-031-09280-0　　　ISBN 978-3-031-09278-7　(eBook)
https://doi.org/10.1007/978-3-031-09278-7

© The Editor(s) (if applicable) and The Author(s), under exclusive license to Springer Nature Switzerland AG 2022
This work is subject to copyright. All rights are solely and exclusively licensed by the Publisher, whether the whole or part of the material is concerned, specifically the rights of translation, reprinting, reuse of illustrations, recitation, broadcasting, reproduction on microfilms or in any other physical way, and transmission or information storage and retrieval, electronic adaptation, computer software, or by similar or dissimilar methodology now known or hereafter developed.
The use of general descriptive names, registered names, trademarks, service marks, etc. in this publication does not imply, even in the absence of a specific statement, that such names are exempt from the relevant protective laws and regulations and therefore free for general use.
The publisher, the authors, and the editors are safe to assume that the advice and information in this book are believed to be true and accurate at the date of publication. Neither the publisher nor the authors or the editors give a warranty, expressed or implied, with respect to the material contained herein or for any errors or omissions that may have been made. The publisher remains neutral with regard to jurisdictional claims in published maps and institutional affiliations.

Cover illustration: History and Art Collection/Alamy Stock Photo

This Palgrave Macmillan imprint is published by the registered company Springer Nature Switzerland AG
The registered company address is: Gewerbestrasse 11, 6330 Cham, Switzerland

Acknowledgements

The completion of this study, which stems from my doctoral project, would not have been imaginable without the support that I have gladly received from a number of people and institutions. A thank you is first and foremost owed to Dimitris Krallis for being an amazing supervisor ready to engage in academic talk at any given moment, as well as a genuine friend, who was always there to help me stay focused and optimistic. I extend my gratitude to all the supervisors and members of the doctorial committee—Thomas Kuehn, Paul Dutton, Cecily Hilsdale, and David Mirhady—whose comments and suggestions have helped me improve this project. Thank you to Sam Stocker for being a very understanding and supportive editor and to Leonora Neville, who initially expressed interest in this project, together with Florin Curta and Shaun Tougher, the series editors of New Approaches to Byzantine History and Culture at Palgrave Macmillan, who took this project onboard.

I owe a thank you to Simon Fraser University's Dean of Graduate and Postdoctoral Studies' Office for the financial support I have received in the form of a Multi-Year Funding Package, which allowed me not to worry about pecuniary matters and to focus on Michael Palaiologos and the public sphere of the Roman Empire in exile. A special thanks goes to the librarians at the Bennett Library at Simon Fraser University who were always able to acquire whatever I requested either through purchase or interlibrary loan, as well as to the baristas of JJ Bean in North Vancouver, who have never failed to provide me with excellent coffee and ambiance at the café I used as my main workspace while writing this book.

A big thank you goes to Adrianna Bakos for being a supportive friend and chair of the Department of History at the University of the Fraser Valley, a place where I have worked since 2018. I extend my gratitude to Nicole Kungle, who made sure that my work schedule left me with enough time to work on my dissertation and then the book project itself, as well as to all my colleagues in the Department of History at the University of the Fraser Valley.

Crossing the Atlantic back in 2014 and settling down in Vancouver took much more patience and courage than I ever could have imagined it would. For being there for me in moments when I lacked both patience and courage, I cannot express enough gratitude to Alex Grammatikos—who has been beyond supportive and patient with me and my peculiarities, while always finding the time to iron out the ESL oddities in my writings, this book included. I am eternally grateful for having had the chance to become friends with Shawna Vickerman, Nicole Vittoz, and Lauren Gilbert, who made my social life in Vancouver pleasant, which in turn allowed me to focus on research and writing with ease.

It would not be possible to conclude this public act of gratitude without mentioning all those who made me what I am today. I am forever grateful to my happily divorced parents, Valentina Šćekić and Dragan Jovanović, for insisting on my learning English from the age of three and for supporting me in all my decisions, even when, at the age of twelve, after having heard several pop songs by Anna Vissi and Despina Vandi (to whom I will always be grateful for introducing the Greek language into my life), I told them I wish to study things Greek, which translated into my graduating with a BA and MA in Classical Philology from the University of Belgrade and a Ph.D. in History from Simon Fraser University. So, thanks for being supportive even when not completely understanding me. Speaking of understanding me, I owe an immense debt to Aleksandra Pavlović for being my friend, even almost a decade into my permanent relocation from Serbia to Canada. Last, but certainly not least, I wish to thank Larisa Orlov Vilimonović for having actively kindled my interest in things Byzantine (in every sense of the term) and for remaining a friend despite the physical distance between us.

Note on Translation and Transliteration

In the present study, I adhere to our contemporary academic standards of naming people, nations, and places by their autochthonous and not Anglicized names. Much as nobody has any qualms (or at least I hope not) with names of people being Aleksandar or Pierre and not exclusively Alexander or Peter, I have decided to extend the same courtesy to the medieval Romans, who are the central actors of the pages to follow. To begin with, then, the term Byzantine and its derivates are used interchangeably with the term Roman and its cognates, although the latter is preferred, for the people under study here perceived themselves mainly as Romans. Also, there is no John or Johannes, but only Ioannes; no Latinized versions of names and places such as Alexius I Comnenus and Dyrrachium, but rather Alexios I Komnenos and Dyrrachion. All this is to say that I have opted to transliterate virtually all Greek proper nouns. At the expense of complete transparency of the graphemes, but for the ease of reading, I have omitted placing lengths on long vowels. Thus, there will be no distinction between ε (*epsilon*) and η (*eta*) or ο (*omikron*) and ω (*omega*). For example, the title hero of the narrative is named Michael Palaiologos and not Michaēl Palaiologos; his arch-nemesis in contemporaneous narratives is named Theodoros II Laskaris and not Theodōros II Laskaris. I have applied the same rules of transliteration to the offices and dignities of the Romans: *megas stratopedarches*, *megas konostaulos*, etc. All other names of Perso-Arabic or Turkish provenance, as well as Italian and

vii

Frankish names, have been transliterated in accordance with existing practices, while, again, omitting placing lengths on long vowels. For example, we find Sulayman ibn Qutlumush and not Solomon ibn Kutlumush, nor the modern Turkish Kutalmışoğlu Süleyman Şah. Finally, it should be noted that there are some exceptions to the rule. Some geographical locations as well as Latin speaking emperors of the Romans have become an integral part of common parlance in English, and thus have been preserved in their Anglicized forms: Constantinople, Constantine the Great, Thessaloniki.

In order to keep up with the consistency of naming practices, I have opted to offer my own translation of all the texts (unless otherwise noted). Having said that, in translating from Greek, I have consulted, where available, existing translations of the sources. Here I wish to emphasize that I have relied heavily on Ruth J. Macrides' translation of Georgios Akropolites' *The History*, as well as Vitalien Laurent's French translation of Georgios Pachymeres' *Historical Relations*.

Contents

1 **Introduction: Meeting the Roman Public**   1
    1.1   *The Empire of the Romans in Exile (1204–1261)*   4
    1.2   *The Empire of Individuals: Communicative Actions and Individual Agency*   11
    1.3   *Biography: A Vehicle for Writing Social History*   16
    1.4   *Places of Communication: The Public Arena*   20
    1.5   *Publics and Actions by Chapters*   27

2 **Making Officials in Exile: The Case of the Palaiologoi**   31
    2.1   *The Palaiologoi: Seven Generations Serving the Empire*   35
    2.2   *Preparing for Greatness: Education at the Imperial Court*   40
    2.3   *Education: A Public Affair*   45
    2.4   *Progymnasmata in Action: Michael Palaiologos' Erudition on Public Display*   52
    2.5   *Like Father Like Son: Andronikos and Michael Palaiologos in the Public Eye*   59
    2.6   *A Useful Life: Andronikos Palaiologos in Provincial Public Service*   62
    2.7   *A Useful Afterlife: The Place of Andronikos Palaiologos in the Public Memory of Thessaloniki*   72

3 **Linking the Golden Chain: The Social Network of Michael Palaiologos**   85
   3.1 *Keeping Checks and Balances Among the Romans*   90
   3.2 *Michael's Trial: A Hot Mess?*   99
   3.3 *A Fresh Start with Old Friends: Imperial Son-in-Law and New Appointment*   106
   3.4 *Theodoros II Laskaris: The Breaker of Chains*   120

4 **"Je veux être calife à la place du calife": Michael Palaiologos in the Saljuq Sultanate of Rum**   129
   4.1 *The Prodigal Son: The Saljuq Sultanate of Rum*   133
   4.2 *The Sultanate of Rum: A Byzantine Haven?*   139
   4.3 *The Roman Diaspora in the Saljuq Sultanate of Rum and Frankish Greece: A Comparison*   144
   4.4 *Flight to the (Un)Known*   151
   4.5 *Michael Palaiologos: A Saljuq Dignitary*   163
   4.6 *There and Back Again*   175

5 **"The Return of the King": Michael Palaiologos Claims Imperial Dignity**   179
   5.1 *Homecoming*   182
   5.2 *The Rhetorical Side of Public Deliberations: Obtaining Public Support for the Mouzalones' Regency*   192
   5.3 *The Violent Side of Public Deliberations: Obtaining Public Support for the Palaiologan Regency*   200
   5.4 *Social Capital and Public Deliberations: Michael Palaiologos, Guardian of the Empire*   205
   5.5 *The Final Countdown: Michael Palaiologos Goes for the Throne*   210
   5.6 PANEM ET CIRCENSES: *Michael Palaiologos and the Public Consensus*   216
   5.7 *The Man Who Wrote the Book*   221

6 **Conclusion**   225
   6.1 *The Publics and Their Wants*   225
   6.2 *Concluding the Conclusion*   229

Bibliography   231

Index   251

Abbreviations

Actes d'Iviron III — Lefort, Jacques, Oikonomidès, Nicolas; Papachryssanthou, Denise, et Kravari Vassiliki éds. *Actes d'Iviron III: de 1204 à 1328.* Paris: Peeters, 1994

Akropolites, *Chronike* — Heisenberg, Augustus, ed. et comm. *Georgii Acropolitae Opera*, I. Lipsiae: B.G. Teubneri, 1903 (editionem anni MCMIII correctiorem curavit P. Wirth, Stuttgart 1978)

Aphthonios, *Progymnasmata* — Rabe, Hugo, ed. *Aphthonii progymnasmata.* Lipsiae: Teubner, 1926

Autoreianos, *Testament* — Migne, Jean-Pail, ed. *Patrologia Graeca* 140. Parisiis: Garnier Fratres, 1865

Blemmydes, *Curriculum* — Munitiz, J.A. ed. *Nicephori Blemmydae Autobiographia sive Curriculum Vitae necnon Epistula Universalior.* Turhout: Brepols, 1984

Blemmydes, *Epitome Logikes* — Migne, Jean-Paul, ed. *Patrologia Graeca* 142. Parisiis: Garnier Fratres, 1863

BMGS — *Byzantine and Modern Greek Studies*
ByzSym — *Byzantina Symmeikta*
BZ — *Byzantinische Zeitschrift*
DOP — *Dumbarton Oaks Paper*
FM — *Fontes Minores*
JÖB — *Jahrbuch der Österreichischen Byzantinistik*

Laskaris, *Letters* — Festa, Nicola, ed. *Theodori Ducae Lascaris Epistulae CCXVII.* Firenza: Istituto di studi superiori pratici e di perfezionamento, 1898

MM	Miklosich, Fraz et Muller, Josef, (eds.), *Acta et diplomata medii aevi sacra et profana* VI vol. Vindobonae: C. Gerold, 1860–1890
ODB	Kazhdan, Alexander P. *Oxford Dictionary of Byzantium*. Oxford: Oxford University Press, 1990
Pachymeres, *Chronikon*	Failler, Albert, éd. et intro., Laurent, Vitalien transl. *Georges Pachymérès Relations historiques*, I. Paris: Les Belles Lettres, 1984
Palaiologos, *Autobiography*	Grégoire, Henri. "Imperatoris Michaelis Palaeologi *De vita sua*." *Byzantion* 29-30 (1959–1960), 447–474
PLP	Trapp, Erich, ed. *Prosopographisches Lexikon der Palaiologenzeit*. Wien: Verlag der Österreichischen Akademie der Wissenschaften, 1976
REB	*Revue des Études Byzantines*
Res Gestae Divi Augusti	Volkman, Hans, ed. and transl. *Res gestae Divi Augusti das Monumentum Ancyranum*. Leipzig: Reisland 1942
Synopsis Chronike	Sathas, Konstantinos, ed. Μεσαιωνικὴ Βιβλιοθήκη VII. Venice: Phoenix, 1894
ZRVI	*Zbornik Radova Vizantološkog Instituta SANU*

LIST OF FIGURES

Fig. 2.1	The Empire of Nikaia and its neighbours c.1228 when Michael Palaiologos was around five years old	36
Fig. 2.2	The surviving structure of the palace at Nymphaion	50
Fig. 2.3	The Empire of Nikaia and its neighbours in 1255 after the conquests in the Balkans during Ioannes III Batatzes' reign	64
Fig. 3.1	The Byzantine House in Melenikon	92
Fig. 4.1	The Empire of Nikaia and its neighbours in 1257, at the time of Michael Palaiologos' flight to and return from the Saljuq Sultanate of Rum	151
Fig. 4.2	The Temple of Augustus and Roma in Ankyra	156

CHAPTER 1

Introduction: Meeting the Roman Public

At 9:00 PM on 18 March 2014, a group of political activists—most of whom were students—stormed and occupied the Legislative Yuan—Taiwan's parliament. Hundreds of student activists decided to occupy Taiwan's parliament in order to turn the political elites', as well as the wider public's, attention to the ruling party's intention to sign the Cross-Strait Service Trade Agreement. According to the protesters, the free trade agreement with the People's Republic of China would heavily infringe on Taiwan's economic and, in the long run, political independence vis-à-vis its mainland counterpart. After twenty-three days of occupation, the ruling Kuomintang party capitulated and offered a public point-by-point review of the document before signing it. Once the agreement between the activists, by now labelled popularly as the Sunflower Movement, and Kuomintang had been reached, the building hosting both the Legislative and Executive Yuan was evacuated.[1]

The news about the occupation of the Yuan took Taiwan by storm and soon hundreds of thousands took to the streets of Taipei to express their approval or disapproval for the Sunflower Movement. This unprecedented event in Taiwan's political culture shook the state as a whole. Riding on

---

[1] For an overview of the event see: I. Rowen, "Inside Taiwan's Sunflower Movement: Twenty-Four Days in the Student Occupied Parliament, and the Future of the Region," *The Journal of Asian Studies* 74 (2015), 5–20.

© The Author(s), under exclusive license to Springer Nature Switzerland AG 2022
A. Jovanović, *Michael Palaiologos and the Publics of the Byzantine Empire in Exile, c.1223–1259*, New Approaches to Byzantine History and Culture, https://doi.org/10.1007/978-3-031-09278-7_1

the tide of the Sunflower Movement, individuals like Huang Kuo-Chang, one of the most vocal activists within the occupied Legislative Yuan, were able to introduce themselves to the wider public as potential long-term alternatives to the existing political establishment. Indeed, a year after the Sunflower Movement, Huang became the leader of the New Power Party and, as its candidate, managed to secure a place for himself in the Legislative Yuan in 2016.

Academics were fairly quick to address the rise of the Sunflower Movement by focusing on the cracks within the Taiwanese governing establishment that social movements used to their advantage to shake up public opinion on the island.[2] The speeches delivered by leading activists and the president of Taiwan, as well as massive public gatherings in the streets of Taipei—all of which were broadcast by main media outlets domestically and internationally—have enabled scholars to analyze the significance of a primarily student-led social movement in shifting the political paradigm in Taiwan and East Asia more broadly. While theoretical and methodological frameworks of academic inquiry deployed to look at the Sunflower Movement have varied greatly depending on researchers' academic interests and educational background, one common thread can be noted: the unrestricted and rapid flow of information has been taken for granted by every scholar. The Yuan was occupied at 9:00 PM; by 9:30 PM, most Taiwanese citizens were aware of what was going on; and by 10:00 PM most of the world could find relevant information about the event in more than a few languages. Thanks to such a rapid spread of communiques targeted at the voting Taiwanese, Huang Kuo-Chang was able to make himself known to the wider public. In the long run, he used the political capital he accumulated during the twenty-three-day occupation of the Yuan to advance his own position in the country's political life. But what happens when an instantaneous and geographically unlimited flow of information is cut off from an individual blocking the Legislative Yuan? What value does the very act of occupation have if the news

---

[2] For instance, see: M.S. Ho "Occupy Congress in Taiwan: Political Opportunity, Threat, and The Sunflower Movement," *Journal of East Asian Studies* 15 (2015), 69–97; Ho, "From Mobilization to Improvisation: The Lessons from Taiwan's 2014 Sunflower Movement," *Social Movement Studies* 17 (2018), 189–202; and Ho, *Challenging Beijing's Mandate of Heaven: Taiwan's Sunflower Movement and Hong Kong's Umbrella Movement* (Philadelphia: Temple University Press 2019).

about it takes days, weeks, or even months to reach the targeted audiences that are supposed to be influenced by the Sunflower Movement? How would Huang Kuo-Chang have become a democratically elected MP in the Legislative Yuan if nobody had heard of him and his speeches outside his immediate circle at the parliament building during his twenty-three-day stay in the Yuan? This anachronistic opening eases us into the process of conceptualizing the complex premodern techniques of information dissemination. The set of what-if questions make us think about the absence of modern means of communication, so that we can start thinking about the challenges of reaching wider audiences. It is with such thoughts in mind that I turn our attention from our contemporary Huang Kuo-Chang to Michael Palaiologos, a thirteenth-century Byzantine magistrate-turned-emperor of the Romans in order to explore the mechanisms of communication which allowed Byzantine aristocrats and courtiers to reach different audiences across the empire.

The medieval Roman Empire remained a centralized state throughout most of its existence, even after the loss of Constantinople in 1204.[3] Yet, the premodern methods available for dissemination of knowledge and information substantially limited the ease of outreach that the reining emperors or their officials could have in reaching their targeted audiences. Scholarly attention has mostly focused on addressing questions revolving around centralized governance in the premodern empire by looking at imperial legislation, administration, and the army.[4] This study aims to

---

[3] For a comparative approach of the centralized Roman Empire vis-à-vis Western European states see: C. Whickham, *Framing the Early Middle Ages: Europe and the Mediterranean, 400-800* (Oxford and New York: Oxford University Press 2005); for the administrative practices of the central government during the period of exile see: M. Angold, *A Byzantine Government in Exile: Government and Society Under the Laskarids of Nicaea, 1204-1261* (Oxford: Oxford University Press 1975); for the attempts to keep the state centralized in the fourteenth and fifteenth centuries see: R. Estangüi Gómez, *Byzance face aux Ottomans: Exercise du pouvoir et contrôle du territoire sous les derniers Paléologues (milieu XIVe – milieu XVe siècle)* (Paris: Publications de la Sorbonne 2014).

[4] For example, see the titles from the preceding footnote together with: J.-C. Cheynet, *Pouvoir et contestations à Byzance (963–1210)* (Paris: Éditions de la Sorbonne 1996); J. Haldon, *Warfare, State, and Society in the Byzantine World* (London: UCL Press 1999); L. Neville, *Authority in Byzantine Provincial Society, 950-1100* (Cambridge, UK and New York et al., 2004); M.C. Bartusis, *Land and Privilege in Byzantium: The Institution of Pronoia* (Cambridge, UK: Cambridge University Press, 2012); and J. Herrin, *Margins and Metropolis: Authority Across the Byzatine Empire* (Princeton and Oxford: Princeton University Press 2013).

examine the ways in which medieval Roman aristocrats engaged different publics—their peers, bureaucrats, and commoners—in order to advance their own careers in the service of the empire. In doing so, the officials as much as the emperor had to account for the different audiences' socio-economic standing when attempting to gain the publics' support. They also had to keep in mind, unlike their modern counterparts—such as Huang Kuo-Chang who relied on mass-media live-broadcast around the country to reach his potential supporters across Taiwan—the limited scope of each action they performed. For instance, Ioannes II Komnenos' building of the Pantokrator monastery in the capital would turn the citizens' attention to the founder and his endeavours to enrich the public landscape of the city.[5] However, this costly project would affect only immediate audiences—both rich and poor—who could witness it; citizens of other provincial cities had nothing to do with the inauguration of this major monastic complex. This meant that both the emperor and leading officials had to make sure to leave their mark on the provincial populace in order to further secure their own positions in the centre.[6] By securing the public consensus for his regime in the provinces, an emperor could reduce the chances of a successful rebellion against his reign; at the same time, a leading aristocrat hoping to advance his own career could gain solid social cache at the imperial court by gaining the support of a major provincial city or local elites. With the focus of this study being on Michael Palaiologos before his enthronement in 1259, I hope to shed more light on modes of communication that the medieval Roman elites had at their disposal to gain the public support of different socio-economic groups across the empire vis-à-vis the emperor and his endeavours to do the same.

1.1 The Empire of the Romans in Exile (1204–1261)

12 April 1204 was one of the most cataclysmic days in the history of the Roman Empire. On this day, the troops of the Fourth Crusade, which

---

[5] For the Pantokrator's urban significance in the Komnenian period, see: P. Magdalino, "The Foundation of the Pantokrator Monastery and its Urban Setting," in S. Kotzabassi (ed.), *The Pantokrator Monastery in Constantinople* (Boston and Berlin: De Gruyter 2013), 33–56.

[6] For example, see the imperial inscriptions in both secular and sacred spaces in the provinces: D. Krallis, *Serving Byzantium's Emperors: The Courtly Life and Career of Michael Attaleiates* (Cham: Palgrave Macmillan 2019), 60–62; S. Gerstel, *Rural Lives and Landscapes in Late Byzantium: Art, Archaeology and Ethnography* (Cambridge: Cambridge University Press 2015), 13–14, 27–28.

had gone astray, sacked the city of Constantinople and, for a brief period, ended the Roman Empire which was to be reconstituted in Asia Minor with the imperial coronation of Theodoros I Laskaris in 1207.[7] While the Roman Empire ceased to exist in 1204, the Romans continued to exist both within and without the borders of the reestablished exilic polities.

The reestablished Roman Empire in exile, oftentimes called the Empire of Nikaia, has received substantial scholarly attention in recent publications which tackle the polity's social, political, cultural, and economic history.[8] Thus, instead of offering a brief synthesis of the empire in exile's history, I suggest that we look at the people who constituted this polity. The hellenophone inhabitants of the empire in exile together with their once-compatriots living in Epeiros, the crusader states such as the Principality of Achaea or the Lusignan Cyprus, and the Saljuq Sultanate of Rum saw themselves simply as Romans.[9] The preferred ethnonym of the people studied in this book will be used throughout the work unapologetically alongside the more conventional term Byzantine and its derivatives.

However, a few words on the ways in which Romanness was manifested in the thirteenth century is in order. Namely, in modern parlance the terms Roman Empire and Romans are almost exclusively used to denote the Roman state from its foundation in the eighth century BCE to roughly the sixth century CE when the anachronistic term Byzantine becomes preferred. The usual explanation behind the preferred term Byzantine rests on the idea that the *original* Roman identity belongs to

---

[7] For the Fourth Crusade and the crusading kingdoms in the Balkans see: P. Lock, *The Franks in the Aegean, 1204–1500* (New York and London: Routledge 2013[2]); F. Van Tricht, *The Latin Renovatio of Byzantium: The Empire of Constantinople (1204–1228)*, P. Longbottom, transl. (Leiden and New York: Brill 2011). On the foundation of the Roman Empire in exile see: Angold, *A Byzantine Government*, 9–36; D. Korobeinikov, *Byzantium and the Turks in the 13th Century* (Oxford: Oxford University Press 2014); and 51–80, D. Angelov, *The Byzantine Hellene: The Life of Theodore Laskaris and Byzantium in the Thirteenth Century* (Cambridge: Cambridge University Press, 2019), 13–36.

[8] For instance, see: Angold, *A Byzantine Government*; D. Korobeinikov, *Byzantium and the Turks*, D. Angelov, *The Byzantine Hellene* among others.

[9] On the Roman identity of the people inhabiting the empire See: A. Kaldellis, *Hellenism in Byzantium: The Transformations of Greek Identity and the Reception of the Classical Tradition* (Cambridge and New York: Cambridge University Press, 2007); A. Kaldellis, *Romanland: Ethnicity and Empire in Byzantium* (Cambridge, MA and London: Harvard University Press 2019); and D. Krallis, "Villages, Towns, Soldiers and the Search for Elusive Byzantine Commons," *ByzSym* 28 (2018), 11–48; for the period of exile see: Angelov, *The Byzantine Hellene*, 202–207.

the polytheistic Latin-speaking Romans. After all the territorial, social, cultural, and economic transformations that the empire and its inhabitants underwent from Octavian Augustus to, say, Alexios I Komnenos, a new label needed to be introduced in order to label the Christian hellenophone empire of the Romans.[10] Thus, after a bit of trial and error, we have ended up with the term Byzantine to denote the medieval Romans, who would not have known that this term could apply to anything but the archaizing name of the capital city of the empire.

The crux of the problem here lies in our own conception of what it *really* means to be a Roman, as in the twenty-first century we tend to perceive Roman identity as static and never evolving, an identity that belongs to but a fragment of the Roman state's long history. The logic would then be that if the mores of a period do not correspond to the polytheistic Latin-speaking city of Rome and its empire with a specific artistic and architectural expression, then we cannot talk about Rome or the Romans. This view is rather reductive and does not allow us to see or explore the ever-changing nature of any identity, the Roman one included. Since the early modern period, what it means to be Roman has been constructed to look a certain way. Thus, it might feel odd for us today to imagine Romans as also being predominantly Christian speakers of Greek who took pride in building domed churches decorated with intricate mosaics and frescoes while engaging with ancient statues and architecture around their urban landscapes; to the medieval Romans this was the only Romanness known to them.[11] Granted, the intelligentsia was

---

[10] For a history of the nomenclature used for the Roman Empire after 476 CE in scholarship see: A. Kalldelis, *Byzantium Unbound* (Leeds: Arc Humanities Press 2019), 1–28. As an example of an extremely forced and severe decoupling of Romanness from the Empire of the Romans after Herakleios due to its not fitting our own modern preconceptions of what means to be Roman see: "In short, the self-proclaimed imperial Romanness of the rulers of post-seventh century Constantinople is a chimera. The losses suffered at the hands of Islam meant that these emperors were now ruling what was as much a successor state to the Roman Empire as any of the new powers of the Roman west a century earlier. My own preference, in fact, is to use 'Byzantine' rather than 'east Roman' from the mid-seventh century, as a reflection of how great a sea change the rising tide of Islam had created in Mediterranean history" (P. Heather, *Empires and Barbarians: The Fall of Rome and the Birth of Europe* [Oxford and New York: Oxford University Press 2012], 381).

[11] For a nuanced discussion on the transformation and evolution of Roman identity in the empire see: D. Whalin, *Roman Identity from Arab Conquests to the Rise of Orthodoxy* (Cham: Palgrave Macmillan 2021).

much aware of the polytheistic past visible in the landscapes as well as in the texts read by the elites.

Adding to the problem of Romanness is its convoluted legacy in medieval Western Christendom. One of the reasons scholars—mostly from the West—opted to use the anachronistic term Byzantium was that the idea of Romanness was alive outside the empire since Christmas of 800 CE, when the *translatio imperii* and *renovatio* of the Roman Empire became a reality for the kings of the Franks and, from the tenth century, their German successors. The title of the Roman emperor, and with it the idea of a Roman state, was more elusive in Western Christendom. That is, the issue of Romanness was a matter of the elites—specifically the pope and the emperor; the vast majority of people living across Western Christendom did not have any connection with nor claim to Roman identity.[12] Political leaders holding the title of the emperor of the Romans in the West were even willing to let go of their claim in order to win the support of the emperors in Byzantium, as was the case with Frederick II of Hohenstaufen in his letters to Ioannes III Batatzes.[13] Contrary to the Western scenario, in the Roman state centred in Constantinople, the empire's inhabitants belonging to all walks of life knew of themselves as Romans primarily. This is to say, the Romanness to which the people ascribed was ever developing. Thus, the Romans of the medieval period relied on common cultural references they shared across the empire. These references belonged to their own world and their own times and not to an antiquarian elitist sense of Romanness connected to Augustus and other emperors, which was reserved for the empire's intelligentsia. What our medieval Romans cared about were Christian heroes such as the Anatolian

---

[12] On the questions of identity and empire in the West see: R. McKitterick, *Charlemagne: The Formation of a European Identity* (Cambridge and New York: Cambridge University Press 2008); R. McKitterick, *History and Memory in the Carolingian World* (Cambridge and New York: Cambridge University Press 2004); A.A. Latowsky, *Emperor of the World: Charlemagne and Construction of Imperial Authority, 800-1229* (Ithaca and London: Cornell University Press 2013); and M. Gabriele, *An Empire of Memory: Charlemagne, the Franks, and Jerusalem Before the First Crusade* (Oxford and New York: Oxford University Press 2011). On Byzantine models used for Western European imperial expression see: C. Raffensperger, *Reimagining Europe: Kievan Rus' in the Medieval World, 988-1146* (Cambridge, MA and London: Harvard University Press 2012), 10–46.

[13] All those Romans under your rule/πάντας τοὺς ὑπὸ σέ Ῥωμαίους (MM IV: 72.). For Frederick II's reasons for doing so and for the use of the terms *Rhomaioi* and *Graikoi* in the correspondence of the exilic Roman Empire see: Kaldellis, *Hellenism in Byzantium*, 368–379.

border warrior Digenis Akritas—of whom we see depictions on pottery from the Peloponnese to as far as Crimea—who were more relatable to their lived realities.[14]

Somewhat comparable to the antiquarian and elitist view on Roman heritage in the West was the trend introduced by some members of the elites in the Roman Empire in exile, who opted to adopt a Hellenic ethnonym to identify themselves. The best example of this trend is found in Theodoros II Doukas Laskaris and his former teacher Nikephoros Blemmydes.[15] However, while these literati used the term Hellenic in some of their rhetorically embellished works—sometimes even to denote the Empire of Nikaia and its inhabitants vis-à-vis the Roman diaspora—the common people of the exilic empire had "a strong awareness of the collective self as 'the Romans.'"[16] While the Hellenic identification promoted by Laskaris and Blemmydes will have long-term echoes for some intellectuals of the Roman world who started adopting this identity towards the end of the empire's tenure,[17] most literati preferred to use the ethnonym Roman to Hellenic in their works (e.g., Nikephoros Gregoras, author of *The Roman History*).

The term Roman used in this book does not try to make the Romans of the thirteenth century equivalent to the Romans of the first century BCE and CE. Michael VIII Palaiologos is no Octavian Augustus and Georgios Akropolites is no Livy; they are their own people who are products of their own times and circumstances. By the thirteenth century, what it meant to be Roman to the Romans changed quite a bit from

---

[14] On the wide spread of Romannes in the empire see: A. Kaldellis, "The Social Scope of Roman Identity in Byzantium: An Evidence-Based Approach," *ByzSym* 27 (2017), 173–210. For the example of Digenis Akritas see: L. Zavagno, *The Byzantine City from Heraclius to the Fourth Crusade, 610-1204: Urban Life After Antiquity* (Cham: Palgrave Macmillan 2021), 105; J. Vroom, "Medieval Ephesos as a Production and Consumption Center," in S. Ladstätter and P. Magdalino (eds.), *Ephesos from Late Antiquity Until the Late Middle Ages: Proceedings of the International Conference at the Research Center for Anatolian Civilizations, Koç University, Istanbul 30th November–2nd December 2012* (Vienna: Österreichisches Archäologisches Institut 2019), 239–240.

[15] Kaldellis, *Hellenism in Byzantium*, 368–388; Angelov, *The Byzantine Hellene*, 202–216.

[16] Angelov, *The Byzantine Hellene*, 203.

[17] G. Steiris, "Byzantine Philosophers of the 15th Century on Identity and Otherness," in G. Steiris, S. Mitralexis and G. Arabatzis (eds.), *The Problem of Modern Greek Identity: From the Ecumene to the Nation-State* (Newcastle upon Tyne: Cambridge Scholars Publishing 2016), 173–199.

the early centuries of the common era. Other than the major linguistic and confessional transformation of Eastern Romanness, the Romans also stopped living exclusively in one polity and they started forming significant diasporic communities.[18] Since the Islamic conquest of Roman lands in Southwest Asia and North Africa, the Roman diaspora grew significantly without having to move anywhere. The same process occurred with the loss of territories in the Balkans, as well as with the establishment of the Saljuq Sultanate of Rum in Asia Minor.[19] Finally, after 1204, most Romans arguably lived under foreign rule rather than under that of their emperor now in Asia Minor.[20] However, in the polycentric Eastern Mediterranean, there was a common consensus among Roman communities living in several different states that their identity was that of the Romans. This Romanness was expressed in a number of ways: it could entail works of vernacular literature talking about Roman exploits vis-à-vis those of their new masters, as is seen in the Greek version of the *Chronicle of Morea* or it could be seen by looking at "[i]nscriptions in the village churches [which] includ[ed] the names of reigning Byzantine emperors, indicating that Constantinople, the city identified with imperial hegemony, was present in the minds of those who worked the land."[21]

The fragmentation of the Roman Empire after 1204 also meant that the exilic Empire of Nikaia now hosted a very homogenous population in comparison to the Komnenian and Angelid periods when the Roman Empire incorporated some territories inhabited by mainly non-Roman elements, such as the Bulgarians and the Albanians. Alongside the Romans though, numerous diasporic communities of Latins, Cumans,

---

[18] For the transformation of Roman identity from the 7th to the tenth centuries see: Whalin, *Roman Identity*. On the multiethnic cohabitation in the Islamicate caliphates see: J. Tannous, *The Making of the Medieval Middle East: Religion, Society, and Simple Believers* (Princeton and Oxford: Princeton University Press 2018).

[19] For the Saljuq Sultanate of Rum and the Roman Empire see: Korobeinikov, *Byzantium and the Turks*; for the empire's policies in the Balkans see: P. Stephenson, *Byzantium's Balkan Frontier: A Political Study of the Northern Balkans, 900-1204* (Cambridge and New York: Cambridge University Press 2000).

[20] For the crusader states and the Roman populace see: Lock, *The Franks in the Aegean*, 266–309.

[21] Gerstel, *Rural Lives and Landscapes*, 172.

and Turks lived in the exilic empire.[22] Regardless of the diasporic communities' presence in the empire, the vast majority of the people were the Romans who had traditionally inhabited Western parts of Asia Minor for generations. The major shift in the population happened mostly in the higher socio-economic stratum of the Empire of Nikaia with the influx of Constantinopolitan aristocrats, who now had to settle in the provinces.[23] This might have come as a shock to many of the leading *oikoi*, who now had to adjust to a significantly more modest lifestyle compared to what they were accustomed to in Constantinople, even though a number of people who counted themselves among the high elites of the empire grew up in the Roman provinces.

After the initial shock and trauma caused by the events of 1204, the Roman Empire in exile under the leadership of Theodoros I Laskaris (1205–1221), followed by that of Ioannes III Batatzes (1222–1254), managed to reestablish the central government—albeit somewhat reduced in the number of civil servants and offices needed to run the state—and to redistribute the lands and properties among the elite refugees who were supposed to occupy the highest positions of power and responsibility in the empire.[24] From its humble beginnings in 1205 to the reconquest of Constantinople in 1261, the exilic emperors of the Romans succeeded in building a viable state with a centralized government able to tax its inhabitants and build up both urban and rural infrastructure. At the same time, after the initial drawbacks during Theodoros I's reign, the period of Ioannes III's reign was marked by a rapid expansion of the empire into

---

[22] On the pre-1204 ethnic diversity found in the Balkan provinces see: P. Stephenson, *Byzantium's Balkan Frontier*. For foreigners in the service of the Empire of Nikaia see: R.J. Macrides, "Introduction," in Georgios Akropolites, *The History* (Oxford: Oxford University Press, 2007), 98; Korobeinikov, *Byzantium and the Turks*, 75–80.

[23] On the aristocratic families from the 10th to the end of the twelfth centuries see: Cheynet, *Pouvoir et contestation*, 249–286. For the aristocratic *oikoi* that survived from the twelfth century into the Palaiologan period see: A.E. Laiou, "The Byzantine Aristocracy in the Palaeologan Perdiod," *Viator* 4 (1973), 131–151; K.-P. Matschke and F. Tinnefeld, *Die Gesellschaft im späten Byzanz. Gruppen, Strukturen und Lebensformen* (Köln, Weimar and Wien: Böhlau Verlag 2001), 18–31, 158–220. For the aristocratic *oikoi* originating mostly from Constantinople in the Empire of Nikaia see: Korobeinikov, *Byzantium and the Turks*, 61–68.

[24] Angold, *A Byzantine Government*, 147–296; Korobeinikov, *Byzantium and the Turks*, 69–74.

the Balkans, culminating in the reconquest of Constantinople in the early reign of Ioannes IV Laskaris and Michael VIII Palaiologos.

1.2 The Empire of Individuals: Communicative Actions and Individual Agency

The present study explores the ways in which individual agents employed different public arenas in order to establish a widespread popular consensus for their own political agendas among specific societal interest groups operating in the exilic Roman polity centred in Asia Minor. That is, by examining active agency of individuals in the public life of the Roman state in exile (1204–1261), I demonstrate the necessity of transclass engagement with the Roman body politic as a prerequisite to advancing one's political career. Of course, one has to keep in mind the quite limited premodern means of disseminating ideas about one's merit and abilities among the elites and the wider populace alike. In exploring the ways in which individual state officials promoted themselves to a wide range of social groups as ideal candidates for public offices, I chart and analyze specific communicative methods—from pieces of court rhetoric and historiography to vernacular poems and wall inscriptions—employed by statesmen in order to gain the needed support of the empire's publics. By examining the means of public self-promotion in the medieval Roman Empire, I hope to be able to contribute to the wider conversation in the field of Byzantine and Medieval Studies about the complicated role that elites and the general populace played in shaping the governing practices of any medieval polity.

In the second half of the twentieth century, scholars working on the premodern Mediterranean have begun to look towards sociological and anthropological theories to explain the ways in which vast multi-ethnic (or at least multi-lingual) empires operated and endured over time. The introduction of theoretical frameworks led scholars to deploy academic jargon previously unused in the historical examination of premodern polities. Thus, nowadays, we are quite comfortable talking about *public consensus* in Rome, *political and legal culture* in Han China, or the *body politic* in the seventeenth-century Ottoman Empire.[25] The rise of such conceptual models of inquiry has led scholars working on various premodern empires to reexamine the ways in which we imagine the very essence of these polities' social, economic, political, and cultural practices.

Diving into the sea of available concepts, Clifford Ando in his *Imperial Ideology and Provincial Loyalties* employed Jürgen Habermas' theory of communicative action's significance in maintaining consensus in the public sphere of bourgeois societies in Early Modern and Modern Europe.[26] Ando's goal was to adjust Habermas' observations and make them suitable for an examination of the ways in which the Roman Empire of the first two centuries CE established and maintained rather peaceful coexistence for its inhabitants regardless of their social, economic, racial, or linguistic background. There was, however, a catch or two. In his analysis Ando had to disregard such means of information dissemination as newspapers or affordable printed books that were employed by modern Europeans in public debates. Habermas' idea about the value of communicative actions in maintaining public consensus among modern Europeans, however, served as a useful tool for Ando to explain the consensus the Roman state had built through communicative methods, of which sheer force was but a subset. According to Ando's model we see a rather vivid Roman provincial society whose peaceful and willing support becomes crucial for operating the polity:

> For a society like that of Rome, which believed that its legitimacy as a normative order and, indeed, its good relations with the divine derived directly from the *consensus of its participants, communication as a process for reaching understanding was of the utmost importance*. Indeed, the Roman empire achieves its unique status among world empires in no small part through its gradual extension of government by consensus formation to all its subjects. In doing so, it had to create, adopt, or extend the *institutions*

---

[25] For instance, see: Ando, *Imperial Ideology and Provincial Loyalty in the Roman Empire* (Berkley, Los Angeles and London: University of California Press 2000); P.R. Golding, "Han Law and the Regulation of Interpersonal Relations: 'The Confucianization of the Law' Revisited," *Asia Major* 25 (2012), 1–31; and B. Tezcan, *The Second Ottoman Empire: Political and Social Transformation in the Early Modern World* (Cambridge and New York: Cambridge University Press 2010).

[26] J. Habermas, *Communication and the Evolution of Society*, T. McCarthy (transl.) (Boston: Beacon Press 1979); Habermas, *The Theory of Communicative Action*, 2 vols., T. McCarthy (transl.) (Boston: Beacon Press (1984/1987).

of communicative practice throughout its territory. Thus Romans believed that the maintenance of their society depended upon a communicative practice that had to satisfy certain conditions of rationality—although it was in the first instance that Rome defined those conditions. Yet that practice exposed the conditions themselves to question: their validity came to rest not on the power of Rome to assert them, but upon the integrative work of Roman and provincial who together coordinated their social actions through criticizable validity claims.[27]

The consensus reached by every free body in the empire, then, became the means by which the state apparatus functioned for several centuries. In turn, such consensus was maintained mainly through the communicative institutions that state and emperor forged over the centuries of Roman dominance in the Mediterranean. These communicative institutions relied on communicative actions. The communicative actions in the premodern classical and medieval Roman Empire were limited to the following: imperial effigies sent around the empire, imperially sponsored building projects in the provinces, universal legislation, and the ubiquity of imperial legal proclamations around the empire. There was also, the Roman legal system offering justice to whomever was in want of it, and record-keeping in provincial cities.[28] All these practices established public support for the Roman Empire and ensured the willing integration of its subjects into the Roman nation. The success of these communicative actions is best represented by emperor Caracalla's issuance of the *Constitutio Antoniniana* granting Roman citizenship to all the subjects of the Roman state, that is people who had been Romanized (and had influenced the perception of Romanness) over the course of the two centuries of *Pax Romana*.[29]

Building upon Ando's idea that a wider public consensus maintained the Roman polity, as well as existing scholarship in the field of Byzantine Studies,[30] Anthony Kaldellis in *The Byzantine Republic: People and Power in New Rome* offered a framework for the study of the medieval Roman

---

[27] Ando, *Imperial Ideology*, 77 (emphases added are my own).

[28] Ando, 73–130; 206–276.

[29] On the *Constitutio Antoniniana* and its political significance see: O. Hekster, *Rome and Its Empire, AD 193-284* (Edinburgh: Edinburgh University Press 2008), 45–55; C. Ando, *Law, Language, and Empire*, 19–36.

[30] J.B. Bury, *A History of the Later Roman Empire from Arcadius to Irene* (London: Macmillan 1889); H.-G. Beck, *Senat und Volk von Konstantinopel: Probleme der byzantinischen Verfassungsgeschichte* (München: Verlag der Bayerischen Akademie der Wissenschaften

polity's political system that discarded narratives about the theocratic nature of the Byzantine government and introduced public consensus as central to maintaining a regime in power.[31] With *The Byzantine Republic*, then, we are reminded of the role of the people and the Senate of New Rome. That is, while the emperor exercised immense power, his rule would be impossible without the support of the empire's elites, as well as the populace at large.

Examining the ways in which the elites of the Middle Byzantine Period organized themselves as a cohesive group of competing clans and factions, Jean-Claude Cheynet, in his *Pouvoir et contestation à Byzance (963–1210)*, sheds light on the culture of rebellion as well as of subsequent justification of power seizure in Byzantium by members of the aristocracy. In elucidating the nature of rebellions against a regime and the ways in which a new regime had to secure its position, Cheynet argues that the new emperor had to make sure to appease both the elites and the *hoi polloi* of the empire.[32] Those members of the elites supporting the new emperor's initial actions in seizing power were awarded proper office and titles together with privileges vis-à-vis those potentates who kept neutral or opposed the rebellion. When it comes to the wider populaces of the empire, Cheynet points out the new regime's need to win support through public endeavours that would demonstrate imperial care for the people of the empire. Thus, *Pouvoir et contestation* represents a major milestone upon which the present study builds, namely by looking at the ways in which not only the emperor engaged the elites and the commoners to support the regime, but also how the leaders of major *oikoi* in the empire employed a number of strategies to win over the support of their peers as well as the wider populaces in order to advance their own agendas vis-à-vis the empire's goals.

Contributing to the exploration of various aspects of medieval hellenophone Romanness, scholars such as Leonora Neville and Dimitris Krallis have offered focused single-author studies that explore the ways in which one's Romanness was conceptualized and understood by Byzantine authors living in the eleventh and twelfth centuries. Thus, in *Heroes*

1966); and H.-G. Beck, *Res Publica Romana: Vom Staatsdenken der Byzantiner* (München: Verlag der Bayerischen Akademie der Wissenschaften 1970).

[31] A. Kaldellis, *The Byzantine Republic: People and Power in New Rome* (Cambridge, MA and London: Harvard University Press 2015).

[32] Cheynet, *Pouvoir et contestation*, 199–205.

and Romans in Twelfth-Century Byzantium: The Material for History of Nikephoros Bryennios, Neville examines the ways in which Roman heroic ethos was employed by Nikephoros Bryennios, a leading Byzantine courtier of the twelfth century, in writing his historiographic narrative.[33] Moving away from cultural legacy, Krallis in *Serving Byzantium's Emperors: The Courtly Life of Michael Attaleiates* engages with the life of a Roman judge, Michael Attaleiates, in order to explore the ways in which the statesman himself theorized the world around him and the historical memory of the Roman nation in the eleventh century.[34] By examining the ways in which specific historical agents conceptualized the world in which they lived thanks to their own erudition and reading of pre-existing literature, Neville and Krallis capture specific social and cultural trends in the constantly shifting political realities of the medieval Roman state and society and, from it, draw wider conclusions about the medieval Roman polity and what it meant to be Roman in the Middle Byzantine Period. In so doing, both scholars escape a somewhat essentialist approach of grand narratives that seem to argue, intentionally or not, that the Byzantine state and its culture remained monolithic and unchanged over the centuries.

Engaging with such scholarship, this study is the first to look at how individual agents employed specific communicative actions for their own political advancement. That is, I demonstrate how individuals who were not emperors used their active agency in the framework of the existing Byzantine political and social culture in order to advance their own fortunes in the imperial administration. It is my aim to examine the role interactions among people with names and surnames such as Bryennios and Attaleiates played in the grand narratives of depersonalized state bureaucratic apparatuses and defaced masses. In doing so, I hope to contribute to the wider understanding of medieval Roman societal practices in governing the state, albeit not from an aerial view, but from an on-the-ground perspective. In other words, I look at the ways

---

[33] L. Neville, *Heroes and Romans in the Twelfth-Century Byzantium: The Material for History of Nikephoros Bryennios* (Cambridge, UK and New York: Cambridge University Press 2012).

[34] D. Krallis, *Michael Attaleiates and the Politics of Imperial Decline in Eleventh Century Byzantium* (Tempe: Arizona Center for Medieval and Renaissance Studies 2012); Krallis, *Serving Byzantium's Emperors*.

in which individuals could mobilize and even shape Ando's and Kaldellis' faceless "institutions of communicative practice."[35] By focusing on one individual, Michael Palaiologos, though not conducting a single-author study, I move away from a single person's worldview to offer a personalized version of the communicative means Byzantine officials had at their disposal in order to publicly promote themselves to various socio-economic and political factions of the Roman Empire in exile.

1.3 Biography: A Vehicle for Writing Social History

When writing the biography of Ioannes VI Kantakouzenos, Donald Nicol noted that his work attempted to reconstruct the life, including all the personal aspects, of a Byzantine emperor. Thus, as Nicol made clear to his readers: "[the] book does not aim to present a social and political history of the Byzantine Empire in the fourteenth century."[36] In direct opposition to Nicol's biographical narrative about Ioannes Kantakouzenos, the biographical framework of this book serves as a means to present the social history of the thirteenth century. The present biography of Michael Palaiologos should not be read as an attempt at a definite or factual reconstruction of his life. Questions concerning Michael Palaiologos' psyche, desires, emotions, and his personal motivations are not taken into consideration here.[37] Rather, questions that revolve around the choices Palaiologos made in his public career prior to his enthronement in 1259—which have come down to us through multiple sources by a number of authors—make up the central part of this biography. Thus, such questions as whether or not Michael *really* plotted against Ioannes III Batatzes or Theodoros II Laskaris, remain beyond the scope of this project. What concerns us here is that Romans reading accounts of Michael's actions, including accusations of his alleged acts of treason, could find these actions plausible. The very plausibility of actions ascribed to Michael Palaiologos, either by himself or by other authors, is what

---

[35] Ando, *Imperial Ideology*, 77.

[36] D. Nicol, *The Reluctant Emperor: A Biography of John Cantacuzene, Byzantine Emperor and Monk, c.1295–1383* (Cambridge and New York: Cambridge University Press 1996), 2.

[37] For a study of individual emotions, urges, and feelings in the wider political world of Byzantium see: Angelov, *The Byzantine Hellene*.

makes them relevant for our narrative.[38] By looking at these plausible actions, I explore different communicative actions that Michael Palaiologos employed to win over and maintain the goodwill of emperors, elites, and commoners—all three of which comprised different groups in the empire's public sphere. Maintaining a balance between different publics around the empire in exile, in turn, aided Michael Palaiologos in fulfilling his own political aspirations. On the example of Michael Palaiologos' pre-imperial career we can explore the various communicative actions undertaken by high state officials more generally in order to win over the support of different socio-economic groups in the empire, which was necessary to advance their careers and distinguish themselves at the imperial court.

Michael Palaiologos proves an ideal candidate for writing the social biography of imperial officials, as his public career took him around the empire during the Roman polity's exilic era. That is, Palaiologos was born in 1223 in Roman-ruled Bithynia, at a time when the imperial capital, Constantinople, was under the rule of Western European crusaders. The convenience of this time period rests in the fact that, for the first time since, arguably, the reign of Constantine the Great, we see historians and other literati of the empire writing from a non-Constantinopolitan perspective. With the sack of Constantinople in 1204, the traditional dichotomy between the clear image of the central government's *modus operandi* and the blurred provincial social and political realities had come to an end.[39] In following Michael's life and career in Asia Minor and

---

[38] On plausibility, or rather truth-telling as a persuasive technique in Byzantine historiography, see: S. Papaioannou, "The Aesthetics of Historiography: Theophanes to Eustathios," in R.J. Macrides (ed.), *History as Literature in Byzantium: Papers from the Fortieth Spring Symposium of Byzantine Studies, University of Birmingham, April 2007* (Surrey: Ashgate 2010), 3–24; also, on rhetorical practices including the role of plausible truth-telling in historiography see: A. J. Woodman, *Rhetoric in Classical Historiography* (London: Croom Helm 1988); M.J. Wheeldon, "'True Stories': The Reception of Historiography in Antiquity," in A. Cameron (ed.), *History as Text: The Writing of Ancient History* (Chapel Hill: University of North Carolina Press 1989), 33–63; and M. Mullett, "Novelisation in Byzantium: Narrative After the Revival of Fiction," in J. Burke et al. (eds.), *Byzantine Narrative: Papers in Honour of Roger Scott* (Melbourne: Australian Association for Byzantine Studies 2006), 1–28.

[39] For an examination of medieval Roman provincial society before 1204, for example, see: P. Lemerle, *The Agrarian History of Byzantium from the Origins to the Twelfth Century. The Sources and Problems* (Galway: Galway University Press 1979); Neville, *Authority in Byzantine Provincial Society*; and Herrin, *Margins and Metropolis*. For

the Balkans we escape Constantinople's gravitational pull and explore the ways in which provincial notables and populations at large reacted to the Roman state and its high officials. This opportunity to explore officials' ability to mobilize the provincial populaces' support in order to promote their own careers allows us to examine the communicative actions that the likes of Michael Palaiologos had at their disposal in crafting an attractive public persona for their audiences.

Michael VIII Palaiologos' imperial tenure (1259–1282) and the public persona he projected towards the Roman publics has not escaped contemporary scholarly attention. Being the emperor under whom Constantinople was restored to the Romans, as well as a man who obtained the throne solely for himself by blinding a child emperor, Michael had to carefully justify his position. In doing so, as shown by Alice-Mary Talbot and Cecily Hilsdale, Michael embarked on an artistic and architectural programme to emphasize the role of divine providence in his imperial elevation.[40] The emperor did not miss a single opportunity to explain that his imperial ordination was an act of God and not the outcome of actions set in motion by his own will. Thus, statues, images, and coins traditionally represent the emperor in the company of a divine figure. In literary production Palaiologos himself, and his main intellectual mouthpiece, Georgios Akropolites, name divine grace and providence as Michael's Platonic *daimon*.[41] All these communicative actions served to justify Michael VIII's imperial elevation and controversial actions that followed it, which included the blinding of young Ioannes IV and the signing of an ecclesiastic union between the Orthodox and Catholic Churches.[42] Whether these communicative actions served their purpose or not remains open for discussion. On the one hand, the

---

provincial society during the period of exile see: Angold, *A Byzantine Government in Exile*.

[40] M.-A. Talbot, "The Restoration of Constantinople under Michael VIII," *DOP* 47 (1993), 243–261; C.J. Hilsdale, "The Imperial Image at the End of Exile: The Byzantine Embroidered Silk in Genoa and the Treaty of Nymphaion (1261)," *DOP* 64 (2010), 151–199; and Hilsdale, *Byzantine Art and Diplomacy in an Age of Decline* (Cambridge and New York: Cambridge University Press 2014), 31–87.

[41] On the role of divine protectors and providence in the image of Michael VIII Palaiologos see: Hilsdale, *Art and Diplomacy*, 31–87; Macrides, "Introduction," 54–55.

[42] For the opposition to the Palaiologoi and the role played by the image of a blinded young emperor see: T. Shawcross, "In the Name of the True Emperor: Politics of Resistance After the Palaiologan Usurpation," *Byzantinoslavica* 66 (2008), 203–227.

emperor stayed in power until his peaceful death in 1282. On the other, he died excommunicated by both the patriarch of Constantinople and the pope of Rome. Be it as it may, Michael VIII Palaiologos successfully branded himself as both the mighty New Constantine and restorer of Constantinople, as well as the victim of *fatum*, that is of divine providence, in the vein of Virgil's Aeneas.[43] Both imperial images could be used at any given occasion depending on the audience and the desired effect they ought to produce. Through a series of innovations resting on his personal connection with the divine in his public image, Michael VIII Palaiologos managed to keep public consensus on his side until his very last breath.

How did Michael Palaiologos and his associates come up with all these ideas? Why would Michael care to forge an image of a divinely sanctioned New Constantine during his reign? Why was Michael elected emperor in the first place? It is by examining Michael Palaiologos and his career before he became emperor of the Romans that we find answers to these questions. Traditionally, it is imperial reigns that receive scholarly attention, not the formative years and career of an emperor-to-be.[44] In contrast to this approach, I begin the biographical narrative with Michael's formative years and end with his imperial coronation in 1259. By doing so, I hope to emphasize how active individual agency and public relations determined the careers of officials and their promotions. While Michael VIII Palaiologos has been usually labelled as the founder of the Palaiologan dynasty with which the Roman Empire enters the last stage of its development, here I look at Michael Palaiologos, a Roman official and member of the Nikaian generation; that is, as a member of a generation of officials, intellectuals, and generals of high birth raised at the imperial courts and palaces of the Byzantine Empire in exile (1204–1261). The focus on the Nikaian generation shows Michael, as well as other authors who left their accounts of the events during the exilic period, as social and intellectual products of Laskarid educational and cultural policies. The individuals belonging to the Nikaian generation, in turn, shaped the first generation of Palaiologan scholars and bureaucrats serving under Michael

---

[43] R.J. Macrides, "The New Constantine and the New Constantinople—1261," *BMGS* 6 (1980), 13–41; for the role of divine providence and mercy see n.17 and n.18.

[44] For the example of Michael VIII Palaiologos and the exclusive focus on his imperial reign see: D.J. Geanakoplos, *Emperor Michael Palaeologus and the West (1258–1282)* (Cambridge, MA: Harvard University Press 1959).

VIII Palaiologos with whom scholars traditionally begin their accounts of the Palaiologan renaissance of arts and culture.[45]

Examining the ways in which non-emperors were able to employ communicative actions allows us to see how state officials gradually forged a reliable public image of themselves in order to stake out a spot for their own careers on the political scene of the empire. By not exploring the public persona of an emperor, but rather that of his subordinates, I hope to demonstrate the complexities that hide behind the employment of communicative actions by state officials vis-à-vis the emperor. That is, while the emperor had the means and the ideological apparatus (i.e. institutions of communicative practice as Ando names them) to support his public image-building process, state officials had to be careful not to infringe on any of the emperor's prerogatives in their own self-promotion to peers and other Romans. For this reason, I believe studying the social and political agency of Roman statesmen, and not solely that of emperors, becomes pertinent for our conceptualization of power and social relations among various intertwined socio-economic factions within the empire.[46] By shifting our gaze from the centre of power—the emperor—to the prominent aristocrats and even traditionally faceless groupings in contemporary scholarship—bureaucrats, generals, and anonymous citizens—I hope to offer a nuanced reading of medieval Roman governing and social practices. After all, much like his political allies and adversaries, Michael Palaiologos did not shy away from bending expected codes of conduct in order to secure a place for himself in the highest echelons of power in the Byzantine Empire, while, at the same time, relying on the existing governing apparatus and social system.

1.4 Places of Communication: The Public Arena

That emperors and dignitaries employed a plethora of communicative actions—either visual or aural—in order to gain public support for their respective agendas was a commonplace in Byzantium.[47] But what were

---

[45] For example, see: E.B. Fryde, *The Early Palaeologan Renaissance (1261-c. 1360)* (Leiden: Brill 2000).

[46] For instance, both Cheynet in *Pouvoir et contestation* and Kaldellis in *The Byzantine Republic* examine the centre of power, focusing on emperors, imperial image, and consensus in the hands of the emperors.

[47] For Late Byzantine intellectual community in imperial service see: D. Angelov, *Imperial Ideology and Political Thought in Byzantium, 1204–1330* (Cambridge: Cambridge University Press 2007); Matschke and Tinnefeld, *Die Gesellschaft*, 211–385; N. Zagklas,

these spaces in the empire where individuals could gain access to public opinion? That is, where and how could one get the opportunity to mobilize the public for their cause? Furthermore, how far-reaching were the echoes of communicative actions? In dealing with such questions, the basic premise on which I rely here is the concept of the public sphere, which can be defined as "a discursive space in which individuals and groups associate to discuss matters of mutual interest and, where possible, to reach a common judgement about them. It is the locus of emergence for rhetorically salient meanings."[48] So, the public sphere becomes the conceptual space in which individuals like Michael Palaiologos could hope to influence public opinion and gain advantage over their political peers. The task that remains is to try to locate the spaces, be they physical or conceptual, within which the public sphere operated. Since the premodern polity of the Romans is the focus of this study, we have to keep in mind that the limited communicative techniques and technologies available to individuals had to nevertheless be able to influence the very essence of the discursive public sphere.

An important qualifier for our understanding of public opinion, and really the public sphere in the medieval Roman Empire, comes from the very fact that there was not just one faceless public that reacted in the same way to communicative actions across the empire. Rather, there were multiple coexisting publics that to some extent had shared interests.[49] In referring to multiple publics in the Byzantine Empire, I turn to Gerard Hauser's observation that since the later eighteenth century, European societies have developed numerous publics with different interests and agendas.[50] Hauser's inquiry focuses mainly on socio-economic and class relations in explaining the process of the rise of civil society in

---

"'How Many Verses Shall I Write and Say?': Poetry in the Komnenian Period (1081–1204)"; A. Rhoby, "Poetry on Commission in Late Byzantium (13th–15th Century)," in W. Hörandner, A. Rhody and N. Zagklas (eds.), *A Companion to Byzantine Poetry* (Leiden and Boston: Brill 2019), 237–263, 264–304.

[48] G.A. Hauser, *Vernacular Voices: The Rhetoric of Publics and Public Spheres* (Columbia: University of South Carolina Press 1999), 60.

[49] For different interest groups in Middle Byzantine Constantinople see: Cheynet, *Pouvoir et contestation*, 199–205; for multiple socio-economic strata in Late Byzantine cities see: Matschke and Tinnefeld, *Die Gesellschaft*, 99–157; A. Kontogiannopoulou, "The Notion of δῆμος and Its Role in Byzantium During the Last Centuries (13-15th c.)," *ByzSym* 22 (2012), 101–124.

[50] Hauser, *Vernacular Voices*, 19–39.

Europe that allowed for several separate public spheres to coexist. These groups with different agendas were oftentimes in conflict with the interests of the state or with other socio-economic groups. This brought about the fragmentation of the state's monopoly over public discourse which could now be mobilized by various entities.[51] Thus, according to Hauser, "discursive spaces within this network displaced the state's claim as the domain in which social will was articulated and executed."[52] This remark becomes pertinent for our understanding of premodern publics and their employment of discursive spaces both physical and conceptual.

In the medieval Roman Empire, public discourse had never been the exclusive domain of the state and its head, the emperor. The production and preservation of knowledge was more often than not in the hands of state and ecclesiastic officials, who fairly frequently criticized and challenged the regime.[53] As such, discursive spaces were influenced by multiple voices. Even though discursive spaces were heavily reliant on Aristotle's rhetorical model in which political animals' service for the good of the state as a whole played a pivotal role in praising or criticizing given regimes, the discourse about the state was never dominated by a single regime. For instance, one of the main narrative sources for the period of exile is Georgios Akropolites' *The History* which, one could argue, was an official apology of Michael VIII Palaiologos' rise to power.[54] In the same generation, another author offered a paraphrase of Akropolites' narrative in which he excluded all encomiastic references to Palaiologos in his *Synopsis Chronike* in the hopes of changing the discourse promoted by the Palaiologan regime in the Roman elites' public memory. It is with such zeal that the literati under study here attempted to dominate the public discourse about the state by inevitably entering a dialogue with

---

[51] ibid., 23.

[52] ibid., 23.

[53] For an overview of Byzantine history writers, and their views and agendas see: L. Neville, *Guide to Byzantine Historical Writing* (Cambridge and New York: Cambridge University Press 2018).

[54] Macrides, "Introduction," 60–65; R.J. Macrides, "George Akropolites' Rhetoric," in E. Jeffreys, (ed.), *Rhetoric in Byzantium: Papers from the Thirty-fifth Spring Symposium of Byzantine Studies, Exeter College, University of Oxford, March 2001* (Aldershot: Ashgate 2003), 201–210.

their political opponents.[55] The state, with all its resources, could not do much to halt this process, but rather had to engage with the literary production of the empire's intellectuals cum officials in order to try and dominate public discourse. So, the public sphere was open to anybody who had the social and economic means to try to sway some degree of public opinion to their side.

The first public that I am concerned with is the one comprised of the most affluent state officials who monopolized a lion's share of the public discourse and spaces in the empire together with the emperor, who himself originated from this group. The discursive space of their operation was at times physical—meetings of the senate, ecclesiastic and state ceremonies, military camps, *theatra*—and at times confined to their personal reading and literary production—i.e. the case of Georgios Akropolites' *The History* and his interlocutor's ideologically modulated paraphrasis. Thus, narrative sources, on which the present study mostly relies, belong to the realm of conceptual discursive spaces: the texts written for the authors' peers who were educated and, importantly, affluent enough to be able to read and afford book manuscripts.[56] Of the literary sources used here, the histories of Georgios Akropolites and his namesake Pachymeres together with Palaiologos' autobiographical narrative found in the *typikon* (foundation chart) of the monastery of St Demetrios in Constantinople are the base for most of the reconstructed biography of Michael Palaiologos' public life prior to 1259.[57] In addressing Michael's position in the Roman state, the three narratives are in direct dialogue with one another. Akropolites' *The History,* composed either in the seventh or eighth decade of the thirteenth century, is the oldest of the three narratives.[58] As has been noted, *The History* was a piece of Michael VIII's

---

[55] D. Krallis, "Historiography as Political Debate," in A. Kaldellis and N. Siniossoglou (eds.), *The Cambridge Intellectual History of Byzantium* (Cambridge: Cambridge University Press 2017), 599–614.

[56] On book production in the medieval Roman Empire see: N.G. Wilson, *Byzantine Books and Bookmen* (Dumbarton Oaks: Centre for Byzantine Studies, 1975); D.M. Gorecki, "Books, Production of Books and Reading in Byzantium," *Libri* 14 (1984), 113–129.

[57] Both Michael VIII Palaiologos in the typikon and Georgios Akropolites in *The History* provide us with an abundance of details about their lives. On autobiographical trends in Byzantine literature see: M. Angold, "The Autobiographic Impulse in Byzantium," *DOP* 52 (1998), 225–257.

[58] On composition date see: Macrides, "Introduction," 32–34.

propaganda offering a plausible explanation for the rise of Palaiologos to the imperial throne. In writing what was in effect an encomium in the form of history, Akropolites hoped to dominate those public spaces inhabited by intellectuals and, in turn, cement a brilliant image of Michael VIII Palaiologos in the memory of these elite Romans. In the same vein, Palaiologos' self-eulogizing autobiography dating from 1282, the last year of the emperor's life, served the same purpose, together with the monastic structure he had built in the centre of Constantinople as part of his pious public endeavours.[59] Georgios Pachymeres' *Chronicle*, on the other hand, was composed from a very different perspective and stands in opposition to the two mentioned sources. Writing in the fourteenth century, during the reign of Michael VIII's son Andronikos II, Pachymeres, in the first two books of his *Chronicle*, offers a rehabilitation of Ioannes III Batatzes and, up to a point, Theodoros II Laskaris, whose reputations had been tarnished in Akropolites' narrative. Furthermore, in explaining Palaiologos' rise to power, Pachymeres represents the emperor-to-be in a rather negative light, with only a few lesser merits ascribed to his name.[60] Relying on these three sources, to begin with, we can think of the intellectual publics and their engagement with the production and preservation of knowledge for the Roman aristocracy. In doing so, the public sphere they were concerned with was one that revolved around learned discussions of the *theatra* and literary political dialogues of composed works.[61]

---

[59] On the autobiography and the *typikon* see: A. Thomas and A. Constantinides Hero (eds.), *Byzantine Monastic Foundation Documents* 1 [Dumbarton Oaks Studies XXXV] (Washington, DC: Dumbarton Oaks Research Library and Collections 2000), 1237.

[60] On Pachymeres see: A. Failler, "Chronologie et composition dans l'Histoire de Georges Pachymérès," *REB* 39 (1981), 145–249.

[61] For the performative nature of Byzantine rhetoric *inter alia* see: M. Mullet, "Aristocracy and Patronage in the Literary Circles of Comnenian Constantinople" in M. Angold (ed.), *The Byzantine Aristocracy, IX–XIII Centuries* (Oxford and New York: Oxford University Press 1984), 173–201; M. Mullet, "Rhetoric, Theory, and the Imperative of Performance: Byzantium and Now," in E. Jeffreys (ed.), *Rhetoric in Byzantium. Papers from the Thirty-Fifth Spring Symposium of Byzantine Studies, Exeter College, University of Oxford, March 2001* (Aldershot and Burlington, VT: Ashgate 2003), 151–170; N. Gaul, "Performative Reading in Late Byzantine Theatron," in T. Shawcross and I. Toth (eds.), *Reading in the Byzantine Empire and Beyond*, (Cambridge and New York: Cambridge University Press 2018), 215–233, Neville, *Heroes and Romans*, 28–32, A. Riehle, "Rhetorical Practice," in S. Papaioannou (ed.), *The Oxford Handbook of Byzantine Literature* (Oxford and New Yorks: Oxford University Press 2021), 294–315; and

The content of the three aforementioned narratives, together with other documents used for this project, also provides us with the information necessary to conceptualize other publics and how these engaged in the empire's public sphere. Leaving the *theatra* and reading rooms of the high-born elite, these elite texts provide us with a vivid image of the squares, streets, churches, palaces, courts, taverns, and other places of mass and socially diverse congregation. It is by following the narrative descriptions of these places, in which individual agents such as Michael Palaiologos operated in order to win over a specific public's support, that I conceptualize the communicative actions employed by state officials in attempts to dominate the wider public discourse. The methods used varied from the delivery of public speeches to the erection of structures dotted with public inscriptions commemorating the *ktetor*. The great care individuals took to promote themselves and their families to different interest groups in the empire becomes clearer once we contrast the communicative actions upon which these political agents relied to attract the attention of distinct publics. It was thus one thing to write elaborate accounts for the elites and a completely different thing to dominate the so-called vulgar discourse of the wider populace, which was marked by gossip.[62]

The question of which communicative actions pair best with which public has so far been addressed to a greater or lesser extent in the terms of class-related interest groups: the highly educated elites read long histories in complex classicizing Greek, while the people in the streets prefer short texts in vernacular *rhomaika*.[63] Another dimension which we have to keep in mind when dealing with premodern states, as was mentioned, is that of time and distance. For instance, Michael VIII Palaiologos' consecration of the monastery of St Demetrios in 1282 was witnessed by several

---

D. Krallis, "Urbane Warriors: Smoothing Out Tensions Between Soldiers and Civilians in Attaleiates' Encomium to Emperor Nikephoros III Botaneiates," in M. Lauxterman and M. Whittow (eds.), *Being in Between: Byzantium in the Eleventh Century* (London and New York: Routledge 2015), 154–168.

[62] Habermas finds gossip and the opinion of the masses to be part of vulgar speech which does not meaningfully affect the rationale of the public sphere: Jürgen Habermas, *The Structural Transformation*, 27. On the other hand, Hauser emphasizes the importance of this vulgar speech in public rhetoric: Hauser, *Vernacular Voices*, 42.

[63] On classicizing vis-à-vis vernacular Greek see: G. Horrocks, *Greek: A History of the Language and Its Speakers* (Hoboken: Wiley Blackwell 2010), 211–392; On the politization of Rhomaika in the empire see: Kaldellis, *Romanland*, 83–113.

different publics: the ecclesiastic elites, the state officials, members of his family, and the commoners of Constantinople.[64] The people of Thessaloniki, on the other hand, could not witness the event taking place in Constantinople. Thus, Michael VIII, the same as every other emperor, bureaucrat, or random citizen of the medieval Roman polity, had to think of the spatial outreach of his deeds and, when needed, instigate several parallel projects independent from one another to maintain the consensus of various publics under his control. The *typikon* and the very structure of St Demetrios in Constantinople were a unifying communicative action undertaken by Michael VIII to display his piety publicly—at the time in question, given his excommunication by both the patriarch and the pope—to the attention of both the commoners and the elites. On the other hand, for the people of Thessaloniki or, say, the recently recovered areas of the Peloponnese, the emperor had to employ different means by which to demonstrate his presence and piety to local elites and commoners alike.[65]

Ultimately, as much as they tried to show their care for everybody in the empire, the lack of imperial physical presence in the provinces meant that the discursive life of provincial cities remained, for the most part, uncontrolled by the central government. It was much easier to maintain popular consensus in the capital where the emperor dwelled and could always manifest himself publicly than it was in the provinces where the ruler had to rely on such communicative actions as inscriptions, coinage, and invocation of his name during liturgies in maintaining the support of the locals. As effective as these actions were, the emperor understood that the threat to the imperial reputation and power in the provinces came from the local elites as well as the centrally appointed governors and officials who could always use their physical presence to win over the sympathies, and at times allegiances, of the provincials for their own political goals. Every emperor, then, had to be weary of the governors he himself appointed. In turn, every state official, as was Michael Palaiologos, could only hope to start building a base of public support in the

---

[64] Michael VIII Palaiologos most likely intended this monastery to be his final resting place: T. Shawcross, "In the Name of the True Emperor," 218–221.

[65] For example, see inscriptions on two churches in Mani and Kythera in the Peloponnese: V.A. Foskolou, "In the Reign of the Emperor of Rome...": Donor Inscriptions and Political Ideology in the Time of Michael VIII Paleologos," Δελτίον της Χριστιανικής Αρχαιολογικής Εταιρείας 27 (2011), 455–462.

provinces away from the imperial centre of power. In other words, it is the periphery that becomes the key to political promotion and security once one had reached the highest echelons of power in the imperial centre.

1.5 Publics and Actions by Chapters

Following the public life of Michael Palaiologos from his early days and upbringing to imperial elevation opens for us a whole new world of communicative interactions between members of various publics. Exploring multiple narratives, primarily composed by intellectuals and clerks other than Michael Palaiologos, this book's narrative might at times correspond more to depersonalized narratives about governing mechanisms, power relations, transclass actions, and other concepts than an individual's history. On the other hand, by using the figure of Palaiologos as the focal point of the book, I hope to offer a narrative that emphasizes the importance of individual political agents in exploring the role of communicative actions within the sphere of multiple publics whose support was essential if one were to successfully govern the exilic Roman state in the thirteenth century.

In the opening chapter, I chart Michael's early life by focusing on his education at the imperial court and his early career under the service of his father Andronikos Palaiologos, whom Ioannes III had elevated to the rank of *megas domestikos*. By looking at the imperial education programme put in place by Ioannes III, I explore the interactions Michael had with officials and bureaucrats in his childhood while being educated at the court. These two groups, officials and bureaucrats, based on their shared ways and spaces of interaction, formed a core public of Michael's social engagement. Other than social interactions, examination of literary and other texts employed in the educational system sets the stage for the exploration of communicative actions undertaken by individuals like Michael Palaiologos, whose way of thinking was surely influenced by their very *morphosis* at the imperial court. The second part of the chapter focuses on Michael's early career as governor of Serres and Melenikon under his father Andronikos. Andronikos Palaiologos and his career become the centre of the analysis as I explore his interactions with the notables of Thessaloniki on whom, after his father's death, Michael relied in order to forge a solid support base for the Palaiologoi in the city. The chapter ends with Michael's first independent communicative action taken in Thessaloniki. Away from the emperor in Asia Minor,

Michael had ample room to publicly commemorate his father and his deeds. To do so he hired an intellectual by the name of Iakobos, who was the nominal archbishop of Bulgaria, to compose a funerary speech and three poems in celebration of his father's accomplishments in Thessaloniki. The rhetorical programme Michael Palaiologos sponsored was the first step in gaining the support of various interest and class groups in Thessaloniki. The nature of those diverse groups is revealed by the genre of those poems, which were written in different registers of Greek.

The following chapter looks at the ways in which members of the highborn elite working for the imperial government interacted with the people of provincial cities in which they operated. Here we encounter Michael learning how to engage with the wide audience of provincial citizenry, just as he did in Thessaloniki after his father's death, as well as a separate public comprised of local elites with their own interests and ways of communication which differed from those of the wider urban populace. In this aspect, the case of Michael Palaiologos is rather telling since, unlike his father, he ran into conflict with the local notables headed by a certain Nikolaos Manglavites. Manglavites, according to Akropolites, went as far as to accuse Michael Palaiologos of treason in front of the emperor, which led to Michael's deposition and subsequent trial. The case of Nikolaos Manglavites allows us to explore the not always smooth path that individuals had to tread in order to gain public support in the provinces. For once, we see that a major official, and member of the highborn elites, was accused by a local notable, likely a merchant, who knew how to use Roman law in order to protect his own interests. This chapter, then, focuses on the communicative actions taken by both aristocratic and local elites in the provinces in order to extend our understanding of the centre-periphery relationship in the Byzantine Empire. It was not only the imperial officials who served as a link between the centre and the periphery, but in order to neutralize their social or political opponents, affluent members of provincial society knew exactly the ways in which they could engage with the central authorities. In doing so, we see that the state was very much present in the empire's European provinces, much as it was in the traditional Laskarid imperial centres in Magnesia and Nikaia. The second part of the chapter deals with Michael's trial. Here we explore the social networks of the Palaiologoi as a clan and Michael Palaiologos as an individual. It is thanks to these networks in the highest echelons of power, as well as with the soldiery of the imperial army (a special public of their own), that Palaiologos managed to get

1 INTRODUCTION: MEETING THE ROMAN PUBLIC   29

away unharmed and even enjoy promotion after the trial. The last part of the chapter is concerned with the change on the throne and the ways in which Theodoros II wished to alter the existing power constellation at the very centre of power. Looking at Theodoros II's political maneuvers, I examine the extent and limits of both imperial and elite power in relationship to one another.

The subsequent chapter represents a break in the narrative as we follow Michael Palaiologos on his self-imposed exile in the Saljuq Sultanate of Rum. The opportunity to view Michael, a Roman general and senator, serving a ruler of a different polity allows us to see how communicative actions as well as the public sphere at large operated in a different political system. This is pertinent as, in the thirteenth century, the majority of the urban population in the Sultanate of Rum was still Roman. This chapter, then, explores the ways in which Romans of Rum negotiated their new position in a Muslim polity. We look at both the Romans occupying positions of power in the government as well as the commoners who comprised the majority population of the sultanate. In reconstructing the public lives of Romans under Saljuq rule, I rely on both textual and material sources that have come down to us. Furthermore, in order to explore the street life of Saljuq cities, I employ Romaic textual production of non-Roman elements in the sultanate. In doing so, I hope to demonstrate the vividness and active presence of Romans in the social fabric of the Saljuq Sultanate of Rum, showing that their voices could not be overlooked by the central authorities in Ikonion. The Romans of Rum were a public that neither the sultan nor Palaiologos could afford to ignore.

In the final chapter, we follow Michael Palaiologos' return to the Roman Empire and pick up the thread of social relations among different publics in the imperial centre—that is, the officials and dignitaries, the ecclesiastics, the commoners, and the soldiers—on whose support the regime had to rely. After the death of Theodoros II, the regency of three brothers, who belonged to the family of Mouzalones, and which was established for the young emperor, lacked the support necessary to maintain itself in power. The regency serves as a good case study for the importance of forging closer ties with the empire's various publics before coming to power. Where the Mouzalones family failed, however, Michael Palaiologos did not. In the second half of the chapter, we follow the ways in which Michael cashed-in his accumulated social capital with different public interest groups and managed to claim the regency and subsequently the imperial throne for himself. A series of rhetorical communicative actions taken by Michael Palaiologos in the last months of 1258 allow us to examine the ways in which he, holding more power than before, further reinforced existing social support and gained new allies as he sought to claim the imperial dignity for himself. With the imperial coronation in January 1259, Michael VIII Palaiologos' career, and with it all his communicative actions, experienced a drastic change. No longer did Michael Palaiologos need to maneuver carefully among emperors, elites, and the wider Byzantine populace in order to carve out a spot for himself in the social and political life of the empire. Now his main goal was to maintain his imperial position by promoting the image of his own splendour and by carefully preventing anybody else's attempts to carve out too big a spot for themselves in the public sphere of the Roman polity. It is with this drastic shift in his political life that we bid farewell to Michael Palaiologos, the Roman official.

CHAPTER 2

Making Officials in Exile: The Case of the Palaiologoi

In *The History*, written well after the Roman reconquest of Constantinople in 1261, Georgios Akropolites, *megas logothetes* and renowned teacher, joyfully reminisces about advice he allegedly received from Ioannes III back in 1234, at the beginning of his own studies in Nikaia:

> These [young men] I have taken from Nikaia and handed them over to the school, but you I have taken from my household and sent you to be taught together with them. Demonstrate that you indeed come from my household and engage in your studies accordingly. For if you were to become a soldier by occupation, you would have so much from my majesty by way of sustenance and perhaps a little more because of your illustrious *genos*. But should you prove to be versed in philosophy, you will be deemed worthy of great honours and rewards. For, alone of all people, the emperor and the philosopher are the most known.[1]

---

[1] τούτους μὲν ἐκ Νικαίας λαβὼν τῷ διδασκαλείῳ παρέδωκα, σὲ δὲ τοῦ ἐμοῦ ἐκβαλὼν οἴκου τουτοισὶ συναφῆκα διδάσκεσθαι. δεῖξον οὖν, ὡς ἀληθῶς τῆς ἐμῆς οἰκίας ἐξήεις, καὶ οὕτωσὶ τῶν μαθημάτων ἀντιποιήθητι. στρατιώτης μὲν γὰρ τὸ ἐπιτήδευμα γεγονὼς ὁπόσα ἂν ἔσχες τὰ τοῦ σιτηρεσίου παρὰ τῆς βασιλείας μου, τοσαῦτα ἂν ἴσως ἢ καὶ ὀλίγον πλείω διά τοι τὸ τοῦ γένους περιφανές· ἔμπλεως δὲ φιλοσοφίας φανεὶς μεγάλων ἀξιωθήσῃ τῶν τιμῶν τε καὶ τῶν γερῶν· μόνοι γὰρ τῶν πάντων ἀνθρώπων ὀνομαστότατοι βασιλεὺς καὶ φιλόσοφος (Akropolites, *Chronike*, 32.7–16).

© The Author(s), under exclusive license to Springer Nature Switzerland AG 2022
A. Jovanović, *Michael Palaiologos and the Publics of the Byzantine Empire in Exile, c.1223–1259*, New Approaches to Byzantine History and Culture, https://doi.org/10.1007/978-3-031-09278-7_2

Here, Akropolites highlights the importance of extensive education and training for civil officials-to-be from a young age.[2] Such advice is worth paying attention to since it served Akropolites well, for our historian successfully navigated his way through imperial administration over three successive imperial tenures. Having received an education as a gift from his imperial patron Ioannes III, Georgios served both this emperor and his son, Theodoros II, as well as Michael VIII Palaiologos. Securing an important position even under the administration of Michael VIII, which was cleansed of officials close to Theodoros II, testifies to Georgios' political acumen.[3]

Not long after Georgios composed *The History*, his younger contemporary Michael VIII Palaiologos[4] takes pride (not unlike Akropolites) in his upbringing in the imperial household of Ioannes III and boasts in an autobiographical narrative that:

> Before I had outgrown my infant years, my uncle took me up in the imperial palace (this was the late Ioannes [III]). He raised me and instructed me diligently as if I was his own, striving to appear more affectionate toward me than my own father in matters of education and studies in all fields. Whether I made use of the instructions of this great mind and was a worthy student of such a pedagogue, others can say. As soon as I joined among the young lads and was able to carry weapons, I was deemed suitable for command by the late [emperor] himself, so not to mention that I was selected over those who many years earlier had begun this career.[5]

---

[2] For educational practices and curricula see Angold, *A Byzantine Government*, 174–181; C.N. Constantinides, *Higher Education in Byzantium in 13th and Early 14th Centuries (1204–ca.1310)* (Nicosia: Cyprus Research Centre 1982): 5–27; Angelov, *The Byzantine Hellene*, 70–87.

[3] For Michael's cleansing of imperial administration see Akropolites, *Chronike*, 77 and Pachymeres, *Chronikon*, 113.15–115.6.

[4] Georgios Akropolites was born in 1217 (Macrides, "Introduction," 6); Michael Palaiologos around the year 1224 (Geanakoplos, *Emperor Michael Palaeologus*, 17).

[5] ἄρτι μὲν γὰρ οὔπω καθαρῶς τὴν βρεφικὴν παρήμειβον ἡλικίαν, καί με ὁ θεῖος ἐν τοῖς βασιλείοις ἀνελόμενος (ὁ ἐν βασιλεῦσιν ἀοίδιμος Ἰωάννης οὗτος ἦν) ἐπιμελῶς ὅσα καὶ αὐτοῦ γνήσιον ἔτρεφε καὶ ἀνῆγε, φιλονεικῶν ταῖς περὶ πάντων πραγμάτων ἐκπαιδεύσεσι καὶ σπουδαῖς καὶ αὐτοῦ δὴ πατρὸς περὶ ἐμὲ φανῆναι φιλοστοργότερος• εἰ δὲ καὶ τῶν εἰσηγήσεων τῆς μεγάλης ἐκείνης φρενὸς ἀπωνάμην καὶ τὸν μαθητὴν ἄξιον παρεσχόμην τοῦ παιδευτοῦ, ἄλλοι λεγόντων, ἐγὼ δὲ ὡς εἰς μείρακας ἤδη πρώτως παρήγγελλον καὶ ὅπλα φέρειν ἦν ἱκανός, ὑπ' αὐτοῦ δὴ ἐκείνου στρατηγεῖν ἐκρινόμην ἵνα μὴ λέγω ὅτι καὶ τῶν πολλοῖς ἔτεσι πρότερον ἀψαμένων τοῦ πράγματος προὐκρινόμην (Palaiologos, *Autobiography*, 4.4-15). Here Michael

Both Georgios and Michael VIII emphasize their physical proximity to and acquaintance with the imperial court from a young age to explain their social success and rise on the Roman political scene. The prime value of this familiarity with the imperial household, however, lay beyond the obvious direct contact with the emperor and other members of the Laskarid family. Georgios as much as Michael relished the fact that elite contacts afforded them both an exquisite education and a sense of politics that only life among high officials could offer. Ioannes III himself was at the palace throughout the year. He usually spent the warm season (and sometimes even winter) away from Nikaia and Nymphaion in the Balkans reconquering and then administering Roman lands.[6] As a result, young notables at the court had the time to engage with other members of the court that included their senior peers of high birth. Michael, just like Georgios, was able to make use of this opportunity and excel in his training. This raised his profile at court where he was noticed by the emperor and other senior officials. Michael's well-known surname certainly helped his case, but in equal measure, he had to prove himself worthy of his *genos*' reputation. To do so, he had to complete his studies under imperial supervision. While Georgios and Michael took different career paths—the former became a prominent civil servant and the latter a popular military commander—they both originated from the imperial household. How did they end up there? How were they chosen and subsequently enrolled in imperially sponsored schools that promised to provide the best training possible?

The Roman polity before 1204 had its own share of prominent educators. Whether around churches and monasteries, to which schools were attached, or through private tutors for those who could afford them, ambitious Romans had access to all levels of education. Taking advantage of such educational practices, ambitious and affluent young men trained in hopes to catch the imperial eye in order to secure a position in imperial service.[7] The reputation of a teacher would depend not only

---

echoes traditional Roman credo that skill and virtue have the precedence over kinship in building a successful military career under good emperors. For example, see Leo VI's thoughts on good generals in *Taktika*: G. Dennis (ed., transl. and comm.), *The Taktika of Leo VI* (Washington, DC, Dumbarton Oaks 2010), 16–36.

[6] On Ioannes III's calendar and itinerary see Akropolites, *Chronike*, 19–52.

[7] On educational practices of the eleventh century see G. Weiss, *Oströmische Beamte im Spiegel der Schriften des Michael Psellos* (München: Verlag der Bayerischen Akademie der

on one's teaching skills but also on one's connections with the imperial household and other prominent families in the empire that could help individuals' careers. Michael Psellos, in the eleventh century, attracted students to his classroom not just because he was a good lecturer. He was also a well-connected member of the Constantinopolitan central administration.[8] Like Michael Psellos, Eustathios, in the twelfth century, before becoming archbishop of Thessaloniki, was able to promote his own pupils to the emperor. Thus, even newcomers to the city of Constantinople who could afford a teacher had a decent chance of catching the imperial gaze. Eustathios' student from the provincial city of Chonai, a young man by the name of Michael Choniates, succeeded in making a name for himself at the court of Manouel I Komnenos. Once at the court, Michael was able to secure a decent ecclesiastical position for himself. What is more, he leveraged his new courtly connections to put his younger brother Niketas on course for a career at court.[9]

While the catastrophe of 1204 left the Roman polity paralyzed for a number of years, most state officials and members of the courtly elite, the Palaiologoi included, gathered around Theodoros I Laskaris as he reconstituted the imperial administration in Bithynia (Fig. 2.1). Since the polity and its apparatus, much as the Romans themselves, were recovering from the trauma caused by the loss of Constantinople, the production of a new class of state officials was not of immediate concern. By the 1220s, however, many existing officials were well past their prime and the task of keeping the central administration of the state running became

---

Wissenschaften 1973); P. Speck, *Die Kaiserliche Universität von Konstantinopel* (München: Verlag der Bayerischen Akademie der Wissenschaften 1974); P. Lemerle, "Le gouvernement des philosophes: notes et remarques sur l'enseignement, les ecoles, la culture," in *Cinq études sur le XIe siècle byzantin* (Paris: Centre National de la Recherche Scientifique 1977), 195–248; F. Bernard, *Writing and Reading Byzantine Secular Poetry 1025–1081* (Oxford: Oxford University Press 2014), 210–213.

[8] For Michael Psellos' biography and teaching see S. Papaioannou, *Michael Psellos: Rhetoric and Authorship in Byzantium* (Cambridge: Cambridge University Press 2013), 4–4; Bernard, *Writing and Reading*, 213.

[9] Michael Choniates' network-building during his lifetime (including the relationship with Eustathios of Thessaloniki) is discussed in Φ. Κολυβού, *Μιχαήλ Χωνιάτης. Συμβουλή στη μελετή του βίου και του έργου του το Corpus των Επιστολών* (Αθήνα: Ακαδημία Αθηνών 1999), 37–51. For Niketas Choniates's social networking see A. Simpson, *Niketas Choniates: A Historiographical Study* (Oxford: Oxford University Press 2013), 24–36.

a burning issue.[10] For this reason, Ioannes III took it upon himself to create new cohorts of capable officials. He did so by organizing a new way of imperially sponsored training for ambitious young individuals.[11] Much like the Choniates brothers in the twelfth century, individuals from (well-off) provincial families now sought to obtain training that would help draw imperial attention onto their persons. While *novi homines* were by no means a *rara avis* among Laskarid officials, more often than not the trainees came from already established families in the central government, the so-called *archontopouloi*. It was precisely this mix of intelligence and pedigree that placed Georgios and Michael in the rarefied world of imperial education. The Akropolitai had, after all, been attested in civil administrative positions since the early eleventh century,[12] while the Palaiologoi had held high positions next to the Komnenoi since Alexios I's enthronement in 1081.[13]

2.1 The Palaiologoi: Seven Generations Serving the Empire

Before we proceed to see how Michael Palaiologos benefitted from Ioannes III's system of sponsored education, it would be worthwhile to look back at the familial milestones of the Palaiologoi from the later eleventh century until the enthronement of Ioannes III. As much as the propagandists of the Palaiologoi traced the family's origins back to the senatorial elites of elder Rome in the times of Constantine the Great—as was customary for the eulogist of the Komnenian elites—the origins of this genos are much more recent and more local.[14]

---

[10] Constantinides, *Higher Education*, 9–10.

[11] Angold, *A Byzantine Government*, 174–181; Constantinides, *Higher Education*, 9–17.

[12] Macrides, "Introduction," 6–7.

[13] D.I. Polemis, *The Doukai: A Contribution to Byzantine Prosopography* (London: Athlone Press 1968), 152–164; J.-C. Cheynet and J.-F. Vannier, *Études Prosopographiques* (Paris: Éditions de la Sorbonne 1986), 123–187.

[14] For detailed prosopography as well as the hypotheses about the Palaiologoi and their familial relations that follow in this section, see Cheynet and Vannier, *Études Prosopographiques*, 129–186. For the propaganda around the alleged Palaiologan Italian origins see ibid., 130.

Fig. 2.1 The Empire of Nikaia and its neighbours c.1228 when Michael Palaiologos was around five years old

The Palaiologoi most likely originate from Phrygia and by the eleventh century they had managed to amass enough wealth and reputation that one of the clan's members succeeded in crafting a formidable career for himself in Constantinople. This man, Nikephoros Palaiologos, entered the imperial service during a period of great uncertainty for the empire.[15] The tumultuous period from 1057 to 1081, which coincides with the prime time of Nikephoros' career, saw no less than five emperors enthroned and deposed—Isaakios I Komnenos, Konstantinos X Doukas, Romanos IV Diogenes, Michael VII Doukas, and Nikephoros III Botaneiates.[16] Nikephoros Palaiologos was in no way special, though, as he acted much like a number of other members of the provincial elites throughout the tenth and eleventh centuries by deciding to try his luck and move to Constantinople to improve his position in hopes

---

[15] On Nikephoros Palaiologos, see Cheynet and Vannier, *Études Prosopographiques*, 133–135.

[16] For the rebellions and changes of imperial regimes in the eleventh century, see Cheynet, *Pouvoir et contestation*, 337–357; M. Angold, *The Byzantine Empire 1025–1204: A Political History* (Cambridge and New York: Cambridge University Press 1997), 35–80.

of joining the highest echelons of power in the capital.[17] The migration of the provincial potentates fueled Constantinople with the needed cadre to run the empire and some of these men, like those belonging to the Phokai clan, managed even to occupy the imperial throne in the later tenth century.[18] By the mid-eleventh century, the Phokai gave room to the new *oikoi* competing for the throne. Namely, the two factions competing for the throne in the mid-eleventh century were the Doukai and the Komnenoi—the latter, originating from Kastamon, were relative newcomers to Constantinople.[19] Thus, not unlike the Palaiologoi or the Phokai, the Komnenoi were tied as a clan to their roots in Asia Minor. It was in these circumstances that Nikephoros Palaiologos found himself spreading his roots in Constantinople by securing his position among the capital's elites through a marriage arrangement with the family of the Kourtikioi, who had occupied a prominent position in the empire since the times of Basileios I.[20]

As if the internal struggles were not enough both for the empire and Nikephoros Palaiologos, the Roman state was also facing two immediate external threats from the Normans in Italy and, somewhat more pressingly, from the Saljuq Turks in Asia Minor.[21] It is exactly during the imperial tenure of Romanos IV Diogenes that Nikephoros Palaiologos comes into the picture as one of the opponents of the emperor's decisions, which led to the catastrophe at Manzikert in 1071. While the empire found itself in crisis mode after the defeat in 1071, Nikephoros

---

[17] For the provincial elites moving to Constantinople see Cheynet, *Pouvoir et contestation*, 207–248.

[18] For the aristocratic *oikoi* and their connections in Constantinople see ibid., 261–286.

[19] For the Komnenian family and state politics see ibid., 359–377; Angold, *The Byzantine Empre 1025–1204*, 115–170, V. Stanković, *Komnini u Carigradu (1057–1185) evolucija jedne vladarske porodice* (Beograd: Vizantološki institut SANU 2006). For the administrative changes that happened in the Komnenian period see J. Shea, *Politics and Government in Byzantium: The Rise and Fall of the Bureaucrats* (London: I.B. Tauris 2020), 125–159.

[20] On the Kourtikioi see А. П. Каждан, *Армяне в составе господствующего класса Византийской империи в XI—XII вв* (Ереван: Изд-во АН АрмССР 1975), 14–17.

[21] For military conflicts in the eleventh century see J. Haldon, *The Byzantine* Wars (reprint Brimscombe: The History Press 2008), 164–193; for the early stages of Turkic presence in Asia Minor see A.D. Beihammer, *Byzantium and the Emergence of Muslim-Turkish Anatolia* (New York: Routledge 2017).

found himself on the winning side during the tumultuous 1070s as he supported the Doukai against Romanos IV.

A few years after Manzikert, we encounter Nikephoros occupying an important position in the eastern realms of the empire, surely thanks to the choices he made before the dethronement of Romans IV and the rise of young Michael VII Doukas. First, Palaiologos served as an imperial ambassador to the Alans in the Caucasus in 1075 and then as *megas doux* in the thema of Mesopotamia during the reign of Michael VII. It is while staying in the eastern provinces, however, that Nikephoros Palaiologos decided to turn against the emperor and support a general by the name of Nikephoros Botaneiates in his bid to claim the throne in Constantinople. From 1077 until Nikephoros III Botaneiates' abdication in 1081, Nikephoros Palaiologos remained a faithful companion to the emperor.

Nikephoros Palaiologos was prudent and lucky enough to have supported the right claimant to the throne until his preferred emperor Nikephoros III's abdication and the enthronement of Alexios I Komnenos in 1081. Nikephoros was yet again fortunate as his son Georgios sided with Alexios I during the rebellion against Nikephoros III and thus cemented the support of the cadet members of the Palaiologoi to the Komnenoi. Just as his father must have vouched for his son, who sided with Michael VII, to Nikephoros III, so too, we can imagine, Georgios Palaiologos was able to repay the debt and have his father integrated into the ascending Komnenian elites.

While Nikephoros had achieved quite a bit for himself and his family, it is with Georgios Palaiologos that the family reached new heights in the empire.[22] Namely, Alexios I Komnenos, now emperor in Constantinople, consciously or not, created a system of intertwined elites through various marital arrangements from which the Palaiologoi were to profit.[23] In his attempts to strengthen the position of the Komnenoi and to eliminate the threat of the Doukai, Alexios I married Eirene Doukaina, thus solidifying

---

[22] On Georgios Palaiologos, see Cheynet and Vannier, *Études Prosopographiques*, 137–141.

[23] See footnote 77.

the newly established order among the imperial elites. Georgios Palaiologos, a close associate of the emperor, married the empress's sister Anna Doukaina and was granted an elevated courtly title of *sebastos*.[24]

The fortunes of the Palaiologoi continued to be solidified throughout the twelfth century as the immediate offspring of Georgios and Anna—Nikephoros, Andronikos, and Alexios—are all found bearing the title of *sebastos*, just like their father.[25] Furthermore, Alexios Palaiologos married Alexios I Komnenos' great niece with whom he had a son by the name of Georgios. This Georgios Palaiologos carried the family tradition into the fourth attested generation of the Palaiologoi in Constantinople and secured the title of *sebastos*, as well as an office of *megas hetaireiarches* granting him proximity to emperor Manouel I Komnenos.[26] The son of this *megas hetaireiarches* named Alexios Palaiologos furthered the position of the family by marrying the daughter of the emperor Alexios III Angelos and securing a title of *despotes* for himself—a title oftentimes used to designate preferred heirs to the throne.[27] However, Alexios died in 1203 before he could even be considered for the imperial role, leaving behind him his daughter Theodora. Another Palaiologos of the same generation, Andronikos, was the next in the family who secured the title of despotes for himself after 1204 by marrying Eirene Doukaina Laskarina, the daughter of the first emperor in exile Theodoros I Laskaris.[28] Not unlike Alexios, Andronikos too died before his imperial father-in-law, depriving the Palaiologoi of their second chance to seize the throne.

The prominent positions in the empire's armies were not secured only for the aforementioned branch of the Palaiologoi. Rather, the line established by Nikephoros, the eldest son of Georgios Palaiologos and Anna Doukaina, continued to thrive alongside that of his brother Alexios. Both Nikephoros' son Michael and his grandson Alexios occupied positions at the court, while eventually his great grandson Andronikos Palaiologos

---

[24] On the place and the value of the Doukai in the Komnenian system, see L. Vilimonović, *Structure and Features of Anna Komnene's* Alexiad: *Emergence of a Personal History* (Amsterdam: Amsterdam University Press 2018), 163–268.

[25] On the four sons of Georgios Palaiologos and Anna Doukaina, see Cheynet and Vannier, *Études Prosopographiques*, 145–151.

[26] On *megas hetaireiarches* Georgios Palaiologos, see ibid., 156–158.

[27] On *despotes* Alexios Palaiologos, see Cheynet and Vannier, *Études Prosopographiques*, 170–172.

[28] On *despotes* Andronikos Palaiologos, see ibid., 172–174.

became the megas domestikos of the imperial armies during the reign of Ioannes III Batatzes.[29] It is this megas domestikos Andronikos Palaiologos who fathered four children with his cousin Theodora Palaiologina, the daughter of despotes Alexios, the son-in-law of Alexios III Angelos, among whom was Michael Palaiologos, who in time would bring the Palaiologoi to the imperial throne.

The emperor-to-be Michael Palaiologos, as well as his two older sisters Maria and Eirene and his younger brother Ioannes, all had potential for a bright future thanks to their family's pedigree and prudent marital choices that spanned over seven generations. While having an extremely well-connected family was certainly a major aid to one's career, young Michael Palaiologos still had to receive a proper education and martial training before hoping to become more prominent in the imperial service. In the end, the Palaiologoi were far from the only ones who married smart; careful family alliances had become a trend since the reign of Alexios I Komnenos for most elite *oikoi*. Thus, in the sea of high-born sons, Michael had also to rely on his education and training in advancing his career in the service of Ioannes III Batatzes and the Roman Empire in exile.

2.2 Preparing for Greatness: Education at the Imperial Court

Thanks to Theodoros I's efforts to gather most of the pre-1204 notable families under his imperial authority, his successor Ioannes III had quite a few literati to choose from when he looked for teachers to train his new cohort of capable civil and military officials.[30] Early education—*grammatike* or *hiera grammata* which introduced students to writing, grammar, and basic Homeric poetry—was not part of Ioannes III's educational master-plan.[31] This was to be obtained by trainees elsewhere at their own expense. Ioannes III took in the best among a number of affluent young pupils, providing them with the next level in their

---

[29] On Michael Palaiologos and Alexios Palaiologos, see ibid., 153–155, 168–170. On *megas domestikos* Andronikos Palaiologos, see 176–178.

[30] On the intellectuals and other members of the elite who joined Theodoros I see Constantinides, *Higher Education*, 5–8; Angold, *A Byzantine Government*, 9–22.

[31] Bernard, *Writing and Reading*, 213–222.

formation—the *enkyklios paideia* that taught students more elaborate rhetorical composition. The selection process was based on recommendations from the polity's literati-teachers. In a sense, the circle of people who could attract imperial attention was limited to families affluent enough to provide a head start for their male offspring with a formidable early education. Academic merit notwithstanding, finding a teacher well-connected to the imperial court was a paramount goal of any ambitious *novus homo*.[32]

This imperially sponsored educational initiative was only introduced in the 1230s. Before this period, ambitious individuals were left to their own devices when it came to acquiring their first letters and, hopefully, garnering imperial attention. Thus, a leading erudite of the Nikaian period, Nikephoros Blemmydes, obtained his entire education completely on his own, or at least on his family's dime. After obtaining *grammatike* and *enkyklios paideia*, Nikephoros went to study philosophy under a hermit by the name of Prodromos around the Skamander region (which was under Latin control until 1224).[33] Having completed his education under Prodromos, he continued his studies of the Holy Scriptures at Nymphaion. Without imperial patronage for young erudite men, how did Nikephoros, an utter newcomer to the court elites, catch Ioannes III's attention? He did so precisely thanks to personal connections he made during his early education. In his *Autobiography*, Nikephoros explains that he was invited to Nikaia by the patriarch Germanos II, who introduced him to the imperial court where he underwent an examination before the emperor.[34] Nikephoros' knowledge was tested by the *hypatos ton philosophon* Demetrios Karykes, who was in charge of higher education at the court. The examination was held in the presence of a larger audience of *logades*. In this public event, Nikephoros managed to shine and prove himself worthy of an office in the state administration.[35] Ioannes III offered him a position immediately, but Nikephoros chose a career in the Church under Germanos II's patronage.

---

[32] For instance, see the case of Ioannes Bekkos later in this chapter.

[33] On Nikephoros' early education see Blemmydes, *Curriculum*, i.304; for his studies and curriculum under Prodromos: ibid., i.6–8.

[34] ibid., i.12.1–4.

[35] For Nikephoros' education in Nymphaion and public examination see ibid.: i.14–21; Constantinides, *Higher Education*, 9.

While the how and where of Nikephoros' first encounter with Germanos II remain unknown, it is clear that this earlier social connection, one most likely established through education, gave Nikephoros access to the aforementioned examination and selection process. We therefore see that even before the emergence of an imperially endowed education, Ioannes III's court nourished the idea of recruiting potential officeholders among the well-off members of the polity through examination with the trusted *logades*. For, as Floris Bernard points out for the eleventh century:

> [e]ducation is the cornerstone on which the meritocratic ideal of the intellectual elite is built. It transmits necessary competences and skills, forges ties of long-lasting friendship, and serves as a criterion on the basis of which careers are assigned. [...] it was also put up as a barrier for determining who could appeal for membership of the elite and who could not.[36]

By the time of Nikephoros Blemmydes' examination, notable pre-1204 intellectual offices had been re-established. There was at Nikaia an *hypatos ton philosophon* and *logades*, who were all involved in public examinations of prospective candidates.[37] The court at Nymphaion became a place where young literati could attract the attention of both established notables and the emperor.[38] This allowed *archontopouloi* as well as newcomers to secure unbiased witnesses to their budding erudition. By putting their intellectual wares on public display, these aspiring young men could be in no doubt that regardless of social connections, the truly talented among them would indeed be offered a position in the administration.

Early in the 1230s, Ioannes III sought to regularize the process of selection for the central administration by establishing an imperially sponsored educational system open to those pupils who had distinguished themselves during their initial privately funded early education. While teachers received their salaries directly from the emperor, instructors and

---

[36] Bernard, *Writing and Reading*, 209.

[37] Constantinides, *Higher Education*, 5–9.

[38] Blemmydes emphasized that Ioannes set up the imperial court in Nymphaion (and not Nikaia): τὴν ἀνακτορικὴν σκήνωσιν ἔχειν ἐν Νυμφαίῳ προείλετο (Blemmydes, *Curriculum*, i.12.9–10). For presence of imperial palaces in various cities of the empire (Nymphaion, Magnesia, Smyrne, Philadelphia, and Nikaia), see Angelov, *The Byzantine Hellene*, 44.

schools continued to operate outside the court. For instance, Nikephoros Blemmydes' institution—attached to his monastery of St George the Wonderworker by Ephesos—accepted imperial donations and students, while retaining curricular independence. Georgios Akropolites was one of the first pupils in this imperially endowed academy for future officials. In his own words, Georgios describes his parents sending him to the emperor once he had finished the *grammatike* in Constantinople. We learn that he was placed at that school in 1233 along with four other students.[39] From this point on Georgios' official training lasted for about five years. He began his higher education at the age of 17 under Theodoros Hexapterygos, who dwelled mostly on rhetoric and "he was," as Georgios put it, "a man not very versed in philosophy but good at matters of speech, since he had dwelt extensively on rhetorical studies and had studied skilful expression and had acquired great reputation because of this."[40] After Theodoros' death, the group of five studied under Nikephoros Blemmydes. This time, Georgios was exposed to philosophy, astronomy, and theology. Despite having rejected an official position, Nikephoros remained close to the court and as a monk obtained a grant to build his own monastery and school in the region of Ephesos.[41] In exchange for such imperial support Nikephoros was to play a part in educating future court officials.

By employing already existing teachers in their respective schools, Ioannes III, as well as his successor Theodoros II, kept institutions of learning alive, while at the same time making the imperial imprint prominent in the provinces away from the court. Not only were the pupils at schools aware that their education was paid for by the imperial household, but the textbooks used in class made it clear that their instructors were also dependant on imperial patronage. For instance, in *Epitome Logikes* composed to teach philosophy to Georgios Akropolites and his four classmates, Nikephoros Blemmydes opened the textbook with an appropriate proem:

---

[39] Akropolites, *Chronike*, 32.1–6; 17–18; on the total number of five students see Blemmydes, *Curriculum*, i.49.3–5.

[40] ἀνὴρ οὐ πάνυ μὲν ἐπιστήμων ἐν τοῖς μαθήμασιν, ἀγαθὸς δὲ φράζειν, οἷα ῥητορικοῖς λόγοις κατάκρως ἐνδιατρίψας καὶ τὸ ἐξαγγέλλειν εὐφυῶς μεμελετηκὼς καὶ πολλοῦ διὰ τοῦτο ἠξιωμένος ὀνόματος (Akropolites, *Chronike*, 32.19–22).

[41] Ibid., 32.24–29.

Imperial sovereignty and philosophy have a lot in common and are of the same kind. They both represent the greatness of divine power and they both strive to the same goal: the former to rise high in dignity and to control [imperial] power; the latter to govern arts and sciences and to enact laws for all of them. For this reason, [philosophy] is called the art of arts and the science of sciences, just as the imperial sovereignty is called the dignity of dignities and the authority of authorities.[42]

While the *prooimion* pays necessary lip service to the regime, it also encourages students to exceed in their studies by comparing the role of philosophy to that of the emperor. In order to become good servants of the empire, students had to emulate the greatest of public officials, the emperor of the Romans. The relation between education and imperial dignity is made clear by comparing the two: just as philosophy is held in the highest esteem among arts and sciences, so is the imperial office among public dignities. By proclaiming emperorship a dignity to be emulated, Nikephoros masterfully displayed a sense of gratitude to Ioannes III (who held the dignity thanks to his own exceptional qualities) for imperial patronage.

Georgios and his four colleagues remained with Nikephoros until two of the students accused their teacher of embezzling money from the metropolitan in Ephesos. Even though he was cleared of charges at both imperial and ecclesiastic courts, Nikephoros decided not to take on any more imperially sponsored students.[43] An exception was made several years later, when he agreed to tutor young Theodoros, son of Ioannes III. The emperor, however, had to look for new places of learning for his officials-to-be. Fortunately for Ioannes III, having completed his education, Georgios Akropolites was immediately accepted into the imperial administration, while on the side, he also started teaching. By the 1240s, the governing of the state as well as the training of future officials was in the hands of individuals such as Georgios, who were raised and educated after 1204. With them the Nikaian generation came to the fore.

---

[42] Βασιλείας καὶ φιλοσοφίας πολὺ τὸ συγγενές τε καὶ ὁμοιότροπον. Καὶ ἄμφω γὰρ τὸ μεγαλεῖον τῆς θεαρχίας ἐξεικονίζουσι, καὶ τὸ ἴσον προτίθενται σκοπὸν ἑαυταῖς, ἡ μὲν τῶν ἀξιῶν ὑπερέχουσα, καὶ ταῖς ἀρχαῖς ἐπιτάττουσα. ἡ δὲ τῶν τεχνῶν ἐξάρχουσα καὶ τῶν ἐπιστημῶν, καὶ νομοθετοῦσα ταύταις ἁπάσαις καὶ καλουμένη δία ταῦτα τέχνη τεχνῶν καὶ ἐπιστήμη ἐπιστημῶν, ὥσπερ καὶ ἡ βασιλεία τῶν ἀξιῶν ἀξία καὶ ὑπεροχὴ τῶν ὑπεροχῶν (Blemmydes, *Epitome Logikes* [PG 142], 689).

[43] Constantinides, *Higher Education*, 12.

2.3 Education: A Public Affair

If we are to trust the author of the *Synopsis Chronike*, Ioannes III "assembled libraries around the cities from books pertaining to all kinds of arts and sciences."[44] These establishments were certainly staffed with the intellectual progeny of Nikaian teachers. The organization of higher education allowed the emperors to make themselves (as well as the potential lucrative careers they had to offer) known to the provincial elite throughout the lands of the polity, thus opening a path that led from local affairs to central administration. Providing this path was a good way to secure the provincial notables' allegiance to the regime. To reinforce such links between centre and periphery, the emperors employed teachers from among the court circles in Nikaia, Nymphaion, Philadelphia, Smyrne, and Magnesia. Such men could be trusted in their recommendations of prospective officials-to-be. A good example of this process is an otherwise unknown teacher by the name of Georgios Babouskomites, who worked at a school outside the capital cities.[45] Georgios kept in touch with his friends Michael Theophilopoulos, Ioannes Makrotos, and Nikolaos Kostomyres, who were imperial secretaries, in order to promote his students to them.[46] Thus, a well-connected and credible teacher, even one far from the major administrative centres of Nikaia and Magnesia, would advocate for capable students by mobilizing his friends in the civil service.[47] The most famous student Georgios launched into a public career was Ioannes Bekkos, who eventually followed the ecclesiastic track; this was a well-made decision, one could argue, since he ended up on

---

[44] βιβλιοθήκας κατὰ πόλεις συνήθροισεν ἐκ βίβλων πασῶν τεχνῶν καὶ ἐπιστημῶν (*Synopsis Chronike*, 507.19–20).

[45] V. Laurent, "La correspondance inédite de Georges Babouscomitès," in *Εἰς μνήμην Σπυρίδωνος Λάμπρου* (Ἀθῆναι: Ἐπιτροπὴ ἐκδόσεως τῶν καταλοίπων Σπυρίδωνος Λάμπρου 1935), 87.

[46] ibid., 83–100.

[47] Constantinides, *Higher Education*, 17, argues that Georgios Babouskomites's school was on imperial payroll; however, the letters do not provide us with any information on the topic. The fact is that he was in touch with imperial secretaries and that he promoted his students to them. Whether these students paid for their education from their own pockets or the imperial one remains an open question. In the fifth letter, however, we learn that Ioannes Bekkos left the school in order to pursue his education elsewhere only to come back to Georgios. While it is not implausible that one would leave a place at the school with imperial patronage, it is also possible that young Ioannes wished to spend his money elsewhere.

the patriarchal throne. Ioannes, however, initially had doubts about his prospective career path. Georgios refrained from giving his pupil advice. He simply noted in a letter that while his school would serve his pupil well in both ecclesiastic and state careers, it was up to the young intellectual to decide which path he wished to take.[48]

The imperial court did not stop at opening schools around the empire and hiring trusted teachers. The regime kept a close eye on the training process itself in order to ascertain the quality of future cadres. We have already seen how Nikephoros Blemmydes was examined by the *logades* in imperial presence. Examining individuals who had completed education at their own expense was one way to assess one's capability to serve the imperial administration. Another was to randomly summon students while they were still at school to test their progress. In a letter written between 1254 and 1258 to Andronikos Phrangopoulos and Michael Senachereim, teachers at the imperially endowed school of St Tryphon in Nikaia, Theodoros II, now the sole emperor of the Romans, congratulated the two teachers on training their students well by acknowledging that "the group of six [students] sent before me testifies to your presence [at the school], wise men worthy of praise."[49] The letter suggests that the emperor, randomly chose and examined a cohort of students to make sure that specific schools and students were worth the investment. Another peculiarity of the letter is that the emperor summoned a group of five students who were at the same level, while the sixth one was at a different stage of education.[50] It thus seems that the cohorts were not particularly large and that the number of five students per class was standard in state-sponsored schools—from Georgios Akropolites' cohort of 1233 to the one of the mid-1250s at St Tryphon. This means that the selection of students for imperially sponsored schools was open only to the most promising candidates. Also, groups of five were easier to examine whenever it was deemed necessary. On the other hand, groups

---

[48] Laurent, "La correspondance inédite," 93, 13–15. Post-1204 education retained the early practice of not separating secular and ecclesiastic education (see Bernard, *Writing and Reading*, 211–212).

[49] καὶ τὴν μαρτυρίαν ἄγει πρὸς τοὐμφανὲς ἡ τῶν νέων ἑξὰς ἡ πρός με πεφθακυῖα, ὦ σοφώτατοι ἄνδρες καὶ ἀξιέπαινοι (Theodoros II Laskaris, *Epistulae*, 217.92–94).

[50] οὗτοι γὰρ πεντὰς καὶ ἑξάς· ἡ μὲν πεντὰς ὡς ἀρχὴ αἰσθητικῆς καὶ ζωικῆς ὑπάρξεως, γραμματικῆς δηλονότι· ἡ δὲ συντελεστικὴ μονὰς τῆς ἑξάδος ποιητικῆς ἐστι προσβολή (ibid., 217.94–96).

of five students per cohort in schools around the empire could surely secure enough recruits for the upper rungs of central and even provincial administration, which was humbled in size after 1204.[51] This is especially true since more than one cohort of five was enrolled at a single school as is seen from Theodoros II's letter where a complete group of five is counted, plus one younger student.

One's education did not, however, end once that individual became a state official. Rather, officials and bureaucrats could take time off in order to further their education.[52] In Theodoros II's correspondence, we encounter letters in which the heir apparent asks secretaries of the fisc about the benefits of further education. In one of the letters to his secretaries, Theodoros II notes that "the career of those circulating at the court is complicated" and wonders how their further training was going: "how do you go through the matters of philosophy? Partially or overall, completely?"[53] This letter sent to his secretaries shows that Theodoros II was deeply invested in the bureaucrats' training. He kept in touch with those who were absent from their workplaces by posing reflective questions to them.[54] In demonstrating his care for his secretaries, Theodoros II also managed to send a clear message that he was vigilant of major and lesser officials' deeds—for better or for worse. The combination of examination during one's studies as well as occasional briefing during one's career allowed the court of the post-1204 Roman polity to keep track of the central administration at various levels. On the other hand, the bureaucrats were reminded that keeping their skills polished could only help them in advancing even further in their careers.

Michael Palaiologos was brought up in this very system of education and selection. Unlike the *novi homines* or even members of families that

---

[51] For comparative purposes see the number of intellectuals present at the court in the tenth century (prior to the establishment of the office of *hypatos ton philosophon*): Paul Lemerle, "Élèves et professeurs à Constantinople au Xe siècle," *Comptes-rendus des séances de l'Académie des inscriptions et belles-lettres* 113 (1969), 576–87; idem, *Byzantine Humanism: The First Phase* (Canberra: Australian Association of Byzantine Studies 1986), 281–309. On the fewer people needed to run the administration of the state see Angold, *A Byzantine Government*, 147–236.

[52] Constantinides, *Higher Education*, 21.

[53] πολύτροπος ἡ διαγωγὴ τῶν ἐν βασιλείοις περιπατούντων [...] πῶς τὰ τῆς φιλοσοφίας διέρχεσθε; μερικῶς, ἢ ὅλοις καθολικῶς; (Theodoros II Laskaris, *Epistulae*, 121, 24–25, 39–40).

[54] See, for example: Theodoros II Laskaris, *Epistulae*, 121.

had served the state for generations, such as Georgios Akropolites' *oikos*, Michael originated from one of the leading families of the empire. That is, the Palaiologoi actively occupied some of the highest positions in the empire since the later eleventh century and by the thirteenth century they formed integral linkages of the golden chain households. While Michael had to prove himself worthy of high office, as he explained in his writings, he could rest assured that a position would be found for him, if only based on his family's illustrious background.[55] For the very same reason, however, Michael was under greater scrutiny than his peers at court. For, just like Akropolites, Palaiologos was brought up at the court. Unlike Georgios, though, Michael operated close to his parents and relatives who were frequenting the court and did not dwell in Latin occupied Constantinople. So, why was Michael raised—as he himself notes—by the side of the imperial family? Having a young Palaiologos close to the imperial administration served a number of purposes. First, just like lesser state officials-to-be, Michael would be aware of the court's vigilance and care for him. He would internalize the imperial gaze and would be raised to think twice before trying to betray his benefactor. Secondly, by being at court, Michael had a chance to obtain a better sense of the duties and obligations that were the purview of the polity's great notables.[56] Finally, on a more personal level, while Michael was from a well-off family, he was brought up by his sister Maria Palaiologina before he had moved to the court, since his mother died while Michael was a child and his father busied himself with a career that took him all around the empire.[57]

Where Michael received his early education—the *grammatike*—remains unknown. Once he was taken up by Ioannes III, however, his whereabouts and actions become better known to us. From the time of his *enkyklios paideia*, Michael lived in one of the imperial palaces, close to the imperial family, the senate, and other institutions related to the court. We have already seen young individuals such as Georgios Akropolites sojourned at the court before they were sent to be educated

---

[55] On Byzantine offices' interrelation with kinship, family background, and patronage see J. Haldon, "Bureaucracies, Elites, and Clans: The Case of Byzantium, 600–1100," in P. Crooks (ed.), *Empires and Bureaucracy in World History: From Late Antiquity to the Twentieth Century* (Cambridge, UK: Cambridge University Press 2016), 147–169.

[56] On Byzantine governing practices and the place of the great notables in it, see A. Kaldellis, *The Byzantine Republic*.

[57] On Michael's elder sister Maria, religious name Martha, see *PLP*, 21,389.

elsewhere. Much like Georgios, Michael was surrounded by other *archontopouloi*, since this was apparently a common practice at the court. Being at the court meant that Michael, as much as his young peers, was able to get acquainted with the imperial family. However, the emperor and his family had a few palaces to choose from, which meant that they were not constantly present at a specific location where Michael grew up. Adding to this, we should keep in mind that Ioannes III spent quite a few months out of a year campaigning in the Balkans. Thus, young Michael Palaiologos had a chance to be familiar with the imperial family, but he was not a regular member of their entourage.

Another important factor limiting the mobility of courtiers and other people present at the court was the very infrastructure of the palace. Later Byzantine imperial palaces, such as Blachernai and Tekfur Saray in Constantinople, as well as the one in Nymphaion, were not built in the fashion of traditional Late Antique and Medieval Roman aristocratic domus.[58] The layout of these palaces was quite different from the Great Palace at Constantinople, which stayed in parallel ceremonial and administrative use with other residences taken up by various emperors since the tenth century.[59] While the Great Palace was a vast ground floor structure, subsequent palaces consisted of several multi-storeyed buildings arranged around a central courtyard. Taking into account the layout of the palace in Nymphaion and the Tekfur Saray in Constantinople, as well as the reconstruction of the palatial complex of Blachernai based on narrative texts, it is easy to see how several interconnected buildings allowed for *archontopouloi* to dwell within the palace without at the same time having unfettered access to all quarters of the imperial palace.[60] The emperor

---

[58] On Late Antique origins of Byzantine palatial architecture see P. Niewöhner, "The Late Antique Origins of Byzantine Palace Architecture," in in M. Featherstone, J.-M. Spieser, G. Tanman, and U. Wulf-Rheidt (eds.), *The Emperor's House: Palaces from Augustus to the Age of Absolutism* (Berlin, München, and Boston: De Gruyter 2015), 31–52.

[59] On the Great Palace see A. Berger, "The Byzantine Court as a Physical Space," in *The Byzantine Court: Source of Power and Culture* (Istanbul: Koç University Press 2013), 3–12; M. Featherstone, "The Everyday Palace in the 10th Century," in *The Emperor's House*, 149–158.

[60] On the reconstruction of the Blachernai palatial complex based on Pseudo-Kodinos' ceremonial handbook and other narrative sources, aided by the material remainings of Tekfur Saray and the palace at Nymphaion, see R. Macrides, "The 'Other' Palace in Constantinople: The Blachernai," in *The Emperor's House*, 159–168. Also, see R. Macrides,

Fig. 2.2 The surviving structure of the palace at Nymphaion

and his family could therefore be so close and yet so far away, completely secluded from unwanted contact with those who spent time within the palace. Such distance notwithstanding, future imperial officials, who had the opportunity to live within the palatial complex, were able to witness the daily workings of the central administration (Fig. 2.2).

Learning by observing how the governing apparatus functioned was therefore undoubtedly one of the greatest benefits of growing up at the court. The imperial palace was the seat of administrative units such as the *scriptoria* and the fisc. It housed both imperial secretaries and governing bodies such as the senate.[61] At court, young Michael and his peers also observed how the palace as a space interacted with the outer world. The essence of the court's communication with the outside was the admission

---

J.A. Munitiz, and D. Angelov, "The Palace of the Ceremonies," in *Pseudo-Kodinos and the Constantinopolitan Court: Offices and Ceremonies* (Aldershot: Ashgate 2013), 367–378.

[61] On imperial governing bodies c.1204–1261 see Angold, *A Byzantine Government*, 147–236.

of peoples' petitions either by the emperor or his representatives during his absence. If we are to trust Theodoros II's description of his daily agenda, dealing with petitions and passing judgement consumed quite a few hours of his day:

> As the sun appears, care for soldiers is awakened with us from bed. While the sun is rising further and is being carried higher, care for ambassadors and their reception and dismissal [occupies us]. As the sun is still rising, the order of the troops is settled by us. When the sun is positioned in the middle at noon, the matter of petitioners is attended and resolved. We then go out on horseback to hear those who could not enter with those at the gates of the palace. As the sun is setting down, we pass the judgements for our subjects.[62]

By having, albeit limited, access to various aspects of state administration and by seeing individuals of all manner of rank and provenance circulating around different parts of the palace, students developed a sense of the court as a public space. Many people, oftentimes unrelated to the imperial family, dwelled in the palace. Aside from the high-ranking officials, bureaucrats, and servants permanently employed in offices by the court, other Romans and foreigners passed through the palace on business, as it seems, smoothly. All these men—be it monks and *paroikoi* at each other's throats, contesting the possession of public land,[63] a soldier seeking a *pronoia*,[64] a local citizen displeased with a lack of attention from the emperor,[65] or a grand Mongol embassy sent by the Great Khan[66]—contributed to making the palace a vibrant meeting place for conducting all manner of business. By maturing in such an environment rather than in the private and more secluded household of the Palaiologoi, Michael

---

[62] ἀνατέλλοντος τοῦ ἡλίου περὶ τῶν ὁπλιτῶν ἡμῖν ἡ φροντὶς ἐκ τῆς κλίνης συνανεγείρεται, ἀνερχομένου τε καὶ ἀναφερομένου περὶ τὰ ὑψηλότερα ἢ τῶν πρέσβεων μέριμνά τε καὶ εἰσδοχὴ καὶ ἀπεκβολή, ἔτι δὲ ἀναφερομένου ἡ τῶν φαλάγγων τάξις τάττεται παρ' ἡμῶν, ἱσταμένου δὲ περὶ τὸ ἡμερήσιον μέσον ἡ τῶν δεομένων μελέτη μελετᾶταί τε καὶ κατασκευάζεται, καὶ ἵππῳ βαίνομεν ὡς τῶν μὴ πρὸς τοὺς ἐν ταῖς πύλαις τῶν βασιλείων εἰσελθεῖν δυναμένων ἀκροασόμενοι, ὑποκλίνοντος δὲ τὰς κρίσεις τῶν ὑποκλιθέντων ἀποπληροῦμεν (Theodoros II Laskaris, *Epistulae*, 50.63–71).

[63] *MM*, 36–39.

[64] Bartusis, *Land and Privilege*, 213–24.

[65] *Synopsis Chronike*, 463.

[66] Akropolites, *Chronike*, 41.

did not only obtain a first-hand experience about the ways in which the administration operated, but also had an opportunity to learn a thing or two about the psyche and mores of his compatriots who did not belong to his social group.

2.4 Progymnasmata in Action: Michael Palaiologos' Erudition on Public Display

While learning by observing the dynamics of the imperial court helped prepare Michael for serving the empire, the most significant portion of his education came from the classroom. Here, Palaiologos received his education just like Georgios Akropolites and other officials-to-be. This included extensive training in rhetoric and, up to a point, philosophy. Even though Michael eventually chose a military career path, he did not skip the basic upper-level education. After all, it was not uncommon for young *archontopouloi* and other individuals like young Bekkos to receive formidable education by the age of seventeen and then decide which way they wished to direct their careers. Regardless of the path they chose, the art of rhetorical persuasion was always welcome both at court and the battlefield for "to speak and to exhort the public properly, I think, is of greatest use to the army."[67] While we can hypothesize that Michael employed his rhetorical skills in the army, his scholarly erudition is best displayed in the extensive autobiographical portrait he included in the *typikon* of the Monastery of St Demetrios in Constantinople.

In the third and fourth centuries CE, teachers and theorists of rhetoric composed textbooks on writing, style, and the art of eloquence that contained a number of examples and exercises for the purposes of instruction.[68] These rhetorical textbooks, called *progymnasmata*, served as a base for any education one was to receive in the Roman Empire all

---

[67] Λέγειν δὲ καὶ δημηγορεῖν ἱκανόν· ἡγοῦμαι γὰρ τὰ μέγιστα ὠφελεῖν διὰ τοῦτο τὸ στράτευμα (*The Taktika of Leo VI*, G. Dennis ed. and trans. (DO 2010), 20, 58–59). On the need of generals and emperors to be ready to engage in oratory in front of the soldiers see *Maurice's Strategikon. Handbook of Byzantine Military Strategy*, G. Dennis ed. and trans. (Philadelphia: University of Pennsylvania Press 1984), 270; *The Taktika of Leo VI*, 20; *The Taktika of Leo VI*, 20–21.

[68] On *progymnasmata* see G.A. Kennedy, *Progymnasmata: Greek Textbooks of Prose Composition and Rhetoric* (Atlanta: Society for Biblical Literature 2003); G.A. Kennedy, *A New History of Classical Rhetoric* (Princeton: Princeton University Press 1994), 202–208; R.F. Hock, "General Introduction," in R.F. Hock et al. (eds.), *The Chreia in*

the way to 1453. All *progymnasmata*, be it the ones originating from Late Antiquity—such as those of Libanios, Hermogenes, or Aphthonios— or the ones from later periods—by Psellos, Basilakes, Hexapterygos, or Pachymeres—contained virtually the same exercises and rules followed by different examples.[69] At the time of Michael Palaiologos' education, the most widely used textbooks, alongside those of contemporary teachers, were the *progymnasmata* of Hermogenes and Aphthonios.[70]

Rhetorical exercises emphasized the importance of clarity and good style in composing orations of any sort. Rhetorical training, however, also prepared one for public service; being a good writer and speaker had a lasting impact on one's career. As we have seen, secretaries of the imperial administration took "sabbaticals" in order to perfect their existing training so that they would be able to keep up with the requirements of their own office and even achieve promotion to higher positions. Clarity and persuasiveness in writing and speaking was crucial for both civil and military officials who were all expected to relate effectively and cohesively their own or other people's ideas, requests, and affairs. Furthermore, polished language and urbane witticism were norms of communication among the elites of the empire.[71] Thus, rigid training in *rhetorike techne* helped students polish their communication skills and draft official speeches and documents.[72] Such training went beyond memorizing and mimicking classical authors and their language, as is seen by the very content of the exercises. For example, students had to write appraisals and refutations

---

Ancient Rhetoric (Atlanta: Society for Biblical Literature 1986), 3–60. For *progymnasmata* in Byzantium see H. Hunger, *Die hochsprachliche profane Literatur der Byzantiner* I (München: C.H. Beck 1978), 92–119. On rhetorical education in Byzantium see A. Riehle, "Rhetorical Practice," in S. Papaioannou (ed.), *The Oxford Handbook of Byzantine Literature* (Oxford, 2021), 304–310.

[69] C. Barber and S. Papaioannou (eds.), *Michael Psellos on Literature and* Art (Notre Dame: Notre Dame University Press 2017); Nikephoros Basilakes, *The Rhetorical Exercises of Nikephoros Basilakes*, ed. and transl. J. Beneker and C.A. Gibson [Dumbarton Oaks Medieval Library 43] (Cambridge, MA: Harvard University Press 2016); W. Hörander, "Die Progymnasmata des Theodoros Hexapterygos," in W. Hörander et al. (eds.), Βυζάντιος. *Festschrift für Herbert Hunger zum 70. Geburtstag* (Wien: Österreichische Akademie der Wissenschaften 1984), 147–162.

[70] For example, see Blemmydes, *Autbiographia*, i.4.

[71] On acquired urbane qualities, including the well-polished rhetorical skills in conversation expected of a general see Krallis, "Urbane Warriors," 154–168.

[72] For example, Akropolites oversaw drafting documents for Ioannes III since 1246 (Akropolites, *Chronike*, 44).

of specific individuals or concepts.[73] By being exposed to such training, selected young men learned how to craft persuasive arguments for their respective side, while seeking to outmanoeuver their opponents in public debate of any sort, a skill much appreciated in medieval Roman society.

Michael, who made a career for himself in the military, nevertheless took pride in showing off his eloquence. Throughout his autobiography, Michael adhered to the rules of rhetorical composition he had learned as a teenager at school. In order to forge a positive image of himself, he relied heavily on the rules for composing an *enkomion* (praise)[74] in the *progymnasmata* of Hermogenes and Aphthonios that instruct:

> These are then the traits of *enkomion*. You should work through it with the following chapters. You will make a preface proper for the subject; then you will state the origin, which you will divide into nation, homeland, ancestors, and parents; followed by the upbringing, which you will divide into habits, acquired skill, and principles of conduct; then you will compose the greatest chapter of the praise, the deeds, which you will divide into those of mind, body, and fortune: mind, as courage or prudence; body, as beauty, swiftness, or strength; fortune, as power, wealth, or friends; after these a comparison, attributing superiority to the praised by juxtaposition; then an epilogue with a prayer at hand.[75]

Michael adapted this rhetorical blueprint to his own needs: to celebrate his own career in the rules of a monastery he built before his death in 1282. Thus, the narrative begins with Michael's glorious ancestry—emphasizing the antiquity of his family line, the Palaiologan position in Constantinople, as well as his grandfather's and father's illustrious careers, followed by the mother's reputable ancestry. Once he had pointed out the greatness of his lineage, Michael turned to his own upbringing, the excellent education he had received, and his excellence in it, which exceeded

---

[73] Kennedy, *A New History*, 3–60.

[74] On *enkomion* see Hunger, *Die hochsprachliche profane Literatur*, 120–132.

[75] Ἡ μὲν οὖν διαίρεσις αὕτη τοῦ ἐγκωμίου· ἐργάσαιο δ' αὐτὸ τοῖσδε τοῖς κεφαλαίοις· προοιμιάσῃ μὲν πρὸς τὴν οὖσαν ὑπόθεσιν· εἶτα θήσεις τὸ γένος, ὃ διαιρήσεις εἰς ἔθνος, πατρίδα, προγόνους καὶ πατέρας· εἶτα ἀνατροφήν, ἣν διαιρήσεις εἰς ἐπιτηδεύματα καὶ τέχνην καὶ νόμους· εἶτα τὸ μέγιστον τῶν ἐγκωμίων κεφάλαιον ἐποίσεις τὰς πράξεις, ἃς διαιρήσεις εἰς ψυχὴν καὶ σῶμα καὶ τύχην, ψυχὴν μὲν ὡς ἀνδρείαν ἢ φρόνησιν, σῶμα δὲ ὡς κάλλος ἢ τάχος ἢ ῥώμην, τύχην δὲ ὡς δυναστείαν καὶ πλοῦτον καὶ φίλους· ἐπὶ τούτοις τὴν σύγκρισιν ἐκ παραθέσεως συνάγων τῷ ἐγκωμιαζομένῳ τὸ μεῖζον· εἶτα ἐπίλογον εὐχῇ μᾶλλον προσήκοντα (Aphthonios, *Progymnasmata*, 21.20–22.11).

all expectations. After these introductory chapters, the author continued by showcasing his own deeds. These he divides in three categories. He starts with the deeds of mind, which are courage in battle from a young age and prudence in dealing with domestic and foreign affairs. Then he turns to the deeds of the body: swiftness in the battlefield. Michael leaves fortune last in this three-part account. Aware of the problematic nature of his elevation to the imperial office, Michael decided to frame this topic as a matter of fortune: "I was elevated to emperor of your people by you [God]."[76] By following the tripartite division of deeds, Michael was able to completely circumvent his somewhat problematic enthronement that was anything but scandal-free. Finally, in place of comparison, Michael positions himself vis-à-vis other emperors and mentions that his son will be the next ruler of the Romans. In place of "an epilogue rather fitting a prayer," Michael introduces St Demetrios, his protector saint, and offers a prayer to him in exchange for protecting himself and the imperial family.

It does not come as a surprise that Michael deployed a rhetorical *deus ex machina* to avoid compromising himself on the issue of elevation to the throne. On the other hand, he went to a great deal of trouble to also explain away his flight to the Saljuq Turks. In openly addressing his abandonment of the Romans and his running away to the Turks of Ikonion, truly an act of betrayal, Michael notes:

> Then there were military commands again and battles again, but anew God granted me fame and success in everything. Then I was entrusted with the war against the Latins, who occupied the queen of the cities, much to her misfortune. Being with the army across the city in Asia, I cannot say that I did not persecute them to the furthest extremities with God as my ally. From all the sides, I prevented them from disembarking, I repelled their assaults, and I cut off their vital supplies. All this happened while he [Ioannes III] was alive and we advanced from glory to glory always becoming greater and greater with God leading us to prosperity. However, when the empire of the Romans passed on to his son, it happened that we were to be tested by the arrows of jealousy with which many others have been tested. How did God deliver us at that time and how did He bring us from the oppression to the wide place? To state it briefly, he saved us with the Persians. There God took me by my right hand and elevated me with glory. Even nowadays, they can still be heard signing about our

---

[76] ἀναλαμβάνομαι εἰς βασιλέα τοῦ σοῦ λαοῦ παρὰ σοῦ· (Palaiologos, *Autobiography*, 6.9–10).

resistance and assault against the Massagetai [i.e. the Mongols], about the effort and the great victory over those who appeared unstoppable before. This was not achieved amid Persian lands by us, but God [acting] through us. Henceforth, many embassies and letters were sent to us by the emperor who was summoning us back to our kin and fatherland.[77]

Here Michael masterfully deals with the scandal that followed his flight to the Turks by promoting an image of himself as a faithful citizen of the empire who was forced to run for his life by an overtly envious emperor. Furthermore, Michael singles out divine grace as his protector in exile. Because of God's patronage, the fame of his deeds among the Persians echoed in the hearts of his fellow Romans, who still sung paeans about his militarily exploits in exile. According to Michael, his reputation was so strong that even the emperor relented for plotting against him and invited him back to Roman lands. But why did Michael need to address this unpleasant episode in an autobiographical narrative attached to a monastic *typikon*? Why did he not deploy yet another *deus ex machina* and avoid the scandalous affair at any cost? To grasp the magnitude of Michael's image problem we have to consider the optics of his Saljuq escape. While blinding and removing Ioannes IV was an odious act, it had at least been a domestic affair. Flight to the Turks, on the other hand, was a betrayal, not of the regime per se, but of the Roman Empire as a whole. Even Georgios Akropolites, who cast Michael as the otherwise impeccable hero of *The History*, ascribed his protagonist's escape to the Turks to a weakness of

---

[77] Ἐντεῦθεν στρατηγίαι πάλιν καὶ ἀγῶνες πάλιν καὶ θεὸς αὖθις εὐδοκιμοῦντας ἐν πᾶσι καὶ κατορθοῦντας δείκνυσιν ὁπότε καὶ τὸν πρὸς Λατίνους οὓς ἐπὶ κακῷ τῷ ἑαυτῆς ἡ βασιλὶς ἐφρούρει τῶν πόλεων ἐγχειρισθεὶς πόλεμον, καὶ τὴν ἀντιπέραν τῆς πόλεως Ἀσίαν ἔων στρατόπεδον, οὐκ ἔχω εἰπεῖν ὡς οὐκ εἰς τοὔσχατον ἀπορίας αὐτοὺς ὑπὸ θεῷ συμμαχοῦντι συνήλασα. ἀπανταχόθεν αὐτῶν εἴργων τὰς ἀποβάσεις, καὶ τὰς ὁρμὰς ἀναστέλλων καὶ περικόπτων τὰς τοῦ ζῆν ἀφορμάς. ἀλλὰ ταῦτα μὲν ἦν ἕως ἐκεῖνος ἦν ἐν τοῖς ζῶσι, καὶ προὐβαίνομεν ἀπὸ δόξης εἰς δόξαν μείζονες ἀεὶ ἐκ μεγάλων γινόμενοι, θεοῦ διὰ τῶν εὐθυμοτέρων ἄγοντος. ἐπεὶ δὲ τὰ Ῥωμαίων κράτη ἐπὶ τὸν ἐξ ἐκείνου μετῆλθε καὶ τῶν τοῦ φθόνου βελῶν σὺν πολλοῖς καὶ ἄλλοις τοῖς πεπειραμένοις ἐχρῆν καὶ ἡμᾶς πειραθῆναι, πῶς ἐξάντεις ποιεῖ καὶ τότε θεὸς καὶ πῶς ἐκ θλίψεως ταύτης ἐξάγει εἰς πλατυσμόν; σώζει πρὸς Πέρσας, ἵνα συντεμὼν εἴπω· κἀνταῦθα κρατεῖ τῆς ἐμῆς δεξιᾶς καὶ μετὰ δόξης προσλαμβάνει με· ὑμνούντων ἔστιν ἀκούειν ἐκείνων ἔτι καὶ νῦν, τὴν κατὰ τῶν Μασσαγετῶν ἀντιπαράταξιν καὶ τὴν ὁρμήν· καὶ τὴν συμπλοκὴν καὶ τὸ κατ' αὐτῶν ἀνυποστάτων τέως δοκούντων μέγα τρόπαιον ὅπερ οὐχ ἡμεῖς ἐν μέσῃ τῇ Περσικῇ, θεὸς δὲ δι' ἡμῶν ἵστησι· πρεσβείας μὲν οὖν τοὐντεῦθεν παρὰ βασιλέως καὶ γράμματα ὅσα πρὸς ἡμᾶς ἀπελύετο, πρὸς τὸ γένος καὶ τὴν πατρίδα παρακαλοῦντα (Palaiologos, *Autobiography*, 5.1–23).

human nature.[78] If members of the elite, who had supported the emperor after 1258 felt the need to denounce him on account of this incident, we can only imagine how useful this scandal could prove for Michael's political opponents. Fully aware of this fact and wishing to tackle the issue at hand, Michael embraced yet another rhetorical technique he had learned and apparently mastered in school. He employed what is known as "the statement of confirmation," which in any of the major *progymnasmata*, was described as such:

> Confirmation is validation of a matter at hand. Matters that should be confirmed are neither very clear nor completely impossible, but those that are in the middle. Those who are confirming should employ arguments opposite of those in refutation and first mention the good reputation of the subject, then, in turn, provide an exposition.[79]

Reading these instructions in relation to Michael Palaiologos' autobiography, the emperor's rhetorical training comes to the fore. The episode of the flight begins with Michael's faithful and successful defence of the empire and the emperor against the invading Latins. This allows the author to "first mention the good reputation of the claimant." Then Michael exposes an affair that lies in unclear waters. Having God by his side (let us not forget that the whole narrative is appended as an introduction to a *typikon* and divine providence played a major role in the emperor's public image), Michael builds a case for himself as an honest and just person who enjoys divine protection. The only logical way to explain his flight then is to cast the blame on irrational imperial policies for which the escape to the Saljuq Turks was the only and, more importantly, godly sanctioned, solution. Furthermore, to counter the malicious gossip (that we can imagine echoing in the streets of Constantinople),[80] Michael emphasized the heroic songs that circulated

---

[78] Akropolites, *Chronike*, 64.22–40.

[79] Κατασκευή ἐστι προκειμένου τινὸς βεβαίωσις πράγματος. Κατασκευαστέον δὲ τὰ μήτε λίαν σαφῆ μήτε ἀδύνατα παντελῶς, ἀλλ' ὅσα μέσην ἔχει τὴν τάξιν. Δεῖ δὲ κατασκευάζοντας τοῖς ἐναντίοις χρήσασθαι τῆς ἀνασκευῆς καὶ πρῶτον μὲν εἰπεῖν εὐφημίαν τοῦ φήσαντος, εἶτα ἐν μέρει θεῖναι τὴν ἔκθεσιν (Aphthonios, *Progymnasmata*, 13.20–14.1).

[80] On the Constantinopolitans' love of gossip and public ridicule, see Niketas Choniates' description of the people's reaction to Qilij Arslan II, during his visit to Constantinople, and Manouel I's *pretending* to limit the citizens' freedom of speech (τὸ ἐλευθερόστομον) in the streets on Qilij Arslan's bequest (Choniates, *Annales*, 120.14–21).

among the populace to commemorate his campaigns with the Turks against the Mongols. That is, instead of public gossip about his fidelity to the Romans, Michael introduces public acclamations of himself among the populace of Constantinople.

Michael's school years came to an end while he was still a young man.[81] His formation now took him out of the classroom and into the army camp where, by holding his first military ranks, Palaiologos entered the final stages of his formation. This time, however, young Palaiologos was on the battlefield under the careful watch of Ioannes III and his entourage. It was not uncommon, that young men would follow the imperial camp to demonstrate and further advance skills obtained at school. This sort of internship was practiced by both military men and civil servants who attended military campaigns in order to write reports and draft diplomatic documents. As Nikephoros Blemmydes states "this too was called education."[82] All emperors in exile, unlike some of their predecessors, were active in the battlefield. They led the armies themselves and oftentimes were present when treaties with enemies were being discussed and negotiated. For this reason, part of the imperial cabinet was always on the move with the emperor, while other officials remained in Nymphaion, Nikaia, and Magnesia to regulate affairs of Asia. Georgios Akropolites took pride in his internship under Ioannes III, whom he followed on his campaigns and for whom he drafted numerous imperial documents.[83] Michael, unlike Georgios who took up a career in civil administration, dedicated himself to the arts of war and was acknowledged by the emperor as an exquisite warrior from his young age. Given his education in rhetoric, philosophy, and other disciplines, as well as his illustrious background, Michael was assured a bright future in the imperial government. Time spent at court was also used to build personal networks with other students and courtiers. Among students and recent graduates at the court were Michael Palaiologos' future long-term allies: Georgios Akropolites and Alexios Strategopoulos.[84]

---

[81] ἐγὼ δὲ ὡς εἰς μείρακας ἤδη (Palaiolgos, *Autobiography*, 4.11–12).

[82] παίδευσιν καὶ ταύτην καλοῦσιν (Blemmydes, *Autobiograhia*, i.6.3–4).

[83] Akropolites, *Chronike*, 44.

[84] According to Georgios, all three men were together in the imperial camp on one of Ioannes III's campaigns in 1253 (for the date see Macrides, *The History*, 251): Akropolites, *Chronike*, 49.36–40.

2.5 Like Father Like Son: Andronikos and Michael Palaiologos in the Public Eye

Taking up children of established state officials and notable Roman families into imperial care was also advantageous for the *paterfamilias*, who did not have to think about educating and preparing his offspring for officialdom. In the exilic Byzantine Empire the imperial court could assume this task, as we have seen. In turn, mature officials could focus on their official duties, assured that their progeny was on the royal road to imperial service. Andronikos Palaiologos, Michael's father, was one such high official who was able to focus on the advancement of his own career, while the state occupied itself with his son's education.

Little is known about Andronikos Palaiologos' youth and early career under Theodoros I Laskaris. He was born into a wealthy household of the Palaiologoi around 1190 in Constantinople. His father was *megas doux* Alexios Palaiologos who had married Eirene Komnene around 1180. By getting married into the household of the Komnenoi, Alexios had boosted his immediate family's reputation among other notables.[85] Cashing in on this reputation, Andronikos entered public service during Theodoros I's reign, only to reach the zenith of his career under his successor, Ioannes III. Most likely, just a few years after his accession to the throne in 1222, Ioannes elevated Andronikos to the rank of *megas domestikos*.[86] The first major task we are aware of that Andronikos conducted for the state was the *exisosis* of 1224—a large-scale fiscal survey—with an eye to land reorganization in the newly reconquered region of Skamander.[87]

After the fall of Constantinople to the crusaders and the fragmentation of the Byzantine polity, power relations among the Romans shifted drastically as Constantinopolitan monastic and ecclesiastic foundations, as well as aristocratic families, lost their holdings in Asia Minor and in lands now held by the crusaders. In these new chaotic conditions, Theodoros I

---

[85] On Andronikos Palaiologos's family and background see Polemis, *The Doukai*, 156–157; Cheynet, Vannier, *Etudes prosopographiques*, 176–178.

[86] Polemis ascertained that Andronikos was invested into the office of *megas domestikos* by Theodoros I, more recently, Cheynet and Vannier (*Etudes prosopographiques*, 176) suggested it was more probable that Ioannes III elevated Andronikos into this office.

[87] On *exisosis* and *apographe* see footnote 158.

Laskaris had to tackle local magnates and villagers who appropriated officially unoccupied land in order to reclaim it for the state.[88] While this conflict with local magnates and other parties caused new domestic troubles for the regime, the emperor was able to acquire significant swaths of territory for the public fisc. These possessions needed to be surveyed anew to ensure effective collection of adequate tax revenues.[89] They often also had to be assigned new owners from among the populace. A well-regulated and accurately measured countryside would assure that the imperial treasury remained full, so that the emperor could afford his expensive wars against Latins, Epirotes, and Bulgarians in the Balkans, as well as Saljuq and nomadic Turks in Asia Minor.[90]

During Ioannes III's reign, the polity entered a new stage of constant expansion, first in the Marmara region, followed by conquests in the Balkans. The size of the newly reconquered territories meant that the state acquired more land that it could effectively tax, grant, or cultivate. In order to efficiently turn acreage into substantial sources of income, the state had to survey the land. The task of meticulously surveying these lands was entrusted to high state officials directly connected to the court.[91] By putting members of court elites in charge of such surveys, the imperial regime sent a clear message to the local populace: whether a plot was recognized as private property of Roman citizens or as public land, the state remained vigilant and asserted its capacity to tax and protect private and public property from any kind of threat. As the state asserted its authority over the newly conquered lands, the surveys became a necessity in the Laskarid polity. The main mode of land surveying was conducted through an *exisosis* which could be defined as:

> [p]eriodic inspections of properties followed by revisions (*exisoseis*, literally "equalizings") of the tax lists were a basic feature of late Byzantine fiscal policy in the thirteenth and fourteenth centuries. They had a number of purposes: to increase state revenues by reevaluating the values of property; to ensure that everyone was holding his property lawfully, and especially to ensure that imperial grants, including *pronoiai*, were still in the possession

---

[88] Bartusis, *Land and Privilege*, 185, 191.

[89] Angold, *A Byzantine Government*, 202.

[90] On relations of the Byzantines with the Saljuq and other Turks in the thirteenth century see Korobeinikov, *Byzantium and the Turks*.

[91] Angold, *A Byzantine Government*, 210.

of those to whom they had been granted; and to locate available properties to confer as *pronoia* grants. This is when *perisseia* would be found. A fiscal assessor (*apographeus*) traveled through a particular region reevaluating the *posotetes* of properties, rights, and *paroikos* households, and then creating new, revised *praktika*.[92]

Adding to the *exisosis* an occasional *apographe* would be conducted as well, which is defined as:

> a periodic survey made by an official (in the thirteenth century, a *doux*; in the fourteenth century, usually an *apographeus*) of the current holdings of private individuals and religious foundations. Following the *apographe*, the fiscal official might supply the individual landholder with a revised *praktikon*, reflecting changes since the landholdings were first granted or since the last *apographe*.[93]

Both of these surveys, at least during the period of exile, were carried out by two officials.[94] This minimized the chance of manipulation and bribery of the officials by local notables who wished to retain the land they occupied after the commotion of 1204.[95]

The significance of Laskarid land surveys was underlined by the author of the *Synopsis Chronike*. In this account, Ioannes III's fiscal arrangements clearly benefited the wider Roman population. The historian praises the emperor for filling up the imperial treasury in Magnesia, opening trade routes from India to Egypt, as well as for establishing schools and libraries, only to conclude with the emperor's meticulous surveys of Roman land.[96] The newly acquired land was to be surveyed and then redistributed as either *pronoiai* or taxable property.[97] The *exisosis* was a means by which

---

[92] Bartusis, *Land and Privilege*, 414.

[93] ibid., 212–213.

[94] On the two types of land surveys in the period of exile, see Angold, *A Byzantine Government*, 210–214. While Angold ascertains that the *apographe* was conducted by high officials of the central government, as was the *exiosis*, I suggest that enough room was left for local notables to conduct the *apographe*. For examples see the case of the *apographe* of Thessaloniki conducted by two members of the city's urban elite in 1262 (*Actes d'Iviron* III, no. 59, 96–103).

[95] MM IV: 217–218; 320–321; 327–329.

[96] *Synopsis Chronike*, 507.14–18, 535.26–536.4.

[97] ibid., 507.21–24.

the state affirmed its presence in the province, while also it helped in projecting the image of present imperial government in local affairs. Such reorganization of land and ownership in provinces could only be undertaken by the central administration. No local notable or administrator was allowed to obstruct the process. By managing this process throughout the empire, the polity showed it had both the means and the will to impose itself as the sole caretaker of public affairs. The men employed to conduct the land survey were deemed pious men of utmost integrity in the society. There was little room to doubt their judgement. What is more, by conducting *exisoseis* and *apographai*, the state was able to accumulate wealth from taxation or, alternatively, to distribute *pronoiai* to those who were found deserving of this tax-based income.[98]

In 1224, Andronikos Palaiologos and the otherwise unknown *kaisar* Romanos conducted an *exisosis*.[99] As an *exisotes* of the public fisc, Andronikos Palaiologos carried out one of the first major land surveys of Ioannes III's reign. Serving as a representative of the state he did not simply survey land for the state but also demonstrated to the local Romans that the polity was present, as well as capable of managing its affairs and taking care of its citizens. Having a notable from a famous *genos* in the province certainly left a mark in the minds of local landowners, since it was not the *doux* otherwise in charge of civic and military affairs of a province who was taking care of the taxation, but rather a different pair of individuals sent directly from the centre with only one task at hand: to conduct an *exisosis*.

2.6 A Useful Life: Andronikos Palaiologos in Provincial Public Service

After the *exisosis* of 1224, which coincided with the year of Michael's birth, the sources remain silent about Andronikos' career until 1233 when "[the emperor Ioannes III] gave to Andronikos Palaiologos, whom he had appointed *megas domestikos*, about whom I spoke a little earlier, the troops and their generals and dispatched him to the island of Rhodos with an adequate number of triremes and other ships so that he might attack the renegade with greater force and inflict damage upon him with those

---

[98] On *pronoiai*: Bartusis, *Land and Privilege*.
[99] Pachymeres, *Chronikonapht*, 222.1–6.

methods of strategy he knew."[100] The renegade in question was Leon Gabalas, whose family had ruled independently over Rhodos and some more distant Kykladic islands ever since 1203.[101] While Georgios tells us little about the outcome of this, we discern that Andronikos was experienced in warfare since he employed "those methods of strategy he knew." Most likely then, Andronikos spent the years between the *exisosis* of 1224 and the military expedition of 1233 in active service to the imperial army.

Another piece of information Akropolites shares with us is that Andronikos was given command over imperial troops (including their generals), which means that he was not in charge of any specific province at the time. Rather, instead of commanding provincial troops as a *doux*, Andronikos was sent on campaign with an imperial mandate. Much as he had been sent to conduct the *exisosis* of 1224, taking his orders directly from the imperial court he was once more on imperial duty. We can thus conclude that at least during Michael Palaiologos' childhood, his father Andronikos had held offices at the imperial court, close to the emperor as well as his own family. This meant, in turn, that when the time came for Michael to pursue higher education, it was only logical that he was sent to the imperial household, which his father had served for over a decade.

While Michael studied at the court, his father was active in the Balkans waging war against the empire's enemies by Ioannes III's side. In fact, ever since the Rhodian expedition, we keep encountering Andronikos in the emperor's entourage "directing the affairs of the armies."[102] We learn from Georgios, who was for the most part present in the imperial camp as a fresh graduate of an imperially sponsored school, that Andronikos assumed an important role in the imperial council. For instance, after the

---

[100] τῷ Παλαιολόγῳ Ἀνδρονίκῳ, ὃν μέγαν δομέστικον εἶχε, περὶ οὗ καὶ μικρὸν πρόσθεν εἰρήκειν, τὰ στρατεύματα καὶ τοὺς στρατηγοὺς παραδοὺς καὶ περὶ τὴν νῆσον Ῥόδον τριήρεσιν ἱκαναῖς καὶ λοιπαῖς ἐξαποστείλας ναυσίν, εἴ πως βριαρώτερον ἐπιτεθείη τῷ ἀποστάτῃ καὶ καταβλάψειεν οἷς οἶδε λόγοις τῆς στρατηγίας (Akropolites, *Chronike*, 28.2–7).

[101] Macrides, *The History*, 188. On his coinage, which he minted himself as an independent ruler, Leon did style himself as *kaisar* and servant of the emperor (M. Hendy, *Catalogue of the Byzantine Coins in the Dumbarton Oaks Collection and the Whittemore Collection* iv (Washington: Dumbarton Oaks 1999), 649–650), so it would not be completely unfeasible that he had accepted Nikaian rulers as his nominal masters prior to Andronikos's expedition. Furthermore, Georgios Akropolites employs the term renegade to describe Leon vis-à-vis Ioannes, which indicates that at least officially Ioannes was recognized as the emperor in Rhodos too.

[102] τὰ τῶν στρατευμάτων διεξάγων πράγματα (Akropolites, *Chronike*, 40.44).

Fig. 2.3 The Empire of Nikaia and its neighbours in 1255 after the conquests in the Balkans during Ioannes III Batatzes' reign

death of the child-emperor of the Bulgarians, Kaliman, in 1246, Ioannes was deliberating whether to reclaim the city of Serres for the Romans. This was an opportune moment, though the emperor did not in fact have enough troops for a proper siege. While most generals opted not to attack the city, Andronikos convinced the emperor to roll the dice. It was a good call, as the Bulgarian governor of Serres, Dragotas, surrendered the town to Ioannes III, promising to also deliver Melenikon to the Romans (Fig. 2.3).

Andronikos' career reached a new high that same year with the surrender of Thessaloniki to the imperial forces. He now became *praitor* of the Balkans, in charge of civilian and military administration.[103] While based in newly conquered Thessaloniki, Andronikos' jurisdiction covered all Balkan lands of the Roman polity. He therefore had to deal with all

---

[103] On Andronikos's title of *praitor* see Macrides, Introduction, 27. For the role of *praitor* see H. Glykatzi-Ahrweiler, "Recherches sur l'administration de l'empire byzantin aux IX-XIème siècles," *Bulletin de Correspondance Hellénique* 84 (1) (1960), 75–78; J. Herrin, "Realities of Byzantine Provincial Government: Hellas and Peloponnesos, 1180–1205," *DOP* 29 (1975), 266–267. The *praitor* in the Balkans had the same authorizations as did the *doukes* in Asia Minor (Herrin, "Realities," 266); for the *doukes* in Asia Minor see Angold, *A Byzantine Government*, 250–258.

manner of people, from different ethnic backgrounds, at different levels of provincial civil and military institutions. Luckily for Andronikos, around that time his son Michael—a fresh graduate from an imperial school— became governor of Serres and Melenikon, two important cities in the wider hinterland of Thessaloniki.[104] Having his son in control of public affairs in two important centres close to his own capital surely made Andronikos more secure in his position since he was now more protected from potential conspiracies and uprisings from his immediate surroundings. On the other hand, Michael, still a young man, was to hold his first public post under the supervision of his own father. Even though his days of training in both classroom and military camp were behind him, Michael was able to perfect his governing skills under the caring and vigilant eye of his own father.

The *megas domestikos* remained in charge of Thessalonian and Balkan affairs until his death sometimes between 1247 and 1248.[105] Governing a major city such as Thessaloniki—second only to the Queen of Cities— was a demanding but potentially rewarding business. The city with its proud populace stands as an example of Byzantine urban social and political life after 1204.[106] A few months before the city opened its gates to the imperial forces in 1246, several members of local notable families, such as Demetrios Spartenos and Nikolaos Kampanos, decided to get in touch with emperor Ioannes III, having deemed their own *despotes* Demetrios Angelos incapable "to rule a state and be in lawful command."[107] It was deemed that the *despotes*, who had nominally recognized the emperor as his master, eventually started to rule on his own right without taking

---

[104] Akropolites, *Chronike*, 46.14–19.

[105] ibid., 46.25–26.

[106] For the intellectual scene of Late Byzantine Thessaloniki see F. Tinnefeld, "Intellectuals in Late Byzantine Thessalonike," in *DOP* 57 (2003),153–172; H. Ahrweiler, "Philadelphie et Thessalonique au début du xive siècle: à propos de Jean Monomaque," in H. Ahrweiler (ed), *Philadelphie et autres études* (Paris: Sorbonne 1984), 9–16. For the civic identity of cities in Middle and Late Byzantium, including Thessaloniki see C. Sode, "The Formulation of Byzantine Urban Identity on Byzantine Seals," in B. Bedos-Rezak (ed.), *Seals—Making and Marking Connections across the Medieval World (The Medieval Globe)* (Leeds 2019) 150–165. For the medieval Romans own perception of different class structures in the cities see A. Kontogiannopoulou, "The Notion of δῆμος,' 101–124; idem, "Κοινωνική διαστρωμάτωση στις βυζαντινές πόλεις (11^{ος}–15^{ος} αι). Η Περίπτωση των καστρηνῶν," *Μεσαιωνικά και Νέα Ελληνικά* 11 (2014), 9–28.

[107] πολιτείας κατάρχειν καὶ νομίμως ἐπιστατεῖν (Akropolites, *Chronike*, 45.15–16).

the empire's benefit into consideration.[108] Demetrios and Nikolaos were supported by other local notables, like Iatropoulos and Koutzoulatos,[109] as well as "the distinguished ones [such] were Michael Laskaris and Tzyrithon, whom emperor Ioannes honoured as *megas chartoularios*,"[110] who organized a successful conspiracy against Demetrios Angelos. In order to crown the endeavour with success, Demetrios and Nikolaos had to secure not only the support of the notables and distinguished men, but rather of the wider populace once the city came into Ioannes III's hands. They had done so by paying a visit to the emperor "in reality to obtain a common chrysobull which included the customs and rights which from the beginning were attached to Thessaloniki, and provided for their own freedom."[111] Keen to get the city under his control, the emperor conceded to this request and once Thessaloniki was in his hands, a chrysobull in the public interest was promulgated in order to swiftly bring the populace to his side. The fact that the conspirators opened the gates for the emperor, and nobody was hurt during the takeover of the city helped immensely in reinforcing the perception of Ioannes III as a righteous and merciful ruler.

The account of Thessaloniki's affairs before the conquest of 1246 reveals a great deal about the importance of public support in running a Roman city. Practically speaking, this event demonstrates that both local notables as well as those distinguished men connected directly to the imperial court relied on the populace when seeking to govern Thessaloniki. To be sure Demetrios Spartenos and Nikolaos Kampanos first sought and secured the support of other notables in the city, most likely members of the council with a recognized legal right to manage the city's

---

[108] Akropolites, *Chronike*, 45.

[109] We know nothing about these two men; however, their offspring continued to play a significant role in Thessaloniki in the later thirteenth century. This means that the two men's households played an important role in local affairs prior to their involvement with the conspiracy against Demetrios Angelos in 1246, which brought them further benefits.

[110] οἱ δὲ τῶν ἐπισήμων ὅ τε Μιχαὴλ ὁ Λάσκαρις καὶ ὁ Τζυρίθων, ὃν καὶ μέγαν χαρτουλάριον ὁ βασιλεὺς Ἰωάννης τετίμηκεν (Akropolites, *Chronike*, 45.18–20).

[111] τῇ δ'ἀληθείᾳ κοινοῦ χρυσοβούλλου ἐπευμοιρῆσαι, τῶν ἀνέκαθεν προσαρμοσάντων Θεσσαλονίκῃ ἐθίμων τε καὶ δικαίων περιεκτικοῦ καὶ τῆς σφῶν ἐλευθερίας παρεκτικοῦ (ibid., 45.25–28).

On the chrysobull see D. Kyritses, "The 'Common Chrysobulls' of Cities and the Notion of Property in Late Byzantium," *ByzSym* 13 (1999), 229–245.

affairs.[112] Then they communicated with the emperor's representatives. Eventually, however, they obtained a chrysobull granting rights and privileges to the city. The common benefit of all citizens became the pivotal point of the conspiracy. This was after all framed as the removal of a tyrant, which was to grant the people their sovereign rights. Though mostly born after 1204, Thessalonians were nevertheless still aware of their Romanness and of all the rights that sprung from it. For this reason, the emperor did not hesitate to grant the status that the city had enjoyed before the events of 1204. With one stroke of a pen the rule of the Franks and the "tyranny" of the Epirot *despotai* was expunged from Roman history. For the Thessalonians, Ioannes' rule was legitimate because he was the lawfully acting ruler of the Romans (and they too were Romans), who brought them back into the Roman orbit from which they were forcefully removed.

Needless to say, the conspirators and their families benefited personally from the conspiracy. During Theodoros II's reign, about fifteen years after the events of 1246, Demetrios Spartenos led the embassy to the papacy. In similarly good books, we encounter Nikolaos Kampanos holding the high office of *prokathemenos* of Thessaloniki.[113] In 1284, well after the death of our protagonists, Demetrios's son Ioannes Spartenos occupied the office of *prokathemenos* of Thessaloniki. With imperial support, members of such local notable families as the Spartenoi and the Kampanoi controlled the municipal affairs of Thessaloniki under both the Laskarides and Palaiologoi. By granting positions of authority to the more affluent members of Thessaloniki's society, Ioannes secured this group's undisputed support much as he secured the support of the populace at large by protecting their rights. In this way, the emperor established a direct connection with all of Thessaloniki's social groups. The Thessalonians returned the favour by supporting his regime. Obtaining their support

---

[112] On city councils in Late Byzantium see Α. Κοντογιαννοπούλου, *Τοπικά συμβούλια στις βυζαντινές πόλεις: Παράδοση και εξέλιξη (13ος-15ος αι.)* (Αθήνα: Ακαδημία Αθηνών 2015). For the case of Thessaloniki see ibid., 49–89; 90–94; Τ. Κιουσοπούλου, "Το *βουλευτήριον* της Θεσσαλονίκης," Α. Κοντογιαννοπούλου (επιστημονική επιμέλεια), *Πόλεις και εξουσία στο Βυζάντιο κατά την εποχή των Παλαιολόγων (1261–1453)* (Αθήνα: Ακαδημία Αθηνών), 109–120.

[113] *Prokathemenos* was at the head of the municipal administration and his position would usually be approved by the emperor and not the provincial administrator such was the *doux*. For more on *prokathemenos* see Angold, *A Byzantine Government*, 264–266. On the Kampanoi and Spartenoi see Macrides, *The History*, 238–39, n.6–7.

granted Ioannes III calmer seas on which to sail the ship of state. With his actions, Ioannes III made it clear that he was the caretaker and benefactor of the people.

Another way for the emperor to demonstrate his care for the people in his absence was to appoint capable men as governors of cities and provinces. In this respect, Andronikos Palaiologos was a sensible choice. He was a high official experienced in affairs pertaining to both the army—having been a general and member of the imperial military council—and civil administration—having managed the *exisosis* of the Skamander region. The post of governor of Thessaloniki and *praitor* of the Balkans was also a boon for Andronikos, as it helped him promote himself and his *genos* in two different directions. First, by handling local affairs without turmoil, he demonstrated his continued administrative and militarily competence to the emperor. Second, by taking care of the local people's safety and well-being, Andronikos established himself as their caretaker. Andronikos was able to make it clear that he was the one directly providing for them by being constantly physically present in Thessaloniki's public life. These two directions of self-promotion were in fact intertwined since any actions by the empire's representatives in the provinces were perceived as an imprint of the state itself.

Archbishop Iakobos of Bulgaria, an inhabitant of Thessaloniki at the time, tells us that Andronikos secured the citizens' gratitude (and thus gained in popularity) by maintaining the city-walls and by proving a just governor and judge when dealing with city affairs.[114] By promoting himself as an effective caretaker of the Roman populace, during his rather short tenure in the city, Andronikos mirrored traits that the emperor himself sought to associate with his public image. Unlike the emperor though, whose public image remained more generic, in order to appeal to Romans all around the empire, Andronikos' public image was carefully calibrated to the peculiar needs of the city of Thessaloniki, where the Palaiologoi were building a power base. It is for this reason, after all, that emperors usually reassigned governors of provinces on a nearly annual basis.[115] In doing so, the administration sought to undermine

---

[114] S.G. Mercati, *Collectanea Byzantina* I (Bari: Edizioni Dedalo 1970), 69.18–70.5; 70.13–28.

[115] On the limited term of office holders in the provinces during the period of exile see Angold, *A Byzantine Government*, 250; Ahrweiler, "L'histoire et la géographie de la région de Smyrne entre les deux occupations turques (1081–1317), particulièrement

a popular governor's local support, by ensuring that a respected and well-entrenched public servant could not rise against his more distant emperor.

Local notables of Thessaloniki were fully aware that they owed their posts to the emperor of the Romans. They still did not shy away, however, from building cordial relations with the *megas domestikos*, who was in charge of overseeing their affairs. Whether Andronikos went out of his way to actively accommodate the needs of local influential citizens in Thessaloniki or even turned a blind eye to some of their less laudable actions, we will never know. For whatever reason, Andronikos was able to gain the support of both the populace at large and the more affluent members of the society. By keeping on good terms with the Palaiologoi, people like Demetrios Spartenos and Nikolaos Kampanos secured positions for their families not just during Ioannes III's and Theodoros II's reigns but well into the Palaiologan period. The local elites' best chance of maintaining their prestigious status in the local community was to connect themselves with the high representatives of the imperial administration. Such associations opened new opportunities for them. As we have seen, the otherwise unknown Demetrios Spartenos was sent as an ambassador to the pope by Theodoros II. Surely, Demetrios' role in the events of 1246 and direct correspondence with Ioannes III made him known to the imperial court and to Theodoros II. For let us not forget that the emperor would read letters of political interest before his council and Georgios Akropolites was present as a member of that council when the fate of Thessaloniki was being decided.[116] It would not be implausible to suggest that Demetrios established a good report with Akropolites, who in turn promoted the Thessalonian's career on the grand imperial stage. Demetrios' as well as Nikolaos Kampanos' good rapport with Akropolites and Andronikos Palaiologos surely helped them in gaining the offices of

---

au XIIIe siècle, *TM* 1 (1965), 138–148; F. Dölger, "Chronologisches und Prosopographisches zur byzantinischen Geschichte des 13. Jahrhunderts," *BZ* 27 (1927), 307–310.

[116] For example, see the account by Akropolites about a meeting of which he was an attendee together with selected generals and officials convoked by Ioannes III in order to discuss the course of action based on messages the emperor received about the situation in Serres in 1246: Akropolites, *Chronike*, 43.

apographeis and conducting an *apographe* of the theme of Thessaloniki during Michael VIII's reign.[117]

Apart from the local elites, during his tenure as the *praitor* of the Balkans, Andronikos had to deal with the local populace at large. Andronikos' presence in the province made the local populace mindful of the fact that, if need be, they could quickly take their affairs and concerns beyond the level of local administration and even above the regional authority of the *doux*. In Andronikos the provincials had access to the emperor and his immediate representatives. In this way, the state of Ioannes III was able to present itself in the provinces and expand its direct influence on-the-ground at the expense of local notables. That is, instead of looking to the local magnates for protection, the villagers and town-dwellers could rely on the imperial government. On the other hand, local notables as well as minor landholders were able to take their business to the imperial court and thus circumvent the provincial administration that served as an intermediary between authorities around the emperor and the local populace. This allowed the Laskarid state, at least in theory, to be present at all levels of private and public life in the empire. In practice, of course, local courts in cities and villages as well as major provincial courts overseen by the *doux* were as busy as the central administration when it came to landownership disputes and other affairs.[118] For instance, in the region of Smyrne, we encounter legal disputes between villagers that are settled by a local *oikodespotes* who was no more than a major village figure.[119] On another occasion, we see a provincial *doux* conducting an official investigation around the province to disperse justice.[120]

Judging by all the cases from Andronikos' times that have come down to us, whether they were investigated and settled at a local level or by the imperial administration, we clearly see that public discourse was alive and well in the Laskarid polity. It was not just the emperor or even such courtiers as the Palaiologoi and Tornikoi, who openly expressed their opinions and grievances. Local *pronoiars*—for the greater part of Ioannes

---

[117] *Actes d'Iviron* III, no. 59, 96–103.

[118] Blemmydes, *Curriculum*: 17, 29–30; Theodoros II Laskaris, *Epistulae*, 298–299. On rural lives in later Byzantium see Gerstel, *Rural Lives and Landsapes*.

[119] *MM* IV, 81.

[120] ibid., 36–37.

III's reign soldiers obtained *pronoiai* to arm and support themselves[121]—and *paroikoi* also took to the courts to protect what they saw as their rights.[122] Once at court, *paroikoi* employed appropriate legal language well enough to frame their case in a manner that accorded with the legal traditions of the empire. Such well-versed Roman citizens, regardless of their social standing, would have made Andronikos' work in the province less difficult to cope with vis-à-vis his previous career focused around the imperial centre. While, unfortunately, not a single case that was conducted under Andronikos' supervision has come down to us, we still have enough material to imagine the type of individuals and cases he must have dealt with. For instance, in the case of the monks of Lemviotisa vs. the *paroikoi* of the village Potamou which was given as *pronoia* to a certain *kavalliarios* Syrgares,[123] we see how far both sides were willing and able to go to prove their case.[124] Both sides, that is the monks and the *paroikoi* in question, took the case of *pronoia* ownership to the emperor. The villagers, much as the more educated representatives of the monastery, directly addressed the emperor, who listened to their grievances and the case they presented against their accusers. It was only after the initial trial that the *pronoiar* Syrgares took up the role of the defender of his *paroikoi* at court. Thus, the *pronoiar*, benefiting from helping the *paroikoi* to ascertain their rights against other *paroikoi* or institutions (such as the monasteries), acted as a patron of his clients otherwise independent from him; for it was these clients who initiated the defence and who were accused by the monastery, not the *pronoiar*. Cases such as this one allow us to understand that public discourse in local and imperial courts was not reserved for the selected few. Rather, the emperor and his men, as was Andronikos, had to be present, in both theory and practice, to listen and settle disputes of all the empire's citizens.

---

[121] On *pronoia* before 1204 as well as under the Laskarids see Bartisis, *Land and Privilege*: 112–240.

[122] On social dynamics in Byzantine villages, as well as sense of collectivity, see Gerstel, *Rural Lives and Landscapes*. For the sense of the villagers belonging to the Roman nation in rural parts of the empire see Krallis, "Villages, Towns, Soldiers," 11–48.

[123] On *kavallarios* Syrgares see *MM* IV, 209–210.

[124] ibid., 36–9.

2.7 A Useful Afterlife: The Place of Andronikos Palaiologos in the Public Memory of Thessaloniki

Whether or not Andronikos was supposed to be rotated into a new post before he became too close to the local elites, we will never know, since he died in 1247 or 1248, after having served in Thessaloniki anywhere between a few months to just over a year. On his deathbed, Andronikos took monastic vows and assumed the monastic name Arsenios.[125] This transition from secular to monastic life suggests that he had time to make arrangements for a peaceful death in Thessaloniki. While Theodoros Philes replaced the deceased *megas domestikos*,[126] the connections Andronikos made during his short tenure in the city remained at his son's disposal. The network of local support Andronikos started to build in Thessaloniki is perhaps best represented by the prominent careers of the Spartenoi and Kampanoi well into the reign of his son Michael Palaiologos. Furthermore, the impact of Andronikos' tenure on the city and the public support generated by it for the Palaiologoi comes to the fore in the carefully crafted image of Andronikos that survives in the city's public memory. Almost immediately after the death of his father, Michael Palaiologos hired the logographer Iakobos who, having served as metropolitan of Ochrid, was certainly a prominent ecclesiast in the Balkans.[127] Employing Iakobos, a known figure among the empire's literati, to commemorate Andronikos was a smart move on Michael's part.[128] A respected figure such as the titular archbishop of Bulgaria would surely attract more people to the congregation than a less known priest or rhetorician. To enhance the populace's fond memory of the *megas domestikos*, Iakobos produced a funerary oration as well as three poems commemorating Andronikos and his deeds.

---

[125] Mercati, *Collectanea*, 72.1.

[126] Akropolites, *Chronike*, 46.28–9.

[127] On Iakobos see Mercati, *Collectanea*, 99–103.

[128] Iakobos was a well-known intellectual who even served as an encomiast to Ioannes III Batazes when the emperor visted the city in 1252/1253 (Angelov, *Imperial Ideology*, 168–169).

To live up to the literary expectations of the time, Iakobos followed the rules prescribed by rhetoricians in *progymnasmata* for encomiastic prose.[129] He praised Andronikos for his illustrious origins, birth, upbringing, career, good deeds for the people, and faithful service to the emperor.[130] An image of a morally righteous person comes to the fore from the bishop's speech. Hearing about the exquisite character of the deceased in a funerary oration is by no means surprising; after all, one would not commission a speech on mediocrity. What is special about Iakobos' oration is its content and context. While following the expected formulae for speech writing, Iakobos rooted his oration entirely in the affairs of Thessaloniki. For starters, he addressed his audiences directly throughout the speech, alluding to their active participation in the urban life of the city. The author refers to the community of the Thessalonians by either using the first-person plural *we* or by personifying the city of Thessaloniki itself. By doing so, Iakobos also made sure to boost the pride of the people in the city by emphasizing its historic role with such lavish statements as "the celebrated and truly happy Thessaloniki, after the city of Constantine the most renowned of all the Roman places in Europe" and "you, the city of Thessaloniki with wide streets of great name—to you I turn back the countenance of the speech right away."[131] With such statements about the city, the author was able to boost the local patriotic feelings his listeners had for their city. Simultaneously, by emphasizing that they, the Thessalonians, are the focus of his narrative, Iakobos managed to create a sense of active communal agency among the

---

[129] On epitaphs and monodies see Hunger, *Die hochsprachliche profane Literatur*, 132–165; on Iakobos of Bulgaria and his funerary opus see A. Sideras, *Die byzantinischen Grabreden. Prosopographie, Datierung, Überlieferung 142 Epitaphien und Monodien aus dem byzantinischen Jahrtausend* (Wien: Verlag der Österreichischen Akademie der Wissenschaften 1994), 246–248.

[130] Mercati, *Collectanea*, 66–73. For the rules of composition for a funerary speech see D.A. Russel and N.G. Wilson, *Menander Rhetor: A* Commentary (Oxford: Oxford University Press 1981), 171–178.

[131] ἡ περίπυστος πόλις καὶ πανολβία Θεσσαλονίκη, ἡ μετὰ τὴν Κωνσταντίνου μεγαλωνυμουμένη παρὰ πάσας τὰς ἐν Εὐρώπῃ ῥωμαϊκάς (Mercati, *Collectanea*, 68.25–26); σύ, πλατυάμφοδον ἄστυ Θεσσαλονίκη καὶ μεγαλώνυμον – πρὸς σὲ καὶ γὰρ αὖθις ἐπιστρέφω τοῦ λόγου τὸ πρόσωπον (ibid., 71.24–25).

listeners in order to keep their attention on his performative reading of the funerary oration.[132]

Speaking to this specific audience of Thessalonians then, Iakobos focused solely on those deeds which Andronikos accomplished for the sake of the citizens of Thessaloniki. He is completely silent about the *megas domestikos*' earlier endeavours such as the *exisosis* of Skamander and the conquest of Rhodos. This narrower focus on Thessalonian affairs allowed the listeners to associate the deceased with local affairs since those were already familiar to them. More importantly, Iakobos recognized that it was local affairs that truly mattered to his listeners and not Andronikos' other accomplishments. By framing his speech around facts and deeds known to the audience, Iakobos crafted Andronikos' public image as a devoted benefactor of Thessaloniki. In doing so, the orator's speech fulfilled a specific political goal: he shored up public support, or at least sympathy, for the Palaiologoi in Thessaloniki.

In painting a portrait of a desperately missed governor in his funeral oration, Iakobos often deployed the first-person plural *we* to designate the community of citizens with which he self-identified. By doing so, he was able to cast his personal grief as that of the whole community and, again, contribute to the listeners' sense of being active agents in the speech. For instance, he ascertained that everybody was in distress because of the loss of such a marvelous governor by exclaiming "we are all gazing at the common penalty, the collective shipwreck of citizens and their surroundings."[133] Creating a sense of despair and ruin after the death of the *megas domestikos* was a good way to introduce the great deeds Palaiologos accomplished on behalf of the city and its dwellers. Having primed his audience by emphasizing their communal relationship with the deceased, Iakobos took the narrative back to Andronikos, who fought off the Latin

---

[132] On loud reading and public performance in Byzantium see P. Magdalino, *The Empire of Manuel I Komnenos* (Cambridge, UK: Cambridge University Press 2002³), 339–353; M. Mullet, "Aristocracy and Patronage in the Literary Circles of Comnenian Constantinople," in M. Angold (ed.), *The Byzantine Aristocracy, IX–XIII Centuries* (Oxford: Oxford University Press 1984), 173–201; A. Kaldellis, *Hellenism in Byzantium*, 235–237; Neville, *Heroes and Romans*, 28–32; Ch. Messis and S. Papaioannou, "Orality and Textuality (with an Appendix on the Byzantine Conceptions)," in S. Papaionnou (ed.), *The Oxford Textbook of Byzantine Literature* (Oxford: Oxford University Press 2021), 241–272.

[133] τὸ πάνδημον θεώμεθα πρόστιμον, τὸ κοινὸν τῶν πολιτῶν καὶ τῆς περιοικίδος ναυάγιον (Mercati, *Collectanea*, 69.1–2).

imposters and then refurbished the city and its walls around the harbour. Since reminding the people of their turbulent past before the Laskarid takeover and Palaiologan governance was a useful tool for instilling a sense of gratitude in the Thessalonians, Iakobos inserted in his oration a brief digression on the crusaders to emphasize the previous misfortunes of the city. These "barbarian dogs"[134] are mentioned in strictly pejorative terms, which would have heightened the audience's attention to, and appreciation for, its benefactors, not least of all Andronikos Palaiologos. Lest we forget, Thessaloniki was one of the cities that experienced Latin occupation, which was still fresh in the communal memory of its citizens. By dwelling on common knowledge about the city's recent history, the author successfully created a bond between the deceased and the populace, who should be eternally grateful to Andronikos, and by extension to the Palaiologoi, for their toils and labours on the city's behalf.

While Andronikos was cast as the utmost benefactor of the city, Iakobos was very careful to not infringe on the rights of the emperor in the city and the state. When addressing the deceased for the first time in the oration, the author introduces the emperor as well: "alas, oh great-named Andronikos, who with the greatest emperor surpasses all men, besides him [the emperor], in strength of your wisdom, capability of your hands, and prudence."[135] By introducing the comparison with the emperor from the onset, Iakobos avoids creating tension between praising the deceased and respecting the throne. The author promotes an image of Andronikos as a just official faithful to the regime by noting that: "since he [Ioannes III] became the master of our paradise, he established you [Andronikos] as a flaming sword irresistible in meeting opponents in battle, bringing fire to them, and to us deliverance."[136] The audience then received a twofold message: first, Andronikos was a faithful subject of the emperor and the benefit of the people he worked for was also to the benefit of the emperor. Second, while Andronikos was the utmost caretaker of Thessaloniki, he was able to be so only because the

---

[134] σκύλα βαρβαρικά (ibid., 69.10).

[135] Φεῦ φεῦ, Ἀνδρόνικε μεγαλώνυμε, μετὰ τὸν μέγιστον αὐτοκράτορα ὁ πλὴν ἐκείνου πάντας ἄνδρας νικῶν τῇ στερρότητι τῶν φρενῶν, τῇ δεξιότητι τῶν χερῶν, τῇ εὐβουλίᾳ (ibid., 68.30–69.1).

[136] ἀφ' οὗ οὖν οὗτος ἐκυρίευε παραδείσου τοῦ καθ'ἡμᾶς, οἷόν τινα φλογίνην ῥομφαίαν ἐγκατέστησέ σε τοῖς ἀντιμάχοις ἀπρόσμαχον, ἐμπύριον μὲν αὐτοῖς, ἡμῖν δὲ καὶ λίαν σωτήριον (ibid., 69.15–17).

emperor was wise and just in placing such a marvelous man in charge of public affairs. Imperial prudence was in no way threatened by the *megas domestikos*' exceptional personality; rather, it was in fact enhanced through Andronikos' wise governing. Thus, Thessaloniki's prosperity was a result of masterful imperial governance to which Andronikos pledged his abilities and loyalty.

While the speech was written to commemorate Andronikos, its main goal was to promote the Palaiologoi family to the citizens of Thessaloniki, especially, the *megas domestikos*' son Michael, who was already serving as governor of the neighbouring cities of Serres and Melenikon. In the introduction of the speech, Michael is mentioned by Iakobos vis-à-vis Andronikos: "olden hope, golden wreath of your brightness, who after you is the heir of your charisma and of the capable *genos* of the Palaiologoi, after the first, the second no lesser brilliance, the very famous Michael."[137] By receiving such a laudable mention in the speech, Michael was openly promoted as a worthy heir to Andronikos. Thus, Iakobos introduced his benefactor to the people of Thessaloniki, who were expected to embrace him as a worthy substitute for Andronikos, even if the young Palaiologos did not hold an official office in the city.

Much like the speech, the three poems by Iakobos addressed the same occasion and issue.[138] But why did Michael commission these three poems together with the funerary oration? The answer to this question might be simpler than expected: it was a common practice for the medieval Romans of the Middle and Late Byzantine periods to include pieces composed in verse to the funerary programmes. The fact that we have a speech accompanied by three distinct poems written by Iakobos simply means that we have a chance to look at one of the fully preserved funerary programmes which has come down to us intact. To sustain this claim, we can start by looking at the opus of Iakobos' younger contemporary Georgios Akropolites, which includes a funerary speech to Ioannes III composed in 1254. Fourteen years before bidding the final farewell to Ioannes III, Akropolites produced a funerary poem for the deceased empress consort to the emperor, Eirene Laskarina. This poem was accompanied by another poem from the pen of Nikephoros Blemmydes. By

---

[137] ἡ γηρωκόμος ἐλπίς, ὁ χρύσεος τῆς σῆς λαμπρότητος στέφανος, ὁ μετὰ σὲ τῶν σῶν χαρίτων ὄντως διάδοχος καὶ τοῦ τῶν Παλαιολόγων γένους ἀριπρεποῦς μετὰ τὸν πρῶτον ὁ δεύτερος οὐκ ἐλάσσων φωστήρ, ὁ παγκλεέστατος δηλαδὴ Μιχαήλ (ibid., 67.26–29).

[138] ibid., 73–79.

looking at these pieces together, we can discern that the poems for Eirene Laskarina and the funerary speech for Ioannes III are just surviving fragments of more complete programmes that included both classicizing speeches in prose and epitaphic poetry in verse. Adding to this, if we turn our attention back to the ninth century, we encounter an interesting statement by Ignatios the Deacon. After having recovered from illness, Ignatios sent a letter to a friend, who, had the deacon died, "would have had to scan for me a funerary elegiac poem and fashion epic verses in hexameter, and weave the major ionic in due measure with the minor, and so sing to me a burial song."[139] By simply referring to the two funerary poems, without any further elaboration, Ignatios allows us to infer that his contemporaries were aware of the existence of specific poems at funerals. Also, Ignatios' side remark about his friend having to compose two funerary poems makes it clear that such encomia were not reserved for emperors alone, but were expected to be delivered at funerals or other events commemorating the deceased.[140] While over four hundred years separate Ignatios the Deacon's comment and the deaths of Andronikos Palaiologos and Ioannes III, the example of Georgios Akropolites' poem for the deceased empress testifies to the continued performance of burial songs into the Late Byzantine period. In conclusion, then, it appears that having four distinctive pieces commemorating Andronikos Palaiologos was not that unusual in the thirteenth century. The only oddity we encounter here is that the complete literary commemorative programme for the departed *megas domestikos* has been passed down to us intact.

While producing more than a single commemorative piece was not that unusual for the Romans of the thirteenth century, the nature of the three poems invites us to take a closer look at them. By looking at the language

---

[139] C. Mango in collaboration with St. Ethymiadis, *The Correspondence of Ignatios the Deacon. Text, Translation, and Commentary (CFHB 39)* (Cambridge, Mass 1997), 146–147. For context and analysis of these lines, see M. D. Lauxterman, *Byzantine Poetry from Pisides to Geometers, Texts and Contexts I* (Vienna: Verlag der Österreichischen Akademie der Wissenschaften 2003), 213–214.

[140] For the proliferation of encomiastic literature which happens under the Komnenoi see Magdalino, *The Empire of Manuel I*, 180–227, 510–512. For commissioned poetry, including funerary verses, by the later Byzantine elites see N. Zagklas, "'How Many Verses Shall I Write and Say?'," 237–263 and A. Rhoby, "Poetry on Commission," 264–304 For epigrams being inscribed next to the visual representations of the deceased see A.-M. Talbot, "Epigrams in Context: Metrical Inscriptions on Art and Architecture of the Palaiologan Era," *DOP* 53 (1999), 75–90.

and content of the poems, it becomes clear that they were written in different registers of Greek. The first poem celebrating the deceased *megas domestikos* was written in highly archaizing hexametric and elegiac Homeric Greek, employing defunct Aiolic, Doric, and Ionic morphology. The second was written in standard iambic, that is dodecasyllabic, *koine*. Finally, the third was composed in the form of *erotapokriseis*—that is, in a question-and-answer format.[141] The content is fairly similar across all three poems and resembles that of the funerary oration. The poems open with Andronikos' illustrious birth. They focus on his Constantinopolitan origin, his background and ties to the Palaiologoi, Komnenoi, and Doukai. What follows is a narrative of the *megas domestikos*' service under Ioannes III, with an account of his deeds for Thessaloniki and its people, and finally, his death. In all three poems, as well as in the speech, Michael Palaiologos is cast as the natural heir to his father's dedication to and works for the public's benefit.

While the topic of all four works is rather similar, they had different target audiences based on the language and cultural themes employed in each poem. In the thirteenth century, Thessaloniki was surely home to a vibrant intellectual scene, as the presence of men like Iakobos suggests. Judging by his career as an encomiast to the Palaiologoi and, as of the 1250 s, to Ioannes III himself, Iakobos was no stranger to the circles of educated Roman literati. The first poem, then, was written in Homeric Greek to cater to the refined tastes of these very same cultured individuals. In addition to the Homeric language, all the references in the poem are exclusively based on the *Iliad* (without a single Christian reference being made). All these features would have made the poem rather incomprehensible to wider audiences and it is quite possible that the very performance of this poem happened in a *theatron*-like setting in the city. By commissioning an archaizing poem both in terms of language and theme, Michael

---

[141] *Erotapokriseis* was a popular form of didactic literature in Late Antiquity and remained in use until Photios' times. After the tenth century, the genre falls out of use and makes a comeback in the Late Byzantine era. According to the surviving sources, Iakobos' *erotapokriseis* might be the first encounter of this format in the post-Macedonian period. For *erotapokriseis* and their authors in Byzantium see A. Kazhdan, "*Erotapokriseis*," in *ODB* II, 727; Y. Papadoyannakis, "Instruction by Questions and Answer: The Case of Late Antique and Byzantine *Erotapokriseis*," in S.F. Johnson (ed.), *Greek Literature in Late Antiquity* (Routledge 2015), 91–105; S. Efthymiadis, "Questions and Answers," in A. Kaldellis and N. Siniossiglou (eds.), *The Cambridge Intellectual History of Byzantium*, (Cambridge: Cambridge University Press, 2017), 47–62.

was able to cast himself as a patron of fine arts, a quality certainly appreciated by ambitious literati who would often offer their services to generous patrons.[142] Michael's patronage did not go unnoticed by Iakobos, as the archbishop singles Michael out from Andronikos' surviving offspring:

> But the one resembling his divine parent the most.
> with trustworthy ethos and sagacious heart,
> is Michael the famous, staunch in battles, of marvelous posture.[143]

With such a clear reference depicting Michael in the likeness of Homeric heroes, Iakobos made sure that the city's intelligentsia did not miss out on the fact that Michael is the main patron of the piece. For Michael this was an important message to be sent, as having such men at his disposal meant that he could always rely on them for well-crafted propaganda, even if Iakobos were unavailable.

The second poem was composed in the rather more approachable *koine*. We can imagine that, like the funerary speech, this piece was read at a church during one of the commemorative events. The local and imperial elites sitting in the front rows of the church—the Spartenoi, Kampanoi, and others from among Thessaloniki's notables—could certainly have engaged with the poem's *koine*, as could have other churchgoers attending the event. They would not have had problems understanding its content. This is in fact truer for the poem since it was composed in verses that conveyed Iakobos' message directly, while the oration was filled with overly elaborated and rhetorically ornamented syntax. On top of the approachable language, the poem's reliance exclusively on biblical motifs made it more intelligible to the audience, as references to David's psalms and Solomon's sayings were an integral part of ecclesiastic sermons:

> The shifty nature of Earthly things,

---

[142] On artistic and literary patronage in Byzantium see Magdalino, *The Empire*, 413–488; Mullet, "Aristocracy and Patronage," 173–201; I. Drpić, *Epigram, Art, and Devotion in Later Byzantium* (Cambridge: Cambridge University Press 2016). On the literary scene in Late Byzantine Thessaloniki see D. Bianconi, *Tessalonica nell'età dei Paleologi. La pratiche intellettuali nel riflesso della cultura scritta* (Paris 2005).

[143] σφῶν δ' ὁ πρόατος ἐϊκόμενος γενετῆρι δίῳ.
ἤθεσι κεδνοτέροις πευκαλίμοις φρεσί τε.
Μιχαὴλ ἀγακλεής, μενεχάρμης, εἶδος ἀγητός, (Mercati, *Collectanea*, 75.43–45).

long ago, Solomon delineated.
and this, he registered under vanity.
David represented the essence of the mortals.
as a withering flower, as the first shoot of grass
that temporarily sprouts from the hollowness of the soil,
only to fall back in the hollows of the earth,
experiencing growth and then dryness towards its end.[144]

After setting the stage with the proverbial advice of Solomon and David, Iakobos moved on to address the passing of human beings only to continue by praising the life of the famous Andronikos Palaiologos, emphasizing again all the good deeds he was able to perform because of the emperor's prudent choice. By invoking Ioannes III, much as he had done in the speech, Iakobos sought to present the Palaiologoi as fully faithful to the regime. Finally, Iakobos introduces the deceased's grieving children with a familiar twist:

leaving behind in life three daughters
with the same number of excellent sons,
of whom Michael the strong-willed leads forth,
three times first in every measurement.
The images of his father fit him,
like resemblance [fits] with indistinguishability,
mind with purity and bravery,
with the purity of the soul and with military command.[145]

[144] Τὴν τῶν χθονίων ἀστατουμένην φύσιν.
πάλαι προλαβὼν Σολομὼν διαγράφει.
ἐν οἷς ματαιότητος ἐντὸς ἐγγράφει.
Δαβὶδ παριστᾷ τῶν βροτῶν τὴν οὐσίαν.
ὡς ἄνθος εὐμάραντον, ὡς χόρτου χλόην.
πρόσκαιρον ἐκθάλλουσαν ἀγροῦ κοιλάδων,
αὖθις δὲ συμπίπτουσαν ἐν γῆς λαγόσιν,
βλάστην παθοῦσαν καὶ τρύγην πρὸς τῷ τέλει (ibid., p. 76.1–8).

[145] βιοῦν δὲ λιπὼν τὴν τριθηλυτεκνίαν.
μετ' ἰσαρίθμων παναρίστων υἱέων,
ὧν καὶ προάρχει Μιχαὴλ ὁ στερρόφρων,
τρισὶν ὁ παμπρώτιστος ἐν πᾶσι μέτροις·
ᾧ καὶ προσαρμόζουσι πατρὸς εἰκόνες,
ὡς ἐμφερεῖς γε σὺν ἀπαραλλαξίᾳ,
νοὸς καθαρότητι κἂν εὐανδρίᾳ,
ψυχῆς καθαρότητι καὶ στρατηγίαις (ibid., 77.59–78.66).

As seen here, again, Michael Palaiologos, most likely present at the event, is singled out as the main heir and caretaker of his father's legacy, including the role of the protector of Thessaloniki. The approachable language of the poem ensured that this message was not lost in translation on its way to the audiences present at the commemorative event. It becomes clear, then, that the audience for the iambic poem was wider than that of the hexametric and elegiac Homeric poem.

The final poem by Iakobos commemorated Andronikos in a mostly unaffected *koine* that was not, however, completely devoid of archaizing impulses. The Q&A format of the *erotapkoriseis* allowed the author to pose brief and intelligible questions, while offering short answers that everybody could understand. For instance:

A: O tomb, do tell whose remains you carry.
B: If you wish, learn of famous Andronikos.
A: Who is he, expose by talking subtly.
B: He from the bright family of the proud Palaiologoi.
A: Let us hear of his ancestral roots.
B: Hear of Komnenian and Doukaian sprout.
A: Where did he move then? B: To the expanse of Asia.
A: And tell us what was his title?
B: *Megas domestikos* in Roman land.[146]

From the very first verse of the question-and-answer poem, Iakobos draws the listeners' attention to a speaking tomb, introduced in tandem with a random passerby curious about its contents. Talking graves are by no

---

[146] (α) Ὁ τύμβος, εἰπὲ < τίν > α < τ > ὸν νέκυν φέρεις.
(β) τὸν κλεινὸν Ἀνδρόνικον, ἢν βούλῃ, μάθε.
(α) ὁποῖος οὗτος, ἰσχνομυθῶν ἐκτίθει.
(β) ὁ λαμπρὸν αὐχῶν Παλαιολόγων γένος.
(α) καὶ ῥίζαν ἀκούτισον ἀρχικωτέραν.
(β) Κομνηνικὴν ἄκουε Δουκοφυῖαν.
(α) θρέπτειραν οἵαν ἔσχε; (β) τὴν Κωνσταντίνου.
(α) ποῖ δ' αὖ μετέστη; (β) πρὸς πλάτος τῆς Ἀσίας.
(α) τὴν ἀξίαν ἔπειτα τίς ἐστι φράσον.
(β) δομέστικος μέγιστος ἐν Ῥωμαΐδι (Mercati, *Collectanea*, p. 78.1–10).

means a novelty in the Mediterranean world, as we often encounter gravestones with inscriptions narrating the lives of the people entombed.[147] The people of the city were then familiar with inscribed gravestones, which were present all around them, and funerary poems and epigrams with speaking tombs were still being composed in the Komnenian period.[148] For instance, Andronikos' namesake who was the son of Georgios Palaiologos and Anna Doukaina received a funerary poem framed as a conversation between a passerby and his tomb from the pen of Nikolaos Kallikles.[149] The diverse audiences listening to Iakobos' poem must have appreciated the author's wit in translating the familiar landscapes of Thessaloniki and its countryside into a dynamic narrative piece. Testifying to the popularity of question-and-answer format in funerary poetry of the later Byzantine period are two poems composed by Manouel Holobolos, who, just like Iakobos in the 1250s, thrived under the patronage of Michael VIII Palaiologos in the decades to come.[150] Interestingly, Manouel Holobolos too has one of the two funerary poems framed as a conversation between a tomb and a passerby.[151] Thus, we see that two different authors close to Michael Palaiologos' literary

---

[147] For the presence of dialogues on tombs in pre-modern Mediterranean landscapes see S. Kauppinnen, *Dialogue Form in Greek Verse Inscriptions with some Non-Inscriptional Parallels*, PhD dissertation, Helsinki, 2015; M. A. Tueller, "The passer-by in archaic and classical epigram," in M. Baumbach, A. Petrovic, and I. Petrovic (eds.), *Archaic and Classical Greek Epigram* (Cambridge: Cambridge University Press, 2010), 42–60. For the interaction between inscriptions and readers see I. Drpić and A. Rhoby, "Byzantine Verses as Inscriptions: The Interaction of Text, Object, and Beholder," in *A Companion to Byzantine Poetry*, 430–455; A. Rhoby, "Text as Art? Byzantine Inscriptions and Their Display," in I. Bert, K. Bolle, F. Opdenhoff, and F. Stroth (eds.), *Writing Matters Presenting and Perceiving Monumental Inscriptions in Antiquity and the Middle Ages* (Berlin and Boston: De Gruyter 2017), 265–284.

[148] For instance, see the grave inscription of the tenth-century general Katakalon in Thessaloniki in Lauxtermann, *Byzantine Poetry*, 226. For later Byzantine epigrams see A.-M. Talbot, "Epigrams in Context," 75–90; A. Rhoby, *Byzantinische Epigramme auf Stein* (Vienna 2014), 64–69.

[149] Nicola Callicle, *Carmi: Testo critico, introd., trad., cennentario e lessico*, R. Romano (ed.) (Napoli: Napoli Bibliopolis 1980), 83–85.

[150] For analysis and references of the two poems see Rhoby, "Poetry on Commission," 273.

[151] G. Andrés, "Versos inéditos de Manouel Holóbolos a la tumba de Andrónico Tornikes," *La Ciudad de Dios* 175 (1962), 83–88.

circle decided to engage with their surroundings in order to deliver performatively enticing funerary poems.[152]

While it becomes clear that the poem's content and language were widely accessible to Thessalonians from all walks of life, how and where the piece was performed remains unknown. Based on the composition of the poem, though, we can reasonably argue that there was more than a single performer involved. The very form of the poem demands at least two readers: one asking and one responding. The dramatic dialogue between the orator asking the questions and a possible stand-in for Andronikos' tomb would have made for an interesting and engaging experience for the audiences. With the need for at least two readers in mind, my suggestion is to situate the performance of this piece in a church setting during a commemorative service for Andronikos Palaiologos.[153] The poem is not as rich in biblical references as the iambic one is, but the very genre of *erotapokriseis* makes it ideal for an ecclesiastic performance; after all, the Christians of Late Antiquity mainly employed the genre in ecclesiastic settings and the most prominent authors of *erotapokriseis* were men of the church. Also, an ecclesiastic commemoration would have had a priest—in this case perhaps Iakobos himself—present at the altar, as well as other members of the church, including the cantors who could step in for either of the two roles required for this piece to be performed effectively. Thus, the brief poem could have been performed as a dialogue in a swift manner that would resonate with the audiences even after they had left the church congregation. Later on, it could have been potentially inscribed on the tomb itself.

Iakobos' four works about the deceased Andronikos Palaiologos stand as testimony to Michael's careful crafting of his public persona from the

---

[152] Manouel Holobolos had shown himself to be a careful viewer of the objects in his surroundings. For example, in an encomium to Michael VIII Palaiologos, Holobolos crafts an image of the emperor's alliance with Genoa by taking in the motifs from a *peplos* sent from Nymphaion to Genoa to mark the bonds between the two states: C.J. Hilsdale, "The Imperial Image at the End of Exile: The Byzantine Embroidered Silk in Genoa and the Treaty of Nymphaion (1261)," *DOP* 64 (2010), 151–199.

[153] For dramatic performances of saints' lives in churches and monasteries that attracted significant crowds coming to appreciate the art of performance see the introduction to and the translation of Michael Psellos' encomium to Ioannes Kroustoulas: S. Papaioannou, "Encomium for the Monk Ioannes Kroustoulas Who Read Aloud at the Holy Soros," in S. Papaioannou and C. Barber (eds.), *Michael Psellos on Literature and Art: A Byzantine Perspective on Aesthetics* (Notre Dame, IN: University of Notre Dame Press 2017), 218–244.

early days of his career. The Thessaloniki-based content of the speech and poems strongly suggests that the target audience for these pieces were indeed the citizens of this great Balkan metropolis. The different registers of language employed in each of these works testify to Michael's attempts to engage as wide an audience as possible while trying to satisfy the tastes of influential groups in the city. Hiring a single author to compose these diverse works of literature speaks to Iakobos' status as a renowned logographer and preacher in the city. Having such a celebrity writer compose four very different pieces in form, yet similar in content, enabled Michael to draw attention to his person from the widest possible cross-section of the city's population.

Having obtained his education and early experience in public affairs at the imperial court, Michael certainly knew how to use rhetoric to his own benefit. Crafting a relatable image of a popular public figure in a major city such as Thessaloniki, on whose social fabric the Palaiologoi had been leaving an imprint since the twelfth century, was a smart move on Michael's part. Whatever his aspirations, having the support of the publics at all levels—from people on the streets to local elites—made governing the province easier and secured Michael's future. Unfortunately for Michael, he was about to learn that maintaining the support of local notables was not as easy an endeavour as his initial successes among the Thessalonians may have suggested.

CHAPTER 3

Linking the Golden Chain: The Social Network of Michael Palaiologos

Surviving narratives about the early life of Michael Palaiologos and his immediate family members offer a vivid image of social realities at the imperial court and provincial administration, while speaking to the role of the Palaiologan *genos* in the Roman polity after 1204. The situation changes drastically for a brief but crucial period of Michael's life: roughly from the moment he was accused of high treason and incarcerated in 1253 to his enthronement in 1259. The accounts for this period tend to be brief and seem somewhat incomplete, even though these six years were marked by a high-profile trial, incarceration, marriage into the imperial family, flight to the Saljuq Turks of Rum, yet another arrest, and Michael Palaiologos' eventual election to the imperial office in late 1258. The fact that both Michael and his main apologist, Georgios Akropolites, left these six years unaddressed in their narratives should not surprise us. After all, being accused of treason and running away to a foreign polity to escape potential trial certainly leaves little to no room for praise. Thus, the two authors muddied the flow of their narratives and managed to describe the period of 1253–1258 in unclear fashion. Nevertheless, swimming through the murky waters of Michael's pre-imperial career still offers enough material to conceptualize the public sphere in the empire of the Romans and Michael's potential role in it.

© The Author(s), under exclusive license to Springer Nature Switzerland AG 2022
A. Jovanović, *Michael Palaiologos and the Publics of the Byzantine Empire in Exile, c.1223–1259*, New Approaches to Byzantine History and Culture, https://doi.org/10.1007/978-3-031-09278-7_3

In his autobiographical *typikon* of St Demetrios' monastery, Michael addresses none of these issues save his escape to the Turks and eventual enthronement. Both, however, he de-historicizes by emphasizing the role of divine providence.[1] Georgios Akropolites, for his part, provides a very colourful account of the trial, to which he had been witness.[2] Here Georgios cast Michael as the arch-hero, with Ioannes III and his circle playing the role of antiheroes. This substantial narrative of the trial by a first-hand witness offers a rather rare opportunity to examine a high-profile public trial in Later Byzantium, concerns about objectivity notwithstanding. In contrast to Akropolites, Georgios Pachymeres dedicated a chapter of *The History*'s first book to Michael's incarceration around the time of the trial, which he does not address. He also wrote about Michael's reconciliation with Ioannes III and subsequent marriage with the emperor's niece.[3] Unlike Akropolites' narrative, which serves as an apology of Palaiologos' rise to power, Pachymeres' is a hostile account that builds a case against Michael in the course of his work. Thus, we are left with two conflicting narratives of Michael's life from 1253 to 1259. Regardless of these two authors' conflicting agendas, they both had to bow to the essential rule of history writing: *truthful telling*.[4] That is, in crafting their arguments, they both had to rely on retelling the known facts from Michael's life. By focusing on the known facts, they could inflect them in ways that revealed the image of Michael Palaiologos' character that they wished to promote to fit their respective agendas. Stemming from the idea of truthful telling of the story, Akropolites and Pachymeres guide us into the world of social, cultural, and political practices and expectations of the thirteenth century. Their political agendas aside, both authors employed

---

[1] Palaiologos, *Autobiography*, 5–6.

[2] Akropolites, *Chronike*, 50–51.

[3] Pachymeres, *Chronikon*, 37.2–39.14.

[4] On truth-telling as a persuasive technique in Byzantine historiography: Papaioannou, "The Aesthetics of Historiography," 3–24; Neville, *Heroes and Romans*, 32–33. On rhetorical practices including the truth in historiography: Woodman, *Rhetoric in Classical Historiography*; M. J. Wheeldon, "'True Stories,' 33–63; Mullett, "Novelisation in Byzantium," 1–28. On different techniques used by historians vis-à-vis rhetoricians to depict emperors in Byzantium see: A. Angelov, "In Search of God's Only Emperor: *Basileus* in Byzantine and Modern Historiography," *Journal of Medieval History* 40 (2014), 123–141. For an example of the audiences' engagement with the facts known to them in the works of history see: Neville, *Heroes and Romans*, 31.

arguments and reasoning as they built their cases about Michael Palaiologos which stemmed from the contemporaneous worldview and anxieties of the Romans.

By gradually unpacking the intertwined narratives of Palaiologos, Akropolites, and Pachymeres, I chart out a crucial period in Michael's life without attempting to pass my own judgement on whether Michael *really* conspired against Ioannes III or not. The following chapter, however, does not try to offer a rehabilitation of Michael Palaiologos either. Instead, it follows the surviving narratives, focusing on examining the ways in which both Akropolites and Pachymeres employed arguments and reasoning as they built their cases about Michael Palaiologos which stemmed from the contemporaneous worldview and anxieties of the Romans in the thirteenth century. Reconstructing Michael's biography in these six tumultuous years in turn leads us to explore the Nikaian elites' employment of public support, spaces, and events in maintaining or even enhancing their socio-political standing within the polity of the Romans.[5] All the sources covered in this chapter were, after all, meant for public distribution. Michael's autobiographical narrative as part of a monastic *typikon* was available to the public gaze, while the two histories written by a state and a church official found their target audience in their peers, that is, in the empire's educated officials.[6] The very emphasis on specific aspects from Michael's life in these sources was an endeavour in and of itself to project a carefully crafted image of the emperor to a wider public, either to praise or criticize him.

---

[5] For the Byzantine polity and the populace see: Kaldellis, *The Byzantine Republic*; D. Krallis, "Popular Byzantine Agency," 11–48; for the alliances of Byzantine elites during the twelfth century see: Magdalino, *The Empire of Manuel Komnenos*.

[6] For the public display of inscriptions in Byzantium see: A. Rhody, "Interactive Inscriptions: Byzantine Works of Art and Their Beholders," in A. M. Lidov, (ed.), *Spatial Icons. Performativity in Byzantium and Medieval Russia* (Moskau: Indrik 2011), 317–333; id., "*Tower Established by God, God Is Protecting You*: Inscriptions on Byzantine Fortifications—Their Function and Their Display," in C. Stavrakos, (ed.), *Inscriptions in the Byzantine and Post-Byzantine History and History of Art* (Wiesbaden: Harrassowitz Verlag 2016), 341–370; I. Drpić, *Epigram, Art, and Devotion*; id., "Painter as Scribe: Artistic Identity and the Arts of *graphē* in Late Byzantium," *Word & Image* 29 (3), 334–353; and P. Agapitos, "Poets and Painters: Theodoros Prodromos' Dedicatory Verses of His Novel to an Anonymous Caesar," *JÖB* 50 (2000), 173–185. For Byzantine performativity of works of history see: Magdalino and Macrides, "The Fourth Kingdom and the Rhetoric of Hellenism," in P. Magdalino, (ed.), *The Perception of the Past in Twelfth-Century Europe* (London and Rio Grande: Bloomsbury Academic 1992), 117–156.

Before engaging with Michael's high-profile trial, we follow him into provinces where we pick up the thread of public influence in the empire by unspooling the tale of Michael's role in the city of Melenikon. Moving away from the relationships that Byzantine high-born notables forged with the wider populace, which was the theme of the previous chapter, I shift our focus to Michael's relationship with local notables. Going a step up the social ladder, in the remainder of the chapter I explore Michael's social network in the highest circles of society. Examining the social network Michael formed around himself serves as a good example of alliance building and power brokerage among the empire's elites, including the imperial family. In the process of constant power struggle among the elites, the imperial household was wary of other prominent clans building up their own system of alliances and allegiances at the expense of the imperial family in whose service they thrived. It is this peculiar power relationship that appears as a common theme throughout the chapter.

In order to focus on the relevance and intersection of social connections with local and high elites of the empire, I centre our story on Michael's public effort to defend his person from accusations of treason before and after the trial. I also draw links between the account of the trial and Michael's position as governor in the city of Melenikon. By examining the actions of a prominent member of Melenikon—Nikolaos Manglavites—vis-à-vis Michael Palaiologos in the context of the trial, a rather complex image of social and power relations arises before our eyes. This set of relations among a high-born Roman (Michael Palaiologos), a local notable (Nikolaos Manglavites), and the emperor (Ioannes III) reveal the complexities caused by the state administration's direct presence and interest in its provinces. Exploring the physical setting of the trial and the audience present at it, as described by Georgios Akropolites, affords one clearer insight into wider social dynamics of a public event of this sort. Furthermore, following the entire process enables us to conceptualize the limits of imperial authority in a public trial as well as the role of the *kritai* and witnesses in building the case for and against Michael Palaiologos.[7]

---

[7] On Byzantine legal culture see: Z. Chitwood, *Byzantine Legal Culture and the Roman Legal Tradition, 867–1056* (Cambridge, UK: Cambridge University Press 2017); for legal practices in Middle and Late Byzantium see: A. Γκουτζιουκώστας, *Η απονομή δικαιοσύνης στο Βυζάντιο (9ος-12ος αιώνες): τα δικαιοδοτικά όργανα και τα δικαστήρια της πρωτεύουσας*

Michael's subsequent reintroduction to public service and marriage into the imperial family gives us insight into the carefully orchestrated manoeuvres that were supposed to protect the emperor from other notable officials in the empire. By concluding a marriage between an aristocrat of dubious allegiance and a member of his family, Ioannes III reveals the limits of imperial autocracy.[8] This constrained imperial authority draws the emperor into constant negotiations with the aristocrats "for whom the *golden chain* of high birth was welded."[9] Pachymeres' reference to the Homeric *golden chain* becomes an apt label for the empire's elites. The balance of power between the emperor and the *golden chain oikoi* also depends on the ability of either side to muster public support by building alliances among them and by directly communicating with the Roman populace. In this context, Michael's efforts to publicly celebrate and shape the common memory of Andronikos Palaiologos in Thessaloniki become more meaningful for our own understanding of Roman politics in the thirteenth century.

The chapter concludes with the examination of Theodore II Laskaris' rise to power and his promotion of certain aristocrats—first and foremost the Mouzalones—to the highest-ranking offices. I argue here that in his attempt to introduce new families of provincial stock to prominent positions, Theodore II did not wish to eradicate the aristocratic families of

---

(Αριστοτέλειο Πανεπιστήμιο Θεσσαλονίκης: Σχολή Φιλοσοφική 2004) (PhD Thesis); N. Oikonomides, "The 'Peira' of Eustathios Rhomaios: an Abortive Attempt to Innovate in Byzantine Law," *FM* 7 (1986), 169–192.

[8] For a take on the imperial power as a Roman office that had to be maintained through power brokerage see: Beck, *Senat und Volk*; Kaldellis, *The Byzantine Republic*; Krallis, *Michael Attaleiates and the Politics*. For a sacral image of a Later Byzantine emperor (conveniently enough Michael VIII Palaiologos) as a means of imperial public propaganda that served to bolster the emperor's prestige vis-à-vis other Romans see: Hilsdale, *Byzantine Art and Diplomacy*, 31–87. For the system of intertwined family clans established by Alexios I Komnenos from 1081 to 1204 see: Cheynet, *Pouvoir et contestation*, 359–473; V. Stanković, *Komnini u Carigradu*; L. Vilimonović, *Structure and Features*, 163–338. For the post-1261 aristocratic *gene* whose privileged positions were cemented during the Komnenian period see: Matschke–Tinnefeld, *Die Gesellschaft*, 18–32; Laiou, "The Byzantine Aristocracy," 132–136.

[9] Pachymeres, *Realtiones*: 1.21.

the *golden chain*.[10] Rather, he strove to add new links—albeit loyal exclusively to him—to the existing chain in order to weaken the individual influence of certain aristocrats. To this end, the emperor had to remove a number of prominent individuals from their offices, but he never tried to eliminate families that had been connected to the imperial administration at least since the times of the Komnenoi. Unfortunately for Michael, he found himself among those officials to be removed. For this reason, Michael Palaiologos had to choose whether to remain in the polity and suffer demotion or seek refuge beyond the empire's borders.

3.1 Keeping Checks and Balances Among the Romans

During his public service in Melenikon and Serres, under the wings of his father Andronikos, Michael Palaiologos came in contact with the local urban elite for the first time. Much like Andronikos, who kept on good terms with such families as the Spartenoi and Kampanoi of Thessaloniki, Michael had to rely on and occasionally accommodate the aspirations of the elites at Melenikon. This was all rather new for Michael, who so far in his career had to do business only with his peers of the *golden chain*. Fortunately for Michael, he benefited from his father's instruction. Another factor that made Michael's job easier was that the region he was assigned to govern was far from underdeveloped. In the thirteenth century, Melenikon retained its pre-1204 urban characteristics and was an important commercial centre of the region.[11] Traces of Melenikon's

---

[10] Traditional scholarly depictions of Theodoros II represent the emperor as the most 'anti-aristocratic' monarch of the three Laskarid emperors (Angold, *A Byzantine Government*, 60–79). Recently, Dimiter Korobeinikov pointed out that we should be cautious in labelling the three Laskarid emperors (Theodoros I, Ioannes III, and Theodoros II) 'anti-aristocratic' rulers (Korobeinikov, *Byzantium and the Turks*, 40–80, especially 58–75). Here, I push Korobeinikov's argument further by ascertaining that not even Theodoros II had any intention of eradicating the influential families from the public scene.

[11] On the role of Melenikon as the regional mercantile and administrative centre see: M.S. Popović, "Zur Topographie des spatbyzantinischen Melnik," *JÖB* 58 (2008), 107–119; id., "Die Sieldungstruktur der Region Melnik in Spatbyzantinischer und Osmanischen Zeit," *ZRVI* 50 (2010), 247–276. On Melenikon's local governing structure see: Κοντογιαννοπούλου, *Τοπικά Συμβούλια*, 100–102. For the socio-economic stratification of Byzantine cities, see footnote 126. Comparable to Melenikon was Serres that was also governed by Michael Palaiologos at the time. For the structure of the governing classes in Serres, which include both the local and imperial landowning aristocrats as

prosperity are best preserved in archaeological sites such as the so-called Byzantine House—a dwelling place of affluent merchants of the city that was modelled on the palaces of Asia Minor and Constantinople (Fig. 3.1).[12] Structures like the Byzantine House and the geographical distribution of settlements in the vicinity of Melenikon attest to the presence of an affluent local elite, whose members had the means to advertise themselves to the city's populace. By ensuring that they were well regarded by their fellow citizens, the elites of Melenikon strove to obtain high positions within the city and further their *oikos*' reputation in the region. If we are to trust Akropolites' account, Nikolaos Manglavites, member of a major landowning family, "was one of the most prominent people among the inhabitants of Melenikon."[13] Nikolaos became a pivotal figure in regional politics when, according to Akropolites, he gave a fiery public speech to the people in the streets of Melenikon in 1246. Manglavites sought to persuade local Roman and Bulgarian dwellers of the city to willingly join Ioannes III. As Nikolaos put it "our land belongs to the empire of the Romans [...] and all of us originate from Philippopolis, pure Romans by origin."[14] As a leader of the citizens of Melenikon, Nikolaos negotiated the terms upon which the city would join Ioannes III and support his cause in the Balkans against the Bulgarians and the Epirotes. Nikolaos' dealing with the emperor certainly made him a major public figure in Melenikon, once the city successfully passed from Bulgarian to Roman rule. We have no way to assess Nikolaos' political role at Melenikon during Michael's tenure in the city. We can, however, think of him as a vocal representative of the urban elites' interests in the city. Michael surely could not afford to dismiss his intercessions on their behalf. We can also presume that both Michael and

---

well as the *mesoi* such as local magistrates, merchants, and others: A. Κοντογιαννοπούλου, "Μεταξύ Κωνσταντινουπόλεως και Θεσσαλονίκης: Διοικητική και κοινωνική οργάνωση στις Σέρρες (1261–1383)," *Πόλεις και εξουσία*, 121–160.

[12] For the Byzantine house in Melenikon's features that correspond to palatial architecture of Byzantine Asia Minor see: P. Neiwohner, "Houses," in P. Niewohner, (ed.), *The Archaeology of Byzantine Anatolia: From the End of Late Antiquity until the Coming of the Turks* (Oxford: Oxford University Press 2017), 115.

[13] εἷς ἦν τῶν ἐπιφανεστέρων ἐν τοῖς τοῦ Μελενίκου οἰκήτορσιν (Akropolites, *Chronike*, 44.10–11).

[14] ἡμέτερος χῶρος τῇ τῶν Ῥωμαίων προσήκει ἀρχῇ [...] ἡμεῖς δὲ πάντες καὶ ἐκ Φιλιππουπόλεως ὁρμώμεθα, καθαροὶ τὸ γένος Ῥωμαῖοι (ibid., 44.29–30, 32–33).

Fig. 3.1 The Byzantine House in Melenikon

Nikolaos were politically active in the public eye. Michael was an imperially appointed governor of Melenikon and Serres. On top of his official appointment, Michael belonged to the well-known *oikos* of the Palaiologoi, who had occupied some of the highest offices in the empire since the reign of Alexios I Komnenos.[15] Such genealogy and concurrently held public office surely made Michael the talk of the town. Nikolaos, on the other hand, was a local man. He made a name for himself in Melenikon while the city was under Bulgarian rule, certainly becoming even more prominent after his successful direct dealings with emperor Ioannes III. Having men such as him on his side would have eased Michael's efforts in running the city's affairs.

Michael, however, did not share in his father's good fortune in doing business with the local elites. Akropolites explains that Nikolaos accused Michael of treason against the emperor, on account of popular rumors spreading around Melenikon.[16] This was something that

---

[15] For Palaiologoi under the Komnenoi see: Chenyet et Vannier, *Études*, 133–187; Polemis, *The Doukai*, 152–164.

[16] For the trial of Michael Palaiologos due to the accusations brough about by Nikolaos Manglavites, see: G. Prinzing, "Ein Mann τυραννίδος ἄξιος: zur Darstellung der rebellischen Vergangenheit Michaels VIII. Palaiologos," in I. Vassis, G. S. Henrich, D.

Michael's deceased father Andronikos had never experienced during his career, at least according to the surviving sources. Michael had to learn how to deal with this issue on his own. Thanks to Georgios' fervent defence of Michael, we have in our hands a forensic account of the criminal trial of Michael Palaiologos in 1253.[17] Akropolites dedicated a whole chapter to this trial, which is also the first in the series of scandals that will plague Michael until his death almost thirty years later. In building the case for Michael, Akropolites inevitably offered a detailed—albeit rhetorically embellished—report of the events surrounding the trial in order to suit his agenda of dismissing any accusations against Michael.[18]

According to Akropolites, the accusations against Michael were nothing but rumors swirling around the streets and taverns of Melenikon; after all, at the time Michael was the talk of the town. These rumours reportedly sprung from a misunderstanding between two men engaged in a conversation about Michael. Their discussion had focused on Michael's sadness for the passing of Demetrios Tornikes, who "had a wife who was the first cousin of the *megas domestikos* [Andronikos Palaiologos]."[19] In the conversation, one of the two men noted that the two Palaiologoi in charge of the region were great men and that Michael should perhaps marry the sister of the Bulgarian monarch. A secret marriage alliance between Michael and the Bulgarian princess would certainly have raised alarm bells at the imperial court. According to Akropolites, Michael knew nothing of these conversations. Word had, however, spread out before he could stop it and Nikolaos rushed to lay charges against Michael before the emperor. Interestingly enough, Akropolites did not use the term treason, leaving accusations against Michael vague.[20] Georgios Pachymeres fills in the blank for us by emphasizing that Michael was accused of high treason against the crown for allegedly conspiring

---

R. Reinsch (eds.), *Lesarten. Festschrift für Athanasios Kambylis zum 70. Geburtstag dargebracht von Schülern, Kollegen und Freunden* (Berlin and New York: Walter De Gruyter 1998), 181–188.

[17] Akropolites, *Chronike*, 50.

[18] For Akropolites' employment of literary techniques in the depiction of the trial in order to build a case supporting Michael Palaiologos see: Macrides, "George Akropolites' Rhetoric," 201–211.

[19] σύζυγον ἔχων τοῦ μεγάλου δομεστίκου πρωτεξαδέλφην (Akropolites, *Chronike*, 50.16–17).

[20] Macrides, *The History*, 246, n.12.

with his namesake Michael Angelos, the *despotes* of Epeiros. According to Pachymeres, Palaiologos was to marry the daughter of Angelos and they were to rule the empire together after Ioannes III's assassination.[21]

The imperial reaction was swift, and Michael was removed from public office and incarcerated,[22] which meant that the accusations fell under civil criminal procedure.[23] Akropolites for his part did not mention Michael's removal from office and his incarceration. He rather noted that once learning of the accusations the emperor set the case aside until a suitable hour, "since it was not the time for inquiry into such affairs but for campaign and battle."[24] Pachymeres, as we saw, complements Akropolites' account by writing that Michael was put under arrest. We should not disregard how Michael's presumed actions at Melenikon must have looked to the members of the imperial household. He was closely tied to the imperial family through upbringing and kinship. He was also carefully building a successful career and a good name for himself in the newly reconquered territories in the Balkans under the supervision of his father Andronikos Palaiologos. In those lands, which were newly reintegrated into the Roman polity, the local populace was not accustomed to the imperial regime from Nikaia. In the absence of strong allegiances to a distant emperor, court elites charged with the administration of these lands had breathing room to carve out their own share of public support at the expense of the common consensus behind the reigning emperor. Through their positions, charitable deeds, and patronage, Andronikos and Michael Palaiologos could win over the populace of Northern Greece for themselves rather than for the imperial household. That is, by being at the very outskirts of Ioannes III's empire and so close to the Bulgarians and the Romans of Epeiros, Michael surely looked well positioned to challenge the emperor's authority, if not in the empire as a whole then at least in Roman Macedonia where his deeds made him popular among

---

[21] Pachymeres, *Chronikon*, 37.3–20.

[22] For Michael's incarceration, which Akropolites does not refer to, see: Pachymeres, *Chronikon*, 39.2–3.

[23] For civil criminal procedure see: "Civil Procedure," in *ODB* I, 467. For operating of the ideal court see: R. J. Macrides, "The Competent Court," in A. Laiou, (ed.), *Law and Society in Byzantium, Ninth-Twelfth Centuries* (Washington: Dumbarton Oaks 1992), 117–129.

[24] ἐπεὶ δὲ οὐκ ἦν καιρὸς τοιούτων πραγμάτων ἐρεύνης ἀλλ' ἐκστρατείας καὶ μάχης. (Akropolites, *Chronike*, 50.6–8).

the locals. This was by no means a benign threat to Ioannes III, who had experienced a fair share of conspiracies against his rule.[25]

While Nikolaos' reasons for turning on Michael remain obscure, the preserved description of the entire criminal procedure against the accused Palaiologos extends our understanding of socio-political and legal practices in the later Byzantine period. Serendipitously, it also sheds light on the complex relationships forged among the emperor, court elites, and provincial Roman citizens. For it is telling that a local affluent Roman citizen from a provincial city such as Melenikon was able to generate enough commotion to have a member of the court aristocracy arrested under changes of treason. Another important aspect of the story, so vividly reported by Georgios Akropolites, is that Ioannes III did not, or rather could not, simply have Michael condemned without a trial. Rather, the emperor had him incarcerated before the trial. Akropolites does not commend the emperor for not acting hastily. He might have avoided doing so because he was casting Ioannes III as the villain of the story in *The History*. It is also possible that by not staging the trial or execution immediately, the emperor was simply following established legal practice. A law promogulated by Theodosius I, which, as Michael Attaleiates informs us, was revived in the later eleventh century by emperor Nikephoros III Botaneiates stipulated "that no man could be executed before a span of thirty days had elapsed after the final verdict against him."[26] Attaleiates introduced the story of Theodosius I's law and Nikephoros III's revival of it in order to praise the emperor.

---

[25] For instance, see Akropolites, *Chronike*, 22–23 for the separate conspiracies against Ioannes III by the brothers of Theodoros I Laskaris and by Andronikos Nestongos.

[26] Michael Attaleiates, *The History*, transl. A. Kaldellis and D. Krallis (Cambridge, MA and London, UK: Harvard University Press 2014), 571. Theodosius I's original proclamation jointly with his co-emperors Gratian and Valentinian goes as follows: "Imppp. Gratianus, Valentinianus et Theodosius aaa. Flaviano pf. p. Illyrici et Italiae. Si vindicari in aliquos severius, contra nostram consuetudinem, pro causae intuitu iusserimus, nolumus statim eos aut subire poenam, aut excipere sententiam, sed per dies XXX super statu eorum sors et fortuna suspensa sit. Reos sane accipiat vinciatque custodia, et excubiis solertibus vigilanter observet. Dat. XV. kal. sept. Verona, Antonio et Syagrio coss. Interpretatio. Si princeps cuiuscumque* gravi accusatione commotus quemquam occidi praeceperit, non statim a iudicibus, quae ab irato principe iussa sunt, compleantur, sed triginta diebus, qui puniri iussus est, reservetur, donec pietas dominorum iustitiae amica subveniat." (*C.Th.* 9.40.13.) For the date of the law's issuance see: J. F. Matthews, "'Codex Theodosianus' 9.40.13 and Nicomachus Flavianus," *Historia: Zeitschrift für Alte Geschichte* 46 (1997), 196–213.

The eleventh-century historian left us with another trace of why this law might have remained in practice after Nikephoros III's tenure: "he [the emperor] read the law aloud to the assembly of the Senate, all of whom were in agreement and greatly pleased by this."[27] Presenting the law to the Senate meant that the senators became very well aware of such a law which provided them with a sort of Byzantine *habeas corpus* for imperial associates. Ioannes III, who just like the emperors before him, had to constantly negotiate his own position and authority vis-à-vis other members of the *golden chain*, was probably aware (or maybe even reminded by his entourage) of this law.[28] Theodosius I's law was certainly there to remind the emperor of his precarious position and the constant need to maintain a healthy relationship with the Roman elite. Michael's position was not then as desperate as it might have initially seemed: he was expected to be judged first and then punished if convicted after a potential lapse of thirty days. The emperor assembled a tribunal with judges chosen from the ranks of imperial administrators to examine whether or not Michael, a Roman citizen and aristocrat, plotted against the crown. By putting together a public trial, Ioannes III ensured that he would not fall victim of his own wrath.

For his part, Nikolaos, a landowning notable in the backcountry of Thessaloniki, accused a state official and a member of a major aristocratic family by taking the case to the emperor. The fact that he did not, at least not to our knowledge, try to bring the case against a person of Michael's position to the local courts, which was technically under Michael's supervision, tells us that Nikolaos was aware of the limits of local authority in cases against major political figures. Furthermore, taking the case to the emperor meant that Nikolaos followed the rules of Roman law as prescribed in the *Ekloga Basilikon* of the mid-twelfth century.[29] According to this text, "the law gave to every man a competent judge and ordained that he [the defendant] can be judged only by him [the assigned judge]. Thus, a cleric and a monk [are] under the jurisdiction

---

[27] Attaleiates, *The History*, 573.

[28] This case is comparable to Ioannes III's clemency towards the perpetrators of Andronikos Nestongos' conspiracy, most of whom were liberated unharmed while the emperor "applied the law more compassionately" to the head perpetrators (Akropolites, *Chronike*, 23).

[29] On *Ekloga Basilikon* see: Chitwood, *Byzantine Legal Culture*, 33–35; Macrides, "The Competent Court," 118–119.

of a local bishop or the patriarch, a senator under the emperor, and a guild member under the eparch."[30] Nikolaos, at least through the pen of Akropolites, was sufficiently aware of legal practices to know that Michael as a senator fell directly under the jurisdiction of the emperor to whom Nikolaos had to file a complaint.[31] We see no attempt by Nikolaos to denounce Michael to the *praitor* in Thessaloniki under whom Palaiologos technically served. Rather, he took the case straight to Ioannes III. The example of Nikolaos seems to suggest that pre-1204 Roman legal practices continued well into the thirteenth century.

The case of Nikolaos Manglavites vs. Michael Palaiologos also stands as a testament to the central government's presence in the empire's provinces. Following the trajectory of Michael's tenure in the city of Melenikon, we can see the administrative practices of the imperial government unravel before our eyes. Michael was appointed by the emperor to govern the region of the city of Melenikon. Being sent directly from the imperial centre, Michael served as a link between the centre and the province. Michael was there to make sure that the region operated smoothly on behalf of the emperor and simultaneously he was there to offer Roman services to the local populace. On the other hand, by sending an imperially trained official, the emperor did not just send a capable administrator, but also made sure that the local notables did not end up accumulating too much unchecked power in their hands.

What about the interests of the citizens living in the provinces of the empire, though? How were their interests safeguarded from potential maladministration coming from the top? The case of Nikolaos Manglavites reads as a direct legal remedy to this very issue. Nikolaos, in order to protect his own interests, took his case against the administrator Palaiologos to emperor Ioannes III. Either because Nikolaos sincerely felt his allegiance lay with Ioannes III—in which case he appears to have served as the emperor's eyes and ears in the city ever since the two men

---

[30] ὁ νόμος ἑνὶ ἑκάστῳ τῶν ἀνθρώπων δέδωκε δικαστὴν πρόσφορον καὶ ὥρισε παρ' ἐκείνου κρίνεσθαι μόνον, οἷον τῷ κληρικῷ καὶ τῷ μοναχῷ τὸν κατὰ χώραν ἐπίσκοπον ἢ τὸν πατριάρχην, τῷ συγκλητικῷ τὸν βασιλέα, τῷ συστηματικῷ τὸν ἔπαρχον (*Ecloga Basilicorum*, 7.3.23.2: 35–38).

[31] The case of Nikolaos Manglavites against Michael Palaiologos was not by any means a precedent in Roman legal history. For example, see the case in the eleventh-century legal manual *Peira* composed by Eustathios Rhomaios about a group of villagers taking their case against the local official Romanos to the higher authorities: Panagiotes Zepos (ed.), Πεῖρα Εὐσταθίου τοῦ Ῥωμαίου (Athens: Fexis 1931; repr. Aalen: Sciencia Verlag 1962).

negotiated the surrender of Melenikon to the Romans—or because he was displeased with Michael Palaiologos, this local notable was prepared to seek help outside provincial boundaries. In doing so, Nikolaos demonstrated that people in the provinces had the very same expectations of access to state services and justice as those displayed by Constantinopolitans in the era before 1204. By avoiding provincial administration and taking his issue to the imperial court, Nikolaos shows us that exercising rights from the bottom-up kept the whole system in check. To be sure, Nikolaos had enough influence and funds to get the emperor's attention. A less fortunate citizen might not have had the means to directly invoke imperial attention. This did not mean that this citizen's problems would necessarily stay short of imperial attention. A harmed citizen without the adequate funds would have to rely on his patron to deliver the message. In the absence of such a patron, one would have to put his trust in the collectivity of citizens whose violent reaction against an administrator could provoke an adequate imperial reaction.[32]

The emperor, on his side, had the duty to take care of the plaintiff's petition. In our specific case, the emperor could be grateful that the plaintiff was a well-off individual and not a mob roaming around Melenikon. According to Akropolites, Ioannes III was eager to put together a trial against Michael for he saw him as a threat to the throne.[33] All this does not mean that any of the three parties—Manglavites vs. Palaiologos vs. the crown—did not try to play one against the other through backchannels and informal communication. Unfortunately, Akropolites' ardently pro-Palaiologan account does not offer any insight into potential lobbying against Nikolaos by Michael or his family and associates; his storyline only sheds light on the ways in which the emperor himself wished to influence the trial in order to secure Michael's condemnation. Akropolites' bias is clearly on display in his work, and yet the machinations depicted in the trial, as fictitious or exaggerated as they might be, nevertheless cast light on Roman legal procedure and the judgments the Byzantines produced about their compatriots' actions.

---

[32] On urban agency in Byzantine cities see: D. Krallis, "Historians, Politics, and the Polis in the Eleventh and Twelfth Centuries," *TM* 21 (2017), 419–448.

[33] Akropolites, *Chronike*, 50.

3.2 Michael's Trial: A Hot Mess?

In order to exonerate Michael Palaiologos, Georgios Akropolites carefully discredited his hero's adversaries. He thus did his best to convincingly depict both Ioannes III and Theodoros II as incapable and unjust monarchs.[34] Akropolites avoided simply labelling Ioannes III as incapable or unjust, however, and instead attacked the emperor's very right to rule over the Romans by describing his actions as unworthy of an imperial office holder. Akropolites rhetorically crafted his entire narrative as a cohesive whole, which should, by its end, discredit Ioannes III to the readers. He did this while, at the same time, withholding personal judgement. The task was by no means an easy one, as Ioannes III appears to have entered the pantheon of excellent Roman rulers almost immediately after his death. Thus, Akropolites employed all his rhetorical skill to cast the trial of 1253 as evidence on which to undermine Ioannes III's virtue in the eyes of his readers. In the process, Akropolites left us with a substantial description of the whole juridical process: from evidence collection, to interrogation, trial, final verdict, and lastly the expectations Romans had of their judicial practices.

Akropolites opens his account by focusing on the investigation and collection of proofs that would have enabled Ioannes III to condemn Michael Palaiologos. From the onset of the story, Akropolites tells us that both men, who were conversing about Michael, "were detained and questioned about their conversation."[35] The man who reported the conversation to Nikolaos repeated his claims to the emperor. The other man, who uttered the very words that raised the spectre of treason, adamantly ascertained that "he [the first man] has spoken truthfully, since he heard this from me. However, I did not speak so with the knowledge of Komnenos [Michael], but I myself have brought forward these words."[36] In this scene of interrogation Akropolites uses passive constructions to present the line of questioning, thus occluding the identities of the interrogators. The man who uttered the words of treason was then tortured—a

---

[34] For the critical description of Ioannes III and Theodoros II see: Macrides, "Introduction," *The History*, 55–65.

[35] κατασχεθέντες οὖν καὶ ἄμφω ἠρώτηνται περὶ τῶν λελεγμένων (Akropolites, *Chronike*, 50.42–43).

[36] ἀληθῶς μὲν οὑτοσὶ εἴρηκει, παρ' ἐμοῦ γὰρ ἀκήκοεν· ἀλλ' οὐκ εἰδήσει μοι εἴρηται τοῦ Κομνηνοῦ, ἀλλ' ἐξ ἑαυτοῦ τοὺς λόγους τούτους προήνεγκα (ibid., 50.44–47).

common practice used to obtain confessions from defendants in criminal procedures.[37] Since the torment was to no avail and no fingers could be pointed towards Michael, the accused man together with the one who brought the charges to Nikolaos Manglavites were armed and—for the lack of witnesses—engaged in the trial by combat.[38] The tortured man lost, which was taken as evidence that his testimony was false. He was, however, left alive and was questioned again, only to once more refuse to change his statement. At this point, Akropolites abandons the passive voice and introduces the emperor as instigator of torture and trial by combat. In his words: "since it appeared that the emperor would find out the truth by greater torture, as he was such a person who made examinations more exact, he applied the ordeal by death to the man."[39] Thus the active Ioannes III, who wishes to condemn Michael Palaiologos at any price, staged the execution of the poor man, who, even though exhausted by torture and under the impression that he was about to be killed, still assured the judges that Michael knew nothing of what he himself had said in private conversation. Since he did not change his statement under the threat of death, Ioannes III had no choice but to spare the man's life and incarcerate him for his own treasonous words and ideas. By marking Ioannes III as the perpetrator of the misfortunate simpleton's trial by death and subsequent incarceration, Akropolites played on his readers expectations of justice: the emperor acted harshly by applying a series of ordeals and punishments against a helpless subject.

This story preceding the very central point of the chapter—the trial itself of Michael Palaiologos—served Akropolites well in casting Ioannes III as a vicious monarch who put his own convictions and wishes above the well-being of his fellow Romans, and even above truth itself. Despite his political and rhetorical agenda, Akropolites, nevertheless, touches upon several points that illuminate the early procedure of a high-profile

---

[37] For torture in Byzantine court to extract confession see: "Torture," in *ODB* III, 2098–2099.

[38] For the Romans' acceptance of trial by combat, which was a novelty coming from the West in the times of Alexios I Komnenos, by the time of Michael's trial see: Macrides, *The History*: 265.n.18; idem., "Trial by Ordeal on Whose Order?," in P. Armstrong, (ed.), *Authority in Byzantium* (Farnham: Ashgate 2013), 31–46.

[39] ἐπεὶ δὲ διὰ πλείονος βασάνου ἔδοξεν ἐπιγνῶναι τὸν βασιλέα τὸ ἀληθές, οἷος ἐκεῖνος τὰς ἐξετάσεις ἀκριβεστέρας ποιούμενος, τὸν διὰ θανάτου ἐπήγαγε τῷ ἀνδρὶ ἔλεγχον (Akropolites, *Chronike*, 50.58–61).

trial. First, both parties were extensively interrogated. The defendant was in fact tortured and, given the lack of witnesses the two men met in combat. Obtaining a confession from a defendant who had already admitted to uttering treasonous words about Michael's plausible future actions was pertinent to the trial. Not even the emperor, who heavily rested his hand on the scales of justice, could afford to publicly condemn Michael Palaiologos given the lack of evidence. While it was necessary for the monarch to get involved in the trial of a senator, Ioannes III's insistence on Michael's guilt, as described by Akropolites, suggests that the public saw such actions as bad governance. Applying torture and trial by combat per se were not the actions contested by Akropolites. What Akropolites saw as unjust were Ioannes III's constant interventions in the process in an effort to extort a confession through a feigned trial by death.

Having successfully laid the ground for depicting Ioannes III as a jealous and unjust ruler, Akropolites comes to the central point of the narrative: the interrogation of Michael Palaiologos. From the narrative, we learn that Akropolites was one of a number of otherwise unnamed judges.[40] The trial took place in an army camp in the vicinity of Philippi in Northern Greece. We can picture a large audience comprised of soldiers and other retinue around the camp attending the trial. The presence of a large crowd meant that whatever the outcome of the trial, it would have to be accepted by the soldiers who might otherwise start a not so peaceful commotion. Akropolites employed his rhetorical skills to juxtapose Michael, the true hero of the trial, to a villainous Ioannes III, who was assisted in his inequity by his friend Phokas, the metropolitan of Philadelphia. With emphasis on staging and the opposition of good and bad, the official account of the trial is almost completely omitted. Rather, Akropolites framed the affair as a private conversation between the corrupt Phokas and a dignified and witty Michael. Somehow Akropolites happened to overhear this conversation and relates it to his readers:

> Taking Michael aside, for I [Akropolites] have overheard this conversation, he [Phokas] told him: 'you are a noble man and were born of nobles. For this reason, you must think now and act accordingly to what behooves you for the sake of your reputation, your good faith, and all your *genos*. Since

[40] Macrides, *The History*, 264.n.7.

in your case there is no proof of witnesses, you must present the truth through the red-hot iron.'[41]

In this alleged statement, Phokas suggested that in the absence of concrete proof of treason Michael should undergo trial by hot iron. The metropolitan insisted that Michael do this in order to once and for all clear his own name and that of the Palaiologoi of all charges. While this was a suggestion offered in private, Michael was not subjected officially to the ordeal by iron since the very practice was considered uncanonical by jurists in the years following the sack of Constantinople. Ordeal by fire originated in Western Europe and sole instances of its application (or rather suggestions of its application) come from the period of exile. In the writings of two major exilic ecclesiastic jurists—Demetrios Chomatenos and Ioannes Apokaukos—we find instances when the ordeal by fire was suggested.[42] Both jurists write from Epeiros and find the practice to be barbarian in origin. Chomatenos goes as far as to deny its validity in the eyes of either ecclesiastic or secular civil law.[43] As has been noted, trial by hot iron was employed only if valid proof was lacking. The ordeal was performed by secular authorities and only if the accused agreed (or themselves proposed) such a trial.[44] While some jurists, such as Apokaukos, might accept trial by fire as a legitimate way to prove one's innocence, it becomes clear that in every recorded case that has come down to us, the defendant had to explicitly accept to undergo the ordeal.

Akropolites, knowing his laws and judicial opinions, made much of this scandalous proposal and cast Michael as an intelligent young man of 27 years who was quick to respond:

> I do not know how such a thing is called holy, oh lord, but I am a sinful man and cannot work such wonders. But if a metropolitan, who is a man of God, advises me to undertake such action, you yourself should put on

---

[41] παραλαβὼν Μιχαήλ, κἀμοῦ τῶν λόγων ἀκροωμένου, ταῦτ' εἶπεν ὡς 'εὐγενὴς μὲν ἀνὴρ σὺ καὶ ἐξ εὐγενῶν γεγέννησαι. δεῖ οὖν σε τὸ δέον ὑπὲρ τῆς σῆς ὑπολήψεώς τε καὶ πίστεως καὶ παντός σοι τοῦ γένους καὶ νοῆσαι καὶ διαπράξασθαι. ἐπεὶ δὲ οὐκ ἔλεγχος παρὰ μαρτύρων ἐν σοί, δεῖ σε τῷ μύδρῳ τὴν ἀλήθειαν παραστήσασθαι (Akropolites, *Chronike*, 50.100–106).

[42] D. Chomatenos, *Demetrii Chomateni Ponemata Diaphora*, G. Prinzing (ed.) (Berlin and New York: De Grutyer 2002), 397–399, 302–303; Α. Παπαδόπουλος-Κεραμεύς, *Βυζαντίς* 1 (Ἀθῆναι: κ. κ. Ελευθερουδάκη καὶ Μπαρτ 1909), 27–28.

[43] Chomatenos, *Ponemata*, 303.22-4.

[44] Macrides, "Trial by Ordeal," 31–46.

all your holy attire, as you have the custom when you are entering the holy shrine on foot and when you are appealing to God. Then heat up the iron for me with your own hands which touch the holy sacrifice, the body of our lord Jesus Christ sacrificed for the entire world and which is ever sacrificed by you, priests and hierarchs, and with these holy hands of yours place the iron in my hand, I confide in lord Christ to overlook my every sin and work the truth through miracle.[45]

After Michael's convincing retort that resembles the arguments produced by such jurists as Chomatenos and Apokaukos,[46] Phokas changed track and noted:

'Oh, my good young man, not only is this not a Roman practice of ours, but it is not in ecclesiastical tradition, nor did it proceed from the laws or, earlier, from the divine and holy canons. The fashion is barbarian and unknown amongst us; it is put into practice only by imperial order.' And [Michael] said, 'O the greatest hierarch of God, had I myself been born of barbarians and had grown up with barbarian traditions or had been brought up from childhood in such laws, I would pay my penalty in barbarian fashion. However, if I am a Roman and [originating] from Romans, let this trial of mine come to a conclusion in accordance with Roman laws and written traditions'.[47]

---

[45] 'οὐκ οἶδ' ὅπως τὸ τοιοῦτον κέκληται ἅγιον, ὦ δέσποτα' ἔφη· 'ἀλλ' ἐγὼ μὲν ἁμαρτωλός εἰμι ἄνθρωπος καὶ τερατουργεῖν τοιαῦτα οὐ δύναμαι. εἰ δέ μοι συμβουλεύῃ μητροπολίτης ὢν καὶ θεοῦ ἄνθρωπος τουτὶ διαπράξασθαι, ἔνδυσαι μὲν αὐτὸς τὴν ἱεράν σου πᾶσαν στολήν, καθὼς εἴωθας ἐν τῷ θείῳ εἰσέρχεσθαι βήματι καὶ ἐντυγχάνειν θεῷ· εἶτα δὴ ταῖς σαῖς χερσὶν ἐκπύρωσόν μοι τὸν σίδηρον, αἷς τοῦ θείου ἐφάπτῃ θύματος, τοῦ σώματος τοῦ κυρίου ἡμῶν Ἰησοῦ Χριστοῦ τοῦ ὑπὲρ παντὸς τοῦ κόσμου τεθυμένου καὶ ἀεὶ θυομένου παρ' ὑμῶν τῶν ἱερέων τε καὶ ἱεραρχῶν, καὶ ταύταις δὴ ταῖς ἱεραῖς σου χερσὶν ἐπίθες τῇ χειρί μου τὸν σίδηρον, καὶ τεθάρρηκα εἰς τὸν δεσπότην Χριστόν, ὡς πᾶσαν μὲν οὗτος ἁμαρτίαν μου παροράσεται, θαυματουργήσειε δὲ τὴν ἀλήθειαν' (ibid., 50.107–121).

[46] For the ordeal by fire and the judicial opposition to it see: R. Macrides, Trial by Ordeal, 31–46.

[47] 'ὦ καλὲ νεανία,' ἔφη, 'τοῦτο οὐκ ἔστι τῆς ἡμετέρας καὶ Ῥωμαϊκῆς καταστάσεως, ἀλλ' οὔτε τῆς ἐκκλησιαστικῆς παραδόσεως, οὔτε μὴν ἐκ τῶν νόμων οὔτε δὴ πρότερον ἐκ τῶν ἱερῶν καὶ θείων κανόνων παρείληπται. βαρβαρικὸς δὲ ὁ τρόπος καὶ ἀγνὼς ἐν ἡμῖν, προσταγῇ δὲ μόνον ἐνεργεῖται βασιλικῇ.' καὶ ὅς 'ὦ μέγιστε ἱεράρχα θεοῦ, εἰ μὲν καὶ αὐτὸς ἐκ βαρβάρων γεγέννημαι καὶ βαρβαρικοῖς τοῖς ἤθεσιν ἀνατέθραμμαι ἢ καὶ νόμοις τουτοισὶν ἐκπεπαίδευμαι, καὶ βαρβαρικῶς ἐκτισαίμην τὴν δίκην μου· εἰ δὲ Ῥωμαῖος καὶ ἐκ Ῥωμαίων, κατὰ νόμους Ῥωμαϊκοὺς καὶ παραδόσεις ἐγγράφους ἡ κρίσις τερματωθήτω μοι' (Akropolites, *Chronike*: 50.122–132).

Michael thus chose not to undergo the ordeal by fire, and this seemed to have been a legitimate choice as not even the emperor could impose such a demand on the defendant. Rather, Michael had the opportunity to reject the ordeal twice: once when some of the judges suggested it and then when Phokas proposed it. Both times, the argument employed was that trial by fire was the quickest way to clear his name and his family's reputation. Likewise, both times, Michael had quick and witty answers to the proposals emphasizing the illegitimacy of the very trial, much in the same vein as Chomatenos had done some twenty years earlier.

The History's account of the whole episode, often cited by scholars as evidence of the Byzantines' adoption of the ordeal by hot iron, is therefore a rhetorical set piece, as Ruth Macrides has suggested, that emphasizes the barbarity of the procedure and shows such practices to hold no solid legal ground.[48] The whole episode was an off-the-record conversation and the only witness to the conversation was, conveniently enough, Akropolites himself. Michael was not really expected to undergo ordeal by fire since, as the hero of *The History* emphasized in the narrative, it was neither a Roman practice nor a Christian one. It is exactly for this reason that Akropolites decided to insert this epyllion in prose into the larger narrative. Akropolites' depiction of the supposed conversation reflects on the anxieties of contemporaneous elites, who, in the end, are the main audience of the work. Even the pro-Laskarid historian Pachymeres had to admit that under Theodoros II the option of undergoing the ordeal by fire was sometimes imposed on the high-born Romans whose reputation the emperor sought to tarnish. After Michael's takeover in 1259, any ordeal by fire was made officially illegal. Akropolites employs the story of the ordeal by fire under the Laskarides to discretely remind the high-born Romans of Michael VIII Palaiologos' just governance.

Leaving the ordeal by fire aside, Michael's formal trial, itself a major public event in an army camp at Philippi, was less exciting than the exchange between the metropolitan and the young Palaiologos. Akropolites quite simply notes:

> Even though the emperor made a great effort, he did not find a single fault to hold against Michael Komnenos, but [along the way] he led the guiltless to guilt with the force of words or whips. When all gave their decision,

---

[48] Macrides, "Trial by Ordeal," 31–46.

both the Latins and the Romans, and especially the Latins, since they tend to speak more freely toward their lords, Michael Komnenos was found guiltless according to everybody. I myself heard this, for I was present at the judgement, and with me was Ioannes Makrotos. We were hastily numbered by the emperor into those passing judgement who, as if they were no different from wood, were made to stand there. For the emperor wanted everyone to vote with him against him [Michael], but we uttered no words since Michael Komnenos was being judged without reason.[49]

The official account of the trial is fairly easy to reconstruct: having spent time in prison and not facing firm evidence against him, Michael was brought to the trial. This was a large tribunal and the attending audiences—the soldiers—were not shy to voice their opinion on the issue of Palaiologos' guilt. Both Roman and Latin soldiers in the camp supported Michael. Then, the council of the highest state officials, including emperor Ioannes III himself, who "wanted everyone to vote with him against him [Michael],"[50] cast their vote. Despite the emperor's exhortation to find Michael guilty, this group apparently also affirmed Michael Palaiologos' innocence with their vote. Ioannes III, who according to the law was the only one who had the right to judge senators, was left with no other choice than setting the defendant free. This was no secret trial behind closed doors, attended only by the senatorial elite. Rather, a larger group was involved, even the non-Roman elements fighting for the Romans. The emperor could not convict Michael all on his own—if indeed that was his intention as argued by Akropolites. This would have placed him against both the senators and regular soldiers, essential constituent members of the Roman body politic. Alienating both senate and army was not something any emperor could afford.[51] Ioannes III,

---

[49] ὁ μὲν οὖν βασιλεὺς διάπειραν πολλὴν πεποιηκὼς οὐχ εὗρε κατά τι τὸν Κομνηνὸν Μιχαὴλ ὑπαίτιον ὄντα, καὶ ταῦτα καὶ τὸν ἀναίτιον εἰς αἰτίαν ἄγων τῇ βίᾳ ἢ τῶν λόγων ἢ τῶν μαστίγων. πάντες γὰρ ἀπεφαίνοντο οἵ τε τῶν Λατίνων οἵ τε τῶν Ῥωμαίων, καὶ μάλιστα τῶν Λατίνων, ἐπεί γε οὗτοι ἐλευθερωτέρᾳ χρῶνται πρὸς τοὺς δεσπότας τῇ γλώττῃ, ἀθῷον εἶναι ἐπὶ πᾶσι τὸν Κομνηνὸν Μιχαήλ· ἤκουσα δὲ καὶ αὐτὸς ἐπὶ τῇ κρίσει παρών, καὶ σὺν ἐμοὶ ὁ Μακρωτὸς Ἰωάννης, τάχα καὶ ἡμεῖς συναριθμούμενοι τοῖς κρίνουσι πρὸς τοῦ βασιλέως, ὡς ξύλων ἄν τινες μηδὲν διαφέροντες ἐνταῦθ' ἵστανται. ἐβούλετο γὰρ πάντας κατ' αὐτοῦ συμψηφίζεσθαι, ἡμῖν δὲ οὐκ ἦν λόγος, ἄνευ λόγου τοῦ Κομνηνοῦ Μιχαὴλ κρινομένου (Akropolites, *Chronike*, 50.139–152).

[50] ἐβούλετο γὰρ πάντας κατ' αὐτοῦ συμψηφίζεσθαι (ibid., 50.150–151).

[51] For the role of public opinion, often forged in military camps, in Byzantium see: Kaldellis, *The Byzantine Republic*, 89–164; Krallis, "Popular Political Agency," 11–48;

from his standpoint, had to constrain himself within the legal parameters of the procedure having failed to sway the judges and the public.

The emperor was not able to have Palaiologos condemned without trial since Michael had too many supporters among the men who were in the camp and likely more broadly among the citizenry of Macedonia's towns. According to Akropolites, the whole case had to be eventually dismissed "because he [Michael] was loved—and love is truth—not just by us alone but also by all those in office, the generals, the soldiers, and the common people themselves."[52] This suggests that prior to the trial Michael had done an exquisite job in securing the support of both the elite and the commoners in northern Greece. His public endeavours, such as the commemoration of his father Andronikos in Thessaloniki, appear to have paid off. Michael's support among the elites as well as popularity among the soldiers and civilians around the army camp protected him from the emperor's wrath. In order to smoothly remove Michael from the political scene, the emperor first had to sway public opinion. Otherwise, a backlash from the populace could be expected.[53] In the end, a lack of convincing evidence saved Michael from the emperor's clutches.

3.3 A Fresh Start with Old Friends: Imperial Son-in-Law and New Appointment

Having avoided conviction, Michael knew that the emperor would have to reach out and seek rapprochement. Ioannes III knew this too, for as much as he held Michael in suspicion after the trial, he could not afford to stay on bad terms with the Palaiologoi and other *oikoi* closely affiliated with them.[54] According to Akropolites, the emperor was very much aware

specifically, for the interaction between soldiers and civilians in disseminating ideas about the empire: 23–41.

[52] ἐφιλεῖτο γάρ—φίλη γε ἡ ἀλήθεια—οὐ πρὸς ἡμῶν καὶ μόνον, ἀλλὰ καὶ πρὸς παντὸς τῶν τε ἐν τέλει τῶν τε στρατηγῶν τῶν τε στρατιωτῶν καὶ αὐτῶν τῶν τῆς ξύγκλυδος. (Akropolites, *Chronike*, 50.152–5).

[53] For more on the populace rebelling to express their will see: A. Kaldellis, "How to Usurp the Throne in Byzantium: The Role of Public Opinion in Sedition and Rebellion," in D. G. Angelov and M. Saxby, (eds.), *Power and Subversion in Byzantium: Papers from the Forty-Third Spring Symposium of Byzantine Studies, University of Birmingham, March 2010* (Farnham, UK – Burglinton, VT 2013), 43–56.

[54] Akropolites, *Chronike*, 51; Pachymeres even mentions that Michael was kept imprisoned after the trial since he was still kept in suspicion (*Relations*: 39.2–3).

of the fact that "[Michael's] closeness with other magnates did not allow the emperor to hold grudges against him."[55] After the dramatic narrative of the trial, Akropolites explains how Ioannes III went about achieving reconciliation with the Palaiologoi. Initially, the emperor sought to unite Michael in marriage to his granddaughter Eirene. Such a move was a bit problematic since Eirene was Michael's second cousin and Ioannes knew that the church prohibited such liaisons. Ioannes III could surely rest on precedents to achieve such a union. As Akropolites notes, "even though forbidden by the church, [marriage between cousins] is allowed to the emperors for sake of common welfare and interest."[56] Nevertheless, electing not to aggravate the prelates of the church over such an uncanonical marriage, Ioannes III backed off and sought a different means by which to publicly harmonize relations with Michael Palaiologos.

The emperor, in fact, still involved the church. According to Akropolites, the patriarch Manouel II was to bind Palaiologos with sacred oaths never to conspire against the imperial family.[57] While Akropolites notes that this happened at the emperor's bidding, Pachymeres offers a somewhat different version of the story. According to him, patriarch Manouel II took the initiative by approaching the emperor and suggesting that Michael be sent to him so that oaths of fidelity could be taken.[58] Thus, after patriarchal mediation Michael was brought back to imperial grace. Pachymeres' version enhances the general image of the church that the author promoted in his *History*, by emphasizing the patriarch's role in reconciling the Romans in the name of public benefit.[59] Both historians, with different goals in mind, agree on the fact that Michael was bound to the emperor by oaths offered to the patriarch. To a random observer of the oath-taking event, it becomes clear that the regime of Ioannes III could count on the unconditional support of the church. By involving the patriarchate in the Palaiologos affair, Ioannes III made it a matter of

---

[55] τὸ πρὸς τοὺς μεγάλους γνήσιον τούτου οὐκ εἴα τὸν βασιλέα ἐν περιφρονήσει φέρειν τὰ κατ' αὐτόν (Akropolites, *Chronike*: 51.4–6).

[56] κἂν γὰρ τῇ ἐκκλησίᾳ κεκώλυται, ἀλλὰ τοῖς βασιλεῦσιν ἐφεῖται τῆς κοινῆς προμηθείας χάριν καὶ τοῦ συμφέροντος (ibid., 50.176–177).

[57] ibid., 51.1–15.

[58] Pachymeres, *Chronikon*, 39.3–14.

[59] For Pachymeres' engaged historiography see: Angelov, *Imperial Ideology*, 260–285.

public knowledge that any collusion on Michael's part against the imperial *oikos* would automatically lead to the abrogation of sacred oaths that would result in excommunication. With a publicly staged oath-swearing event before a Church synod,[60] the emperor was able to turn everybody's attention to his rapprochement with Michael. Simultaneously, Ioannes III was sending a clear message to all *golden chain* members: acting against the imperial family in collusion with Michael Palaiologos would lead to church-sanctioned damnation. Acting against the emperor and his family was a criminal offence according to the law, but by making Michael swear oaths to the patriarch, Ioannes III was able to add sacred sanction resonant with the general public.[61]

Taking a public oath of fidelity to the imperial *oikos* was a clear gesture of goodwill on Michael's side, but this meant that Ioannes III would still have to compensate Palaiologos for backing off from the proposed union with his granddaughter. Instead of Eirene, Ioannes III opted for a union between Michael and Theodora, the imperial niece and granddaughter of the emperor's deceased brother, the *sebastokrator* Isaakios Doukas.[62] Theodora grew up at the imperial court under the care of her mother Eudokia since her father Ioannes Doukas died while she was young. Having entered this marriage, Michael was now elevated to the rank of *megas konostaulos*—commander in charge of the Latin troops in the empire[63]—and he was relocated from his office in the Balkans to Bithynia in the winter of 1253/1254. By bringing him closer to the imperial centres in Asia Minor, Ioannes III played it safe and kept Michael under his administration's supervision.

Michael had built solid support for himself and his family around the major city of Thessaloniki and its hinterland, which were only recently

---

[60] Pachymeres, *Chronikon*, 39.15–41.3.

[61] For oath taking see: N. G. Svoronos, "Le serment de fidélité à l'Empereur Byzantin et sa signification constitutionnelle," *REB* 9 (1951), 106–142; J.-C. Cheynet, "Foi et conjuration à Byzance," in M.-F. Auzépy, G. Sant-Guillain (eds.), *Oralité et lien social au Moyen Âge (Occident, Byzance, Islam): parole donnée, foi jurée, serment* (Paris: ARCHByz 2008), 265–280; especially 265–269 on the oaths being sworn by the aristocracy to the emperors alone. On oath-swearing in Late Byzantium see: Estangüi Gómez, *Byzance face aux Ottomans*, 64–67.

[62] Akropolites, *Chronike*, 51. For Theodora see: A.-M. Talbot, "Empress Theodora Palaiogina, Wife of Michael VIII," *DOP* 46 (1992), 295–303.

[63] R. Guilland, *Recherches sur les institutions byzantines* I (Berlin: Akademie Verlag 1967), 471–474.

reincorporated into the empire. We have already seen how Michael employed Iakobos of Bulgaria to commemorate his father Andronikos in Thessaloniki. On his part, Akropolites keeps reminding us that Michael was *loved* by all. His public display of generosity and kind administration were evidence that the emperor had been prudent in the selection of high officials. At the same time, Michael's competence made it possible for him to pose as a benefactor of the populace. His success as a local administrator was all the more significant in newly reconquered lands where the emperor had not had the opportunity to effectively cultivate his own image. All this is to suggest that it is likely that Michael would have been relocated even without the trial. This was, after all, a very common practice that prevented aristocrats from endearing themselves all too much to the local populace.[64] In his new office in Bithynia—the centre of the Laskarid regime—Michael was a horse ride away from the emperor and his men in Nikaia, Nymphaion, and Magnesia. Here any suspicious behaviour would be noted with greater ease. Furthermore, any Palaiologan benefaction would compete here with the heavy patronal footprint of the emperor himself.

Thus, Ioannes III officially pardoned Michael after the swearing of the aforementioned oath of loyalty. Palaiologos was in turn promoted and married into the imperial family—to which he was already connected through kinship. Akropolites offers a straightforward explanation for Ioannes III's leniency to Michael:

> The emperor, having thus dismissed the case, went to the east, while Michael Komnenos, as I said, was held in suspicion. Because of the [Palaiologan] family's nobility and his own kinship with him and, further, his close ties with other magnates did not allow the emperor to hold him in contempt.[65]

Thanks to Michael's personal and familial ties, Ioannes III was not able to downgrade Michael after the unsuccessful trial. Quite the opposite, Ioannes III had to find a way to work with Michael, who, by the

---

[64] Angold, *A Byzantine Government*, 250.

[65] Ὁ μὲν οὖν βασιλεὺς οὑτωσὶ τὰ τῆς ὑποθέσεως διαλύσας εἰς τὴν ἕω ἀπῄει, ὁ δὲ Κομνηνὸς Μιχαήλ, ὡς εἴρηκειν, ὑπεβλέπετο. ἐπεὶ δὲ τὸ τοῦ γένους περιφανὲς καὶ τὸ πρὸς αὐτὸν συγγενές, ἔτι γε μὴν τὸ πρὸς τοὺς μεγάλους γνήσιον τούτων οὐκ εἴα τὸν βασιλέα ἐν περιφρονήσει φέρειν τὰ κατ' αὐτόν (Akropolites, *Chronike*: 51.1–6).

mid-1250s, had already established strong personal connections with members of the empire's elite. On top of his personal social ties, Michael was related to empress Eirene who, like Michael's mother Theodora, was the granddaughter of Alexios III. Not that the sanguine connection to the household meant anything; in 1223/1224, Ioannes dealt with the *sebastokratores* Alexios and Isaakios—his predecessor's rebellious brothers—quite harshly, as they were removed from the public scene.[66] Ioannes was able to deal with his rebellious in-laws with ease because, unlike Michael, they broke into open rebellion by fleeing to the Latins. This action certainly did not resonate with the local populace and Theodoros I's brothers were quickly labelled public enemies. Ioannes used the sentiment against them to mete out brutal, extrajudicial punishment. Michael Palaiologos, on the other hand, was popular (at least in northern Greece) and had supporters among the imperial elites. Michael's case was, in fact, more like the conspiracy of Andronikos Nestongos, Ioannes III's cousin. In 1224, Andronikos with the support of numerous aristocrats from the Tarchaneiotai, Makrenoi, and Synadenoi clans plotted to topple Ioannes and take the throne. Having escaped the plot, Ioannes had to punish all the perpetrators and the penalty for high treason was death. The emperor, however, applied the law more compassionately. Save for Andronikos Nestongos and Makrenos, who were blinded and each had a hand amputated, all other conspirators were restored to their duties.[67] Much like Michael, members of these prominent families were well-connected among themselves, with links even in the imperial *oikos*, so Ioannes in reality had no choice but to spare them. Extended purges would have damaged his relationships with the surviving members of these families, which had been intermarrying since the dawn of the twelfth century.[68] By Ioannes III's time, removing a whole *oikos* from the political scene was nearly impossible without serious negative effects on the functioning of the Roman state whose top offices were occupied virtually exclusively by the members of the *golden chain*. Ioannes III understood this very well.

---

[66] ibid., 22.

[67] ibid., 23.

[68] For family politics in the twelfth century see: Magdalino, *The Empire of Manuel Komnenos*, 180–315.

After 1204, emperors were themselves members of the *golden chain* and relied heavily on the elite that followed them in Asia Minor. Out of the twenty families that occupied high posts in the period of exile, thirteen were politically and socially active in Constantinople of the twelfth century. Another two were on the rise in the later twelfth century, while five came to prominence after the catastrophe of 1204, which surely testifies to the effectiveness of imperially sponsored education in recruiting deserving (and affluent) individuals. If we were to add families occupying middle ranking offices in the empire such as the Akropolitai[69] to the families that were, by the virtue of intermarriages going back to the Komnenian period, connected to the imperial household, the number of pre-1204 families in the administration would swell even more. In this rather complex system of over twenty families connected through marriage, it is quite difficult, if not completely impossible, to identify specific moments in time when Michael became personally associated with prominent individuals from the Laskarid elite. Recreating the Palaiologan social network in the thirteenth century alone would be quite a challenge, if we consider that the Palaiologoi were arguably the most illustrious of the Laskarid high-born families, having occupied the highest offices since Georgios Palaiologos allied himself to Alexios I Komnenos before 1081. The intermarriage of the Palaiologoi with other members of the *golden chain* ensured that one could always find some point of affinity between Michael and other notables. Adding to the illustrious background of the Palaiologoi before 1204, the exilic era Palaiologoi were the only family, but for the Laskarids themselves, who had a member granted the title of *despotes*.[70]

Reconstructing the Palaiologan social network would only partly help in our effort to understand Michael's personal connections to the Roman elite. Nevertheless, the prominent position of the Palaiologan *oikos* and with it the family's blood ties to other aristocratic clans, helps us in understanding why Michael was able to position himself in the centre of a network that was going to shape Byzantine history from the mid-1250s until the final passing of the empire two hundred years later. Recreating Michael's personal socio-political network, on the other hand,

---

[69] The Akropolitai have occupied middle ranking administrative positions since the tenth century (Macrides, *History*, 6–7).

[70] Korobeinikov, *Byzantium and the Turks*, 59.

sheds light on the power dynamics at the very pinnacle of the Byzantine government. We have enough hints to reconstruct at least tentatively the personal circle Michael built around himself to secure his position vis-à-vis Ioannes III and later Theodoros II. It was one thing to have nominal allies as a member of the leading family in the empire, but it was a completely different matter to have ardent supporters in a time of trouble. Michael managed to secure such support by forging strong personal ties of *philia* between himself and quite a few members of the elites.[71] After all, Michael needed allies as much as each and every ally of his needed him and other magnates of the empire in order to maintain a power balance among themselves as well as the emperor. Even the most prominent members of society did not stand a good chance of surviving the competitive world of Roman politics on their own.[72] Anyone in Byzantium could fall easy prey to other magnates with substantial support and of course to the imperial administration. This is something Andronikos I Komnenos learned the hard way in the twelfth century.[73] Operating as a member of aristocratic constellations, which would usually include the imperial family, was the safest way to maintain one's position. This trend was noted by Byzantine authors as well. Scholars have traditionally cited Ioannes Zonaras' critique of Alexios I Komnenos for marrying family with state affairs as an example of this awareness.[74] But it was Georgios Pachymeres, who in his rather pompous Greek style, labelled the court elite as members of the *golden chain*.[75] By employing this

---

[71] For Byzantine family alliances in the form of *philia* see: M. Mullett, "Byzantium: A Friendly Society?," *Past and Present* 118 (1988), 3–24; L. Neville, *Authority*, 90–93. For an analysis of personal network building process see: M. Mullett, *Theophylact of Ochrid: Reading the Letters of a Byzantine Archbishop* (New York: Variorum 2016; first published in 1997), 163–222. For the social network of the Laskarid aristocracy see Vicent Puech's doctoral dissertation: V. Puech, *L' aristocratie et le pouvoir à Byzance au XIIIe siècle (1204–1310)* (I–II. Université de Versailles-Saint-Quentin-en-Yvelines 2000).

[72] For instance, see Kekaumenos' eleventh-century advice on the necessity of *philia* in public relations and office holding: Κεκαυμένος, Στρατηγικόν, Δημ. Τσουγκαράκης (εισ. και μετ.) (Αθήνα: Κανάκη 1993), 80. In the same work, the author also calls for caution against friends with whom, he sees, one maintains contact and cordial relations for no other reason than political gain.

[73] Κ. Βάρζος, Ἡ Γενεαλογία τῶν Κομνηνῶν 1 (Θεσσαλονίκη 1984), 493–638.

[74] P. Magdalino, "Aspects of Twelfth-Century Byzantine Kaiserkritik," *Speculum* 58 (1983), 326–346.

[75] Pachymeres, *Chronikon*, 93.14–15.

evocative metaphor, Pachymeres rightly hinted at the importance of socio-political ties between the elites. If any link were to break, the chain would immediately fragment.

The concept of *philia* was tricky though.[76] While one would have to work hard to maintain close ties with various social and political circles, one had to be cautious about one's friends. It was a general rule that friends bound by *philia* are there for social and political gain, not for emotional fulfillment. Kekaumenos himself was so cautious that, even though admitting that one needs friends to maintain his position, he advised to: "guard yourself more from your friends than your enemies."[77] This maxim, itself a paraphrase of a popular maxim in Byzantine anthologies, certainly found its way to the mind of Michael Palaiogolos. After all, the Palaiologoi had mastered the game of *philia* in order to maintain themselves on the very top of the *golden chain* for two hundred years. Through good fortune and prudence, Michael established a significant personal social network in the empire. Being a member of the Palaiologoi and occupying administrative positions that allowed him to build up a base of popular support made Michael a desired friend in the Laskarid polity. Thus, by the death of Andronikos Palaiologos in the mid-thirteenth century, Michael, who had now become the head of the Palaiologan *oikos*, was in an enviable position, being able to pick and choose his potential associates.

The fastest route to uncovering Michael's socio-political network is to look for allies who left written traces of their affinities. In this regard too, Georgios Akropolites leads the way. It has been noted in analyses of Akropolites' *The History*, not the least by Macrides in the extensive commentary accompanying her translation of his work, that the arch-hero of the story is Michael Palaiologos. The whole history can be read as an apology for Michael's scandalous rise to the throne. Thanks to Akropolites' tendency to insert himself into the narrative we can tentatively pinpoint times and places when *The History*'s author and Palaiologos were both present in the same spot. Michael and Georgios probably met at

---

[76] For friendship as a political mechanism see: Mullett, "Byzantium: A Friendly Society," 3–24; Chitwood, *Byzantine Legal Culture*, 45–75; J. Ransohoff, "'Consider the Future as Present': The Paranoid World of Kekaumenos," *Speculum* 93 (2018), 77–91. For *philia* vis-à-vis other types of personal relationships see: Cheynet, *Pouvoir et contestation*, 287–301.

[77] Κεκαυμένος, Στρατηγικόν, 80.

the court of Ioannes III. Akropolites had been a member of the court since 1234 when he arrived from Constantinople to study under Ioannes III's sponsorship. We see Akropolites actively taking part in courtly philosophical discussions in 1239. He also tutored the young Theodoros II in the 1240s, while simultaneously building a career as an imperial secretary and eventually as *logothetes tou genikou*.[78] Michael, on the other hand, finished his education at the court by 1242/1243 when he was 18 years old, as he tells us in the *typikon* of St Demetrios monastery.[79] Akropolites and Palaiologos therefore overlapped for quite a few years at court. Over this period the two men likely forged amicable ties. They in fact must have found establishing ties of *philia* with one another socially and politically fruitful. Michael saw a useful friend in the imperial secretary in charge of composing letters and decisions on behalf of Ioannes III, while Akropolites understood that forging close ties with Michael, a member of an illustrious *oikos*, was an effective way to improve his sociopolitical standing vis-à-vis other imperial administrators. Both Michael and Georgios, then, had a good grasp of the benefits they could bring each other: Palaiologos gained a friend in the heart of imperial administration, Akropolites a friend from a highly influential family and a potential patron.

After leaving the court, Michael spent most of his time following Ioannes III in his Balkan campaigns. It was precisely at one such military expedition that Michael crossed paths with Georgios. The two men stood side-by-side in the imperial tent, during Ioannes III's Balkan campaign of 1246.[80] After the conclusion of the campaign, Akropolites was in charge of drafting imperial letters and decrees to newly reincorporated cities of the empire: Thessaloniki, Serres, and Melenikon. There may have been shared satisfaction in the knowledge that Akropolites was the one letting those cities know that their new administrators would be the father-son duo of the Palaiologoi. Michael, on his friend Georgios' side, was assured of a glowing introduction to the people of Melenikon and Serres. We can quite reasonably conclude that by the death of Ioannes III in 1254, Akropolites had become closely associated with Michael. Furthermore,

---

[78] For Akropolites' life see: Macrides, *The History*, 5–29; for his titles and honours in the 1240s and 1250s see: Macrides, *The History*, 21.

[79] Palaiologos, *Autobiography*, 4.

[80] Akropolites, *Chronike*, 44–46.

sometime before 1256, Akropolites was joined in marriage with imperial blessings, either of Ioannes III or Theodoros II, to a certain Eudokia, a cousin of Michael Palaiologos.[81] This marriage cemented the ties between the *oikoi* of the Palaiologoi and Akropolitai. Marrying into even a lesser line of the Palaiologan clan assured Akropolites' membership in the *golden chain*.

Alliance with Akropolites, an ambitious and capable stateman as well as a rising intellectual of the empire, turned Michael into a potential patron for men of letters in the Roman polity. One such fortunate man was the famed rhetorician and once-archbishop of Ochrid, Iakobos. While Iakobos produced an encomium for Ioannes III's visit in Thessaloniki, the greater part of this author's surviving works was dedicated to commemorating the deceased Andronikos Palaiologos who left behind him a *glorious offspring* in the person of Michael.[82] Having Iakobos on his side in Thessaloniki boosted Michael's prestige in Northern Greece. Aside from having Iakobos as intellectual support, Michael could hope to tap into the ex-archbishop's social connections as well. Iakobos, it appears, was on good terms with yet another prominent member of the Nikaian elites: Nikephoros Blemmydes, arguably the most influential intellectual, teacher, and theologian of the period. Around the year 1253, Blemmydes sent a friendly tract on the procession of the Holy Spirit to Iakobos, who at the time was already in Thessaloniki.[83] The amicable relations between the two ecclesiastics and scholars could not have escaped Michael's attention. Ioannes III held the scholar in high regard ever since the public examination at the very beginning of Blemmydes' career. The emperor entrusted Blemmydes with the education of his son, offered the patriarchal throne to him on several occasions, and even used his imperial prerogatives to free Nikephoros of charges filed against him by a certain

---

[81] The exact relationship between Eudokia and Michael is unknown, but, during his reign, Michael did refer to Georgios Akropolites as his *gambros* (Macrides, *The History*, 79.n4); Georgios' son Constantine Akropolites refers to his mother in his *Testament* ("Constantini Acropolitae hagiographi byzantini epistularummanipulus," H. Delehaye, (ed.), *Analecta Bollandiana* 51 [1933], 282).

[82] For Iakobos and his role in Palaiologan activities in Thessaloniki see: Chapter I.

[83] *PG* 142, cols. 533–566. For the date of the tract see: Blemmydes, *Curriculum Vitae*, 46; Angelov, *Imperial Ideology*, 66, 66.n.137.

Romanos, one of his students.[84] Here we see, once more, Ioannes III interfering in the judicial process, albeit this time to protect an individual from charges and not to convict the defendant as was the case with Michael Palaiologos.

Beside Blemmydes' friendly relations with Iakobos, we cannot overestimate the relationship that the star tutor and intellectual maintained with his former student, Georgios Akropolites. The social and political ties between the two were so strong that, when compared, Blemmydes' *Autobiography* and Akropolites' *The History* characterize their contemporaries almost identically.[85] Thus, for instance, of the aforementioned patriarch Manouel II who acted as mediator between Michael and Ioannes III, Akropolites has to say: "a man of devotion and chaste in life and demeanour, even though he had been married; otherwise, though, he had no experience of letters and was unable to discern the meaning of what he read."[86] This account of a patriarch whom Ioannes III handpicked in order better to control the church corresponds well with Blemmydes' own negative account.[87] Furthermore, it seems that Blemmydes and Akropolites, who had both at some point taught Theodoros II, experienced a major falling out of favour with this monarch. Their shared predicament certainly helped keep the two intellectuals close. It is by no means a stretch to conclude that the three intellectuals—Nikephoros Blemmydes, Georgios Akropolites, and Iakobosbecame associates of the aristocratic Michael Palaiologos by the mid-1250s. Michael could rely on Iakobos to memorialize his deeds among the people of Thessaloniki, much as his contact with Blemmydes and Akropolites—both men influential at the imperial court—bought him influence at the centre of power. Such influence could perhaps ensure that Ioannes III would pardon him

---

[84] For Blemmydes' career see: Blemmydes, *Curriculum*; Constantinides, *Higher Education in Byzantium*, 9, 12–15; Angelov, *Imperial Ideology*. For the charges by Romanos and imperial intervention see: Constantinides, *Higher Education*, 12; Angelov, *Imperial Ideology*, as well as Blemmydes' poem composed in gratitude for imperial intervention in his favour: Blemmydes, *Curriculum*, 100–108.

[85] Macrides, *The History*, 9, 47–49.

[86] ἀνὴρ εὐλαβοῦς καὶ βίου καὶ πολιτείας σεμνῆς, εἰ καὶ γυναικὶ συνεζύγη, ἄλλως δὲ οὐ πεπειραμένος γραμμάτων οὐδὲ ὧν ἀνεγίνωσκεν ἀνελίττων τὴν ἔννοιαν (Akropolites, *Chronike*, 51.8–10).

[87] Blemmydes, *Curriculum Vitae*, 1.69.11–18.

when faced with an accusation of treason, much as he had pardoned the conspirators in the much more dangerous case of sedition by Nestongos.

With these three influential intellectuals on his side, Michael forged ties of *philia* outside the *golden chain*. While making socio-political alliances within the court elite was a given, Michael gained an advantage over his peers of the senate by aligning himself with two *novi homines*. Blemmydes was after all a son of a physician and Akropolites came from a mid-tier administrative family. Both were close to Ioannes III but had no ties of any sort with other members of the *golden chain*. Seizing the opportunity to further strengthen his *philia* with Blemmydes and Akropolites, Michael hired Iakobos to eulogize the deceased head of the Palaiologoi, the *megas domestikos* Andronikos. The relationship Michael fostered with Iakobos corresponded more to the traditional Komnenian, patron–client relationship. Still, as an associate of Blemmydes' Iakobos was a welcomed client in Michael's circle in the Balkans. At the same time, promoting himself as a generous patron of the arts, Michael could hope to attract other rhetoricians too to his family's service.

Having close associates among the relative newcomers to the central imperial administration was useful for Michael as he sought to obtain access and information about the imperial centre. As advantageous as these relationships might have been, they would count for nothing had Michael not worked to further bolster the *philia* with other aristocratic families occupying high offices. Forging ties with the members of the *golden chain* was somewhat easier since earlier connections of kinship and *philia* had existed between the Palaiologoi and other notable *oikoi* for generations. On the other hand, this also meant that Michael was not the only one seeking to develop these existing relationships. Other members of aristocratic *oikoi* were trying to promote their own names in the wider socio-political circles of the empire. Thus, Michael had to lead a delicate dance of forging alliances with other high elites while, at the same time, trying to establish himself as the epicentre of multiple alliances among the empire's notables. Thanks to Michael's famous father and even more famous surname, it is somewhat impossible to pin down the moment when Michael and the Palaiologan *oikos* allied with specific individuals: were the Palaiologoi allied with the households of Tarchaneiotai and Akropolitai before or after Michael's takeover of the *paterfamilias* role? In order to try to untie the Gordian knot of interfamilial relationships and Michael's place in those, the best starting point is to look at the individuals who supported Michael's cause in the trial for high treason. At this point, we would have to leave Akropolites' flattering remarks that all the senators, soldiers, and civilians were against Michael being condemned because he was so much loved and focus on specific individuals who could be singled out for making a strong case on Michael's behalf with Ioannes III. Needless to say, tracing these individuals is somewhat tricky. Offices occupied in the imperial service cross listed with familial ties to the Palaiologoi become the main tool in the attempt to reconstruct Michael's links with the *golden chain*.

The strongest potential intercessor between Michael and Ioannes III was *epi tes trapezes* Nikephoros Tarchaneiotes, who was held in high esteem by the emperor, especially since his triumphant military leadership at the siege of Tzouroulos in 1237.[88] The role of Nikephoros Tarchaneiotes in Ioannes III's government testifies to the degree of flexibility the monarch demonstrated in managing relationships with the notables. Thirteen years before the triumph in the name of that emperor at Tzouroulos, Nikephoros' predecessors in the *oikos* of the Tarchaneiotai had supported Andronikos Nestongos' rebellion. The emperor, as we have seen, forgave all the perpetrators of the rebellion, who mostly retained their offices. Nikephoros, a member of the not-so-long-ago renegade *oikos*, became Ioannes III's right hand in military campaigns. It was only by flexibly and continuously renegotiating relations with his closest associates (who were also most likely to rebel) that an emperor could maintain the throne. The means employed by both the emperor and the aristocrats to negotiate their share in power were clemency, popular support, and military skill. Ioannes III played the clemency card with the Tarchaneiotai, which won over Nikephoros.

On his side, Nikephoros employed his military genius to gain the emperor's attention. He was so successful that Ioannes III, after Andronikos Palaiologos' death, invited Nikephoros "to execute the duties of the *megas domestikos*."[89] While occupying offices of great importance and remaining in the trust of the emperor, Nikephoros also secured his position on the chain by marrying Andronikos Palaiologos' daughter

---

[88] On Nikephoros Tarchaneiotes see: Cheynet and Vannier, *Études*, 176–178; Macrides, *The History*, 36.n5, 49.n8. For the Tarchaneiotai in Byzantine service since the tenth century see: K. Ἄμαντος, "Σύμμεικτα: Πόθεν το όνομα Ταρχανειώτης," Ἑλληνικά 2 (1929), 435–436; Cheynet, *Pouvoir et* contestations, 210, 232, 281, 371.

[89] οἷον τὰ τοῦ μεγάλου δομεστίκου διεκπληροῦντα (Akropolites, *Chronike*, 49.25).

Maria.[90] The marital union with the Palaiologoi improved Nikephoros' social standing in the empire. The Tarchaneiotai were a politically active family since the tenth century. During the Komnenian period, however, the family continued to occupy offices but not the highest ones. Under Theodoros I and Ioannes III the family reached its political zenith.[91] Thus, Nikephoros' marriage to Maria Palaiologina was a clear sign of the family's prestige in the empire. Marrying Michael's sister came at a price, for now Nikephoros' interests became closely entwined with those of the Palaiologoi. Other than having Michael as brother-in-law, Nikephoros witnessed the lavish commemoration Michael organized for his deceased father in the city of Thessaloniki. This posthumous commemoration of Andronikos Palaiologos was an ideal event for Nikephoros to witness the influence Michael wished to exercise in the region. At the same time, this was an opportunity for Nikephoros Tarchaneiotes to publicly show support for his brother-in-law Michael Palaiologos. Given the family connections and social links, Nikephoros could be counted on to present the case of the Palaiologoi to the emperor, if the need ever arose.

By the end of Ioannes III's reign in 1254, we see Michael Palaiologos personally linked to several important figures of the Roman state. First, by marrying an imperial grandniece, Michael's closeness to the imperial *oikos* was confirmed. Secondly, by having his sister Maria married to Nikephoros Tarchaneiotes, Michael bolstered his ties with a major Laskarid household. More, by marrying his distant cousin Eudokia to Georgios Akropolites, Michael secured the friendship of an influential member of the central administration. Akropolites' own intellectual ties with Blemmydes only further helped Michael secure his position in the aristocratic constellation. He now had allies in virtually all spheres of public life: the court elite, central administration, intellectual circles, as well as public support through his soldiers and citizens of northern Greece. We get a much clearer sense of the number of Michael's potential allies—men, who just like Michael sought support in one another

---

[90] Macrides, *The History*, 36.5; A. Heisenberg, *Aus der Geschichte und Literatur der Palaiologenzeit* (München: Verlag der Bayerischen Akademie der Wissenschaften 1911), 11.

[91] For the Tarchaneiotai before 1204 see: А.П. Каждан, *Социальный состав господствующего класса Византии XI–XII вв.* (Москва: Институт всеобщей истории (Академия наук СССР) 1974), 116; Angold, *The Byzantine Government*, 69; Korobeinikov, *Byzantium and the Turks*, 58, 63–65; *ODB*III, 2011–2012.

without necessarily trying to overthrow Ioannes III or his son—when we turn to the reign of Theodoros II who, during his brief reign, systematically sought to undermine the privileged position of grandees from among the Palaiologoi, Tarchaneiotai, Philai, Strategopouloi, and Rhaoul.[92] It is likely that the rapport and understanding between individuals from these families developed during their early careers. Thus, for example, before assuming his duties as governor of Melenikon and Serres, Michael had served in the army alongside Alexios Strategopoulos and Ioannes Makrenos, his future close associates.[93] We cannot know if such affinities involved the Palaiologoi more broadly or if they ultimately represented Michael's personal inner social circle. It is certain, however, that in Theodoros II Laskaris many members of the *golden chain* found a common opponent who actively sought to break their ties. Thus, with the accession of Theodoros II to the throne, both Akropolites and Pachymeres in order to point out the families whose authority in the empire had been weakened by the new imperial office holder, gave us a glimpse into the personal network of the affected *oikoi*. In Theodoros II's breakdown of the *golden chain* standing next to the Tarchaneiotai, Philai, Strategopouloi, and Rhaoul, we find Michael Palaiologos.

3.4 Theodoros II Laskaris: The Breaker of Chains

Upon his accession to the throne, Theodoros II embarked on a campaign to weaken the overly influential members of old-established families. Many individuals honoured during the reign of Ioannes III found themselves removed from offices and brutally punished by the young emperor.[94] Even Pachymeres, who generally offers a positive portrait of the Laskarides said of Theodoros II that "he was rash in all things and also [believed that] he was thought little of – for the illness which

---

[92] On Theodoros II's reign and work see: Angelov, *The Byzantine Hellene*; Angleov, *Imperial Ideology*, 204–252.

[93] Akropolites, *Chronike*, 49.

[94] Akropolites, *Chronike*, 75; Pachymeres, *Chronikon*, 41.6–43.3.

has struck him and afflicted him greatly persuaded him to pay attention to terrible things."[95] Because of his alleged illness,[96] Pachymeres claims, Theodoros II "introduced measures to bring down the brow of those related to him."[97] It is somewhat surprising that even a supporter of the Laskarides had to comment on the irrational fears that spurred the emperor to purge many deserving high-born Romans. In the same passage, Pachymeres reveals that Theodoros II incarcerated or dismissed Alexios Strategopoulos[98] and Alexios Rhaoul[99]—both members of aristocratic families securely entrenched in the administration for centuries. Some other prominent officials fared even worse. For instance, one of Strategopoulos' sons, Konstantinos, was blinded. The same fate befell Theodoros Komnenos Philes,[100] the "unlawful *praitor*" of the emperor's correspondence.[101] Philes took over the office from the deceased *praitor* of the Balkans, Andronikos Palaiologos, and served until his deposition in 1254. Both Philes and Strategopoulos were blinded for alleged lèse-majesté. Akropolites also mentions the sufferings of *megas primmikerios* Konstantinos Tornikes,[102] *protovestiarites* Georgios Zagarommates,[103]

---

[95] θερμὸς ἦν ἐκεῖνος πρὸς πάντα, ἔτι δὲ καὶ τὴν τοῦ καταφρονεῖσθαι δόξαν—ἡ γὰρ νόσος ἐπεισπεσοῦσα καὶ μᾶλλον τρύχουσα ἔπειθε δεινὰ ὑπιδέσθαι (Pachymeres, *Chronikon*, 41.6–8).

[96] On the question of Theodoros II's condition, see: Angelov, *The Byzantine Hellene*, 11, 176–177, 381–389.

[97] ἐκαινοτόμει, τὴν ὀφρὺν τῶν πρὸς αἵματος καθαιρῶν (ibid., 41.19-43.1).

[98] The Strategopouloi have been connected to the side branches of the Komnenian *oikos* since the times of Alexios I (Βάρζος, *Γενεολογία*, 306–307).

[99] The Rhaoules were relative newcomers to the list of the highborn families managing to intermarry with the imperial family only under the Angeloi (Каждан, *Социальный состав*, 113–14, 119, 129).

[100] The family of Philai came to prominence only after 1204 (Жаворонков, "Состав и эволюция," 88, 90).

[101] For blinding of the incarcerated and blinding of officials see: Akropolites, *Chronike*, 75. On Theodoros Philes see Macrides, *The History*, 75.n10; for Theodoros II' expression of disdain towards Philes see: *Epistulae*, 105.23–106.41.

[102] The Tornikai have been around the prominent aristocrats since the Komnenoi, never occupying the highest posts until the Laskarid period (Каждан, *Социальный состав*, 116; Βάρζος, *Η Γενεολογία*, 446; Polemis, *The Doukai*, 185).

[103] Georgios Zagarammates was a *protovestiarios*, serving as a good example of provincial elite advancing into the central administration under Ioannes III (Ahrweiler, "Smyrne," 177–178).

epi tou kanikleiou Nikephoros Alyates,[104] as well as the four sons of Alexios Rhaoul.[105] Some, like Nikephoros Blemmydes, managed to avoid the imperial wrath, even when they did have a fallout with Theodoros II. Akropolites, beaten under imperial orders, nevertheless managed to profit from the whole situation and become the new *praitor* of the Balkans.[106]

Around the time of his promotion to *praitor* in the Balkans in 1256, Akropolites also wed Michael Palaiologos's cousin, Eudokia, a marriage most likely arranged by Theodoros II in his attempts to dilute the accumulated power of the families of the *golden chain*.[107] While it certainly served Michael, who managed to connect himself with every *praitor* in Thessaloniki succeeding his father, to have a prominent ally so close to the emperor, he was not so lucky with the other favourites of the emperor. Akropolites explains that the emperor appointed to positions of the highest authority in the state men with ancestors in the provincial and central administration from outside the *golden chain*. This assured him of the allegiance of the newly promoted individuals. Akropolites had choice words for the men Theodoros II promoted:

> On the spot he appointed to command the armies Manouel Laskaris, whom he named *protosebastos*, an utterly useless simpleton who was in horrible shape to command, and Konstantinos Margarites, who was pointed out earlier in the narrative, a peasant man born of peasants, reared on barley and bran and knowing only how to grunt.[108]

---

[104] The Alyates served in the imperial chancery before 1204 (I. Ševčenko, "On the Preface to a *Praktikon* by Alyates," JÖB 17 [1968] 65–72).

[105] Akropolites, *Chronike*, 75.

[106] Macrides, *The History*, 12, 66.9, 82.5; Akropolites, *Chronike*, 66, 68, 72, 79, 82. His career in the post was short-lived for he was soon captured by Michael Angelos of Epeiros in the siege of Prilep and was held in custody until Michael Palaiologos managed to secure his release in 1259.

[107] Macrides, "Introduction," 27.

[108] αὐτόθι γοῦν εἰς ἡγεμόνας τάξας τόν τε Λάσκαριν Μανουήλ, ὃν καὶ πρωτοσεβαστὸν κατωνόμασεν, ἀνθρώπιον ἀφελέστατον καὶ κακῶς εἰδὸς στρατηγεῖν, καὶ τὸν Μαργαρίτην Κωνσταντῖνον, ὃν προφθάσας ὁ λόγος ἐδήλωσεν, ἄνδρα ἀγροῖκον καὶ ἐξ ἀγροίκων γεγενημένον, μάζῃ καὶ πιτύροις ἀνατεθραμμένον καὶ λαρυγγίζειν μόνον εἰδότα (Akropolites, *Chronike*, 60.3–9).

Having pointed out how these *nouveau riche* individuals had no refinement and how undeserved epithets such as *megas* now appeared next to their names, Akropolites explained how:

> Georgios Mouzalon, whom he loved above everybody else, who was *megas domestikos*, he honoured as *protosebastos*, and *protovestiarios*, as well as *megas stratopedarches*; his brother Andronikos, who was *protovestiarites*, he named *megas domestikos*; Ioannes Angelos, who was *megas primmikerios*, he honoured *protostrator*; pitiful fellas, worth no more than three obols, brought up in childish games and songs accompanied by cymbals, to whom the Homeric phrase 'false of tongue, nimble of foot, peerless at beating the floor in dance' suits perfectly.[109]

The historian's rant openly marks these individuals as people from outside his personal social network, even though Akropolites himself was as much of a *novus homo* in the administration as Georgios Mouzalon and his relatives. In his characterization of the Mouzalones and the others, Akropolites exaggerated in pointing out that these men had nothing to do with the administration. The household of Mouzalones had been significant in the provincial administration of Asia Minor since the twelfth century. Granted no member of the family ever extended the family's influence outside the provinces, yet in the thirteenth century Asia Minor was the empire.[110] While the Mouzalones did not come from those circles of society that usually occupied the highest posts in the empire, Theodoros II knew well the men he chose as his main advisors and administrators. Despite Akropolites' protestations, they were far from undereducated and inexperienced officials. Pachymeres in fact informs us that the Mouzalones "had been attached as *paidopouloi* when [Theodoros

---

[109] καὶ τὸν μὲν Μουζάλωνα Γεώργιον τὸν ὑπὲρ πάντας ἄλλους τούτῳ φιλούμενον, ὄντα μέγαν δομέστικον, πρωτοσεβαστόν τε καὶ πρωτοβεστιάριον καὶ μέγαν στρατοπεδάρχην τετίμηκε, τὸν δὲ αὐτοῦ ἀδελφὸν Ἀνδρόνικον, πρωτοβεστιαρίτην ὄντα, μέγαν δομέστικον κατωνόμασε, τὸν δὲ Ἄγγελον Ἰωάννην, μέγαν πριμμικήριον τελοῦντα, τετίμηκε πρωτοστράτορα, ἀνδράρια μηδενὸς ἢ τριῶν ὀβολῶν ἄξια, παιδιαῖς ἀνατεθραμμένα καὶ κυμβάλων μέλεσί τε καὶ ᾄσμασι, πρὸς οὓς τὸ Ὁμηρικὸν εὐστόχως ἂν ἀπετόξευσε· 'ψεῦσταί τ' ὀρχησταί τε χοροτυπίῃσιν ἄριστοι.' (ibid., 60.31–41).

[110] On the Mouzalones brothers, as well as the family's pedigree before 1204, see: V. Puech, "The Aristocracy and the Empire of Nicaea," in J. Herrin & G. Saint-Guillain (eds.), *Identities and Allegiances in the Eastern Mediterranean after 1204* (Farnham: Ashgate 2011), 69–79, Angelov, *The Byzantine Hellene*, 111.

II] was still an heir to the throne."[111] Thinking about the social and spatial dynamics of the imperial palace, we can see that Ioannes III would not have allowed random lowborn Romans to serve as his son's companions (*paidopouloi*). Quite the contrary, entering the court and receiving imperially endowed education, room, and board was reserved for affluent members of society. Akropolites made sure to reproach the Mouzalones and other associates of Theodoros II for their lack of prestige, a statement that comes off as quite ironic when we consider that Akropolites himself was a sort of newcomer since none of his family members had ever before reached the ranks he had. Among Akropolites' (as well as Michael Palaiologos') allies we see other families that came into prominence relatively recently (e.g. the Strategopouloi) and some even only after 1204 (e.g. the Philai).

The reasons behind Mouzalones' unpopularity with the members of the *golden chain*, then, do not have much to do with their ancestry since men like Georgios Akropolites were welcomed into the circles of the high state officials. If we were to look at other *novi homines* in the empire, we would see that they integrated successfully into the *golden chain*. For instance, a certain *novus homo* from the Balanidiotes family, who grew up as a *paidopoulos* to Theodoros II, was a promised fiancé to Theodora, Michael Palaiologos' niece by his sister Maria. When Theodoros II decided to break the engagement and marry Theodora off to Basileios Kaballarios, a member of a prominent household, the Palaiologoi protested. That is, Theodora herself as well as her mother Maria preferred the *novus homo* than a Kaballarios to enter their family.[112] Cases such as the ones of Balanidiotes or Akropolites clearly demonstrate that the *novi homines* were more than welcome in the highest echelons of power, despite occasional snotty comments about one's background. The Mouzalones brothers, on the other hand, were disliked by their peers not so much because of their background but because of their exclusive ties with the emperor. In other words, Georgios and his two brothers owed

---

[111] εἰς παιδοπούλους δὲ αὐθεντοπουλευομένῳ τεταγμένους αὐτῷ. (Pachymeres, *Chronikon*, 41.14–15).

[112] For Balanidiotes's linkage to Theodoros II: Pachymeres, *Chronikon*, 55.18–21; Angold, *A Byzantine* Government, 176. For Balanidiotes' engagement with Theodora and her subsequent marriage to Basileios Kaballarios see: Pachymeres, *Chronikon*, 55.17–26. For Balanidiotes' origins and relationship with Theodoros II see: Angelov, *The Byzantine Hellene*, 110, 112, 161, 177.

their whole careers to Theodoros II.[113] They did not try to engage with other aristocrats in the central administration, nor with the urban populace, not even with the soldiers. Because of this exclusive dependence on imperial grace, the Mouzalones became naturally disliked by the *golden chain* households. They also, unlike Michael, proved dispensable.

Theodoros II might have decimated the ranks of the high officials from his father's reign, men from among the empire's prominent families, but by no means did he wish, nor could he afford, to completely oust these families from the empire's political and social life. Rather, as Pachymeres explains, Theodore strengthened the ties of his new high officials with the families of the old aristocracy he had just attacked. And so, Pachymeres explains how the old grandees were crushed only for their families to find themselves in marriage alliances with the new rich:

> He dismissed Alexios Rhaoul from his office, who had been in the honour of *protovestiarios*, placing in honour Georgios Mouzalon of Atrammytion, whom he had married to Theodora of the Kantakouzenoi, who was a niece of [Michael] Palaiologos, while he installed Georgios' younger brother, Andronikos, as *megas domestikos* and betrothed him to Rhaoul's daughter, and the third brother he promoted to *prothiekarios*.[114]

By pointing out that Mouzalones were married into the families whose members were incarcerated by the emperor, Pachymeres strongly hinted at Theodoros II's plans for the empire's elites. It is hardly believable that the emperor wished to eradicate the existing aristocratic families, some of which had been around for two or more centuries. Rather, he envisaged a path for new local elites, whom he could trust unconditionally, to join society's high rungs. In order for these men to be fully accepted, though, they needed to *ennoble* themselves and the best way to achieve this was marriage into the very families whose members were

---

[113] On the relationship Theodoros II had with the Mouzalones and his other friends who took an active role in the empire's government see: Angelov, *The Byzantine Hellene*, 109–127.

[114] παραλύει μὲν τοῦ ἀξιώματος εἰς πρωτοβεστιαρίου τεταγμένον τιμὴν τὸν Ῥαοὺλ Ἀλέξιον, ἀντεισάγει δ' εἰς ταύτην τὸν ἐξ Ἀτραμμυτίου Γεώργιον τὸν Μουζάλωνα, συνοικίσας αὐτῷ καὶ τὴν ἐκ Καντακουζηνῶν Θεοδώραν, τοῦ Παλαιολόγου οὖσαν ἀδελφιδῆν, τὸν δὲπαραλύει μὲν τοῦ ἀξιώματος εἰς πρωτοβεστιαρίου μετ' ἐκεῖνον Ἀνδρόνικον μέγαν δομέστικον καθιστᾷ, τὴν τοῦ Ῥαοὺλ θυγατέρα οἱ συναρμόσας, τὸν δέ γε τρίτον τῶν ἀδελφῶν προβάλλεται πρωθιερακάριον (Pachymeres, *Chronikon*, 41.8–14).

forcefully removed from high office. In this way, the emperor managed to demonstrate that he did not plan to crush the families that occupied high positions for generations. He simply wanted to weaken their position in order to strengthen his own authority and, ultimately, increase the state's vigour and revenues, while enjoying strong support from his staff. Theodoros II was no breaker of the *golden chain*. He simply loosened its grip on power by adding new links to it. After all, while Theodoros II might have been more radical in his attempts to weaken all the high-born families, let us not forget that among the purged families were the Philai who came to prominence by *ennoblement* through marriage only after 1204. Thus, Theodoros II clearly did not have any major plans to deal solely with the pre-1204 Komnenian elite, but rather with all the families that were intertwined by kinship in the 1250s regardless of the period when they came to prominence. The same Philai, for instance, found no major opposition from the older members of the *golden chain* in the early thirteenth century. Rather, they were able to build up alliances even with the most ancient of the high-born families such were the Palaiologoi. It was within this socio-political landscape that Michael Palaiologos had to operate during the mid- to late 1250s.

Michael followed Theodoros II's rise to the throne from his post in Bithynia. The last year of Ioannes III's reign brought no further trouble for him as he successfully commanded the armies in Bithynia and managed to defeat the Latins of Constantinople in their attempts to occupy Roman lands in Asia Minor.[115] Michael spent the first year and half of Theodoros II's reign in Western Asia Minor where "he had been entrusted with the command of the entire place."[116] His duties seem to have been similar to those at his post in Melenikon and Serres; only this time, Michael was closer to the ever weary and all-seeing imperial centre. As Pachymeres explained: "[Michael] was always held in suspicion of [wanting] the imperial majesty [for himself] and it was clear, from his insidious disposition, that he would attempt a revolution if he could seize an opportunity."[117] Truly, witnessing the purges of his allies, Michael knew that he should

---

[115] Michael, *Autobiography*, 5; Akropolites, *Chronike*, 64; Pachymeres, *Chronikon*, 43.6–45.12.

[116] τὴν τῆς ἁπάσης ταύτης χώρας ἡγεμονίαν ἐμπεπιστεῦσθαι (Akropolites, *Chronike*, 64.10–11).

[117] ὕποπτος μὲν εἰς βασιλείαν ἀεί ποτ' ὢν καὶ δῆλος, ἐξ ὧν ὑποκαθημένως εἶχε, νεωτερίσων, εἰ καιροῦ λάβηται. (Pachymeres, *Chronikon*, 37.7–8).

remain cautious in regard to the new emperor. His close associates were one-by-one falling out of favour with the emperor. Even Theodoros II's two beloved teachers (and Michael's allies), Nikephoros Blemmydes and Georgios Akropolites, were not able to keep their relationship with the emperor intact. Generally speaking, Michael and Georgios shared similar relationships with the reigning emperors. Akropolites had no known fallouts with Ioannes III. This does not mean that he was not on good terms with Michael Palaiologos who, both before and after the trial, occupied high positions under the very same emperor. On the other hand, Akropolites surely had a reason to hold grudges against Theodoros II, even though this emperor for the most part was benevolent and generous to him. According to his own biased narrative, Theodoros II had him beaten in the army camp when the latter expressed an opinion the emperor did not like.[118] Nevertheless, Akropolites was promoted by Theodoros II to the rank of *praitor* in the Balkans, where he was captured and taken to Epeiros in the siege of Prilep in 1256. It was Michael Palaiologos who secured Akropolites' release once he was emperor in 1259. During Theodoros II's reign, however, Blemmydes too came into open conflict with his ex-student over the issue of taxation—this conflict was to last until the emperor's death in 1258.[119] At this time Blemmydes composed an advisory piece, the *Imperial Statue*, in which he criticized the emperor by promoting as ideal imperial actions opposed to those of Theodoros II. The time of Blemmydes' fallout coincides with Akropolites' own strained relationship with the emperor. These series of conflicts with the emperor left Michael, by now a shrewd politician, wary of his own position. If men such were Blemmydes and Akropolites did not avoid conflict with Theodoros II, what could Michael, the perpetual suspect of the regime, expect from the emperor?

In the summer of 1256, Michael's associate Kotys, who worked at the imperial court, visited Michael in Bithynia to warn him about the emperor's intention to incarcerate him.[120] Kotys advised Michael to take drastic measures by saying that "both of us must desert to the Persians,

---

[118] Akropolites, *Chronike*, 63.
[119] Angelov, *Imperial Ideology*, 292–296.
[120] Pachymeres, *Chronikon*, 43.6–20.

if you care to keep your eyes."[121] At the conclusion of his discussion with Kotys, Michael knew that he had been blacklisted, much like the Strategopouloi, Philai, Rhaoul, and even Blemmydes. Being aware that he was aligned more with the deposed officials than with his in-law Georgios Akropolites, Michael accepted Kotys' advice and, finding himself in dire straits, fled to the safety of the Saljuq court. A life in shameful self-imposed exile was preferable to immediate disgrace and imprisonment. And so, in the summer of 1256, Michael embarked on a journey to Ikonion, the dwelling place of the sultan of Rum, where he sought refuge against Theodoros II's wrath.[122] The shameful act of cowardice and even treason, as we will see, arguably remained a permanent stain on Michael's reputation for the rest of his life.

---

[121] αὐτομολητέον πρὸς Πέρσας καὶ ἀμφοτέροις, εἴ σοι μέλει τῶν ὀφθαλμῶν (ibid., 43.12–13).

[122] For the story of Michael's flight to the Turks see: Prinzing, "Ein Mann τυραννίδος ἄξιος," 188–192.

CHAPTER 4

"Je veux être calife à la place du calife": Michael Palaiologos in the Saljuq Sultanate of Rum

Sultan Kaykhusraw I lost his life in the battle of Antioch on Menander against Roman forces in 1211. Following his death, the sultan's successor, Kaykaus I, had to assert his position by outmaneuvering other members of the Saljuq family as well as their political supporters at both the court and in the provinces.[1] During the tumultuous months of 1211, the Romans of Attaleia, nominally subjected to the sultan, rebelled against Saljuq rule and embarked on a four-year rebellion by "putting to the sword of vengeance the noble and the ignoble, the adult and the child, all wounded and murdered."[2] The insurrection in Attaleia soon became a burning issue in Kaykaus I's early reign. This was particularly true since the Lusignan Kingdom of Cyprus offered support to the rebels. Without wishing to attract any further foreign intervention the sultan stormed

---

[1] On Kaykhusraw I and Kaykaus II see: C. Cahen, *Pre-Ottoman Turkey: A General Survey of the Material and Spiritual Culture and History (c.1071–1330)* J. Jones and Williams (transl.) (New York: Sidgwick & Jackson 1968); for a critical overview of Saljuq history in the thirteenth century see: Korobeinikov, *Byzantium and the Turks*, 81–110.

[2] شريف ووضيع وكبير ورضيع را جريع وقتيل حسام انتقام كردانيدند. (M. Th. Houtsma ed, *Histoire des seldjoucides d'Asie Mineure d'après l'abrégé du Seldouknāmeh d'ibn- Bībī* [Leiden: Brill 1902], 51).

© The Author(s), under exclusive license to Springer Nature Switzerland AG 2022
A. Jovanović, *Michael Palaiologos and the Publics of the Byzantine Empire in Exile, c.1223–1259*, New Approaches to Byzantine History and Culture, https://doi.org/10.1007/978-3-031-09278-7_4

and conquered the city in 1215 and punished those who rebelled.[3] The remarkable uprising of the Roman populace in Attaleia has come down to us thanks to two Saljuq histories written in the second half of the thirteenth century: the first one was composed by a court official named Ibn Bibi and the second by Bar Hebraeus. Byzantine narratives, on the other side of the border, remain altogether silent about this long-lasting Roman insurgence. Even the main chronicler of the thirteenth century's first half, Georgios Akropolites, refrained from commenting on the rebellion in Attaleia.

Adhering to the unwritten rule of Byzantine historiography in describing solely the affairs of the Roman state and not those of the Romans outside the empire, unless directly related to the affairs of the state, Akropolites, much as Pachymeres, left us with no information about the lives and deeds of those Romans who lived and served in other countries. The two authors focused virtually exclusively on the affairs of the Roman state, save the brief excerpt of Michael Palaiologos' flight to the Turks in Akropolites' *The History*.[4] Venturing outside the expected contextual framework of Byzantine historiography, Akropolites himself admits that he had to broaden the scope of his historical narrative in order to be able to defend his hero's flight to the Turks.[5] While *The History* works as a source of Michael's endeavours in the Saljuq Sultanate of Rum, Akropolites was not particularly interested in describing his hero's surroundings at Ikonion. Akropolites' outline of Michael Palaiologos' escape to the Turks serves more as a vehicle to analyze the footprint of such otherwise unknown Romans as were the rebels in Attaleia dwelling in the Sultanate of Rum than a detailed account of Michael's engagement with the Saljuq polity. By following Michael's travails across the border river Sangarios, I explore here Roman presence in the sultanate. Michael's movements from the border regions to Ikonion and subsequently Aksaray and Kastamon offer us a route to follow as we conceptualize the ways in which a Byzantine aristocrat could have engaged with fellow Romans

---

[3] On the rebellion of 1211 in Attaleia see: *Histoire des seldjoucides d'Asie Mineure*, 51–57; Bar Hebraeus, *The Chronography*, E.A.W. Budge ed. and transl. (London: Oxford University Press 1932), 369.

[4] Akropolites, *Chronike*, 64–65; Pachymeres, *Chronikon*, 43–45.

[5] Ἐνταῦθα δὲ τοῦ λόγου γενόμενοι τὰ τῆς ἱστορίας, ὡς δέον ἐστίν, ἐμπλατύνομεν (Akropolites, *Chronike*, 65.1–2).

of various social standings in the Saljuq polity in Asia Minor. The reconstruction, however partial, of the social and political world of the Romans under Saljuq rule enables us to discuss the ways in which prominent Romans and the Roman populace employed the public sphere in a very Roman fashion in order to advance their careers at the court and in the streets of Saljuq cities.

In order to understand the social and political role of the Romans in the Sultanate of Rum, where Michael Palaiologos fled, we have to rely on Greek language textual production outside the borders of the Roman state, as well as on occasional mentions of Romans in non-Roman sources. Besides the historiographic narratives of Akropolites and Pachymeres, works of Michael Palaiologos' rather famous contemporaries, Jalal ad-Din Muhammad Rumi and his son Sultan Walad, both of whom dwelled in Ikonion, offer rather peculiar insight into the Saljuq capital's public and daily life.[6] The two Sufi intellectuals left a deep mark on Islamic literature.[7] Consciously or not, Rumi and Walad provided enough material with which to seriously reconstruct the urban setting in which the two authors composed their works. While their oeuvre mostly belongs to the realm of contemplative poetry and prose, it also relates to the social and cultural norms of Ikonians and other urban dwellers of the Saljuq Sultanate of Rum. Furthermore, these two authors' ghazals composed in the Greek language offer a unique insight into the cultural negotiation that was taking place in the Sultanate of Rum between the majority Roman populace and the new Persianate settlers.[8]

Complementing textual sources, material artefacts, and infrastructure also helps obtain a better sense of the multicultural character of the Saljuq state in Anatolia. Of specific interest to this chapter is the architectural infrastructure that was built by or for the Romans living in Rum:

---

[6] For the life and opus of Rumi and Sultan Walad see: Lewis, *Past and Present, East and West: The Life, Teachings, and Poetry of Jalal al-din Rumi* (New York: One World Publications 2014).

[7] For the diverse literary legacies coexisting and influencing one another in the Sultanate of Rum see: M. Pifer, *Kindred Voices: A Literary History of Medieval Anatolia* (New Haven and London: Yale University Press 2021).

[8] For the Greek works of Rumi and Sultan Walad see: G. Meyer, "Die griechischen Verse in Rabâbnâma," *BZt* 4 (1895), 401–411; R. Burguière and R. Mantran, "Quelques vers grecs du XIIIe siècle en caractères arabes," *Byzantion* 22 (1952), 63–80; Δ. Δέδες, "Τα ελληνικά ποιήματα του Μαυλανά Ρουμή και του γιου του Βαλέντ κατά τον 13ον αιώνα," *Τα Ιστορικά* 10 (18–19) (1993), 3–22.

churches, monuments of Roman antiquity, and similar exclusively Roman pieces of architecture.[9] However, we should keep in mind that the Saljuq Sultanate of Rum was not a static entity; it developed its own artistic and architectural expression influenced by traditional Perso-Turkic architecture. It left a significant imprint on the urban landscapes of Asia Minor as much as the medieval Roman presence did.[10] By bringing together the architectural and textual evidence of the Romans' enduring presence in Anatolia, I suggest that we can reconceptualize the ways in which we think about the role of the Romans in the sultanate's daily life, as well as in the highest echelons of government.

Thanks to the extant sources, the main focus of this chapter is the issue of *Romanitas* in foreign lands. By following Michael Palaiologos' venture outside the Roman Empire into public service within the Saljuq polity, we have an opportunity to examine how *Romanitas* was negotiated vis-à-vis other communal identities—this time around, without the help of a state deliberately promoting a sense of Roman unity to the populace.[11] The issue of belonging to a specific imagined community becomes even more relevant when we take into account that the sultanate's urban populace was predominantly Roman even in the thirteenth century. In the same vein, Michael's flight to the Saljuq Turks and his service in the Saljuq military certainly raise issues not just about Palaiologos' allegiances but also about his very identity. Was he still Roman—albeit of dubious allegiances—while in self-imposed exile? Was he becoming a Persian of

---

[9] Most existing scholarship focuses on sacral architecture of the Romans in Asia Minor; for Christian architectural endeavours in Saljuq Anatolia as well as the maintenance of old and new ecclesiastic and monastic establishments, see: T.B. Uyar, "Thirteenth-Century 'Byzantine' Art in Cappadocia and the Question of Greek Painters at the Seljuk Court," in A.S.C. Peacoks, B. de Nicola, and S. N. Yıldız (eds.), *Islam and Christianity in Medieval Anatolia* (New York: Routledge 2016), 215–232; M.V. Tekinalp, "Palace Churches of the Anatolian Saljuqs: Tolerance or Necessity," *Byzantine and Modern Greek Studies* 33, 148–167.

[10] R.P. McClary, *Rum Seljuq Architecture, 1070–1220: The Patronage of Sultans* (Edinburgh: Edinburgh University Press 2017); E.S. Wolper, *Cities and Saints: Sufism and the Transformation of Urban Space in Medieval Anatolia* (University Park: The Pennsylvania State University Press 2003).

[11] Questions of Roman identity both from top-down and bottom-up within the Roman polity have received significant scholarly attention in the past decade: Kaldellis, *Hellenism in Byzantium*; Kaldellis., "The Social Scope," 173–210; L. Neville, *Heroes and Romans*; D. Krallis, "Popular Political Agency," 11–48.

Roman origin?[12] Such questions are addressed in our sources, which relate to Michael's pleasant stay at the Saljuq court. Along the same lines, the question of how and whether Michael interacted with other Romans in Saljuq service or even simply under Saljuq rule awaits an answer.

4.1 The Prodigal Son: The Saljuq Sultanate of Rum

The Byzantine loss at Manzikert opened the path to roaming Turkmen tribes in Anatolia. These tribesmen were not, however, particularly interested in conquering Roman cities nor in a systematic settlement of Asia Minor. Neither were they driven by a religious zeal for punishing infidels. Rather, the Turkish tribes in Asia Minor continued living their lives as nomads.[13] The nomadic lifestyle was sustained through transhumant herding and, in the case of stronger communities at least, pillaging of random targets. These Turkmens then, nominally under the rule of the Great Saljuq sultan, who was trying to centralize the new vast empire from Baghdad, formed distinctive autonomous nomadic communities that roamed Asia Minor without much direction from the sultan or any other sedentary entity.[14] The first change in the lifestyle of these nomads was prompted by the Byzantines themselves. Upon understanding that Malikshah or any other sultan was not able to exercise direct control over

---

[12] For Byzantine perception of foreigners see: A. Kaldellis, *Ethnography after Antiquity: Foreign Peoples and Lands in Byzantine Literature* (Philadelphia: University of Pennsylvania Press 2013); for Byzantine views on Persian and Turkic identities see: A. Jovanović, "Imagining the Communities of Others: the Case of the Seljuk Turks," *ByzSym* 28 (2018), 239–273.

[13] For the Turkish settlement in Asia Minor post 1071 see: Beihammer, *Byzantium and the*, 169–304. Beihammer convincingly deconstructs traditional views of religious motivation and rhetoric surrounding the Turkish conquest of Anatolia: ibid., 18–19.

[14] For the state of the Great Saljuqs with its seat in Baghdad see: A.C.S. Peacock, *The Great Seljuk Empire* (Edinburgh: Edinburgh University Press 2015); C. Lange and S. Mecit (eds.), *Seljuqs: Politics, Society and Culture* (Edinburgh: Edinburgh University Press 2011). For the Turkmens see: D. Korobeinikov, "Raiders and Neighbours: the Turks (1040–1304)," in J. Shepard (ed.), *The Cambridge History of the Byzantine Empire* (Cambridge, UK: Cambridge University Press 2008), 692–727; R. Shukurov, "Christian Elements in the Identity of the Anatolia Turkmens (Twelfth-Thirteenth Centuries)," in *Cristianità d'Occidente e Cristianità d'Oriente (secoli VI–XI): 24–30 aprile 2003* (Spoleto: Fondazione Centro italiano di studi sull'alto medioevo 2004), 707–764.

the Turkish groups, Roman notables started hiring the nomads as mercenaries in their own armies.[15] With the loss of significant parts of land that were tenured by the villager-soldiers of the Roman state, apostates turned emperors such as Nikephoros III Botaneiates and Alexios I Komnenos did not shun away from filling their contingents with Turkish and other mercenaries at the expense of the now-collapsing *theme* system.[16]

One such tribal leader who managed to pillage the Roman countryside and even conquer Nikaia and Nikomedia in 1075 was Sulayman ibn Qutlumush, a once-removed cousin to the Great Saljuq Sultan Malik-shah. Two years after the conquest of Nikaia, Sulayman I was allegedly proclaimed sultan of an independent Saljuq entity in Asia Minor.[17] The career of Sulayman ibn Qutlumush was no different from many other Turkish tribal leaders who turned mercenaries for the Byzantines. During his time in Bithynia, Sulayman lent his support to Byzantine emperors and rebels: first to Michael VII Doukas, whom he abandoned to support Nikephoros III Botaneiates. Then, Sulayman joined Nikephoros Melissenos, who in 1080 rebelled against Nikephoros III. Once Nikephoros, for whom he massed popular support in tumultuous Bithynia, decided to support Alexios I Komnenos, the Turkish garrisons were let into Bithynian cities. Alexios I Komnenos, himself not lacking in experience with

---

[15] Beihammer, *Byzantium and the Emergence*, 198–243.

[16] For Byzantine authors' views on the endemic presence of Turkish mercenaries in the armies see: Neville, *Heroes and Romans*, 64–67, 72–74.

[17] Beihammer, *Byzantium and the Emergence*, 215–224. The foundational date of the Saljuq Sultanate of Rum is as problematic as the foundational date of the Byzantine Empire. Just as scholars reached an agreement upon the year 330 CE as a starting point of Byzantium, so too was a consensus reached to date the Saljuq Sultanate of Rum's history from 1077, when Sulayman ibn Qutlumush proclaimed himself sultan in the occupied city of Nikaia. The problems around choice of the year 1077 are greater in number and significance than those surrounding the foundational year of Constantinople. The first major issue is the very act of Sulayman I's sultanic acclamation, which is mentioned for the first time in the twelfth century. The very act of a politically conscious state building process is brought into question. Sulayman ibn Qutlumush, instead, appears to have been a leader of a Turkmen band which in the post-Manzikert havoc managed to occupy the cities of Nikaia and Nikomedia. The story of sultanic proclamation and legitimization through the official recognition by the khalif in Baghdad was conveniently crafted in the twelfth century when the Saljuq state in Anatolia was being consolidated into a cohesive political player in the region. The only recognition that Sulayman received in his lifetime was that by Alexios I Komnenos, who in a treaty with Sulayman acknowledged him as the autonomous ruler in Bithynia.

Turkish mercenaries, recognized Sulayman's position in Bithynia. Thus, from its nascent days, the Sultanate of Rum was tied to Byzantium.[18]

Sulayman conquered the city of Nikaia, allegedly to proclaim himself sultan, and left Bithynia in 1084 to wage war in the east. Sulayman I conquered the city of Antioch but was killed by a Saljuq lord Tutush I in its vicinity in 1086. Sulayman's son, Kilic Arslan I, was sent as a hostage to Isfahan and only managed to return to Asia Minor in 1093. The gap between the father's and the son's reigns was marked by Saljuq absence in Bithynia. Four years later, Kilic Arslan I was besieged in Nikaia by Roman and Crusader armies. During the siege of Nikaia, we see Alexios I continue his previous policies towards the Turks by negotiating independently of the Crusaders with Kilic Arslan the surrender of the city to Roman forces.[19] The withdrawal from Nikaia represented the final act in the Saljuq presence in Bithynia. Kilic Arslan continued fighting the Crusaders actively until 1101, when he settled in the city of Ikonion. This is the first instance in which we learn of Saljuqs settling in that city.[20]

While Ikonion had been under Kilic Arslan I's and his successor Malikshah I's control, it was only under Masud I (1116–1156) that the city became the court's permanent location.[21] Masud I went as far as to construct a dynastic mausoleum, the Alaeddin Mosque, in the city, which helped to establish it as the capital of the Saljuq polity in Rum.[22] Masud I's construction of the Alaeddin complex was the embodiment of the wider socio-political process in Asia Minor: the adoption of a sedentary lifestyle by the Turks. The twelfth century saw the rise of local Turkish lords who settled permanently in Roman urban spaces. Oftentimes, Roman cities, in order to preserve their rights and peace, accepted Turkish overlords. By being exposed to the Byzantine cities' complex mechanisms of political governance and economic production the Turkish

---

[18] For Sulayman ibn Qutlumush see: S. Mecit, *The Rum Seljuqs: Evolution of a Dynasty* (London and New York: Routledge 2014), 23–27; for his relations with the Byzantine notables see: Beihammer, *Byzantium and the Emergence*, 215–224.

[19] For negotiations between Alexios I and the Turks independently of the Crusaders see: Beihammer, *Byzantium and the Emergence*, 309–311.

[20] For the life and tenure of Qilij Arslan I see: Cahen, *Pre-Ottoman Turkey*, 81–90; Mecit, *The Rum Seljuqs*, 27–39.

[21] Beihammer, *Byzantium and the Emergence*, 277.

[22] For the mosque see: S. Redford, "The Alâeddin Mosque in Konya Reconsidered," *Artibus Asiae* 51 (1991), 54–74.

warlords started transforming themselves from raiding tribal leaders and mercenaries in the service of Byzantine nobles into "state builders, who started to focus on the consolidation of their rule and the security of the agricultural and financial resources of the territories they came to control."[23]

The Saljuq sultans of Rum were by no means the only entity that was setting roots in Anatolia. A series of Turkish *beys*, such as Tzachas in Smyrne or the Saltuk dynasty in Erzurum, established *beyliks* in and around Roman cities. Some, namely the Saljuqs of Ikonion and Danishmends, with their centre at Sivas, managed to build larger territorial states that encompassed more than one major city. The Danishmends were so successful that they were able to intercede on behalf of Saljuq princes fighting their siblings for the throne. After all, Masud I came to power thanks to Danishmend support and intervention against his brother Malikshah I.[24] This adoption of urban lifestyles on behalf of the Turks was not, however, a monolithic process. Saljuqs, Danishmends, Artuks, and Saltuks were representatives of certain families and tribes who opted to inhabit Roman and other cities in Asia Minor. Other tribesmen and their *beys* continued roaming around Anatolia nominally recognizing one or the other sedentary dynast as their overlord, but de facto keeping their autonomy from any central government.[25]

The new urban *beys* had to adjust to a sedentary lifestyle that included mastering the arts of agriculture, bureaucracy, taxation, and the minting of coinage. While accepting all the charms of urbane life though, the *beys* found themselves in a peculiar situation: they ruled over a predominantly Christian Roman population that lived in cities and villages. The nomadic Turkmens they commanded for years, whether they had settled down or not, were but a minority.[26] Granted, many Romans escaped

---

[23] Beihammer, *Byzantium and the Emergence*, 245. For settling of the Turks see: ibid., 265–303.

[24] For the reign of Masud I see: Mecit, *The Rum Seljuqs*, 42–53. For the Danishmends role in Masud I's rise to the throne see pages 43–44.

[25] S. Vryonis, *The Decline of Medieval Hellenism in Asia Minor* (Los Angeles: University of California Press 1971), 133–134, 185–194.

[26] For more on the presence of significant Roman populations in thirteenth-century Saljuq Anatolia see: Vryonis, *The Decline*, 59; D. Korobeinikov, "Orthodox Communities in Eastern Anatolia in the Thirteenth and Fourteenth Centuries, Part 1: The Two Patriarchates: Constantinople and Antioch," *Al-Masaq: Islam and the Medieval Mediterranean* 15 (2003), 197–214; and idem, "Orthodox Communities in Eastern Anatolia in

to the Balkans with the advent of the Turks. The majority, however, remained in their dwellings in Anatolia. Alongside the Roman populace, together with the Turkic nomads who were settling down, other Turkish and Iranian urban dwellers—merchants, artisans, intellectuals—moved from Iran to Asia Minor. The new overlords and immigrants to Asia Minor contributed to the further diversification of the Saljuq subject populace.[27] The Romans, in turn, had to learn how to coexist in their traditional dwelling places with the newly settled ethnic and national groups that shared religious, linguistic, and cultural practices with the new conquerors.

That the Roman population retained its position and numbers is best seen in the urban landscapes of such cities as Ikonion.[28] Even though major Byzantine churches were turned into mosques, Christian and Roman architecture continued to be built around the city.[29] The sultans went as far as modeling themselves as pious patrons of churches

---

the Thirteenth to Fourteenth Centuries, Part 2: The Time of Troubles," *Al-Masaq: Islam and the Medieval Mediterranean 17* (2005), 1–29, idem, *Byzantium and the Turks*, 154. For socio-cultural negotiations between the Muslim elite and Christian subjects see: A. Beihammer, "Christian Views of Islam in Early Seljuq Anatolia: Perceptions and Reactions," in A.S.C. Peacoks, B. de Nicola, and S. N. Yıldız (eds.), *Christianity and Islam in Medieval Anatolia* (New York: Routledge 2016), 51–76; D. Korobeinikov, "How 'Byzantine' were the Early Ottomans? Bithynia in ca. 1290–1450," in *Османский мир и османистика: сборник статей к 100-летию со дня рождения А.С. Тверитиновой (1910–1973)* (Москва: Институт востоковедения РАН 2010), 224–230; A. Beihammer, "The Formation of Muslim Principalities and Conversion to Islam during the Early Seljuk Expansion in Asia Minor," in P. Gellez and G. Grivaud (eds.), *Les Conversions a l'Islam en Asie Mineure, dans les Balkns et dance le monde Musulman: Comparaisons et perspectives* (Athenes: École française d'Athènes 2016), 77–108.

[27] Korobeinikov, *Byzantium and the Turks*, 94–95. For comparative purposes, on the issues of amicable and hostile cohabitation between the Romans and the Franks that informed the negotiation of identities and allegiances in crusading Greece see: T. Shawcross, *The Chronicle of Morea: Historiography in Crusader Greece* (Oxford: Oxford University Press 2008), 203–219; 224–237.

[28] While no data is available for Saljuq Asia Minor, it is useful to keep in mind that the process of converstion from Christianity, Zoroastrianism, and other religions to Islam in West Asia was a long one and it took a couple of centuries before Muslims comprised a significant minority or, in some cases, majority of the populace: R. Bulliet, *Conversion to Islam in the Medieval Period: An Essay in Quantitative History* (Cambridge, MA and London: Harvard University Press 2013).

[29] M.V. Tekinalp, "Palace Churches of the Anatolian Seljuks," 148–167.

in Ikonion and elsewhere.[30] The pose of benefactor to the Roman population was a clear sign that the Turkish *beys* and sultans adopted Byzantine imperial rhetoric vis-à-vis the Romans they ruled.[31] The main reason behind this Byzantine modelling was the sheer necessity of keeping the majority of urban dwellers pacified and even supportive of the regime. This becomes even clearer if we keep in mind that some cities preferred to negotiate their surrender to the Turks than put up a fight in order to preserve their ways even after the new mosques were erected in the town squares.

The Turkish *beys*, especially the Saljuq sultans of Rum, were careful in the way they communicated with their subjects. Endowing churches and providing the Romans with security was a way to keep them appeased. On the other hand, the sultans were cautious not to claim themselves as heirs of the Byzantine emperors. Quite to the contrary, the Saljuq sultans were fully aware that they were not ruling a single nation, as the emperor of the Romans did, but rather a multi-ethnic state.[32] In order to keep the Turks, Iranians, Arabs, and others appeased, the sultans crafted the official imagery of themselves as members of the prestigious Muslim Saljuq family, highlighting their successful conquests. Focusing on their Saljuq origins, though, was strictly qualified so as not to infringe on (and provoke an unwanted reaction to) the rights of the Great Saljuq sultan in Baghdad. The situation changed drastically once the Great Saljuq dynasty in Baghdad was no more, and the Saljuq sultans of Rum were the only ones who could claim descent from the famous Saljuq dynasty. Still, throughout the thirteenth century, while the exclusiveness of the Saljuq dynasty was being emphasized, the idea of pious Muslim rule over a multi-ethnic population remained dominant in the sultans' public imagery.[33]

---

[30] O. Turan, «Les souverains seldjoukides et leurs sujets non-musulmans,» *Studia Islamica* 1 (1953), 65–100.

[31] On Byzantine emperors' duties to the populace see: Kaldellis, *The Byzantine Republic*; Angelov, *Byzantine Imperial Ideology*; Blemmydes, *On Imperial Statue*.

[32] Korobeinikov, *Byzantium and the Turks*, 95, 105–106.

[33] Ibid., 100–105; D. Korobeinikov, "'The King of the East and the West': the Seljuk Dynastic Concept and Titles in the Muslim and Christian Sources," in A.C.S. Peacock–S.N. Yıldız (eds.), *The Seljuks of Anatolia: Court and Society in the Medieval Middle East* (London and New York: Routledge 2013), 68–90.

The image of a just Muslim sultan ruling over many different nations became even more important once the Saljuq state of Rum conquered most of the other Turkic entities in Asia Minor, including the strong Danishmend state. Instead of eradicating all the competing families that ruled these independent entities, the Saljuq sultans preferred to integrate them into the sultanate's elite.[34] This was true of both Muslim as well as Roman notables who wished to submit to the sultan of Rum. Since the twelfth century, the sultans were eager to accept not only the conquered elites, but also those who were looking for a refuge from their homelands. The trend of welcoming foreign nobles into the courtly circles of the sultanate continued all the way through the thirteenth century, even after the sultanate lost its nominal independence to the Mongol empire in the battle of Köse Dağ in 1243. Thus, Michael's flight to the Turks was by no means an original or an unexpected move. Michael simply adhered to the over-a-century-old practice of seeking refuge at the court of Ikonion.

4.2 The Sultanate of Rum: A Byzantine Haven?

The Turks' rather swift transformation from nomadic to sedentary lifestyle did not escape the Byzantines' gaze. The swiftness with which Byzantine authors reached a consensus on which names should be employed to denote the various Turkish communities living in Anatolia since the later eleventh century was comparable to that of post-Manzikert Turkish raids. The reason such a virtually instant consensus was made possible was because Byzantine literary tradition offered a plethora of existing ethnonyms to choose from. In order to differentiate between specific groups and polities of the Turks, Byzantine historiographers adopted both already existing vernacular and classicizing ethnonyms, such as Turk and Persian. On the other hand, when need arose, they did not shun away from adopting terms from other languages, such as Turkoman, to label specific socio-political entities.[35] Traditionally, in Greco-Roman historiographic practices, the term Persian was employed to denote a

---

[34] Korobeinikov, *Byzantium and the Turks*, 82–83.

[35] On the origins of the terms Turks and Turkomans in Byzantine literature see: R. Shukurov, *The Byzantine Turks* (Leiden and New York: Brill 2016), 401; for the list of ethnonyms used to designate different Turkic communities see: K. Durak, "Defining the 'Turk': Mechanisms of Establishing Contemporary Meaning in the Archaizing Language of the Byzantines," *JÖB* 59 (2009), 65–78.

series of successive polities that built up their state apparatus on Iranian models drawn from the Achaemenid period onwards. The Great Saljuq Turks' polity was one of these *Persianate* polities—as the main language of administration was Farsi and the whole state apparatus was built on Iranian paradigms—and Byzantine historians did not miss the opportunity to make this clear by applying the ethnonym exclusively to the Great Saljuq dynasty and, later on with the consolidation of power in Ikonion, to the *Persianate* Sultanate of Rum. The nomadic Turks, who did not settle down, were exclusively labelled with the name *Tourkomanos*. The ethnonym Turk, on the other hand, remained reserved for expressing one's racial origin regardless of whether this person was a member of the Persian polity in Anatolia, nomadic communities, or if they were a Roman citizen. Stemming from this then, a Turkmen, a Turkish nomad, could never be a Persian, a member of the Saljuq state, nor could a Persian ever be a Turkmen; but they could all be racially Turks. By looking at the ethnonyms deployed by Byzantine authors, we see that the Romans made a clear-cut distinction between different socio-political entities that emerged in Anatolia and that we, from our present point of view, simply label as Turkish. For the Romans, the name Turk was nothing but an ethic designation; ethnonyms Persian and Turkmen, on the other hand, encapsulated social, cultural, linguistic, and other values that made one entity cohesive and different from others.[36]

Besides the prominent place these newly established Turkish states occupied in the Byzantine social imaginary, they also played a rather prominent role in the lives of Byzantine noblemen. Much in the same vein with the Turkish overlords' willingness to cooperate with the Roman populace, the Saljuq court, itself home to the rebellious branch of the greater Saljuq dynasty, became a haven for dissident members of the Komnenian family and the Roman Empire's elites.[37] The trend of using Turkish lands as a comfortable asylum was inaugurated by the second generation of the Komnenoi in power. Alexios I's son Isaakios, who was honoured with the title of *sebastorkrator* by his brother, emperor Ioannes II, fled to the Turks after his participation in a conspiracy against his sovereign was discovered in 1130. While Isaakios roamed the Turkish

---

[36] Jovanović, "Imagining the Communities of Others," 239–273.

[37] A. Beihammer, "Defection across the Border of Islam and Christianity: Apostasy and Cross-Cultural Interaction in Byzantine Seljuk Chronikon," *Speculum* 86 (2011), 597–651.

lands and eventually returned to Constantinople from where he went into a self-imposed exile in Thrace, his son Ioannes Komnenos, due to his own intrigues against Ioannes II, fled to the Danishmends in 1139 and eventually moved to the Saljuq court where he took permanent residence and was integrated into the court elite. He was so appreciated that he was even given Masud I's daughter in marriage.[38] Thus, Ioannes Komnenos was able to secure a fairly bright future for himself and his family as a Saljuq state official. By the time of Ioannes, grandson of Alexios I Komnenos, the Saljuq court had become a reliable go-to-place for rebellious or otherwise troubled Romans. If we take into consideration that the Saljuq court in the mid-twelfth century was gradually consolidating under Masud I, the flights of such high-profile Roman individuals as Ioannes Komnenos meant that Roman elite had been included in Saljuq governance of Asia Minor and its Roman populace from the very onset of its state-building initiatives. This practice continued all the way into the thirteenth century, when Michael Palaiologos joined other Roman notables in offering his services to the Saljuq sultan.

Having Roman notables at court was beneficial to the sultans in more than one way. First, these men originated from well-known Roman families and resonated with the Roman populace at large. Second, they served as diplomatic capital in the sultans' relationship with the court in Constantinople. This became true especially from the reigns of Kilic Arslan II and Manouel I Komnenos onwards, when the two courts established a fairly regular system of correspondence. Kilic Arslan II even visited Constantinople and entered open negotiations with Manouel I over his submission to the Romans.[39] Turkish high-profile visitors in Byzantium became more common after this visit. This did not mean that the Turkish element in Byzantium had not been present before that. The best example of a Roman of Turkish origin was Ioannes Axouch, but unlike the Turkish lords coming willingly to Byzantium in the later twelfth

---

[38] Ibid., 597–651.

[39] For Qilij Arslan II's visit to Constantinople see: P. Magdalino, *The Empire of Manuel I Komnenos 1143–1180* (Cambridge 1993), 76–77. For Manouel I Komnenos' relationship with Qilij Arslan II see: Magdalino, *The Empire*, 76–78; 95–100; Korobeinikov, *Byzantium and the Turks*, 112–115.

century, Ioannes was captured as a child by Alexios I and became a childhood companion of Ioannes II under whose reign he thrived.[40] Possibly the highest-ranking long-term visitor at the court of Constantinople was the exiled Sultan Kaykhusraw I, who was hosted by Alexios III Angelos for six years (1197–1203). On his way to Constantinople, Kaykhusraw I was also well received by Manouel Mavrozomes, a Byzantine magnate in the Meander Valley. Surely, a Roman notable whose estates were so close to the Saljuq realm was fully aware of the benefits one could derive from having a good personal relationship with a major Saljuq figure. Alexios III was aware of this too. Rumour has it that during his stay in Constantinople, Kaykhusraw I was adopted by Alexios III who also, as the story goes, baptized him.[41] While we have to take this Roman account with a grain of salt, the fact remains that Kaykhusraw I established an excellent rapport with Alexios III as well as other Roman notables such as the Mavrozomai. Even before the sack of Constantinople in 1204, Kaykhusraw I fled the Roman capital and managed to reestablish himself in Ikonion. Once in power, he offered support to Manouel Mavrozomes, who sought to establish himself as lord of the Meander Valley after the sack of Constantinople. After being defeated by Theodoros I in 1205, Manouel fled to Kaykhusraw I.[42] Exiled emperor Alexios III followed suit and after several years of roaming the Balkans ended up in Ikonion.[43] The case of Alexios III shows how great of a political asset Romans at the Saljuq court could be. Under the guise of wishing to see his father Alexios III on the throne, as Akropolites tells us, Kaykhusraw went to war with Theodoros I. Unfortunately for Alexios III, Kaykhusraw I was killed in

---

[40] For Ioannes Axouch see: K. M. Μέκιος, *Ὁ μέγας δομέστικος τοῦ Βυζαντίου, Ἰωάννης Ἀξούχος καὶ πρωτοστράτωρ ὁ υἱὸς τοῦ Ἀλέξιος* (Ἀθῆναι: Ἀκαδημία Ἀθηνῶν 1932). For a general overview of the Turks in Byzantine service, as well as Turkish Romans, see: C.M. Brand, "The Turkish Element in Byzantium, Eleventh-Twelfth Centuries," *Dumbarton Oaks Papers* 43 (1989), 1–25.

[41] R.J. Macrides, "The Byzantine Godfather," *BMGS* 11 (1987), 139–162; idem., "Kinship by Arrangement: The Case of Adoption," *DOP* 44 (1990), 109–118.

[42] For Manouel Mavrozomes and his relationship with Kaykhusraw I see: S.N. Yıldız, "Manouel Komnenos Mavrozomes and His Descendants at the Seljuk Court: the Formation of a Christian Seljuk-Komnenian Elite," in S. Leder (ed.), *Crossroads between Latin Europe and the Near East: Corollaries of the Frankish Presence in the Eastern Mediterranean (12th–Fourteenth Centuries)* (Würzburg: Ergon Verlag 2011), 55–77.

[43] Akropolites, *Chronike*, 9–10.

the battle of Antioch on Meander in 1211 and he himself was captured and subsequently blinded by his son-in-law Theodoros I.[44]

The fate of Manouel Mavrozomes and his offspring was far brighter than that of Alexios III and his adoptee Kaykhusraw I. We do not know much about Manouel Komnenos Mavrozomes, other than he was connected through marriage to the imperial *oikos* of Manouel I Komnenos and that, under the Angeloi, he retained an important position thanks to his family's estates in the Meander Valley. After 1204, Manouel Mavrozomes established himself as a local *prouchon* until he was defeated by Theodoros I Laskaris, whom he opposed, and was forced to flee to the Saljuq Sultan Kaykhusraw I. Whether Manouel was previously acquainted with the sultan (and to what extent) remains an open question since Choniates and Akropolites offer quite different stories about him. A third version is offered by a Persian historian of the Saljuq sultanate Ibn Bibi.[45] What we know is that, once he fled to the Saljuq sultan, Manouel was well received. At Ikonion he even gave his daughter in marriage to Kaykhusraw I and in return Manouel's son Ioannes married Kaykhusraw's daughter.[46] Marrying one's daughter to a Muslim sultan, though, was a rather novel way of building enduring relationships with the Saljuq powerholders. Manouel's son and Kaykhusraw's son-in-law, Ioannes, was promoted to the office of *beglerbey* (commander-in-charge) under Kayqubad I, having helped the sultan defeat his political opponents in battle.[47] At about the same time Ioannes was in charge of rebuilding part of the walls of Ikonion on which he had his name and deeds inscribed in Arabic to commemorate his public endeavours. On the other hand, in letters, this Roman refugee turned Saljuq state official used his Greek-inscribed personal seal.[48] Thus, whenever he would seal a document, we can assume this was done with

---

[44] Ibid. 9.

[45] Yıldız, "Manouel Komnenos Mavrozomes," 55–66.

[46] S.N. Yıldız and H. Sahin, "In the Proximity of Sultans: Majd al-Din Majd al-Din Isqaq, Ibn 'Arabi and the Seljuk Court," in A.C.S. Peacock and S.N. Yıldız (eds.), *The Seljuks of Anatolia: Court and Society in the Medieval Middle East* (London and New York: Routledge 2013), 179; Yıldız, "Manouel Komnenos Mavrozomes," 66–67.

[47] Yıldız, "Manouel Komnenos Mavrozomes," 68–69.

[48] For the Arabic inscriptions of Ioannes Mavrozomes see: S. Redford, "Mavrozomês in Konya," in *1. Uluslararası Sevgi Gönül Bizans Araştırmaları Sempozyumu Bildiriler, İstanbul, 25-26 Haziran 2007 = First International Byzantine studies symposium proceedings, Istanbul 25-26 June 2007* (Istanbul 2010), 48; Yıldız, "Manouel Komnenos Mavrozomes," 68–69. For the Greek seal see: S. Métivier, "Les Maurozômai, Byzance et

his Greek-inscribed seal. A final, rather revealing, trait of the Mavrozomai in Saljuq service comes to us from 1297, half a century after Michael's stay at the court, when the Greek funerary inscription of the family was carved on the marble sarcophagus to commemorate a young *Amir Arslan*, Michael Mavrozomes. The marble slab with the inscription was found in the Church of Panagia Spiliotissa, which was part of the monastic complex located in the fortresses of Gevele, which played a major role in the defence of Ikonion.[49] Thus, the Mavrozomai became members of the Saljuq high elite without even converting to Islam. Quite the opposite, the *oikos* retained its Roman roots and religion for almost a century after the original flight of Manouel and his son Ioannes to the Saljuq court. The cases of Manouel and Ioannes Mavrozomai served as a handy blueprint for Michael Palaiologos to follow once he considered fleeing and offering his services to the Saljuq court at Ikonion.

4.3 THE ROMAN DIASPORA IN THE SALJUQ SULTANATE OF RUM AND FRANKISH GREECE: A COMPARISON

Since the early twelfth century, the largest community of Romans living outside the Roman Empire was found in the Saljuq Sultanate of Rum, which itself was formed in the traditional lands of the Byzantine Empire. As we have seen in the previous sections, the sultans, and other major elites of the sultanate, were more than acquainted with Romans at the court and in the streets. Keeping these Romans at bay and loyal to the sultanate was one of the major tasks that the Saljuq elites had to perform in order to ensure that their state operated smoothly in proximity to the empire of the Romans, who until the later twelfth century continued to dream of eliminating the sultanate and reconquering lost lands.

From the 1180s, during the imperial tenure of the Angeloi—Isaakios II, Alexios III, and Alexios IV—some provinces and territories started to slip out of Constantinople's central control. The reasons for the empire's disintegration were both external and internal as foreign entities such as the Normans continued attacking and even sacking major Roman cities in the later twelfth century, while the Angelid emperors were fighting

---

le sultanat de Rūm. Note sur le sceau de Jean Comnène Maurozômès," *Revue des Études Byzantines* 67 (2009), 197–207; Yıldız, "Manouel Komnenos Mavrozomes," 69–70.

[49] P. Wittek, "L'épitaphe d'un Comnène Konia," *Byzantion* 10 (1935), 505–515; idem, "Encore l'épitaphe d'un Comnène Konia," *Byzantion* 12 (1937), 207–211.

among each other for control over the empire. At the same time, in 1185, a war broke out in the Balkans with the Bulgarian aristocracy seeking independence from Constantinople. If fighting the Normans and the Bulgarians was not enough, not unlike the high aristocrats dwelling primarily in Constantinople, a number of provincial potentates started to act against the central government and establish their own control over the regions in which they lived.[50] For instance, we see men like Isaakios Doukas Komnenos—belonging to a cadet branch of the Komnenoi—usurping Cyprus and proclaiming himself emperor of the Romans on the now seceded island in 1184.

The story of Cyprus after 1184 serves as a good example of the Byzantine world not existing in a vacuum but rather being engaged in wider Mediterranean politics. Namely, Isaakios' reign on the island did not end well for him as he died at the hands of the English crusaders who occupied Cyprus in 1191, a year before it was transferred into the hands of Guy de Lusignan—a king consort of the crusading Kingdom of Jerusalem—who became the first Lusignan king of the newly established crusader Kingdom of Cyprus.[51] The events which took place on seceded Cyprus were a good reminder to the Roman Empire that the crusaders were still around and continued to represent a threat to the Romans.

On 12 April 1204, the empire experienced the unimaginable at the hands of the crusaders who sacked the city of Constantinople and who, in cahoots with Venice, were quick to divide the lands of the Romans among the leaders of the Fourth Crusade according to *Partitio Romaniae*.[52] Since 1204, the traditionally Roman-dominated Eastern Mediterranean became polycentric with the rise of the crusading states in the Balkans. The Saljuq Sultanate of Rum, at the same time, ceased to be the only foreign entity that hosted a significant Roman diaspora which comprised the majority population of the country. Now, the Latin Empire and its vassals, such as the Principality of Achaea in the Peloponnese, also had a

---

[50] For the crisis of the empire under the Angeloi see: Kyritses, "Political and Constitutional Crisis at the End of the Twelfth Century," in A. Simpson (ed.), *Byzantium 1180–1204: 'The Sad Quarter of a Century'?* (Athens: National Hellenic Research Foundation 2015), 97–111.

[51] For an overview of Lusignan Cyprus' history see: A. Nicolaou-Konnari and C. Schabel, "Introduction," in A. Nicolaou-Konnari and C. Schabel (eds.), *Cyprus: Society and Culture 1191–1374* (Leiden and New York: Brill 2005), 1–11.

[52] For the *Paritio Romaniae* see: Lock, *The Franks in the Aegean*, 41–51.

predominantly Roman population, like the Saljuq Sultanate of Rum and the Lusignan Kingdom of Cyprus.

How did the Romans in the newly formed crusading entities fare vis-à-vis those owing their allegiance to, and living in, the Saljuq Sultanate of Rum? For one, it is worth noting that the governments of the crusader states in the Balkans and Cyprus transplanted Western European legal and social traditions such as vassalage and serfdom,[53] as well as the administrative practices relying on the model of the royal household government.[54] Since the new crusader lords of Constantinople and Greece were more than accustomed to their own governing practices, they could also afford to exclude the Roman aristocrats, who held the highest offices in the Byzantine Empire, from running the crusader states.[55] It is for this reason that we mostly encounter the names of the crusaders and their offspring in the highest echelons of power as the elite transfer seems to have been more complete in the crusading entities than in the Sultanate of Rum.[56] Another fact that elucidates the changed composition of the highest elites in the crusading states is the lack of Roman political refugees after 1204, who continue to prefer the Sultanate of Rum as a destination.[57] Granted, Saljuq-Roman relationships were overall less hostile, even though not always peaceful, in the first half of the thirteenth century compared to those of the Romans and the crusading states, at whose expense Ioannes III expanded his own empire.

The governing elites aside, the picture seems rather more complex and diverse when it comes to mid-range officials in the crusading states. To begin with, the by now often-mentioned Georgios Akropolites was born and initially raised in Latin Constantinople. His family members, who

---

[53] D. Jacoby, *La féodalité en Grèce médiévale: Les "Assises de Romanie," sources, application et diffusion* (Paris and The Hague: De Gruyter 1971); A. Papadia-Lala, "Society, Administration and Identities in Latin Greece," in N.I. Tsougarakis and P. Lock (eds.), *A Companion to Latin Greece* (Leiden and New York: Brill 2015), 115–116. On the productivity of the feudal lordships and the serfs' dues see: Lock, *The Franks in the Aegean*, 245–251.

[54] Lock, *The Franks in the Aegean*, 184–189.

[55] Ibid., 161–191.

[56] For the names and roles of the Latin Empire's aristocrats see: Van Tricht, *The Latin Renovatio*, 251–306.

[57] With the notable exception of Alexios and Georgios Laskaris who, after a failed rebellion sponsored by the Latins against Ioannes III, fled to the Empire of Constantinople, see: ibid., 282.

were mid-level bureaucrats since the later tenth century, seem to have chosen to remain in Constantinople and not seek a new home in Asia Minor or Epeiros where two Roman states were formed. Unfortunately for us, Georgios Akropolites does not tell us much about his parents' position in Constantinople, but an image of his father as a man of some relevance to the Latin elites emerges from the few lines about him in *The History*.[58] Nevertheless, with the likes of Akropolites, it becomes apparent that Roman bureaucrats remained active in the civil service of the Latin emperor.

To further explore the role that the Roman diaspora played in the crusading states, let us look at the Kingdom of Cyprus for more signs of Roman activity. Just like in the Latin Empire, the mid- and lower-level bureaucrats could secure employment for themselves in the kingdom's administration.[59] If we look at the surviving sources from the island, we encounter letters preserved in the Greek language. These letters were addressed to foreign dignitaries, such as the emperor of the Romans in Asia Minor or the exiled patriarch of Constantinople.[60] Somewhat surprisingly, the Greek scriptorium was not preserved in Cyprus only to communicate with the exilic Roman Empire, but with the Saljuq Sultanate of Rum as well.[61] This initially surprising fact makes a lot more sense if we look at the two states' cultural backgrounds. That is, the Lusignan Kingdom of Cyprus' culture and administration were rooted in Western European traditions and thus used the Latin language or its derivatives as lingua franca; on the other hand, the Saljuq Sultanate of Rum was tied to Turko-Iranian traditions which promoted the use of Farsi as a preferred language. One common denominator for both Cyprus and the Sultanate of Rum was the Roman populace that lived in the two countries. In order to facilitate faster correspondence and avoid potential misunderstandings caused by translations from Latin to Farsi and vice-versa, the Lusignan

---

[58] Macrides, "Introduction," 7, Lock, *The Franks in the Aegean*, 48.

[59] For the hellenophone Cypriots and their role on the island see: A. Nicolaou-Konnari, "Greeks," in *Cyprus: Society and Culture*, 13–62. For the Cypriot notaries see: J. Richard, "Aspects du notariat public à Chypre sous les Lusignan," in A.D. Beihammer, M.G. Parani and C.J. Schabel (eds.), *Diplomatics in the Eastern Mediterranean 1000–1500 Aspects of Cross-Cultural Communication* (Leiden and New York: Brill 2008), 207–221.

[60] A.D. Beihammer, *Griechische Briefe und Urkunden aus dem Zypern der Kreuzfahrerzeit* (Nicosia: Zyprisches Forschungszentrum 2007), 158–169.

[61] Ibid., 170–173.

administration maintained a Byzantine scriptorium as an integral part of its administration, as much as their Saljuq counterparts did. The same seems to be the case in the Latin Empire where hellenophone interpreters and secretaries maintained an active role in the administration.[62] Furthermore, the contents of the surviving correspondence demonstrate that the Greek scriptorium was used even in cases of high diplomacy, as in the letters where both the king of Cyprus and the sultan of Rum exchange oaths granting free movement to their counterpart's respective subjects in their own lands.[63] Thus, in the much-altered lived realities of the thirteenth century in the Eastern Mediterranean, we encounter the diasporic Romans serving as mediators in cross-cultural communication between Latin Christendom and the Islamic Perso-Turkic world.

After the abrupt and traumatic conquests of 1204, life seems to have continued on as normal in some respects: taxes still had to be paid, cities continued to exist, and the local markets continued to be filled with goods brought in by Venetian and Genoese ships, and mid-range local notables succeeded in finding employment with the new high elites. On closer inspection, however, we see that the social and cultural landscapes changed together with the influx of foreign elites and their ways of governing and doing business. For instance, in the Achaean *Assizes of Romania* we see to what extent livelihood changed for the peasants, who became serfs overnight and now needed their lord's permission to perform a number of daily activities, such as relocating or wedding.[64] Transformation of the social and political landscape was witnessed in urban areas too where, not unlike in the Saljuq Sultanate of Rum, we hear of diverse populaces sharing public spaces.[65] This meant that the local populace had to give room to the Frankish settlers to find a way to express themselves. This also meant that Roman culture lost its position of privilege vis-à-vis customs of the Latins. Thus, both Romans and Frankish settlers now had to learn how to cohabitate and operate within the changed realities in the Balkans. One of the best examples of the cultural hybridity in Frankish Greece is *The Chronicle of Morea* available

---

[62] Lock, *The Franks in the Aegean*, 48.

[63] Beihammer, *Griechische Briefe*, 170–173.

[64] For the *Assizes* see: Jacoby, *La féodalité en Grèce médiévale*.

[65] Lock, *The Franks in the Aegean*, 266–309; Shawcross, *The Chronicle of Morea*, 190–219.

in both French and Greek that invites its audiences "Franks and Romans alike"[66] to engage with the Principality of Achaea's history.

The cohabitation did not mean that the Romans and the Franks were equal though, as much as the chronicler of Morea invites both to listen to him speak. The religious differences between the Orthodox and Catholic Christians became increasingly obvious as the two were in close proximity to each other even outside major cities such as Constantinople.[67] While we see the new lords sometimes adopting Roman expressions to appease the populaces, as was the case with the kings of Cyprus who issued Byzantine-inspired coinage in the first half of the thirteenth century, we also have to keep in mind that the crusader states promoted Catholicism to an overtly Orthodox populace. In a way, the somewhat forced cohabitation between the Romans and the Franks allowed the former to preserve their own identity and a sense of community by contrasting their customs and habits with those of the new settlers, similarly to what they did with their counterparts in the Saljuq Sultanate of Rum.

Finally, the Roman Empire by the later twelfth century had developed a long tradition of high education for its elites that contributed significantly to the Byzantine sense of belonging to the aristocracy of the highest order. Since 1204, outside the Roman exilic states, the traditional Roman spaces for the elites to listen to classicizing pieces of rhetoric, poetry, and historiography had died out and with them so did the higher education in the once imperial lands. As we see with the examples of Cypriot-Saljuq correspondence or the Greek version of *The Chronicle of Morea*, the authors have composed their narratives not in classicizing Greek but in a vernacular register of the language. Was this a deliberate choice targeting wider audiences than a traditional piece of archaizing rhetoric or historiography? Or was this trend adopted out of necessity, as higher education was no longer attainable outside Bithynia and Epeiros? The answer to both questions could be yes. That is, Western European literature in the thirteenth

[66] Ἀκούσατε οἱ ἅπαντες, Φράγκοι τε καὶ Ρωμαῖοι (*Το χρονικόν του Μορέως: Το Ελληνικόν κείμενο κατά τον κώδικα της Κοπεγχάγης μετά συμπληρώσεων και παραλλαγών εκ του Παρισινού*, Π. Π. Καλονάρος (επιμ.), Ρ. Αποστολίδης (εισαγ.), (Αθήνα 1990 (1940)) v.724).

[67] N. Coureas, "The Latin and Greek Churches in former Byzantine Lands under Latin Rule," in *A Companion to Latin Greece*, 145–184, Lock, *The Franks in the Aegean*, 193–221, Shawcross, *The Chronicle of Morea*, 198–202, C. Schabel, "Religion" in *Cyprus: Society and Culture*, 157–218.

century was undergoing a process of vernacularization where spoken variants of languages were being used in composition.[68] It is plausible that hellenophone written literature in the crusading states could have been influenced by Western European standards. It is also important to note that while, traditionally, the written literature of the Romans reserved for the elites was produced in classicizing language, the oral tradition of the wider populaces' literary output was done in the vernacular language.[69] Thus, the authors writing in Greek had a vast body of oral traditions to look to for inspiration in place of traditional Classical Greek literature.

Potential European influences notwithstanding, it is relevant to note that the shift in focus from classicizing to vernacular models of written crusading hellenophone literature was caused by the simple lack of higher education for those who could afford it. The lack of higher education for well-to-do Romans also meant that those born under Latin or Saljuq rule would not be able to live up to the expectations of the previous generation in terms of what it meant to be a noble Roman. This angst caused by the lack of higher education was the reason for the elder Akropolites' decision to send his son Georgios to the court of Ioannes III Batatzes in order for the scion of the household to receive the expected training in belles-lettres and philosophy. The same reasoning echoes from the autobiographical piece of Cyprus-born patriarch-to-be Gregorios II who complains in the mid-thirteenth century that the teachers of Greek on the island were no good and that their Latin colleagues were not much better.[70] The author, having no other options, left Cyprus and ended up in the exiled Roman Empire before moving to Constantinople after the city's reconquest in 1261 in order to refine his speech and mind.

The fragmentation of the Roman Empire gave rise to completely new dynamics in the Eastern Mediterranean in the thirteenth century that left nobody unaffected. The Saljuq Sultanate of Rum, however, remained the main sight of exile and refuge for the Romans fleeing the Empire of Nikaia, despite the existence of the crusading states which also hosted Roman majority populations in their realms. The attractiveness of the

---

[68] Ibid.

[69] R. Beaton, *The Medieval Greek Romance* (New York and London: Routledge 1996²), 91–100, Shawcross, *The Chronicle of Morea*, 123–149, 220–237, G. Grivaud, "Literature," in *Cyprus: Society and Culture*, 219–284.

[70] *Georgii seu Gregorii Cyprii Patriarchae Constantinopolitani Vita* (Venice 1753), i–iii.

4 "JE VEUX ÊTRE CALIFE À LA PLACE DU CALIFE" ... 151

Fig. 4.1 The Empire of Nikaia and its neighbours in 1257, at the time of Michael Palaiologos' flight to and return from the Saljuq Sultanate of Rum

Saljuq court, though, stemmed from the possibility of rather quick integration of the Roman aristocracy, whose members were by no means strangers to the sultanic palace. Thus, Michael Palaiologos continues a century-old tradition and seeks refuge from Theodoros II at the court of the Saljuq sultan of Rum (Fig. 4.1).

4.4 Flight to the (Un)Known

Having been warned by Theodoros Kotys, a member of the imperial administration in Nikaia, about Theodoros II's plan to incarcerate him, Michael Palaiologos did what dozens of high-profile Romans did before him: he fled to the Saljuq court. Recent developments in the Saljuq Sultanate of Rum, though, changed the fortunes of the polity that, at the time of Michael's arrival, found its affairs in disarray. Namely, in the 1243 battle of Köse Dağ, Saljuq forces were defeated by the ever-expanding Mongol armies and the Sultanate of Rum had become a tributary state to the Mongol Ulus.[71] The waning of the Saljuq sultan's authority, as

---

[71] For Saljuq Turks in the thirteenth century see: Cahen, *Pre-Ottoman Turkey*, 119–141; 269–371; Korobeinikov, *Byzantium and the Turks*, 81–110. For the Mongol Ulus

well as the arrival of Mongol nomads, mostly affected the nomadic Turkmens in Anatolia, who had become almost impossible to control.[72] In Akropolites' own words: "[the Turkmens are] a people who occupy the furthest boundaries of the Persians and feel implacable hatred for the Romans, delight in plundering them, and rejoice in booty from wars; this is especially true at the time when Persian affairs were agitated and thrown into confusion by the Tatar attacks."[73] The Roman historian was right to make a causal connection between the restless behaviour of the borderland Turkmens and the weakening of central authority in Ikonion. The Turkmens, then, roamed freely throughout large areas between the sultanate's borders with the land of the Romans and the capital city of Ikonion, which itself was part of the wide Saljuq borderland called the *uj*. The *uj*, unlike in Roman lands, encompassed a rather wide area that even incorporated major cities into it.[74] Michael, in order to reach Ikonion, had to go through these dangerous border regions of the sultanate that were largely controlled by the nomadic Turkmen tribes.

Akropolites corroborates the fact that the Turkmen tribes wandered across the Saljuq lands by informing us that Michael was attacked and stripped of his goods and companions by the nomads in the border regions the moment he crossed into the Saljuq domains; Palaiologos barely saved his own life.[75] While Akropolites provides us with the dramatic story of Michael's unfortunate encounter with the Turkmens of Western Anatolia, he does not offer us the slightest hint about the route

and empire-state building process see: T.T. Allsen, *Culture and Conquest in Mongol Eurasia* (Cambridge: Cambridge University Press 2001), T. May, *The Mongol Empire* (Edinburgh: Edinburgh University Press 2018).

[72] For the Turkmens in the Mongol period see: Korobeinikov, "How Byzantine," 224–232; idem, *Byzantium and the Turks*, 228–234; D. Korobeinikov, "The Formation of the Turkish Principalities in the Boundary Zone: From the Emirate of Denizli to the Beylik of Menteshe (1256–1302)," in A. Çevik and M. Keçiş (eds.), *Uluslararasi Batı Anadolu Beylikleri Tarih, Kültür ve Medeniyeti Sempozyumu-II: Menteşeoğullari tarihi, 25–27 Nisan 2012 Muğla: bildiriler* (Ankara: Türk Tarih Kurumu 2016), 65–76.

[73] ἐν τοῖς οἰκήμασι τῶν Τουρκομάνων ἀφίκετο—ἔθνος δὲ τοῦτο τοῖς ἄκροις ὁρίοις τῶν Περσῶν ἐφεδρεῦον, καὶ ἀσπόνδῳ μίσει κατὰ Ῥωμαίων χρώμενον καὶ ἁρπαγαῖς ταῖς ἐκ τούτων χαῖρον καὶ τοῖς ἐκ πολέμων σκύλοις εὐφραινόμενον, καὶ τότε δὴ μᾶλλον, ὁπότε τὰ τῶν Περσῶν ἐκυμαίνετο καὶ ταῖς ἐκ τῶν Ταχαρίων ἐφόδοις συνεταράττετο (Akropolites, *Chronike*, 65.4–9).

[74] Korobeinikov, "How Byzantine," 224–232 idem., *Byzantium and the Turks*, 228–230.

[75] Akropolites, *Chronike*, 65.10–13.

Michael took in reaching Ikonion. Pachymeres, on the other hand, almost completely omits Michael's ventures outside the Roman lands, including the encounter with the Turkmens, but he does mention that Michael "was invested with the governorship of both Mesothynia and Optimatoi [...], crossed the Sangarios river."[76] Adding to Pachymeres' account is Michael Palaiologos' own testimony about his battles against the Latins during his time in Mesothynia and Optimatoi.[77] Thus, it appears that Michael took flight from the themes of Optimatoi, which was the northernmost theme of the empire, located just opposite the Latin-occupied city of Constantinople and north of Theodoros II's preferred capital at Nikaia.[78] The Sangarios river flows through Optimatoi and passes by Nikaia and all of Bithynia, creating a natural border with the Saljuq lands.[79] While it is possible that on his flight Michael rode down the river on the Roman side and crossed it only once he reached its southern end, it is more plausible that somebody seeking refuge from the regime in power would cross the border as soon as possible and make his way to Ikonion from the Turkish side. Other than following the stark logic of an escapee, the fact that Michael, upon crossing Sangarios, instantly ran into hostile Turkmen raiders further supports the hypothesis that Michael decided to cross the river from the theme Optimatoi. Namely, of the Turkmen tribes, two were particularly notorious for their autonomous and aggressive behaviour near the Roman borderlands and three further east close to Armenian Cilicia.[80] It is the tribal communities inhabiting the northern border region around the river Sangarios, all the way to Kastamon, that deprived Michael of his possessions and retinue.[81] It was only by a stroke of luck, or, as Akropolites would have it, divine providence, that Michael himself managed to escape and reach Ikonion.[82] The encounter with the

---

[76] εἰς κεφαλὴν τεταγμένου Μεσοθινίας καὶ αὐτῶν Ὀπτιμάτων [...] καὶ τὸν ποταμὸν περαιωθεὶς Σάγγαριν (Pachymeres, *Chronikon*, 43.6-7; 44. 25–6).

[77] Palaiologos, *Autobiography*, 5.1–10.

[78] For the themes of Mesothynia and Optimatoi during Michael Palaiologos' stay there, see: K. Belke, *Tabula Imperii Byzantini 13, Bythinien und Hellespont* (Wien: Verlag der Österreichischen Akademie der Wissenschaften 2020), 200–201.

[79] Sangarios River was on the traditional route leading from Nikomedia to Klaudiopolis: Belke, *Tabula Imperii Byzantini* 13, 275–276.

[80] Korobeinikov, *Byzantium and the Turks*, 233–4.

[81] Ibid., 234.

[82] Akropolites, *Chronike*, 65.16–18.

Turkmens must have been a shock for Michael, who had never before forayed into Turkish territory, having served mainly in the Balkans and then in Bithynia where his main duty was to fight off any Latin incursions into Asia Minor. Yet, it appears that despite the initial traumatic encounter with the Turkmens around the border, Michael reached the court of the Sultan Izzeddin Kaykaus II unharmed. Before reaching the sultan's capital, though, Michael had to cross quite a long road, stopping along the way. One of the first cities where Michael could have taken respite after the encounter with the Turkmens of Kastamon on the major ancient highway to Ikonion was Ankyra.[83]

Ankyra was a meeting point on a major crossroads connecting Bithynia with Lykaonia as well as Kappadokia and the Black Sea coast.[84] Since the mid-twelfth century, the Saljuq Turks had successfully occupied the city and had held it all the way into the mid-thirteenth century when Michael likely ventured there.[85] The city itself was a bustling civic community as well as an ancient city-scape with multiple layers of bygone times visible in its streets. Known as a major ecclesiastic centre of the Roman world since the third-century persecutions of the Christians by Diocletian and Galerius, Ankyra hosted one of the first major church councils in 314 CE. As the capital city of Galatia under Roman rule, Ankyra had also become the centre of the regional metropolitan see—a status which the city retained even after the Turkish conquest in the eleventh century, all the way until the twelfth century.[86] The very presence of a metropolitan in Ankyra during the Saljuq period testifies to a strong Roman presence in the city even after the withdrawal of the Roman state from the region. Thus, as was the case with most post-Roman cities in Anatolia, in the thirteenth century the majority of the population was Hellenophone,

---

[83] For the road from Nikaia and Bithynia to Ankyra and from Ankyra to Ikonion dating back to Antiquity see: Belke, *Tabula Imperii Byzantini 13*, 263, 275–276; K. Belke, *Tabula Imperii Byzantini 4, Galatien und Lykaonien* (Wien: Verlag der Österreichischen Akademie der Wissenschaften 1984), 94–96, 106. For Byzantine use of Roman roads see: K. Belke, "Transport and Communication," in P. Niewöhner (ed.), *The Archaeology of Byzantine Anatolia: From the End of Late Antiquity until the Coming of the Turks* (Oxford: Oxford University Press 2017), 30–32.

[84] Belke, *Tabula Imperii Byzantini 4*, 94.

[85] For the history of Ankyra from Augustus to the advent of the Ottomans in the fourteenth century see: Ibid., 126–130.

[86] Ibid., 127.

identified as Roman, and in turn was labelled as such in Saljuq administrative and historiographical sources. While the Romans made up the majority of the city's social fabric, Saljuq governors made sure to leave a permanent Islamic mark on the city's landscape by employing Roman spolia in enhancing the Saljuq imprint on the city. The best example of this practice is the Alaeddin Mosque (homonymous with the better-known family mausoleum of the Saljuqs in Ikonion) commissioned by the governor Muhiddin Masud Shah, son of Kilic Arslan II.[87] The mosque, together with the names of the city's governors, most of whom came from the Saljuq royal family, stands as a reminder of the city's importance in the Saljuq Sultanate of Rum.

Employing spolia in constructing new buildings was rather common practice among Romans and Saljuqs. Yet, since the first-century CE, the epicentre of the city of Ankyra, whose location has been fixed throughout the city's history, had been home to a major temple of emperor Augustus and the goddess Roma.[88] The structure endured the process of Christianization as well as Islamization of the city, surviving, to be sure, as a ruin from classical antiquity, and not as an operating temple to Roma (Fig. 4.2). Unlike many monuments of classical antiquity in Anatolia, the temple did not require uncovering by archaeological teams in the nineteenth and twentieth centuries. Rather, it has remained visible to any passerby over the past two millennia. In the sixteenth century, Ogier Ghiselin de Busbecq, ambassador of the Habsburg Monarchy to the Ottoman Empire, made a one-day stop at Ankyra on his way to meet with the Persian embassy in Amasia. During his short stay in the city, the ambassador went on a day-long quest for ancient coins and Greek or Latin inscriptions which he would record for the benefit of the wider intellectual public in Europe. Much to his surprise, the ambassador stumbled upon the monument of Augustus and Roma in the city centre. He gives a rather surprising description:

> At Angora [Ankyra] we saw a very fine inscription, a copy of the tables upon which Augustus drew a succinct account of his public acts. I had it

[87] Z. Sönmez, *Başlangıcından 16. Yüzyıla Kadar Anadolu-Türk İslam Mimarisinde Sanatçılar* (Ankara: Türk Tarih Kurumu Basımevi 1995), 220.

[88] A. Gökdemir and C. Demirel et al., "Ankara Temple (Monumentum Ancyranum/Temple of Augustus and Rome) Restoration," *Case Studies in Construction Materials* 2 (2015), 55–65.

Fig. 4.2 The Temple of Augustus and Roma in Ankyra

copied by my people as far as it was legible. It is graven on the marble walls of the building, which was probably the ancient residence of the governor, now ruined and roofless. One half of it is upon the right as one enters, the other on the left. The upper paragraphs are almost intact; in the middle difficulties begin owing to gaps; the lowest portion was so mutilated by blows of clubs and axes as to be illegible. This is a serious loss to literature and much to be deplored by the learned, especially since it is generally agreed that the city was consecrated to Augustus as a common gift from the province of Asia.[89]

If the monument's ruins were visible and recognizable in the sixteenth century, despite not having been curated in accordance with our contemporary standards, there is reason to believe that thirteenth-century inhabitants of Ankyra or visitors like Michael Palaiologos could also have cast their gaze on the magnificent ruin. The *Res Gestae Divi Augusti* was probably damaged by the thirteenth century, but, in the worst case, at

---

[89] *The Turkish Letters of Ogier Ghiselin de Busbecq*, E.S. Forster (transl.) (Baton Rouge: Louisiana State University Press 2005), 50.

least the same parts of the text seen by Ogist de Busbecq would have been legible in the times of Michael Palaiologos. The surviving text together with the impressive structure in downtown Ankyra surely provided more than enough material to spark popular imagination about the building and its Roman past. Whether thirteenth-century Romans were aware of the fact that the monument was a temple to Augustus and Roma or imagined it as a residence of a governor as did Ogist de Busbecq, or perhaps something completely different, we will probably never know. We can be sure, however, that the Romans of Michael Palaiologos' times were able to imagine the city's and their own Roman past by reading the surviving parts of the *Res Gestae Divi Augusti*. That any spectator of the ruins was able to engage with Augustus' autobiographical narrative inscribed on the building's walls in both Greek and Latin, either by reading it themselves or by having someone else read it to them, tells us a great deal about the possible impact of structures from bygone times on the people's perception of themselves in the wider world outside their immediate homes and neighbourhoods.[90]

The citizens of Ankyra left us with no written signs of their engagement with the monument. This does not mean, however, that they simply ignored the massive structure which had dominated the city centre for more than a thousand years. Fortunately, we have references to both popular and intellectual engagement with monuments of the Greco-Roman pre-Christian past in Byzantium. For example, the seventh/eighth-century *Parastaseis Syntomoi Chronikai* or the later tenth- to twelfth-century *Patria Konstantinopouleos*, have left us with significant evidence about the ways in which Romans engaged with statues and other

---

[90] For popular imagination around monuments available in local communities in crafting a sense of a unified Roman identity see: Krallis, "Popular Political Agency," 41–45. On landscape theory in examining popular engagement with monuments in Byzantium see: S. Turner and J. Crow, "Unlocking Historic Landscapes in the Eastern Mediterranean: Two Pilot Studies Using Historic Landscape Characterisation," *Antiquity* 84 (2010), 216–229; K. Green, "Experiencing *Politiko*: New Methodologies for Analysing the Landscape of a Rural Byzantine Society," in C. Nesbitt and M. Jackson (eds.), *Experiencing Byzantium: Papers from the 44th Spring Symposium of Byzantine Studies, Newcastle and Durham, April 2011* (London and New York: Routledge 2016), 133–152.

monuments of Constantinople.[91] In the texts, we find numerous references to the popular imagination surrounding specific monuments' past. The statues that were either brought to the city or produced in the city served as an imaginative playground for the citizens of the capital, who invented superstitious stories in order to explain the distant past to themselves. In the story of Kynegion, we hear of a statue that fell on a man and killed him after he boasted that he knew who made it. According to the story, state officials, including the emperor himself, became involved in solving the mystery of a murderous statue, which ends up being buried so that it would not kill anybody in the future.[92] The whole narrative reads as a short story about a magical statue that would fit perfectly into the repertoire of Shahrazad. What matters here, though, is that the Constantinopolitan collective mythologization of the city's past relied heavily on using the state governing apparatus as a well-known reference point in solving the crime. By employing Roman officials in creating a history of an uninscribed artefact, the citizens of Constantinople made it clear that they were fully aware of Roman governing practices which they experienced on a daily basis. In turn, by imagining a common past around the empire's administration and monuments, the Constantinopolitan mass audience was unknowingly revealing a sense of belonging to a single state and a single nation. Popular stories such as the case of the Kynegion accident testify to the dissemination of ideas about a common Roman community among the general populace by the very same populace.[93] In other words, the imperial administration did not have to superimpose any concepts

---

[91] For composition and dating of the two collections see: *Constantinople in the Early Eight Century: The* Parastaseis Syntomoi Chronikai, A. Cameron and J. Herrin (eds., transl., and comm.) (Leiden: Brill 1984), 1–54; *Accounts of Medieval Constantinople: The Patria*, A. Berger ed. and transl. (Cambridge, MA and London 2013: Harvard University Press), vii–xxi. For the *Patria* and its composition and legacy see: G. Dagron, *Constantinople imaginaire: étude sur le recueil des* Patria (Paris: Presses universitaires de France 1984). For the medieval Romans engaging with statues see: P. Chatterjee, *Between the Pagan Past and Christian Present in Byzantine Visual Culture: Statues in Constantinople, 4th-13th Centuries CE* (Cambridge: Cambridge University Press 2021).

[92] *Accounts of Medieval Constantinople*, 64–67.

[93] D. Krallis, "Imagining Rome in Medieval Constantinople: Memory, Politics, and the Past in the Middle Byzantine Period," in P. Lambert and B. Weiler (eds.), *How the Past was Used. Essays in Historical Culture* (London: British Academy 2017), 49–69, here 49–58 for the *Patria* and the *Parastaseis*.

of common belonging to its populace, but only to mobilize and further boost existing sentiments.

If such fantastic, yet fully Romanizing, stories were forged around nameless monuments, it is likely that the citizens of Ankyra created their own narratives around the ruinous temple. Magical in content or not, unlike the Kynegion of Constantinople, the temple of Ankyra bore a major piece of inscribed state propaganda on its walls. The *Res Gestae* carved on the temple must have informed local popular stories about the Roman past. These stories, in turn, became a popular way of constructing and preserving the identity of middle- and lower-class Romans even under foreign rule. Thus, we can think of the Romans in the Sultanate of Rum actively modifying existing narratives about the monument at Ankyra in order to adjust to their new socio-political realities. While the citizens of Ankyra did not live under Roman rule anymore, the traces of their Roman past dominated the city's landscape, and the Muslim governors of the city did not care to alter this fact. Combined with the temple of Ankyra were invocations of the emperor's name in church liturgies, as the Romans of the Sultanate of Rum worked on preserving their Romanness. It was in such a still rather Roman city that Michael Palaiologos arrived after the initial shock of his encounter with the Turkmens on the border.

While his encounter with the Turkmens probably caused a culture shock of sorts for Michael, passing through the cities of Anatolia on his way to Ikonion may have comforted him, for not only did the majority of the populace speak *rhomaika*, that is the vernacular Greek language, but even the cities' landscapes made it impossible to forget the Roman past of Asia Minor. Seeing Roman monuments, inscriptions on buildings and walls, as well as hearing emperors' names in liturgies was one thing; reading the autobiography of the first *imperator* of the Romans on a ruinous façade in a Saljuq city was quite a different affair.[94] For an educated Roman such as Michael Palaiologos, Augustus' autobiography did not represent just a story from a distant past, but an account of one of the best-known Romans in the polity's history. The place Augustus occupied in the minds of Byzantine elites is hard to grasp, but his name and life were discussed by all major historians of the Roman Empire from Cassius Dio to Ioannes Zonaras, as well as by stylistic role models of the

---

[94] For the Ankyra version of the text of *Res Gestae Divi Augusti* see: *Res gestae Divi Augusti das Monumentum Ancyranum*, H. Volkman (ed. and transl.) (Leipzig: Reisland 1942).

Byzantine literati such as Plutarch.[95] Michael would have encountered some of these very accounts during his youth at the court.

Roman intellectuals of Michael's time were not just avid consumers of pre-Christian literature, but also appreciated the art and architecture of Antiquity. The very person Michael was running away from, Theodoros II, has left us with his impressions of ancient ruins at Pergamon, which he visited on his tour of Roman Asia Minor. In the letter to his teacher and official Georgios Akropolites, the emperor wrote:

> [Pergamon] is full of sights, which have aged and withered with time, which show as in a glass their former glory and the greatness of those who built them. These monuments are full of Hellenic ambition and are manifestations of that culture. The city displays them to us, reproaching us as descendants with the greatness of its ancestral glory.[96]

In the opening of the letter, Theodoros II establishes the topic he wishes to discuss: admiration for the pre-Christian, i.e. Hellenic ruins, of Pergamon.[97] Throughout the letter, the emperor points out specific points of interest such as the Hellenistic walls and towers of the lower city. The greatness of the ruins becomes even more emphasized by their comparison to the significantly more modest condition of the existing city up on the acropolis. In order to show off his erudition to Akropolites and philosophize about the passage of time and the glory of bygone times, Theodoros II actively engages with existing ruins of the city; he goes into such detail that he recognizes how "we saw a sanatorium, as it were the home of Galen."[98] The emperor was able to make an informed guess

---

[95] For Byzantines as readers of Plutarch see: Theophili Kampianaki, "Plutarch's Lives in the Byzantine Chronographic Tradition: The Chronicle of John Zonaras," *BMGS* 41 (2017), 15–29. For Byzantines as active readers of Hellenic literature under Roman rule see: Krallis, *Michael Attaleiates and the Politics*, 72–89, Neville, *Heroes and Romans*, 35–38.

[96] θεάτρων οὖσα μεστή, καὶ τούτων οἵων γεγηρακότων καὶ μαρανθέντων τῷ χρόνῳ καὶ ὥσπερ ἐν ὑέλῳ τινὶ τὴν ποτε δεικνυμένων λαμπρότητα καὶ τὸ μεγαλοπρεπὲς τῶν δειμάντων αὐτά. Ἑλληνικῆς γὰρ μεγαλονοίας ὑπάρχει ταῦτα μεστά, καὶ σοφίας ταύτης ἰνδάλματα· δεικνύει δὲ ταῦτα πρὸς ἡμᾶς ἡ πόλις κατονειδίζουσα, ὥσπερ ἀπογόνους τινάς, τοῦ πατρῴου κλέους τῷ μεγαλείῳ (Theodoros II Laskaris, *Epistulae*, 80.4–9).

[97] For Theodoros II's Hellenizing impulses see: Angelov, *The Byzantine Hellene*, 202–216.

[98] παιώνειον δέ τι ὥσπερ τὸν τοῦ Γαληνοῦ οἶκον ὁρῶντες (Theodoros II Laskaris, *Epistulae*, 80.31–32).

about the ruin in front of him by indicating that the ruinous hospital building (that is the temple of Asklepios) might be connected to Galen who was born in Pergamon. The only way Theodoros II could have known about Galen is by reading about the famous doctor during his studies with Nikephoros Blemmydes, and then Georgios Akropolites, both members of Michael's social circles. By drawing links between ancient ruins he was admiring and the texts he had read under Blemmydes' and Akropolites' tutelage, the emperor showcases his erudition before other intellectuals of the time. Doing so, he gives us a sense of how Roman intellectuals of the later Byzantine period were keen to take pleasure in intellectualizing the world around them.[99]

Much as Theodoros II learnedly connected the ruins of the Asklepeion at Pergamon to Galen, about whom he had read, we can imagine Michael Palaiologos gazing in admiration at the temple of Augustus and Roma in Ankyra, with its inscribed autobiography of the first emperor. Even if the text was as damaged as it was in the sixteenth century when the first written account of it came to us, Michael could have read the opening paragraphs of the text in which Augustus boasts about his indispensable role in saving and subsequently running the Roman Republic.[100] Octavian Augustus opted to compose the account of his life in the first person, which he then had translated into Greek, and both versions of the text were engraved on temples dedicated to Roma and himself in the cities around the empire. Reading the imperial autobiography on the walls of the temple could easily have served as an inspiration to Michael Palaiologos, who during the last year of his life inserted a lengthy eleven-chapter autobiographical narrative into the *typikon* of the monastery of St Demetrios in Constantinople, which he consecrated in 1282. While autobiographic information about the *ktetor* is not unique for the case of Michael Palaiologos, the emperor outdid his predecessors by providing a complete narrative of his secular life: familial background, early life and education, administrative and military career both before and during his imperial tenure, both domestically and internationally. By providing the readers of the *typikon* with a detailed boastful account of his life, emphasizing his accomplishments for the public good throughout his life,

---

[99] For Roman intellectuals' engagement with material objects in their narratives see the example of Michael Holobolos describing a silk *peplos* sent to Genoa: Hilsdale, *Art and Diplomacy*, 31–87.

[100] *Res gestae Divi Augusti*, 1–5.

Michael Palaiologos, much as Octavian Augustus, defended the necessity of his imperial election. In other words, both Augustus and Michael cast themselves as indispensable saviours of the Roman polity.

Augustus had to go a long way to justify his monopolization of power in the Roman Republic after the period of civil strife was over. In doing so, *Res gestae* served as a major piece of propaganda that the first emperor introduced in order to obtain public consensus about the necessity of his, at the time, extraordinary position in the empire. Emphasizing his role in terminating the civil war, as well as his accomplishments in running the state for the public good in the aftermath, Augustus was able to cast himself as the saviour of Rome. He emerges from the text as the one in charge of maintaining the *Pax Romana* for the benefit of every free soul in the empire. In justifying his position as the *princeps* of the Roman Republic, Octavian insisted that he did not wish to hold such great power, but that he simply had to obey the will of the senate and the people who wished for him to maintain such authority.[101] In the same vein, Michael, in his attempt to justify his takeover and subsequent reign, focuses on the grave necessity underpinning his tenure of supreme power. The necessity of having Michael Palaiologos on the throne becomes obvious when readers of the *typikon* learn about his toiling for the public good: from fighting off the adversaries of the *politeia* to administering the empire prudently. Furthermore, just like Augustus, who emphasized that the senate and the people alike offered to him many honours and extraordinary powers of which some he could decline but some he had to take upon himself for the sake of the public good, Michael explains his imperial election as a peaceful and divinely ordained process:

> It was not some well-put persuasive speech by me or by my supporters which fell on the ears of the masses, filled them with great hopes, and convinced them to entrust themselves to us, but it was your right hand, Lord, which did this mighty deed. Your right hand elevated me and appointed me as lord of all. I was not persuading but was myself persuaded and forced [to the throne] without bringing force upon anybody.[102]

---

[101] Αὐτεξούσιόν μοι ἀρχὴν καὶ ἀπόντι καὶ παρόντι διδομένην [ὑ]πό τε τοῦ δήμου καὶ τῆς συνκλήτου Μ[άρκ]ωι [Μ]αρκέλλωι καὶ Λευκίωι Ἀρρουντίωι ὑπάτοις ο[ὐκ ἐδ]εξάμην (ibid., 5.1–4).

[102] οὐδὲ λόγος πειθοῖ σύγκρατος εἰς ἀκοὰς τοῖς πλήθεσι, τοῦτο μὲν δι' ἡμῶν τοῦτο δὲ καὶ διὰ τῶν σπουδαστῶν ἐμπεσών, καὶ μεγάλων ἐμπλήσας ἐλπίδων, ἔπεισεν ἑαυτοὺς ἡμῖν ἐγχειρίσαι, ἀλλ' ἡ σὴ δεξιά, κύριε, ἐποίησε δύναμιν· ἡ δεξιά σου ὕψωσέ με· καὶ κύριος

In his narrative, Michael manages to present himself as an unwilling imperial candidate upon whom imperial power was bestowed by divine providence. By insisting that he was elected emperor in untraditional fashion, that is by avoiding the employment of various means of persuasion to obtain the support of the senators, the armies, and the people, Michael attempted to distance himself from his problematic elevation to the throne even further. This point becomes even more striking once Michael's narrative is compared with Akropolites' and Pachymeres' stories of Michael's election to the throne, wherein we read about persuasive speeches delivered by Michael and other notables alongside the armed turmoil that led Palaiologos to the throne.[103] Granted, Akropolites emphasized Michael's reluctance to take over the throne, while Pachymeres presented the whole process as instigated by Palaiologos. By employing the image of divine will that led him to the throne, Michael follows Augustan logic of the necessity of his extraordinary election for the sake of the Romans and not for his own benefit, albeit in a Christianized form that was attuned to monastic sensibilities.

By engaging with remnants of the distant Roman past during his travels through Saljuq lands, in the same way that Theodoros II was able to admire ancient ruins at Pergamon, Michael Palaiologos likely came up with the idea which stayed with him until the latter parts of his reign, when he composed a *Res gestae*-styled account of his own life. At the time of his likely sojourn in Ankyra, however, Michael was probably not contemplating his own imperial autobiography. Rather, he reflected on the challenges of settling down in the Saljuq Sultanate of Rum, like dozens of other notable Romans who had done so in the past. What he must have witnessed in Ankyra, though, stayed with him and may have inspired his future literary endeavours.

4.5 Michael Palaiologos: A Saljuq Dignitary

Leaving Ankyra and its Roman monuments in order to settle comfortably among the Saljuq elite, Michael carried on with his journey to the court of the Saljuq sultan in Ikonion. All of our sources—Akropolites, Palaiologos himself, and Pachymeres—remain silent about the rest of Michael's

---

κατέστην τῶν ὅλων, οὐ πείσας ἀλλὰ πεισθεὶς καὶ βιασθεὶς αὐτός, ἀλλ' οὐκ ἀνάγκην ἐπαγαγών τινι. (Palaiologos, *Autobiography*, 6.12–17).

[103] Akropolites, *Chronike*, 76; Pachymeres, *Chronikon*, 73–79.

trip to Ikonion. We can only assume that Palaiologos arrived in the capital city without once more falling victim to the Turkmens or other bandits. Following the ancient road from Ankyra to Ikonion that was used by the Saljuq dignitaries and merchants probably made his travels safer and easier.[104] Having arrived at Ikonion, Michael found his way to the sultanic court. By the mid-thirteenth century, Saljuq sultans as much as their dignitaries (not a few of whom were of Roman origin themselves) were used to receiving Roman political refugees. At the court, Michael was welcomed with open arms "for [the sultan] had learned of the man's nobility and all the magnates who were with the Persian ruler marveled at his appearance and his disposition."[105] Akropolites emphasized the importance of that first impression that Michael left on the sultan and his retinue. Palaiologos was, however, more than a well-mannered, pretty face for the sultan. Once the sultan learned of Michael's experience with military and administrative affairs, Palaiologos was put in charge of the Christian Roman troops in the Saljuq army.[106]

Taking into consideration the century-long tradition of Roman defectors being welcomed and integrated into the Saljuq polity, Michael's smooth entry into Saljuq high society should not come as a surprise. Georgios Akropolites himself nonchalantly mentioned all these facts— Michael's reception at court and his subsequent honours—which he did not find strange or even worth explaining. By being integrated into the Saljuq court, Michael was not simply received with dignity as a notable refugee whose presence in Ikonion might serve as a bargaining chip in the sultan's hand. Rather, he was received warmly and immediately entrusted with the highly important position of *kundistabl-i rumi* (Roman constable) in the Saljuq military, a rank which closely mirrored his earlier position of *megas konostablos* in the Roman Empire.[107] The Saljuq sultan and his government did not seem to have any qualms about granting such an important office to a Roman infidel refugee. What is more, despite Palaiologos' rather recent arrival to the court, he still, as the commander of the Roman contingents in the Saljuq army, was present

---

[104] For the road networks of the Byzantine period see footnote 411.

[105] τό τε γὰρ εὐγενὲς τοῦ ἀνδρὸς ἐμεμαθήκει, καὶ πάντες οἱ μετὰ τοῦ περσάρχου μεγιστᾶνες τελοῦντες τὸ εἶδος αὐτοῦ καὶ τὸ φρόνημα τεθαυμάκασι. (Akropolites, *Chronike*, 65.19–22).

[106] Akropolites, *Chronike*, 65.24–36. For Michael Palaiologos commanding specifically Roman troops see: Korobeinikov, *Byzantium and the Turks*, 194.

[107] Ibid., 201–203.

at all the major military meetings in the palace. This meant that Michael was deeply involved with the military affairs of the sultanate. In order to understand the sultan's as well as other courtiers' nonchalant attitude toward the inclusion of Roman notables among their ranks, we need to gradually unpack Akropolites' narrative of Michael's flight and set it against what we know about Saljuq social and governing practices. Reconstructing Michael's life at the Saljuq court leaves us with a more nuanced image of the sultanate, its cities, and populace, as well as the court.

As we have seen in the case of Ankyra and its new mosques that coexisted with Christian and other Roman monuments, the urban landscape of once-Roman Asia Minor had undergone a process of transformation by the mid-thirteenth century. Yet, *rhomaika* was widely heard in the streets of towns and villages. Granted, vernacular *rhomaika* took over as the language of textual production, since higher Byzantine education was not as widely available, if at all, in the Saljuq domains. Regardless of this fact, the commoners' lives in the cities were not much affected by this lack of higher education since most urban dwellers would not have sought it in any case. On the other hand, vernacular Greek became more open to evolution and the adoption of Persian and Turkish loanwords. Loanwords, however, travel both ways and many Greek words ended up in Turkish or even in the vernacular Persian language of Asia Minor.[108] Moreover, rather than simply being heard, Greek was also widely seen around cities. For one, places of Christian worship continued to exist under the Saljuqs side-by-side with the new mosques or churches-turned-into-mosques. City walls and buildings often bore Roman inscriptions from both before and after the Saljuq conquest.[109] These inscriptions now had to give some room for others composed in Perso-Arabic script, but they were far from being systematically erased, let alone forgotten

---

[108] Korobeinikov, "How 'Byzantine'," 221–222; R. Shukurov, "Harem Christianity: The Byzantine Identity of Saljuq Princes," in A.C.S. Peacock and S.N. Yıldız (eds.), *The Seljuks of Anatolia: Court and Society in the Medieval Middle East* (London and New York 2013), 129–133.

[109] For Christian architectural endeavours in Saljuq Anatolia as well as maintenance of old and new ecclesiastical and monastic establishments see: T.B. Uyar, "Thirteenth-Century 'Byzantine' Art in Cappadocia," 215–232; M.V. Tekinalp, "Palace Churches of the Anatolian Seljuks," 148–167.

by the local populace.[110] It was, therefore, not particularly unfamiliar landscapes that Michael Palaiologos negotiated in Ikonion.

Other than on buildings bearing inscriptions in Greek, we have seen in the example of Ankyra how the predominantly Roman populace in Saljuq-controlled cities could engage with their Roman past and present more or less unhindered. Ikonion, at the time of Michael's stay, was no different. One might wonder though: if Romans and *rhomaika* were the most visible group in the streets and squares of Ikonion, what was going on with the Persians, Turks, and other city dwellers? Surely, Farsi and Turkish were heard in the streets alongside *rhomaika*; after all, loanwords did not come into Greek out of thin air. Based on the existing literary evidence, we can think of the urban populace as multilingual. That is, if we are to put our trust in the literary opus of Sufi humanists and near contemporaries of Michael Palaiologos, Jalal ad-Din Muhammad Rumi and his son, Sultan Walad—founder of the Mawlawiya Sufi order famous to this day for its whirling dervishes—spoken *rhomaika* was not unknown among the Muslim populace. Poems written in a combination of Persian, Turkish, Arabic, and Greek, all in Perso-Arabic script, were a trend among the urbane populace as we see in Rumi's and Walad's ghazals.[111] Sultan Walad went even further and composed some of his poetry exclusively in vernacular Greek, albeit still in Perso-Arabic script, if we put our trust in the later manuscript tradition.[112] The fact that Perso-Arabic script and not the Greek alphabet were used even for the pieces written exclusively in *rhomaika* hints at Rumi's and Walad's potential inability to read Greek. This would mean that the Sufi duo had to have learned *rhomaika* in the streets and taverns of which they both fondly write. Such works written in *rhomaika* by Persian and Turkish authors complimented the multilingual inscriptions around the cities and were certainly popular among both the Roman and non-Roman citizens of the Saljuq lands. Even intellectuals like Rumi, who were native speakers of Farsi, the lingua franca of the larger Saljuqid world, learned Greek alongside Arabic and Turkish, and used it

---

[110] For instance, a Greek language inscription probably commissioned by a local magistrate is still seen on the walls of Attaleia: H. Gregoire, *Recueil des inscriptions grecques chretiennes d'Asie Mineure* (Paris: Adolf M. Hakkert 1922), 103–104; Korobeinikov, *Byzantium and the Turks*, 152–153.

[111] Korobeinikov, "How 'Byzantine'," 221–222.

[112] G. Meyer, "Die griechischen Verse in Rabâbnâma," 401–411; R. Burguière and R. Mantran, "Quelques vers grecs," 63–80; Δ. Δέδες, "Τα ελληνικά ποιήματα," 3–22.

in their writing.[113] In the realm of language then, Michael had nothing to worry about when he stepped into Ikonion, since he could engage not only with words carved on stone but also with the living dwellers of the town without getting lost in translation.

Michael had the chance to communicate in his mother tongue, albeit employing the unlearned register of the language, with both Roman and non-Roman citizens of Ikonion. The question that arises next is: how would the Muslim, and to a lesser extent Jewish, non-Romans engage with Michael and other mostly Christian Romans? If we, once again, put our trust in Rumi and Walad, the image of a rather cosmopolitan, but spiritually aware, society arises. Rumi himself went as far as composing poems about Jesus Christ, with whom he felt a deep connection.[114] Thus, a popular figure among the populace of Ikonion was merging existing religious trends in his poetry and thus offering an engaging experience to all of his audiences. What is more, Rumi even adjusted some of his Persian poems to fit the tastes of the Roman audience too. For instance, in the ghazal entitled *Chinese and Roman Art*, Rumi inverts the traditional Islamic story found in Al-Ghazali's eleventh-century *Wonders of the Heart* and Nizami's twelfth-century *Iskendername* in which Roman and Chinese artists compete in painting a room in order to decide which nation produces the most refined art. In the traditional version, it is the Romans who paint their walls with lavish and expensive colours, while the Chinese polish their side of the room in a way that will allow the bright colours of the Romans to translate more subtly onto their side of the room, based on the natural flow of light entering the room from windows.[115] This further allowed the Chinese side of the room to be constantly altered by different shades of colour depending on the angle under which light befell the room. Rumi, in his take on the traditional poem, switches the roles played by Roman and Chinese artisans. In his version, it is the Romans

---

[113] Comparatively, for the Greek-language public performers of various songs and epics, as well as their being influenced by Frankish conquerors of Greece in the thirteenth and fourteenth centuries, see: Shawcross, *The Chronicle of Morea*, 116–118. For the multicultural and multilingual nature of Saljuq literature see: Pifer, *Kindred Voices*.

[114] For Rumi's ghazals about Jesus see: *The Essential Rumi*, C. Barks with J. Moyne (transl.) (San Francisco: Penguin 1997), 201–205.

[115] On inverting the content of the story see: A. Schimmel, *A Two-Colored Brocade: The Imagery of Persian Poetry* (Chapel Hill and London: The University of North Carolina Press 2004), 149–150, 380.n.25.

who eventually outsmart the Chinese by polishing their side of the room to reflect the art of the Chinese in a subtler manner.[116] By switching the roles, Rumi catered to the pride and tastes of the local audience in front of whom his multilingual ghazals would be read.[117]

Based on Rumi's and Walad's works in Persian, Arabic, Turkish, and Greek, it appears that matters of religious doctrine or even the basic dichotomy between Christianity and Islam were not of major, if of any, concern to the populace of Ikonion. Jesus Christ is a hero of Rumi's poems as much as the prophet Mohammed and Roman artists are better than their Chinese counterparts: all the works hint towards a rather eclectic and cosmopolitan society. Once we look at the content of Rumi's Persian ghazals or Walad's exclusively *Rhomaic* ones, we see a thread of uniting topics: love, seduction, wine and food consumption, nights in taverns, and sexual escapades. From these ghazals inspired by daily life in Ikonion, an image of a lively and even fun-loving city arises. People congregate in the streets, churches, and mosques, as well as in taverns and hostels where they indulge in hedonistic pleasures regardless of their confessional preferences.[118] How bluntly one's sexual drives were expressed in public is excellently encompassed by Sultan Walad's *Rhomaic* ghazal that goes as follows:

> I'll speak here in *rhomaika*: you've heard, my fair rosy girl,
> what you have seen in my hearth. Come if it seems right to you.
> How you say like a little child: "I'm hungry, I want food!"
> How you say like an old man: "I'm trembling [from cold], I want [to sit in the] corner!"

---

[116] *Essential Rumi*, 121.

[117] On changes in the narrative to fit the needs and the wants of the audiences and their ideologies see: Shawcross, *The Chronicle of Morea*, 187–189 for the changes made in Greek manuscripts of the *Chronicle* in the depiction of the Battle of Prinitsa (c.1261/1263) to depict the loss of the Romans to the Franks in a more neutral light; also, see ibid., 252–254 for making *The Chronicle of Morea* more suitable for Byzantine sensitivities. Rumi, in his poem, undertakes a similar task to adjust the narrative to the wants of his listeners.

[118] *Essential Rumi.*, 1–8, 54–76. For active cultural exchange and original adaptation between Roman and other societies see: C.J. Hilsdale, "Worldliness in Byzantium and Beyond: Reassessing the Visual Networks of *Barlaam and Ioasaph*," *The Medieval Globe* 3 (2017), 57–96. Here, Hilsdale looks at process of "creative adaptation, particularization, and local inflection of a medieval cultural phenomenon so widespread as to be truly global—in a very medieval sense" in order to offer a fresh argument about medieval Roman artistic originality and challenge the traditional scholarly narrative "that reduces Byzantium to a mere storehouse for rich source material on its predetermined journey towards western Europe" (Hilsdale, "Worldliness," 58).

How you say, "my thin one is horny, I want cunt!"
My soul is blackened; I have found water to bathe.[119]

Stylistically and contextually, the ghazal is a far cry from the classicizing court poetry of Byzantine and Saljuq courts, giving us a rare glimpse into the tastes of the wider populace. Its content offers no hint of the self-centred isolationist religious worldview presented in Khazhdan's *homo Byzantinus*; rather, we see a sexually aroused poet who is out to find a partner for intercourse. We can imagine how poems such as this one or the Turko-Perso-*Rhomaic* ghazal—"*If you wish for me to be alive / Come near me tonight, golden lady / Day and night your happiness [comes] from your own beauty* / Come here so that I too see a heart, oh joy of mine!"[120]—coloured the mood of men frequenting various establishments that the city of Ikonion had to offer.

The Perso-*Rhomaic* opus of Rumi and Sultan Walad does not stand in isolation as a unique case of lascivious poetry in wider Roman world. If we are to look at the eleventh and twelfth centuries, we would find more than a singular example of Byzantine lewd humour in verse. From Christopher of Mytilene's eleventh-century satire against a certain monk Andrew who collects alleged relics of saints that he has: "ten hands of Prokopios the martyr, / fifteen jawbones of Theodore, / up to eight feet from Nestor, / on top of this, four hands of George / five breasts from that victorious contender Barbara;"[121] to Ptochoprodromos' twelfth-century

---

[119] Να ειπώ εδώ ρωμαίικα, ήκουσες καλή ρόδινη.
τ' είδες εις ση εστία μου, να έλθης αν σε φαίνη.
Πόσα λαλείς γοιον παιδίτζι, Πείνασα εγώ, θέλω φαγί.
Πόσα λαλείς γοιον το γιόρον, Ρίγωσα εγώ, θέλω γωνή.
Πόσα λαλείς, Η ψιλή μου καυλώθηκεν, θέλω μουνί.
Η ψυχή μου μαυρώθηκεν, ηύρα νερό να λούνη.
(Δέδες, "Τα ελληνικά ποιήματα," 17)

[120] The italicized text of the translation is originally written in Turkish (1a) and Farsi (2a).
كردل سن سن كه بن ديرى الم (1a).
Έλα απόψε κοντά μου, χρυσή κυρά. (1b).
روز و شب شادى تو از خوبى خود (2a).
Έλα 'δώ να ιδώ κ' εγώ καρδιά, χαρά. (2b).
(Δέδες, "Τα ελληνικά ποιήματα," 18)

[121] Προκοπίου μὲν μάρτυρος χεῖρας δέκα,
Θεοδώρου δὲ πεντεκαίδεκα γνάθους.
καὶ Νέστορος μὲν ἄχρι τῶν ὀκτὼ πόδας,

poems about a nagging wife who leaves her husband who now "sleeps alone without comfort / without dinner in darkness and despair;"[122] or Ioannes Tzetzes' dirty jokes wherein he tells a woman "to have a priest fuck [her] cunt"[123] in the *Epilogue on Theogony*, an image of a humorous and lively society comes to the fore. It is with the pre-existing tradition of salacious verses even among Roman literati in mind that we see the Roman populace of both upper and lower classes, under both Byzantine and Saljuq rule, engaging with the sexual and oftentimes inappropriate content of such poems. Unlike the Roman literati who employed popular humour in their learned verses, Rumi and Walad stand hand in hand with the lower stratum of the Roman populace in the streets of Ikonion from whom, in the end, they learned the Greek language.

In the opus of Rumi and Walad, ghazals evoking a beloved one are fairly common and more than a few of them mention sexual longing, but Walad's blatant statement "my thin one is horny, I want cunt!"[124] is not found in other poems of theirs. Rather, a similar form of crass, shameless language can be found in authors such as Ioannes Tzetzes and his employment of the word *mouni(n)*. The fact that the whole ghazal was composed in *rhomaika* hints towards the existence of crass, popular vernacular poetry in Roman Asia Minor from which both Tzetzes, a Byzantine intellectual, and Walad, a populist Sufi mystic, drew their inspiration.[125] Furthermore, the language of the ghazal, *rhomaika*, suggests that Walad was addressing a Roman woman, known in the Muslim world

Γεωργίου δὲ τέσσαρας κάρας ἄμα.
καὶ πέντε μασθοὺς Βαρβάρας ἀθληφόρου.
(*The Poems of Christopher of Mytilene and John Mauropous*, F. Berbard and C. Livanos trans. and eds. [Cambridge, MA and London: Harvard University Press 2018], 242–243).

[122] δὲ μόνος κοιμηθεὶς δίχα παραμυθίας.
χωρὶς δείπνου καὶ σκοτεινὰ καὶ παραπονεμένα. (223–224)

[123] να γαμῇ το μουνίν σου παπάς (H. Hunger, Zum *Epilog der Theogonie* des Johannes Tzetzes, *BZ* 46 (1953), 305.1).

[124] Η ψιλή μου καυλώθηκεν, θέλω μουνί. (Δέδες, "Τα ελληνικά ποιήματα," 17).

[125] For popular inspiration in Byzantine comic literature see: M. Alexiou, "The Poverty of Écriture and the Craft of Writing: Towards a Reappraisal of the Prodromic Poems," *BMGS* 10, 1–40; idem., "Of Longings and Loves: Seven Poems by Theodore Prodromos," *DOP* 69 (2015), 209–224, A. Pizzone, "Towards a Byzantine Theory of the Comic?," in M. Alexiou and D. Cairns (eds.), *Greek Laughter and Tears: Antiquity and After* (Edinburgh: Edinburgh University Press 2017), 146–165; P. Marciniak, "Laughter on Display: Mimic Performances and the Danger of Laughing in Byzantium," in *Greek Laughter and Tears*, 232–242.

as *al-Rumiyya*.[126] The image of *al-Rumiyya*—a beautiful albeit fully emancipated individual, independent of her husband and family, open to flirting and extra-marital sexual escapades—served as a literary *topos* in Islamic literature since the eighth century.[127] Abbasid historians and poets advised their male audience to be extremely cautious when even laying their eyes upon Roman women whose beauty and demeanour would instantly capture their hearts and souls and lead them into peril just like the sirens did to Odysseus' crew.[128] On the other side, Roman intellectuals, as well as the Romans in general, had no qualms composing verses with lascivious content about Roman or other women as we have seen in the examples of Ptochoprodromos and Tzetzes. Thus, by relocating to Ikonion, Michael certainly did not end up traveling to the unknown; he was well acquainted with the mentality of the populace at large even before he had left the Roman Empire for the people were not only communicating in the same language, but they shared the same outlook on the world around them.

Once he left the streets and taverns of Ikonion, though, Michael would be surrounded mostly by other courtiers in the Saljuq state. Dealing with Persianate officials, who dominated the Saljuq court, certainly meant that Michael had to adjust to his new career at the court which differed from the one in which he served and spent his childhood. It is important, however, to keep in mind that a significant number of local Romans occupied positions in the administration of the sultanate. The Greek scriptorium at the Saljuq court appears to have been active in the state's official correspondence both with its Hellenophone neighbour, the Roman Empire, and with other polities around the Mediterranean.[129]

---

[126] A comparable trend emerged across the Mediterranean on the Islamicate Iberian Peninsula where the genre of *kharjat* poems revolving around the themes of love, desire, and lust addressed to women or having female speakers tend to be written in the vernacular Romance language, while male dominated ones are in Arabic: A. Jones, "Sunbeams from Cucumbers? An Arabist's Assessment of the State of Kharja Studies," *La corónica* 10 (1981), 38–53.

[127] N.M. El-Cheikh, *Women, Islam, and Abbasid Identity* (Cambridge, MA and London: Harvard University Press 2015), 77–96.

[128] Ibid., 83–88.

[129] For the Greek scriptorium in the Saljuq court see: Σ. Λάμπρος, "Η Ελληνική ως επίσημος γλῶσσα τῶν Σουλτανῶν," *Νέος Ἑλληνομνήμων* 5 (1908), 40–78; M. Delilbaşi, "Greek as a Diplomatic Language in the Turkish Chancery," in N.G. Moschonas (ed.), *H επικοινωνία στο Βυζάντιο* (Αθήνα: Κέντρο Βυζαντινών Ερευνών 1993), 145–153.

Thanks to surviving records from the Lusignan period, as we have seen, the Kingdom of Cyprus did not employ French, Latin, Persian, or Arabic but rather Greek as its language of correspondence with the Saljuq state.[130] This fact should not come as a complete surprise to us, especially if we take into account that both the Saljuq Sultanate of Rum and Cyprus hosted large numbers, if not majorities, of autochthonous, albeit now arguably subaltern, Roman–Greek speakers. Aside from the staff of the scriptorium, the sultanic harem itself was no stranger to the Greek language; more than one sultan had a Roman mother, who retained their language and probably some of Roman practices while running the harems of their sons.[131] This certainly contributed to the proliferation of Greek language at the Saljuq court. Other than the low- and mid-level officials, as well as the Roman women in the harem, Michael's transition to the Saljuq court was made smoother by a relatively high number of Roman officials who made the Saljuq court their permanent home.[132]

It was with such realities in mind that Michael Palaiologos crossed the river Sangarios and, after the initial unpleasant experience with the Turkmens, reached the haven of the Saljuq court, where a few Roman families were well-established and politically influential. High dignitaries such as the Mavrozomai must have aided Michael in retaining his Roman ways, much as they had over decades of service, as he adjusted to his new position as a Saljuq official. Given that the ethnic composition of the ranks of Saljuq dignitaries informed the social realities of the court at Ikonion, the fact that the Saljuq sultan proved well-disposed to Palaiologos should not surprise us. Michael's own family shared ancestry with the Mavrozomai and, much like other Romans in Saljuq service, Palaiologos was a good ally to have in appeasing the local Roman populace, especially in the capital of Ikonion. Saljuq sultans oftentimes struggled to maintain their position vis-à-vis other powerful families from the Muslim elite of their state. Thus, for instance, Kaykhusraw I was ousted from power by his brother and once he returned to take power in 1205, he had to deal not just with rebellious *amirs* but also with the Muslim religious authorities in Ikonion that found him not to their liking.[133] In such

---

[130] Beihammer, *Griechische Briefe*.
[131] Shukurov, "Harem Christianity," 116–150.
[132] A. Beihammer, "Defection across the Border," 597–651.
[133] Cahen, *Pre-Ottoman Turkey*, 119–141, 173–201, 216–233.

circumstances, Saljuq sultans or claimants to the throne could rely on personal relationships with members of the Roman elite of the sultanate, who remained influential among the Christian Roman subjects in Ikonion and other cities. After all, a Greek-inscribed seal of *amir* Ioannes, the son of Manouel Mavrozomes, was likely used to ratify decisions about the affairs of the Roman subjects of the sultanate. As a new arrival at Ikonion, Michael could assume a similar role at the court: he would help keep the Roman populace loyal while acting as a strong ally to the sultan against potentially dangerous Muslim elites, especially since Michael had no connections with other powerbrokers of the sultanate.

Having proven himself a capable soldier and military commander in Macedonia and Bithynia, Michael was appointed the commander of Roman units in the Saljuq army. Michael therefore stepped into a role similar to that of Ioannes Mavrozomes. He was to keep well-disposed to the regime those Roman soldiers who fought battles on behalf of the sultan.[134] Beyond the battlefield Michael was expected to mobilize the local Christian populace, which was likely more amenable to being managed by a Roman than by a Muslim official of the Saljuq court. The arrival of Michael Palaiologos, a seasoned military commander, to Ikonion was thus convenient for the sultan and his dignitaries. At the time of Michael's flight, the Sultan Kaykaus II refused to grant further pastures and tribute to the Mongol lord Bayju, who was in charge of the Mongol empire's affairs in the Near East, as per the agreement that was made between the Mongol Ulus and the Saljuq Sultanate of Rum after the battle of Köse Dağ in 1243.[135] Since Kaykaus II decided to break the agreement with the Mongols and go to war with them, Michael's flight must have looked almost as a God-sent present to the Saljuq sultan. Based on his previous military experience in Roman lands, Michael seemed like a very reasonable choice to lead the army's Romans: he was both their fellow Roman and a seasoned general. Thus, without much of a break from his career in the Roman polity, Michael now held an important office, albeit this time under a different suzerain.

The very year he arrived at the Saljuq court, Michael had to prove himself in battle. He commanded Roman troops, which he himself led

---

[134] Korobeinikov, "Orthodox Communities," 197.

[135] For Saljuq Turks in the thirteenth century see: Cahen, *Pre-Ottoman Turkey*: 119–141; 269–371; Korobeinikov, *Byzantium and the Turks*: 81–110.

under a banner of the Roman Empire,[136] against the Mongol army encamped by the city of Aksaray. While in his autobiographical *typikon* Michael simply mentions that he had fought for the sultan, Georgios Akropolites provides us with a much more detailed account, focused on Michael's state of mind:

> Being in a foreign land, he considered alliance with the Muslims deplorable, as he used to say, the pious blood of the one falling in battle should never be mixed with unholy infidel blood. He was given courage by divine grace and, having regained his brave spirit, he set out to battle. The part of the army under the command of Michael Komnenos won a victory with strength over the Tatars opposing it, with Michael himself first launching a spear in the chest of the man who rode in advance of the army.[137]

According to Akropolites' rather romanticized depiction of Michael in the Saljuq army, we see that his behaviour as a commander remained pretty much unchanged: he was present on the battlefield in order to boost the morale of his men. Regardless of whether Michael found fighting for the Saljuq sultan an abominable act or not, he was there to offer his service as military commander. In fact, Michael used this battle and his military ability to demonstrate to the sultan that he was worthy of a high position in the sultanate. There was no reason that he and his family could not follow the blueprint of the Mavrozomai, who had occupied high positions in Saljuq society for the last half a century.

Whatever Michael's initial plans in the Saljuq sultanate may have been, they changed at the end of the battle of Aksaray, when the Saljuq army was utterly crushed by the Mongols. Akropolites' eulogizing notwithstanding, Michael took to flight, following the example of the Sultan Kaykaus II and the *beglerbey* Tavtash. Once he joined them, they together rode to *beglerbey*'s estate around Kastamon, which was part of

---

[136] Korobeinikov, *Byzantium and the Turks*: 194.

[137] ὁ δὲ ἐπεὶ ἐν ἀλλοδαπῇ ἐτύγχανεν ὤν, συμμαχεῖν μὲν Μουσουλμάνοις ἀπευκταῖον ἡγεῖτο, μή ποτε, ὡς ἔφασκεν οὗτος, ἐν μάχῃ πεσόντος εὐσεβὲς αἷμα αἵμασι συγκραθείη ἀνοσίοις καὶ ἀσεβέσι, χάριτι δὲ θείᾳ ἀναρρωσθεὶς καὶ γενναῖον ἀναλαβὼν φρόνημα πρὸς τὴν μάχην ἐξώρμησε. τὸ μὲν οὖν μέρος τοῦ στρατεύματος τὸ παρὰ τοῦ Κομνηνοῦ Μιχαὴλ τεταγμένον τοὺς ἀντιτεταγμένους αὐτῷ Ταχαρίους κατὰ κράτος νενίκηκε, τοῦ Μιχαὴλ αὐτοῦ πρώτως δόρατι παρὰ μαζὸν βαλόντος τὸν τοῦ στρατεύματος προηγούμενον (Akropolites, *Chronike*, 65.37–45).

his demesne as well as the historic hometown of the Komnenoi.[138] Thus, Michael ended up visiting his ancestral homeplace some eighty years after it had been ceded to the Saljuqs in 1176.

On a less romantic note, whatever the outcome of Michael's friendship with Tavtash, Palaiologos had to strategize about his future. Remaining in the lands of the sultan who was barely in control of his fate was hardly an ideal option. And so, in 1257, about a year after his flight from the Roman Empire, either on his own or upon invitation by Theodoros II, Michael returned to his position in the empire of the Romans with the emperor's public pardon. Akropolites remains silent when it comes to the question of who initiated the contact. Michael, however, explains that it was the emperor who begged him to come back, having understood that the exiled aristocrat was a priceless asset for the empire.[139] Pachymeres, on the other hand, recalls that it was the metropolitan of Ikonion, operating uninterruptedly in the Saljuq capital, who, on Michael's request, acted as an intermediary between him and Theodoros II, until the emperor swore a public oath that he would not harm Michael. Michael in turn had to follow the emperor's example and swore an oath that he would never plot against the imperial family.[140] Be that as it may, Michael left the tumultuous lands of the Saljuqs and went back to occupy his old post in Bithynia.

4.6 There and Back Again

Michael's brief career at the Saljuq court did not pass unnoticed by Saljuq literati. Writing in the fourteenth century, well past the sultanate's zenith, historian Aqsarayi cast Michael as one of the influential villains at the Saljuq court. In Aqsarayi's rendering of the story of the conflict between Kaykaus II and Bayju, the historian went as far as to ascribe the role of the leader of the Roman party at court to a Roman *constable*, most likely Michael Palaiologos,[141] who drove the sultan's anti-Mongol policies.

---

[138] Korobeinikov, *Byzantium and the Turks*, 42–68; J. Crow, "Alexios I Komnenos and Kastamon: Castles and Settlement in Middle Byzantine Paphlagonia," in M. Mullett and D. Smythe (eds.), *Alexios I Komnenos* (Belfast: The Queen's University of Belfast 1996), 12–36.

[139] Akropolites, *Chronike*, 69.

[140] Pachymeres, *Chronikon*, 45.7–12.

[141] Korobeinikov, *Byzantium and the Turks*, 202.

Michael Palaiologos' image among intellectuals of the Saljuq sultanate was solidified thanks to Aqsarayi some sixty years after the visit had taken place. Regardless of whether Michael exercised such great influence or not, the very fact that Aqsarayi's readers would find the story of a strong Roman faction at the court plausible testifies not to Michael Palaiologos' remarkable personality, but to the importance of the Romans in the Saljuq Sultanate of Rum during its two hundred year lifespan.[142]

As we follow narratives about Michael Palaiologos' travails from the river Sangarios to Ikonion and all the way to Aksaray, the strength of Roman social, cultural, and political presence in Asia Minor gradually unfolds before us. Michael stands at the end of the road of Saljuq dominance in Asia Minor and thus showcases how Roman officials remained welcome at the Saljuq sultan's court throughout the sultanate's history. Living for over a year in the Saljuq Sultanate of Rum, Michael experienced both the transformative power of Turkic presence in Asia Minor, i.e. the Turkmens roaming rural landscapes, as well as the endurance of Roman urban culture in the Saljuq empire at every societal level: from Roman high officials at the court to Sufi mystics reciting *Rhomaic* verses in the streets and taverns of Ikonion. We can even argue that the Greek language was so widely spoken at the court that the *ferman* issued by the grand vizier Mehmed I of Karaman stating that "from now on, nobody present at the court, the divan, the councils, or the palace, will speak another language but Turkish"[143] was not targeted against the Perso- and Arabophone members of the court, but rather against the Roman element, language, and culture omnipresent at the court and in society.

It is the very Roman element that provided the sultanate with much of its political and economic foundations. By following Michael Palaiologos' journey through the Sultanate of Rum, we saw the ways in which public culture continued to thrive albeit in a different form. The main difference lay in the Roman state being exactly that, the state of the Roman nation, and the Saljuq Sultanate of Rum, as the name tells us, being a

---

[142] "Aksaraylı Mehmed oğlu Kerimüddin Mahmud," in O. Turan (ed.), *Müsâmeret ül-ahbâr. Moğollar zamanında Türkiye Selçukluları Tarihi* (Ankara: Türk Tarih Kurumu 1944), 49–51; For the translation and analysis of the relevant part see: Korobeinikov, *Byzantium and the Turks*, 201–203.

[143] Bugünden sonra divanda, dergâhta, bargâhta, mecliste ve meydanda Türkçeden başka dil kullanılmayacaktır (N.S. Banarlı, *Resimli Türk Edebiyatı Tarihi* [Ankara: Türk Tarih Kurumu 1984], 299).

dynastic Muslim entity with the domineering Roman populace among its subjects. Thus, the main difference in the development of the public culture between the Roman Empire and the Sultanate of Rum rests in the amount of political agency that the populace mobilized vis-à-vis the state. As we have seen in the first two chapters, the public relations that Michael Palaiologos and other members of the *golden chain* cultivated in the Roman state transgressed their immediate socio-economic stratum. This agility in being able to converse with their peers, local notables, as well as the urban and rural masses, was the only way for Roman officials' careers to thrive. What is more, it is not just the elites who knew how to employ the public discourse to their benefit, but the peasants and ordinary citizens were well aware of the ways in which they could procure protection or justice individually and collectively by taking their cases publically before designated officials.

Standing in stark contrast to the relevance of public culture in the Roman Empire, in the Sultanate of Rum the positions at the court were dependent on the sultan and his immediate family who oftentimes occupied the highest offices. The Romans serving at the court were a useful governmental instrument to keep the Christian populace (especially the soldiers) at bay by giving them Romaic-speaking officials and generals. Beyond this point, however, the Romans serving in the state administration had to rely solely on the sultan and his retinue in promoting their careers. There was no need for them to go about trying to appease the populace or mobilize them to gain political leverage over their opponents. The connection between the public sphere and the centre of power was rather weak. The dignitaries as much as the sultans showed their generosity and care for the populace by leaving behind them structures and inscriptions that openly celebrated the Saljuq family, and not the populace that made up the social fabric of the empire, who were traditionally mentioned in Roman public political culture. In such circumstances, we saw that Michael Palaiologos was completely reliant on the sultan for his career. The potential outings in the streets of Ikonion would have allowed Palaiologos to experience the similarities in customs and traditions of the Romans in the Sultanate of Rum with those in the Roman Empire, and thus to divert his attention from the oddities of the Saljuq court, but he did not need public support (and did not have to fear public wrath) in order to prosper at the Saljuq court. Without the invigilation and major impositions of the court and administration, public culture in the sultanate continued to develop on its own, relying heavily on preexisting Roman societal and cultural practices. As we have seen, the people of Ikonion, Ankyra, and other cities in the Sultanate of Rum could still engage with the Roman past in the streets and taverns both by gazing at the existing infrastructure or by relating their life and other stories in the Romaic language. The social imprint made by Romans on the public culture of the Saljuq state in Asia Minor is impossible not to notice. The same populace's mark on the political life of the sultanate, though, remained marginal. On his way back to the Roman Empire, Michael, once again, had to get ready to repair the broken, and strengthen the existing, ties in his homeland.

CHAPTER 5

"The Return of the King": Michael Palaiologos Claims Imperial Dignity

During Michael's absence from the imperial court, the empire of the Romans continued to operate without him. His absence was nevertheless noticed by both the emperor and those relatives of his close to the Palaiologan *oikos*. According to Akropolites, the emperor himself was very annoyed with and paranoid about Michael's flight to the Turks.[1] The *oikos* of the Palaiologoi, on the other hand, was left headless since Michael's younger brother Ioannes and half-brother Konstantinos held no official positions in the administration.[2] Following Michael's example by fleeing Theodoros II's potential wrath, fearing for his own life, Ioannes took refuge in Rhodos in 1256.[3] Theodoros II continued to weaken ties among the aristocrats with his policies of marrying off notable women to the *novi homines* of the imperial administration. In this respect, Palaiologos' sister Maria saw her daughter Theodora with Nikephoros Tarchaneiotes married to Basileios Kaballarios, after her prior engagement with a certain Balanidiotes, who was one of the *paidopouloi* to Theodoros

---

[1] Akropolites, *Chronike*, 64.

[2] Pachymeres, *Chronikon*, 91.10–12.

[3] It is not known if Konstantinos was sent on a mission or fled. Since he held no official position at the court or provinces (Pachymeres, *Chronikon*, 91.10–12. It is likely that he sought refuge in the island that was part of the empire.

© The Author(s), under exclusive license to Springer Nature Switzerland AG 2022
A. Jovanović, *Michael Palaiologos and the Publics of the Byzantine Empire in Exile, c.1223–1259*, New Approaches to Byzantine History and Culture, https://doi.org/10.1007/978-3-031-09278-7_5

II, was annulled by the emperor.[4] In arranging and rearranging marital affairs on behalf of the Palaiologan *oikos*, the emperor was able to further break the cohesion of the clan and attach his own men to this notable though leaderless household. With his family affairs in such a precarious situation, Michael returned to his former position of *megas konostaulos* in Bithynia from his self-imposed exile in 1257.[5]

Bringing the narrative back to the affairs of the Roman Empire, the present chapter leaves behind issues of the diaspora and continues the theme of Chapters 2 and 3: the examination of the ways in which public opinions were expressed by both the elites and the populace within the borders of the exilic empire. The case of Michael Palaiologos' gradual elevation from *megas konostaulos* to imperial dignity becomes the main means for exploring Palaiologan endeavours in gaining public support and maintaining the social and political climate favourable to the *oikos* during the delicate process of imperial election. In other words, by looking at the surviving literary depictions of Michael's manoeuvres from the death of Theodoros II to his ceremonial coronation in Nikaia in 1259, the public aspect of the whole electoral process becomes remarkably clear. While behind-the-curtain coercion and political machinations certainly helped the Palaiologan agenda, it is with the public display of the support of the aristocrats, the prelates, the army, and the people that Michael managed to seize the imperial dignity and obtain legitimacy.

Thanks to the oftentimes conflicting narratives of the surviving sources about Michael Palaiologos' election to the throne, we have the opportunity to chart the communicative actions taken by Michael from the beginning of his career to 1258 that made his imperial election possible. The four sources covering Michael's imperial elevation were written by contemporaries of the event, of whom two were present during the events, namely Michael Palaiologos himself and patriarch Arsenios Autoreianos.[6] Unfortunately, though, Palaiologos and Autoreianos employed the imperial election in order to defend their own positions and, thus, remained vague about the bigger picture. We have Michael ascribing

---

[4] For Balanidiotes's linkage to Theodoros II: Pachymeres, *Relationes*, 55.18–21; Angold, 176. For Balanidiotes' engagement with Theodora and her subsequent marriage to Basileios Kaballarios see: Pachymeres, *Chronikon*, 55.17–26.

[5] A. Failler, "Chronologie et composition dans l'Histoire de Georges Pachymérès," *REB* 44 (1980), 16–18.

[6] Arsenios Autoreianos' *Testament* is published in: *PG* 140, 947–957.

his elevation to the throne to divine providence and Arsenios focusing solely on defending his position by dwelling on a set of oaths exchanged between Ioannes IV, Michael VIII, and the notables, while not covering the coronation itself.[7] The two Georgioi, Akropolites and Pachymeres, themselves not present at the election, offer more nuanced versions of Michael's imperial elevation.[8] Both historians, though absent, were politically and culturally active during Michael VIII's reign and were part of the intellectual and political community that had access to the relevant documents and other texts to reconstruct the events of 1258/1259.

The four narratives, despite their differences in genre and sociopolitical agenda, are in direct dialogue with each other. Akropolites and Michael describe the whole process from Theodoros II's departure from life to Michael's official coronation from a pro-Palaiologan perspective. Pachymeres, on the other hand, takes a far more reserved position in terms of the whole process as he explains how Michael managed to persuade different members of the citizenry—from the street crowds to the magnates and the patriarch himself—to support his cause. Finally, Arsenios Autoreianos, in his *Testament*, writing after his deposition at the synod headed by Michael VIII in 1265, composed his own apology that reads as an invective against the emperor.[9] In his narrative, Autoreianos attempts to rehabilitate himself and cast all the blame on the emperor as well as his secular and ecclesiastic supporters. At the time when Autoreianos' text became known to the public, Akropolites could have already been in the process of writing his *The History*. Finally, Palaiologos' autobiographical account was included in a *typikon* issued in 1282.[10] This meant that in crafting their arguments promoting the idea of Michael's reign as irrevocably necessary, both Akropolites and Palaiologos had read

---

[7] Autoreianos, *Testament*, 949.36–953.14.

[8] In 1258/1259 Pachymeres still had not completed his education (A. Failler, "La promotion du clerc et du moine à l'épiscopat et au patriarcat," *REB* 59 (2001), 131–132), while Akropolites was in captivity in Arta (Akropolites, *Chronike*, 72; Macrides, "Introduction," 12, 29).

[9] Autoreianos was deposed in 1265 and had died by 1273 (A.M. Talbot, "Arsenios Autoreianos," in *ODB* I, 187).

[10] Akropolites composed *The History* sometime in the 1260s or, less likely, in the 1270s; he died in 1282 just a few months before Michael VIII (Macrides, "Introduction," 31–4), and Palaiologos' *Typikon* was composed in 1282 (A. Thomas—A. Constantinides Hero (eds.), *Byzantine Monastic Foundation Documents* 1 [Dumbarton Oaks Studies XXXV] (Washington D.C.: Dumbarton Oaks Research Library and Collections, 2000), 1237.).

the deposed patriarch's *Testament* and addressed it in their own narratives by refuting the accusations laid against them one by one. Pachymeres' *Historical Relations*, written in the fourteenth century, addressed the three previous narratives' arguments, while crafting the most detailed account of the four about the imperial election process.[11] It is with these nuances of direct political dialogue between the four authors in mind that we start our journey of exploring political agency and propaganda (to which all these narratives inevitably belong) during the tumultuous period following Theodoros II's death.

All these narratives, though, have one common focal point: the necessity of public approval for all the doings of the senate and the patriarchate. In exploring the ways in which social climate can be influenced by individuals, thanks to the loss of Constantinople to the crusaders, we see, probably for the first time, a wider geographical scope of the Roman constituency actively participating in forging a consensus on an imperial election. All four narratives relate to events that occurred in the imperial dwellings and public spaces in the cities of Magnesia and Nikaia. Thus, a single-city narrative is replaced by a remarkably vivid and active polycentric provincial populace that is aware of its role in the wider politics of the empire. It is with this argument in mind—the willingness of the urban populace to participate in the affairs of the state regardless of their *patria*—that we follow the unfolding of Michael's political career before his rise to imperial stardom.

5.1 Homecoming

Before Michael Palaiologos' definite departure from the Sultanate of Rum in 1257, emperor Theodoros II established a precedent in Roman legal history by swearing a personal oath to Michael promising not to harm him or his family should he return to Romania.[12] Swearing oaths in private and in public was by no means an oddity in Roman history: Roman officials swore oaths as they were invested with their offices, private contracts

---

[11] For Pachymeres' dialogue with Akropolites' narrative see: Macrides, "Introduction," 71–75.

[12] On the oath see Macrides, *The History*, 327–328, n.9; J.-C. Cheynet, "Foi et conjuration à Byzance," 265–280; Estangüi Gómez, *Byzance face aux Ottomans*, 64–67. For Theodoros II's oath being the first of its kind see: N.G. Svoronos, "Le serment de fidélité," *REB* 9 (1952), 138–140.

could be bound by formulaic oaths, or emperors could ask for the aristocracy's oaths to support the imperially chosen successor to the throne.[13] Theodoros II's oath distinguishes itself from the previous ones based on the fact that it is the emperor who, in a publicly proclaimed oath, guarantees the safety of an individual, Michael Palaiologos. The oath given by Theodoros II was also written down under the aegis of the metropolitan of Ikonion, who acted as an intermediary and a witness to the imperial letter between the emperor and Michael. According to Pachymeres' account of the event:

> Since the hierarch [of Ikonion] improvised an intercession with letters [to Theodoros II], the emperor signaled towards a pardon, assuring in imperial writing that he [Michael] would suffer no harm from his anger, and so he returned. The emperor graciously received [Michael] who seemed humbled, embraced him upon arrival, pardoned him when he confessed of being conscious of erring unforgivingly, and restored him to his previous honours.[14]

In this scenario, Theodoros II's written oath served as a guarantee of Michael's safety upon his return to Nikaia; however, the oath itself lacked a public dimension (since it was dispatched to the capital of the Sultanate of Rum). An official ceremony had to therefore be organized in order to demonstrate to the officials and dignitaries that the *oikos* of the Palaiologoi and the imperial household had set their differences aside. The reconciliation was commemorated with a public imperial embrace, an impactful way to announce to magnates and bureaucrats the rapprochement between the two households.[15] Michael's confession, on

---

[13] For customary oaths taken to the new emperor by all serving officials and dignitaries see: Macrides, Munitiz, Angelov, *Pseudo-Kodinos*, 3; Kantakouzinos I, 16.8-14; *Ecloga Basilicorum* VI, 3, 50. For oaths in general in Byzantium see: L. Burgmann, "Oath (ὅρκος)," in: *ODB*III, 1509.

[14] Τοῦ δ' ἱεράρχου γράμμασι σχεδιάσαντος τὴν πρεσβείαν, ὁ κρατῶν κατένευσε τὴν συμπάθειαν, καὶ βασιλικαῖς συλλαβαῖς ἐπ' ἀσφαλείᾳ τοῦ μή τι παθεῖν ἀνήκεστον ἐξ ὀργῆς ἐπάνεισιν· ὁ δὲ καὶ δέχεται τοῦτον πρόφρων ταπεινωθέντα καὶ ἀγκαλίζεται προσιόντα καὶ ὁμολογοῦντα ὡς ἑαυτῷ σύνοιδε πταίσας ἀσύγγνωστα συμπαθεῖ, καὶ ἐπὶ τῆς προτέρας ἔχων τιμῆς. (Pachymeres, *Chronikon*, 45.7-12).

[15] Pachymeres emphasizes that Theodoros II embraced (Pachymeres, *Chronikon*, 45.11: ἀγκαλίζεται) Michael, which implied public physical contact. Imperial embrace was usually reserved for the patriarch (*Book of Ceremonies*, 92.5-8). For general code of conduct in the emperor's presence see: Macrides—Munitiz—Angelov, *Pseudo-Kodinos*, 379-393.

the other hand, "of being conscious of erring unforgivingly"[16] was a sign of penance. It thus justified, in the public eye, the emperor's wrath, which had led to Palaiologos' flight. That said, the confession itself mostly hints towards the flight to the Saljuqs more than at any other specific crime. It is quite possible that the ceremonial reconciliation was followed by an imperial *prostagma*, whose copies would have been sent around the empire to inform provincial officials as well as the populace about Michael's reinstatement to the office of *megas konostaulos*.[17] With a *prostagma* of this kind, Michael's reintegration into the Roman state would have been complete and he could continue to serve in Bithynia as he did before his flight to the Turks.

Michael's stay in Bithynia as the *megas konostaulos* of the Latin forces was brief. After the Roman army captured the city of Dyrrachion, Michael was dispatched to govern that area.[18] In reassigning Michael to a new post, Theodoros II and his dignitaries were following a well-established Roman tradition of, even after 1204, shifting provincial administrators from one province to another every year or so.[19] For Theodoros II it was imperative that Michael be reassigned on a regular basis so that he would not forge strong ties with the local elites and the people as he had done in the city of Thessaloniki. Fortunately for Michael, who was now dispatched to serve in the Balkans, the in-law of the Palaiologan *oikos*,[20] Georgios Akropolites, was appointed to the office of the *praitor* of the Balkans, the same function the late Andronikos Palaiologos occupied at the time of his death.[21] Having a strong supporter as the head magistrate in charge of the Balkans gave Michael a respite from the constant imperial gaze, which looked with suspicion on the household and allies of the Palaiologoi.

---

[16] ἑαυτῷ σύνοιδε πταίσας ἀσύγγνωστα. (Pachymeres, *Chronikon*, 45.11–12).

[17] For *prostagmata* and their functions see: F. Dölger and J. Karayannopolous, *Byzantinische Urkundenlehre: Erster Abschnitt, Die Kaiserurkunden* (München: C.-H. Beck 1968), 109–111. For the practice of sending *prostagamta* around the empire see: Pachymeres, *Chronikon*, 77.32–79.8.

[18] Pachymeres, *Chronikon*, 45.15–20.

[19] See Chapter 1 as well as: Angold, *A Byzantine Government*, 250; Ahrweiler, "L'histoire," 138–148; F. Dölger, "Chronologisches und Prosopographisches zur byzantinischen Geschichte des 13. Jahrhunderts," *BZ* 27 (1927), 307–310.

[20] For Akropolites' marriage into the Palaiologan household see: Chapter 2.

[21] Akropolites, *Chronike*, 66–68.

Georgios Akropolites, whose career was advanced under Theodoros II, was put in charge of the Balkans in 1257 as part of the emperor's crackdown on the *golden chain* households.[22] Georgios came from a family of mid-level bureaucrats and was by no means born into a household of high nobility. As he himself emphasizes, he received his education from the imperially sponsored education scheme under Ioannes III and, as a result, was included in the imperial administration where he managed to prosper in the same manner as Georgios Mouzalon.[23] Looking at Akropolites' own account of his rise and Pachymeres' account of Georgios Mouzalon's speech in the senate in 1258, both men derived prestige from the education they received from Ioannes III.[24] Thus, in Theodoros II's attempts to weaken the traditionally powerful households, Georgios Akropolites, in the same vein as the Mouzalones, was pushed to the fore of state administration. Once in office, Akropolites had quite vast jurisdictions over the peninsula.[25] As he tells us: "I was given permission to do the following: to replace, as I wished, the tax collectors and administrators of fiscal affairs, commanders of the armies and those who hold command of regions."[26] With such broad supervisory authority, the *praitor* was able to make sure that Michael Palaiologos, now governor of Dyrrachion, remained protected from potential opponents in the provincial administration, be they civic or military. In such circumstances, another Nikolaos Manglavites of Serres was less likely to arise from the midst of local notables to make Michael's life more complicated.

In theory at least, Michael's future seemed secured: he was to govern a newly conquered region at the very outskirts of the empire under the supervision of his in-law. Unfortunately for Michael, the emperor had different plans for him, and so he never reached the Adriatic coast. On

[22] Macrides, "Introduction," 27–28.

[23] ibid., 17, 26–27.

[24] Akropolites, Chronike, 32; Pachymeres, *Chronikon*, 65.23–73.5.

[25] For the role of *praitor* see: H. Glykatzi-Ahrweiler, "Recherches sur l'administration de l'empire byzantin aux IX-XIème siècles," *Bulletin de Correspondance Hellénique* 84 (1960), 75–78; J. Herrin, "Realities of Byzantine Provincial Government: Hellas and Peloponnesos, 1180–1205," *DOP* 29 (1975), 266–267. The *praitor* in the Balkans had the same authorizations as did the *doukes* in Asia Minor (Herrin, "Realities," 266.); for the *doukes* in Asia Minor see: Angold, *A Byzantine Government*, 250–258.

[26] ὥριστό μοι καὶ γὰρ ἐπ' ἀδείας ἔχειν με τοιαῦτα ποιεῖν, ἐνεργοῦντας καὶ δημόσια διαπραττομένους καὶ στρατευμάτων προϊσταμένους καὶ χωρῶν ἡγεμονίαν κεκτημένους ἀνταλλάττειν ὡς ἂν βουλοίμην. (Akropolites, *Chronike*, 68.43-46.)

his way to his new post in Dyrrachion, accompanied by his retinue, which included the newly appointed metropolitan of the city, Michael was ordered to join forces with Michael Laskaris, the emperor's uncle, in order to deal with the rebellion of Theodoros, an illegitimate son of *despotes* Michael Angelos of Epeiros, in the region around Berroia.[27] Theodoros' insurrection was part of a grand offensive that the Epeirotes organized in alliance with Stefan Nemanjić of Serbia to push the Romans of Nikaia east of Macedonia.[28] The joint Roman army first plundered the rebellious area around Berroia and eventually engaged the Epeirote troops in an open battle at Vodena where it was aided by the imperially dispatched Manouel Lapardas, albeit with meagre reinforcement. In the battle, Michael managed to kill Theodoros, but the imperial army was defeated by Epeiros' better equipped army. Retreating from Vodena, Michael eventually returned to the city of Thessaloniki via Prilep.

The city of Prilep, itself a major fortress on the Laskarid-Angelid frontier, was an obvious target for the Epeirote-Serbian alliance. Akropolites was himself in the city in his function of *praitor*, ensuring that Prilep was properly defended. He recounts the situation from the perspective of an eyewitness:

> As Michael Komnenos [Palaiologos], Michael Laskaris, and the generals that were present at the campaign were compelled by us to come to Prilep and meet with us; wanting or not they came to us. They stayed with us for a few days, but because they did not have the force to engage in combat and fight the renegade Michael [of Epeiros], they left us and returned [to Thessaloniki]. For they perceived the faithlessness of the inhabitants and they witnessed consciously the doubt of those who had been assigned to guard the town. Then I was left behind in Prilep with those who were there to guard the town. That is what the ruler ordered me to do.[29]

[27] Akropolites, *Chronike*, 70; Pachymeres, *Chronikon*, 45.15–47.6.

[28] For the Epeirote insurrection see: Akropolites, *Chronike*, 68; Angold, *A Byzantine Government*, 289–291. For the alliance with the Serbs see: R. Radić, "Georgije Akropolit i Srbi," T.Z. Živković (ed.), *Kralj Vladislav i Srbija XIII veka* (Beograd: SANU 2003), 89–97.

[29] Ὁ μὲν οὖν Κομνηνὸς Μιχαὴλ καὶ ὁ Λάσκαρις Μιχαὴλ καὶ οἱ ἀμφ' αὐτοὺς ἡγεμόνες τυγχάνοντες τοῦ στρατεύματος, ἐπεὶ παρ' ἡμῶν ἠναγκάζοντο καταλαβεῖν εἰς τὸν Πρίλαπον καὶ ἡμῖν ξυντυχεῖν, ἑκόντες ἄκοντες ἀφίκοντο παρ' ἡμᾶς. καὶ ὀλίγας ἡμέρας προσκαρτερήσαντες μεθ' ἡμῶν, ἐπεὶ μὴ εἶχον δυνάμεως συστάδην ξυνελθεῖν καὶ τὸν ἀποστάτην μαχέσασθαι Μιχαήλ, ἀφέντες ἡμᾶς ὑπέστρεψαν· τήν τε γὰρ ἀπιστίαν τῶν οἰκητόρων διενοήσαντο καὶ τὸ

At Prilep, then, the situation was dire, especially since the populace was more prone to support the Epeirotes than the Romans represented by Akropolites and his troops who were few in number. This time around, there were no prominent local citizens, such as Nikolaos Manglavites in Serres, who could sway public opinion in favour of Ioannes III, and thus Akropolites was left alone with the hostile citizens of Prilep.[30] After Palaiologos and the other generals left, the city was attacked and eventually conquered by the Epeirotes; Akropolites himself was captured and spent the next two years imprisoned in Arta.[31] The downfall of the city was caused by Akropolites' and other officials' inability to maintain consensus among the populace of Prilep in support of Laskarid rule. The political agency of the city's populace proved to be crucial during the siege when the locals opted to offer their support to the Epeirotes who were helped to eventually enter the city.[32] Thus, not only was Palaiologos left without governorship of Dyrrachion, as the whole region was dragged into the conflict, but his main ally, Georgios Akropolites, was not there anymore to offer support and, arguably, protection.

On the other shore of the straits, in Asia Minor, the situation looked as grim for the Palaiologan *oikos*. Accompanying the complete collapse of Michael's fortunes in the Balkans, Palaiologos' elder sister was arrested by the emperor whose worsening health led him to suspect everybody of trying to kill him with poison or magic.[33] Michael's elder sister Maria fell victim to Theodoros II's wrath and he ordered the woman arrested. Once in custody, Maria was tortured under the emperor's orders in order to confess to plotting against the crown. The torment was to no avail and Maria confessed to nothing.[34] Thus Theodoros II now had to worry about once more estranging the Palaiologoi by breaking the public oath he had made in 1257 and torturing a member of the family. Adding to Maria's situation, her daughter with Nikephoros Tarchaneiotes, named

---

ἀμφίβολον τῶν εἰς φύλαξιν αὐτοῦ τεταγμένων νουνεχῶς ἐτεκμήραντο. ἐναπελείφθην γοῦν καὶ αὐτὸς ἐν Πριλάπῳ μετὰ τῶν ὄντων εἰς τὴν φυλακὴν τοῦ ἄστεος· οὕτω καὶ γάρ μοι ὁ κρατῶν προστέταχεν. (Akropolites, *Chronike*, 71.59–70).

[30] For public agency deciding the course of politics see: Kaldellis, *The Byzantine Republic*, 119–125, 150–159; Krallis, "Historians, Politics, and the Polis," 421–436.

[31] Akropolites, *Chronike*, 72.

[32] ibid., 71.65–67.

[33] Pachymeres, *Chronikon*, 53.13–23.

[34] ibid., 57.9–16.

Theodora, was forced to readapt her marital arrangements and change grooms because of the emperor's calculations.[35] Under such conditions, Theodoros II was not willing to risk dubious allegiances, especially at a time when many notables in the Balkans were switching sides to join Michael Angelos of Epeiros. An order to bring Michael Palaiologos back in chains was thus issued by the emperor.[36]

Michael was in the city of Thessaloniki as the imperially dispatched legate, Konstantinos Chadenos, reached the city with the arrest order and instructions for his transfer to Nymphaion. Thessaloniki was by no means uncharted territory for Michael. Quite the contrary, he and the Thessalonians had a history of understanding: after all, Palaiologos began his career in the region governing Serres and Melenikon while his father was the *praitor* in Thessaloniki. We already saw how after Andronikos' death, Michael managed to embroider himself onto the city's social fabric by commissioning a series of works by the rhetorician Iakobos to commemorate his father and the genos of the Palaiologoi. Thus, unable to proceed to the rebellious areas, where he was to take governorship of Dyrrachion, Michael stayed in Thessaloniki surrounded by local elite families, the likes of the Spartenoi and Kampanoi, who were acquainted with and supportive of him.[37]

The news of the pending arrest arrived in Thessaloniki before the imperial legate managed to make his way into the city. According to Pachymeres, having been apprised of the pending arrest and knowing that there was not much he could do to avoid it, Michael turned to the metropolitan of Dyrrachion, who was part of Palaiologan retinue on its way to Albania and was now dwelling in Thessaloniki. The two men went to the monastery of Akapniou to pray for Michael's salvation overnight and during the morning liturgy.[38] The choice of a monastery located in the centre of the city was by no means accidental. Procuring divine protection at such a prime spot in the city was a way for Michael to mobilize the monks around him to spread the news of his pending arrest to

---

[35] ibid., 55.17–57.1.

[36] ibid., 57.16–29.

[37] For the Spartenoi and Kampanoi see: Macrides, *The History*, 238–239. n.6–7.

[38] Pachymeres, *Chronikon*, 47.19–28. For Akapniou monastery and its central location in Thessaloniki see: Th. Papazotos, "The Identification of the Church of 'Profitis Elias' in Thessaloniki," *DOP* 45 (1991), 121–129.

the city's populace.[39] By posing as a pious sinner, Michael was able to both awaken sympathy for himself as well as not to openly accuse the emperor of any wrongdoing. As Pachymeres lets us know: "as soon as dawn came and the hierarch was about to recite the prescribed hours; so that he could perform it, he imposed silence on those outside. He himself conversed with God in private and carried out in complete tranquillity the habitual prayers of the mass."[40] By openly silencing the monks present at the morning liturgy, the designated metropolitan of Dyrrachion, a prominent cleric, was able to turn the congregation's attention to Michael's plight. We can only imagine how the echo of silence resonated with those present in the church. The silencing of the monks was an effective way to grasp the attention of those in attendance since the morning liturgy was proceeding in an unusual way. That is, instead of usual prayers and sermons, the monks did not hear a thing. This was certainly a bizarre turn of events and would likely become the talk of the town. By making sure that his sermon would be talked about in the city in connection to Michael Palaiologos' plight, the metropolitan of Dyrrachion turned God's holy crew into promoters of Michael's case to the citizenry in Thessaloniki, where the Palaiologoi were by no means unknown. This meant that when Michael's situation became a matter of public knowledge, they would be able to relate.

Pachymeres continues the narrative by presenting two versions of the subsequent events. By not providing a singular factual and contextual interpretation of the events, the historian inevitably invites his readers to take a more active role in passing judgement about the events. In the first account of the subsequent events, Pachymeres says that after the liturgy was over, the metropolitan swore he had heard a divine voice saying marpou. Not knowing what it was, the metropolitan of Dyrrachion went to his colleague, metropolitan of Thessaloniki, Manouel Disypatos, who eventually solved the riddle by understanding that M.A.R.P.O.Y. is an acronym standing for: Michael, King of the Romans, the Palaiologos

---

[39] For gossiping monks see, for instance, the career of Nikephoros Blemmydes (Blemmydes, *Curriculum Vitae*).

[40] Ὡς γοῦν ἐπέφωσκεν ἡ ἡμέρα καὶ τὰς νομιζομένας ὥρας διελθεῖν ἔμελλεν ὁ ἀρχιερεύς, ἐφ᾽ ᾧ λειτουργήσειε, σιγὴν μὲν ἐπισκήπτει τοῖς ἔξωθεν, αὐτὸς δὲ κατὰ μόνας ὡμίλει Θεῷ καὶ τὰς συνήθεις καὶ προτελεστικὰς εὐχὰς μεθ᾽ ὅτι πλείστης ἀπεδίδου τῆς ἡσυχίας. (Pachymeres, *Chronikon*, 47.25–28).

will shortly be celebrated.[41] If this story bares any truth, then we see Michael managing to gather the high clergy at his hand to support his cause by spreading the word to the populace of Thessaloniki.[42] Manouel Disypatos, himself a fairly new figure in Thessaloniki's social scene—he started his tenure as the metropolitan of Thessaloniki only in 1258—might have offered his support to Michael, who was known and liked by the Thessalonians together with his father, in order to advance his own position in the city by finding a quick way to gain the general populace's affection and respect.[43]

According to the second account presented by Pachymeres, Disypatos took no part in this event. Rather,

> there are some who say that the [metropolitan] of Dyrrachion did not hear these things nor that the [metropolitan] of Thessaloniki made this prediction but that the latter, being a wise man and interested in such books, which conceive future reigns, had come to know, while arduously researching, such things and he desired to bring this knowledge to the one to whom the summit of imperial power was pledged and, at the same time, relieve this man who feared for his life of distress.[44]

Even if Disypatos was not included in the dissemination of the idea of Michael's bright future, it is still possible to think that the designated metropolitan of Dyrrachion staged the prayer and offered the interpretation favourable to Michael Palaiologos. This same interpretation together with the metropolitan's odd action of silencing everybody in order to pray by himself, while everybody else was waiting outside, could have still

---

[41] Μιχαὴλ γὰρ ἄναξ Ῥωμαίων Παλαιολόγος ὀξέως ὑμνηθήσεται (Pachymeres, *Chronikon*, 49.11–12).

[42] We do not know if Disypatos was willing to help Michael at the time. The same metropolitan, though, was an ardent opponent to Michael's imperial elevation in 1258 (Pachymeres, *Chronikon*, 143.20–23).

[43] For Manouel Disypatos see: *PLP*, no.5544.

[44] Εἰσὶ δ' οἵτινες λέγουσι μήτε τὸν Δυρραχίου τοιαῦτ' ἀκοῦσαι, μήτε τὸν Θεσσαλονίκης τοιαῦτα φοιβάσασθαι, ἀλλά, σοφὸν ἐκεῖνον ὄντα καὶ περὶ τοιαύτας βίβλους, αἳ δὴ καὶ βασιλείας τὰς ἐς τοὐπιὸν διατυποῦσιν, ἐπτοημένον, φιλοπονώτερον ἐρευνῶντα, περὶ τοιούτων ἐγνωκέναι καὶ δή, γνωρίσαι θέλοντα ταῦτα ᾧ γε καὶ ἡ τῆς βασιλείας κατηγγύατο περιωπὴ καὶ ἀναφέρειν οἷον ἐκεῖνον τῆς λύπης, ἐπεὶ καὶ περὶ αὐτῇ τῇ ζωῇ ἐδεδοίκει. (Pachymeres, *Chronikon*, 49.12–18).

become part of the popular discourse in the streets and taverns of Thessaloniki. With or without Disypatos' support, the case for Michael was made to the Thessalonians who were expected to spread the word further around the city.

By the time of Konstantinos Chadenos' arrived in Thessaloniki, the whole affair was known to the populace at large. Moreover, Chadenos himself was Michael's acquaintance and either out of friendship or respect, as Pachymeres relates, the imperial legate decided to have Michael seated freely on a saddled horse and, "so that he [Michael] would not be dishonoured by appearing in chains before the masses of the city, he left at night."[45] By showing respect to Michael and avoiding parading him in chains in front of the Thessalonians, Chadenos averted potential unrest in a city where the popularity of the Palaiologoi in general and Michael specifically could prove to be a challenge to his own authority. If the citizens heard about Michael's apprehension, they could easily be irritated by seeing their champion in chains. Michael's position in Thessaloniki was made more favourable by the fact that, unlike the Palaiologoi, neither Ioannes III nor his successor had spent much time in the city. The emperors had thus not left a permanent mark on the city's infrastructure, as they had been doing in cities across Asia Minor.[46] For these reasons, the populace of Thessaloniki felt more attached to Michael Palaiologos than to the emperor in Asia Minor. The risk of an insurrection in the city was made even greater at the time of Michael's arrest since the area west of Thessaloniki was under Epirot attack, making city-scale sedition even more possible. Taking all these reasons into account, Chadenos smartly opted to lead Michael out of the city in the evening as a free man. Not much was thus made of the exit, ensuring that Michael's "plight" would

---

[45] μὴ καὶ ἐπὶ πολλῶν ἐντὸς ἀτιμῷτο τῆς πόλεως τοῖς σιδήροις πεδούμενος, νυκτὸς ἔξεισιν. (Pachymeres, *Chronikon*, 51.9–11).

[46] For Ioannes III's and Theodoros II's general focus on Asia Minor see: Skoutariotes, *Synopsis Chronike*, 506.19–25; 506.28–507.6, 14–18, 535.26–536.4. For the three Laskarid emperors' inscriptions around the city walls of Asia Minor see: K. Μέντζου-Μεϊμάρη, "Χρονολογημέναι βυζαντιναί επιγραφαί του Corpus Inscriptionum Graecarum IV 2," *Δελτίον Χριστιανικῆς Αρχαιολογικῆς Εταιρείας* 9 (1979), 106.143–145, 107.149, 150, 109.160, 109–10.161. There are no surviving inscriptions on the walls of European cities by the three emperors.

not arouse the populace, whose pity for a man they knew and liked might easily have turned them to violence.[47]

The road to Magnesia seems to have been uneventful and upon arrival Michael was imprisoned without meeting the emperor beforehand.[48] Michael spent the rest of Theodoros II's reign—that is, until the emperor's death on 18 August 1258—incarcerated, awaiting a trial for which the emperor and his allies could not launch due to lack of evidence. The emperor was not able to do away with Palaiologos simply by imposing his imperial will. It was one thing to arrest a notable of Michael's calibre; it was a completely different proposition to execute him without a public trial. The trial, though, was never organized since the emperor died, leaving the throne to his young son Ioannes IV.

5.2 The Rhetorical Side of Public Deliberations: Obtaining Public Support for the Mouzalones' Regency

Before dying, though, Theodoros II worked on his son's regency. To do so, he appointed through stipulations in his will, his onetime associate Georgios Mouzalon—a man he knew from his days as a *paidopoulos*— as *protovestiarios*, imperial regent in charge of running state affairs.[49] All the notables present in Magnesia, including leading generals and senators of the state, as well as a significant number of soldiers stationed around the city, were made to swear an oath to the regent during Theodoros II's last days.[50] The oath, we can imagine, was administered during a

---

[47] The popular reaction to the leniency shown to Ioannes Italos by the ecclesiastic court that was taking place in public serves as a good example of the mobs reacting violently to the officially made decisions regarding prominent individuals: "the whole population of Constantinople ran towards the church looking for Italos. He would most likely have been thrown from high in the middle of the church, had he not hidden in some hole running to the rooftop of the sacred building." (ὁ δῆμος ἅπας τῆς Κωνσταντίνου πρὸς τὴν ἐκκλησίαν συγκεκίνητο τὸν Ἰταλὸν ἀναζητοῦντες. καὶ τάχα ἂν ἀφ' ὕψους εἰς μέσον τῆς ἐκκλησίας ἔρριπτο, εἰ μὴ λαθὼν ἐκεῖνος εἰς τὸν ὄροφον τουτουὶ τοῦ θείου τεμένους ἀνελθὼν ἔν τινι φωλεῷ ἑαυτὸν συνεκάλυψεν. Anna Komnene, *Alexias*, V, 9, 6, 1–5.).

[48] Pachymeres, *Chronikon*, 51.32–53.3.

[49] For Georgios Mouzalon's position in the empire and his proximity to Theodoros II see: Macrides, "Introduction," 24–27; Angelov, *The Byzantine Hellene*, 151–152, 160–162; for the dignity of *protovestiarios* see: Guilland, *Institutions* I, 216–236.

[50] Akropolites, Chronike 75.10–11.

ceremonial event which sought to make the transition of power to both Ioannes IV and Georgios Mouzalon publicly known and accepted by the aristocrats who were at hand. Thus, the whole business was staged as a traditional oath-swearing to the new emperor by the dignitaries and officials. The soldiers present in Magnesia too would have delivered their oaths in public, probably not inside a single room of the palace. Such public and, truth to be told, loud oath-taking would not have been missed by any of the locals dwelling in the city and its vicinity. By pushing for the oaths to Ioannes IV and Mouzalon, Theodoros II was able at least to secure a modicum of popular awareness, if not full support, for his last will.

Despite the oaths taken, Georgios Mouzalon, fearing for his position, convoked the meeting of the senate in order to reach a consensus on the regency.[51] The *protovestiarios*' unease about his safety was not unwarranted, for the *oikos* of the Mouzalones, as we have seen, was not much liked by more ancient *golden chain* households. For that matter he was unpopular even with some of the *novi homines* such as Georgios Akropolites. Other than the volatile cohabitation with other members of the empire's high elites—the imperial family excepted—the Mouzalones were not particularly popular with the masses in Asia Minor even during Theodoros II's reign. According to Pachymeres' account:

> At this moment [Theodoros II's last months of life], because of the frequently recurring illness, the patient, not knowing from where it came, thought that the cause of the wrath was a demon summoned by magic. The masses outside the palace, who tended to believe in such things, attributed the crime to the Mouzalones, who unknowingly became the object of accusations, which they had not expected.[52]

Thus, it appears that rumours of Theodoros II's magic-induced affliction spread like wildfire around the city of Magnesia, and that the populace was quick to suspect the Mouzalones for this, as both Georgios and his brothers were constantly by the emperor's side. Whether

---

[51] Pachymeres, *Chronikon*, 65.8–21.

[52] Τότε τοίνυν ἐπιπιπτούσης συχνάκις τῆς νόσου, οὐκ οἶδ' ὁπόθεν, μήνιμα εἶναι τὸ πάθος ὁ πάσχων ἐκ μαγγανείας δαιμόνιον ὑπελάμβανε. Καὶ οἱ μὲν πολλοὶ τῶν ἔξω, οἷς ἦν τὰ τοιαῦτα πιστεύειν, τὸ ἔγκλημα προσέτριβον τοῖς Μουζάλωσι, παραλόγως καὶ ὡς οὐκ ἂν προσεδόκησαν τῶν ἀξιωμάτων τυχοῦσι. (Pachymeres, *Chronikon*, 53.22–26).

the families of the *golden chain* employed and even promoted these rumours in order to strengthen popular support for themselves at the expense of Mouzalones we cannot tell. We can suppose, though, that the likes of Akropolites or the blinded Philes and Strategopoulos welcomed the commotion in the streets of Magnesia and elsewhere. Taking into account that both Ioannes III, who was popularly proclaimed a saint after his death, and Theodoros II were generally liked by the populace in Asia Minor, the *golden chain* elites could not attract vast support for themselves at the imperial expense.[53] With the Mouzalones losing public support, though, the senatorial elites found convenient scapegoats in order to mobilize the populace around their own political agenda. Much as the populace of Prilep acted on its desire to see the Epeirotes controlling the region or the Thessalonians by displaying public affection to the Palaiologoi without any regard for the central government, thus the citizens of Magnesia were well-placed to directly interfere in state affairs. The senatorial elites and the likes of Michael Palaiologos would not shun away from capitalizing on such an ill-disposed public climate towards the Mouzalones in order to reach their goals. The position of the *protovestiarios* and his brothers was therefore unenviable: they were left in full control of the public affairs without the support of the two pillars that made up the public sphere—the senate and the people of Rome.

Taking into account the lack of basic support for the newly established regime, it should come as no surprise that Georgios Mouzalon convened the senate to discuss issues relating to the regency the moment he took over the reins of the state. Attempting to gain the support of the senate was the first step in reaching a wider public consensus for his regime. The turnout of the senators was astonishing, at least according to Pachymeres, who lets us know that:

> At that time, he [Georgios Mouzalon] convened the entire senate and the entire imperial family, all the archons, and all the military class. Also present were the brothers [Manouel and Michael] of [Theodoros I] Laskaris, the great-grandfather of the emperor [Ioannes IV], who had in the past worn

---

[53] For Ioannes III's popularity see: Skoutariotes, *Synopsis Chronike*; Pachymeres, *Relations* R.J. Macrides, "Saints and Sainthood in the Early Palaeologan Period," in S. Hackel (ed.), *The Byzantine Saint: University of Birmingham Fourteenth Spring Symposium of Byzantine Studies, Volume 1980, Part 2* (London: Fellowship of St Alban and St Sergius 1981), 67–87; For Theodoros II's image among his subjects see: Skoutariotes, *Synopsis Chronike*, 535.5-536.13; Pachymeres, *Chronikon*, 57.32–61.22.

the imperial crown and relieved the Roman state of its confusion. The blind men – Strategopoulos and Philes – were not absent, and all the other magnates completed the gathering.[54]

Adding to the list of attendees, Michael Palaiologos, released from prison after Theodoros II's death, was present as well.[55] While the senatorial elite and the representatives of the army were stationed in Magnesia, the ecclesiastic notables were absent from the meeting with the patriarch himself in Nikaia. With the cream of the crop of all secular civic high officials and dignitaries present at the meeting, Georgios Mouzalon acting as the presiding senator began his speech "from a platform, so that both those in front and those in the back could hear him."[56]

Needless to say, the speech recorded in the *Historical Relations* was either composed or at least heavily edited by Pachymeres.[57] Nevertheless, the surviving peroration had to be based on a typical speech a senator in power would deliver to win over the support of other senators. After all, Georgios Mouzalon had benefited from the imperially sponsored higher education as much as his contemporaries Georgios Akropolites and Michael Palaiologos. With such education, Mouzalon was expected

---

[54] Τότε τοίνυν συγκαλεσάμενος ὅσον ἦν τὸ τῆς γερουσίας καὶ ὅσον τοῦ βασιλείου γένους, ὅσον τε τῶν ἀρχόντων καὶ ὅσον τῆς στρατιωτικῆς τάξεως, παρόντων ἐκεῖσε καὶ τῶν τοῦ προπάππου τοῦ βασιλέως Λάσκαρι αὐταδέλφων, ὃς δὴ καὶ οὗτος τὸ πάλαι βασιλείας διέπρεπεν διαδήματι καὶ τὰ τῆς Ῥωμαΐδος πράγματα συγχυθέντα ὡς εἶχεν ἀνεκαλεῖτο, οὐδὲ τῶν τυφλῶν ἐκεῖθεν ἀπόντων—ὁ Στρατηγόπουλος δ' οὗτοι ἦσαν καὶ ὁ Φιλῆς—, καὶ παντὸς ἄλλου μεγιστάνος συμπληροῦντος τὸν σύλλογον. (Pachymeres, *Chronikon*, 65.12–20).

[55] Pachymeres does not tell us when and how Michael was released. However, at the meeting of the senate, Pachymeres clearly points out Michael's presence by offering a whole speech delivered by the *megas konostaulos* (Pachymeres, Chronikon, 73.19–23).

[56] ἐφ' ὑψηλοῦ στάς, ὡς ἂν ἅμα οἵ τε πρῶτοι ἀκούοιεν καὶ οἱ ὕστατοι. (ibid., 65.20–21).

[57] On composing speeches for characters of histories in Greco-Roman tradition see: A. Tsakmakis, "Von der Rhetorik zur Geschichtsschreibung: Das 'Methodenkapitel' des Thukydides (1,22,1–3)," *Rheinisches Museum für Philologie* 141 (1998), 239–255. For rhetoric in Byzantine historiography see: R.J. Macrides (ed.), *History as Literature in Byzantium: Papers from the Fortieth Spring Symposium of Byzantine Studies, University of Birmingham, April 2007* (Aldershot: Ashgate 2010). Also, on rhetorical practices in historiography: A. J. Woodman, *Rhetoric in Classical Historiography* (Portland: Areopagitica 1988); A. Cameron (ed.), *History as Text: The Writing of Ancient History*, Chapel Hill: Duckworth, 1989. On different techniques used by historians vis-à-vis rhetoricians to depict emperors in Byzantium see: A. Angelov, "In Search of God's Only Emperor: *Basileus* in Byzantine and Modern Historiography," *Journal of Medieval History* 40 (2014), 123–141.

to be versed in rhetoric in order to convincingly address his audience. Indeed, in the speech, should we opt to trust Pachymeres' main outline, the *protovestiarios* was quick to demonstrate his close relationship with the emperor for whom he felt "a mixture of love with fear,"[58] only to acknowledge that many of the senators and their families had suffered under Theodoros II. At this point, all the senators were invited to express their grievances by keeping in mind that Theodoros II was no more and that the young emperor was in need of a good regency. Mouzalon continued by promoting himself as the best option and pointing out that good regents were recognized by their approachability. He thus expanded on the senators' ability "to approach them [the regents] immediately, and to continually poke them with words."[59] Once he had completed the exposé on good regency, Mouzalon continued to further put himself in the hands of the present senators and soldiers:

> I took on the care for the emperor, not through a personal and prearranged choice, or with some goal in mind, but primarily to fulfill the written orders of the emperor [Theodoros II], and, furthermore . . . but I do not want to say more. But it is only with your approval that I wish to devote myself to carrying out of this duty. And if you propose one of you to undertake the duty in the future, it will suffice to me to be placed in the lowest office. If someone takes suitable care of the emperor's safety, I will be content to be nothing but a regular subject, and I would love and beseech the ruler not to become angry if my honours seem to have displeased some of you, because it is better to live in security, serving as one of the soldiers, than live in fear and suspicion through taking high office.[60]

By posing as a modest official reluctant to take upon himself an office that held almost unprecedented power, Mouzalon followed Greco-Roman

---

[58] ἀγάπην φόβῳ μιγνύντες (Pachymeres, *Chronikon*, 65.30).

[59] προσελθεῖν ἐκ τοῦ παραχρῆμα καὶ νύξαι λέγοντα συνεχέστερον (Pachymeres, *Chronikon*, 69.25-26).

[60] Ἐγὼ οὔτ᾽ ἰδίαις καὶ αὐτοβούλοις προαιρέσεσιν, οὔτε μὴν σκοπῷ τινι καὶ μελέτῃ ταῖς τοῦ βασιλέως προσανέχειν ἐπιτροπαῖς ᾕρημαι, ἀλλὰ πρῶτον μὲν ἐπιστολὰς πληρῶν βασιλέως, ἔπειτα δέ ..., ἀλλ᾽ οὐ βούλομαι λέγειν. Πλὴν καὶ ὑμῶν θελόντων, οὕτω καὶ μόνον προσανέχειν καὶ ἔτι ταῖς ἐπιτροπαῖς βούλομαι· εἰ δ᾽ οὖν, ἀλλ᾽ ὑμεῖς μὲν τὸν ἐπιτροπεύσοντα ἐφιστᾶτε, ἐμοὶ δ᾽ ἀρκέσει τὸ ἐπ᾽ ἐσχάτοις τάττεσθαι. Κἄν τις τὴν βασιλικὴν σωτηρίαν πρεπόντως πολυωροίη, καὶ ἰδιωτεύσας ἀγαπήσω καὶ προσλιπαρήσω μὴ ὀργίζεσθαι τὸν δεσπότην, εἰ λυπεῖν τινας ὑμῶν δοκοίη τὸ ἐμὸν ἀξίωμα· κρεῖσσον γὰρ ὡς ἕνα τῶν στρατιωτῶν ἐξυπηρετοῦντα ἀσφαλῶς διάγειν ἢ φόβῳ καὶ ὑπονοίαις μετ᾽ ἀξιώματος ζῆν. (Pachymeres, *Chronikon*, 71.9–18).

rhetorical tradition in his effort to persuade his audience.[61] The reluctance was followed by a shift of focus on Mouzalon's reliability: he noted that he had accepted the office only because the emperor had asked him to. All this, however, was arrived at without the support of the senate and the army, as Mouzalon himself pointed out. At this point, the speech exits the realm of persuasion and leaves the deliberation to the senators and the present soldiers. By employing rhetorical training in order to persuade the political and military elite to support his cause, Mouzalon was testing the waters and seeing whether there was enough goodwill among them to keep him in office.

The education received under Ioannes III seemed to have paid off and the representatives of the army accepted Mouzalon as regent. The senators were initially more reserved than the soldiers, but they too ended up confirming their loyalty to Mouzalon. They collectively picked up on one of the themes of the speech: the blame for their misfortunes was completely associated with the departed emperor, leaving the Mouzalones in the clear.[62] Among the senators, it was Michael Palaiologos who was the most ardent supporter of the Mouzalon regency.[63] Having been only just released from prison, Michael's decision to deliver a speech, according to Pachymeres, was a way for him to reposition himself on the polity's political map. Furthermore, if he had any grievances against the Mouzalones, which was quite possible taking into consideration the fact that he had been arrested and his sister tortured by Theodoros II, while the Mouzalones had occupied the highest dignities, he did not let those bubble up to the surface. Thus, Michael's speech before the senators and the present soldiery was not delivered to simply endear himself to the regents, but to publicly display his comeback from prison as well as his important role in fostering senatorial consensus. All this was done for the eyes of his peers and the polity's military establishment. After Michael's

---

[61] On modesty as a method of gaining sympathy and, in turn, persuading the audience to support the orator see Hermogenes' advice: H. Rabe (ed.), *Hermogenis Opera* (Leipzig: Teubner 1913, reprint 1963), 2.6. For Hermogenes in Byzantine educational curriculum see: Constantinides, *Higer Education in Byzantium*, 7, 11, 152; P. Roilos, "Ancient Greek Rhetorical Theory and Byzantine Discursive Politics: John Sikeliotes on Hermogenes," in T. Shawcross – I. Toth (eds.), *Reading in the Byzantine Empire and Beyond* (Cambridge: Cambridge University Press 2018), 159–184.

[62] Pachymeres, *Chronikon*, 73.13–17.

[63] For the whole of Palaiologos' speech see: ibid., 73.19–77.16.

laudatory speech of support, everybody swore the customary oaths of allegiance to the new emperor and his regents before leaving for their respective posts.

Pachymeres' choice to provide us with his renderings of both Mouzalon's and Palaiologos' speeches, reminds us of the discursive practices shared among educated Romans. The *protovestiarios*' speech was not taken at face value by the senators present at the meeting, but rather it was appreciated for the rhetorical techniques that the educated elites could see deployed within the oration. In the same vein, Michael's laudatory speech was perceived by Georgios Mouzalon as a nicely crafted piece of rhetoric with far greater goals in mind than a simple appraisal of the regent. On the example of these two orations, we see how the elites were able to differentiate themselves from the rest of the society thanks to their exquisite education. That is, through ostentatious displays of their erudition, the notables—be it the members of the *golden chain* or the *novi homines*—were able to establish a communication nebula that was fully understandable and accessible only to them.[64] Those, on the other hand, who did not have the same educational background could never appreciate the intricacies of fine speech and would thus not be able to imagine themselves taking an active role in running the state. Regardless of Pachymeres' level of accuracy in the transmission of the speech's content, these pieces of rhetoric had a twofold goal. First, they established the orators themselves as members of the senatorial echelons on account of their education and merit. This point was important to *novi homines* who had to keep demonstrating their merit through word and acts of the pen or the sword. It was, however, equally significant for the members of the old families, who had to prove that individually there was more to their name than their ancestral surnames. It is in part for this reason that Mouzalon and Palaiologos found it necessary to deliver the respective speeches. Second, the speeches were supposed to persuade the group of commoners, represented by the soldiers stationed at Magnesia, that the regency should remain in the hands of Mouzalones. In crafting their speeches, the two senators then had to use the language and forms of expression that resonated well with the wider, less erudite, audience. Of course, the loud and emphatic pronunciation

---

[64] On the elite Romans' sense of being unique and, arguably, better than those who are not part of the group see: P. Magdalino, "Byzantine Snobbery," in *The Byzantine Aristocracy, IX to XIII Centuries* (Oxford: Oxford University Press 1984), 58–78.

of the speeches helped to sway over the soldiers, who in turn showed their support.[65] Aristocratic virtue signalling notwithstanding, the two speeches also served as a political bridge between senatorial expectations and those of the Roman citizenry at large.

After this mixed session of the senatorial and military establishments adjourned, the Mouzalones had retained their position, albeit after some initial commotion among the senators. Returning to the imperial palace in Magnesia, the regents were quick to notify the wider public of the affairs of the state. As Pachymeres lets us know:

> At this time, *prostagmata* were composed and dispatched all over the cities of the Roman Empire and, among other appropriate news, the principal and the greatest news was to announce the death of the emperor [Theodoros II], and to proclaim the young emperor [Ioannes IV], and to make each person swear the customary oaths of allegiance to him. The decrees were sent out in great numbers, and since the young emperor could not move his hand to sign them, they entrusted the aforementioned *logothetes ton aggelon* to make the imperial signature in red ink.[66]

Sending out imperial notifications—*prostagmata*—around the empire was the fastest way of informing as large a number of the populace as possible about the latest events. This move was supposed to secure a wider level of support for the new regime among the people of the Roman Empire. Making sure that the Romans were aware and hopefully supportive of the regime was particularly necessary at a time when both the emperor and his retinue were not seen with kind eyes by the imperial elites. In the end, securing one stable pillar of societal support was better than none. Furthermore, according to the dispatched *prostagama*, all the notables of the provincial administration had to swear a customary oath of allegiance to the new emperor. In this way, the Mouzalones relied on traditional

---

[65] On tactics for stirring up emotions in public performance see: Rabe, *Hermogenis Opera*, 1.10.

[66] Συνετάττοντο τοίνυν προστάγματα πανταχοῦ πόλεων τῆς Ῥωμαίων γῆς ἀποσταλησόμενα, καὶ κατ' ἄλλας μὲν χρείας ἑτέρας, τὸ δὲ πλεῖστον καὶ μέγιστον κατά τε δήλωσιν τοῦ θανάτου τοῦ βασιλέως, ἅμα δὲ καὶ τῆς τοῦ νέου βασιλέως ἀναρρήσεως, καὶ τοῦ εἰς ἐκεῖνον προστίθεσθαι χάριν συνθήκαις ὅρκων κατὰ τὸ σύνηθες. Καὶ ἐξετίθεντο μὲν τὰ προστατόμενα παμπληθεί, τὰς δὲ δι' ἐρυθρῶν βασιλικὰς ὑποσημάνσεις, ἐπεὶ οὐκ ἦν τὸν νέον βασιλέα χεῖρα κινεῖν καὶ ὑποσημαίνεσθαι, τῷ δηλωθέντι λογοθέτῃ τῶν ἀγελῶν ποιεῖν ἐνεδίδοσαν. (Pachymeres, *Chronikon*, 77.32–79.8).

methods of obtaining publicly acclaimed support by making everybody across the cities of the empire swear oaths of allegiance to the new regime. Thus, the public was involved in the affairs of the polity by means of newly sworn oaths in the empires' provincial centres. The public oath-swearing of the officials from around the empire, following the reception and reading of the *prostagma*, granted legitimacy to the new regime in the eyes of the empire's subjects and allowed for a more favourable view of the new regime. Hoping to reach a consensus among the senatorial elite and anticipating that the Roman populace would be more inclined to support the regency once the *prostagmata* reached their destinations and oaths had been taken, Georgios and his brothers could now focus on running the state.

5.3 The Violent Side of Public Deliberations: Obtaining Public Support for the Palaiologan Regency

The *prostagmata* sent out from Magnesia had not yet reached all the provincial magistrates by the time the volatile cohabitation between the Mouzalones and the other aristocrats came to an abrupt end. The agreements made at the meeting of the senate and the army lasted for about a week.[67] The regime was toppled at the memorial service for Theodoros II at the monastery of Sosandra, where a not insignificant number of lay people, soldiers, bureaucrats, and senators with their families gathered, together with the regents and Ioannes IV, to commemorate the deceased emperor. The event at Sosandra has come down to us in two versions: one by Akropolites and another by Pachymeres.[68] Both of them have a similar outline with Pachymeres providing a far more detailed narrative about the events, while Akropolites cites specific names of participants in the commemoration.

What took place at Sosandra was a riot which unfolded in the following fashion. The monastery at Sosandra was on top of a hill in the vicinity of Magnesia. During the commemoration, Ioannes IV, the Mouzalones, and

---

[67] Akropolites (*Chronike*, 75.11–2) says three days, Pachymeres (*Chronikon*, 81.5) say nine; Gregoras (*Historia* I, 65.15) concurs with the latter. Failler, "Chrolonolgie," 26–27; Macrides, *The History*, 341, n.4.

[68] Akropolites, *Chronike*, 75; Pachymeres, *Chronikon*, 79.11–89.26.

the senators with their families were on top of the hill in the monastery; the people together with the soldiers congregated at the bottom of the hill and observed the ceremony from a distance.[69] As the ceremony was unfolding, the soldiers, especially the Latin contingents which had been under Michael Palaiologos' command, dispersed among the public in order to start a commotion of the masses—the Roman body politic. Pachymeres remains careful in passing any judgement about Michael's or other senators' involvement in staging the rebellion. He does, however, point out that it was the Latin soldiers, usually connected to Palaiologos in his narrative, who started the rebellion.[70] Akropolites' account is not of much help, since it represents Michael and his allies as complete victims of chance. Be that as it may, whether the senators had secretly blessed or even pushed the soldiers to infiltrate the crowds gathered around Sosandra remains less important for our story than the fact that the Mouzalones were not able to change society's mood to their favour. The inability to sway the public their way led to the loss of public support for the regime in less than a week after the oath-swearing ceremony discussed above.

The reason behind the Mouzalones' rather brief tenure in the high offices lies in their failure to cultivate wider social networks around the empire. The three brothers—Georgios, Andronikos, and Theodoros—spent the years of their education and political maturity as *paidopouloi* of Theodoros II. While the close relationship with the designated heir to the throne turned emperor put the Mouzalones into an advantageous position vis-à-vis other notables while their patron was alive, once the emperor was gone, this very connection became their Achilles' heel. It is precisely because of their close ties with the emperor that the Mouzalones did not find it necessary to promote themselves to anybody else in the empire. This turned out to be a fatal miscalculation on their part that would doom their *oikos*. During Theodoros II's concerted campaign to dilute the power of the old senatorial elite, the Mouzalones amassed honours, influence, and ultimately power, which, in turn, alienated them from the persecuted senatorial elite. Unlike some other *novi homines* who were more prudent in their acceptance of imperially granted honours at the

---

[69] For the most likely location of the monastery of Sosandra as well as the hilly terrain around it see: E. Mitsiou, "The Monastery of Sosandra: A Contribution to Its History, Dedication, and Localisation," *Bulgaria mediaevalis* 2 (2011), 665–683.

[70] Pachymeres, *Chronikon*, 79.18–24; 81.9–21.

expense of other members of the elites, the Mouzalones made no effort to tamper the skyrocketing of their careers.[71] The moment Theodoros II was out of the picture, the animosity of the senatorial elite was openly directed towards them. Since the emperor had only attempted to weaken the *golden chain* families rather than break them, their households were quick to consolidate power after the emperor's premature death, putting the integration of new *gene* into the *golden chain* to a definite halt.

While making enemies in the highest echelons of the Roman court was somewhat inevitable for the exclusively imperially supported Mouzalones, they more crucially failed to venture into the arena of wider public discourse. They thus failed to endear themselves to the Roman populace—be it the soldiers or the civilians. When Theodoros II was no more, the Mouzalones would have benefitted from having cultivated the Roman citizenry of Magnesia and other cities in Asia Minor. Unfortunately for the three brothers, they had accumulated little social credit with the masses of the empire. To the contrary, if we are to trust both Akropolites, who has a particularly negative view of the Mouzalones, and Pachymeres, who is far more restrained in criticizing the brothers, we see that during Theodoros II's tenure Georgios and his two siblings managed to estrange the soldiers and other citizenry of the polity. For one, the populace in general was never fond of the Mouzalones who were blamed, both during Theodoros II's life and later, for having conspired to make the emperor sick.[72] Adding to this, popular gossip in the streets suggested that:

> [the Italian soldiers] were deprived by the Mouzalones, especially the elder one, while the emperor was alive, of the assigned remunerations (*rogai*). They had been despised instead of being given their due honours. Under his instructions, they were forbidden their free access to the emperor. They had thus been humiliated by order of the *protovestiarios*.[73]

---

[71] For instance, *protovestiarios* Ioannes Axouch declined to appropriate the belongings of Ioannes II Komnenos' estranged sister Anna (Choniates, *O City of Byzantium*, 8–9).

[72] Pachymeres, *Chronikon*, 53.24–26; 79.14–16.

[73] ὡς παρὰ Μουζαλώνων, καὶ μᾶλλον ἑνὸς τοῦ πρώτου, στεροῖντο, ζῶντος βασιλέως, τῶν εἰς ῥόγας αὐτοῖς ἀποτεταγμένων, ὡς καταφρονοῖντο ἐφ' οἷς ἐδικαίουν ἑαυτοὺς τετιμῆσθαι, ὡς τῆς πρὸς τὸν βασιλέα ἀποκλείοιντο παρρησίας εἰσηγήσεσι ταῖς ἐκείνου, ὡς ἀτιμοῖντο, τοῦ πρωτοβεστιαρίου προστάσσοντος. (Pachymeres, *Chronikon*, 79.20–24).

Such actions—whether real or perceived—made it impossible for the Mouzalones to find allies among the general Roman populace. To their disadvantage, members of the *golden chain* carefully cultivated their public image and were more deliberate in rewarding soldiers under their command with due honours and weaving a visible mark of their respective families into the social fabric of the Roman polity. After all, Michael's endeavours in Thessaloniki to commemorate the *genos* of the Palaiologoi were not unique as an example of a noble attempting to imprint positive images of an affluent household in the public memory. Such strategies aimed at securing public sympathies were no doubt also deployed by other members of the golden chain. Thus, when the time came for the public to take an active role, it was pretty clear it was going to support those members of the Roman elite who had invested in the careful cultivation of popular favour.

The attempt made to appease the senators and the Roman public by deploying rhetorical craftiness was certainly a useful tactic; however, Georgios appears to have come to the public sphere a bit too late in the game. In such circumstances, older allies would have been welcomed, but the three brothers had nobody by their side who would willingly and unconditionally support them. By making their political careers completely dependent on the emperor, the Mouzalones, ironically enough, followed the model that worked for Roman officials in the Sultanate of Rum where personal connections to the sultan almost always guaranteed promotion and stability.[74] In the political culture of the Roman Empire being an imperial favourite was a powerful political tool to be sure. Imperial support, however, was not enough. It had to be combined with the cultivation of social strategies of engagement with other magnates through kinship, tutelage, and amicable relationships. It also required careful courting of Roman citizens via public displays of public care and benevolence.[75] On its own imperial favour could hardly come in handy

---

[74] For governing practices in the Saljuq Sultanate of Rum see: Korobeinikov, *Byzantium and the Turks*, 81–110.

[75] For the regime's loss of public support see: A. Kaldellis, "How to Usurp the Throne in Byzantium: The Role of Public Opinion in Sedition and Rebellion," in *Power and Subversion in Byzantium: Papers from the Forty-Third Spring Symposium of Byzantine Studies, University of Birmingham, March 2010*, D. G. Angelov—M. Saxby (eds.), (Farnham, UK, and Burlington, VT: Ashgate, 2013, 43–56); For *paidopouloi* in Theodoros II's administration and their exclusive ties with the emperor see: Angold, *A Byzantine Government*, 76, 176–177.

once the emperor was gone and the favourites were left on their own to defend their position in the public political arena.

At Sosandra, Mouzalones experienced quite viscerally what it meant not to be in the public's good books. The commotion started during the commemoration, when the soldiers in the crowds at the bottom of the hill demanded to see the emperor. In referring to their young master, they spoke of him as the captive of his father's murderers, i.e. the Mouzalones. The crowd was quick to join in with the soldiers since in the court of public opinion the Mouzalones had already been judged and condemned for the previous emperor's death. The negative social climate towards the Mouzalones was amplified by the fact that Theodoros II, much as his father Ioannes III, was remembered as a good emperor of the people. Thanks to the public memory of the two emperors, the masses gathered at Sosandra saw in Ioannes IV an emperor who would continue the tradition of his forefathers. Since the people did not wish to see Ioannes IV harmed by the murderous brothers, they demanded to see the young emperor. The elites gathered around the young emperor had to comply and Ioannes IV waved at his subjects from the top of the hill. The young emperor was also asked to give the sign to the masses to leave. The sign that the emperor gave, however, was interpreted in two ways, or as Pachymeres' own words tell us:

> When the youth [Ioannes IV] appeared, the voices grew louder, and the [soldiers] caused commotion in an very disorderly fashion. Those in his retinue instructed him to make a gesture with his hand. This gesture could do one of two things: restrain the commotion or approve it. To those around the young master the assenting gesture of the hand was seen as a sufficient sign for the lords to defend them and bring the rioting under control; the rest, however, took it as an encouragement to go ahead. A shout arose, that the emperor approved, and at once the crowd rushed forward, and everybody moved as if to defend the emperor, ready to expose themselves to danger.[76]

[76] Ὡς δὲ φανέντος τοῦ νέου, καὶ μείζων ἤρετο ἡ φωνὴ καὶ ἀτακτότερον ἐθορύβουν, χειρὶ κατανεύειν οἱ ἀμφ' ἐκεῖνον ἐκεῖνον διδάσκουσι· τὸ δ' ἦν ἅμα κροῦον καὶ πρὸς ἀμφότερα, ὅτι τε ἀναστέλλοι τὸν θόρυβον καὶ ὅτι ἐκχωροίη διδούς. Καὶ τοῖς μὲν περὶ τὸν νέον ἄρχοντα ἱκανὸν εἰς ἀπολογίαν ἐσύστερον πρὸς τοὺς ἄρχοντας ἡ τῆς χειρὸς κατάνευσις ὑπολέλειπτο, ὡς δῆθεν ἐπισχεῖν οἰκονομοῦσι τὸν θόρυβον, τοῖς δὲ καὶ λίαν ἀρκοῦν ἐνομίζετο πρὸς ἐκχώρησιν. Εὐθὺς οὖν βοὴ ἤρθη, ὡς ἐκχωροῦντος τοῦ βασιλέως, καὶ ἅμ' ἐχέοντο παμπληθεί, καὶ ὡς τιμωρὸς τῆς βασιλικῆς σωτηρίας συνέθεεν ἕκαστος, ὡς καὶ προκινδυνεύσειν. (Pachymeres, *Chronikon*, 81.29–83.8).

By using the young emperor as bait, the soldiers in the crowd, possibly with the assent of the senators, attacked the monastery and the regime was brutally toppled. The Mouzalones tried to hide around the monastery, but to no avail: they were found and killed *ek topou* by the enraged soldiers and citizens. The regency came to an end even before it had properly begun at the hands of the Roman citizens. It was thus through employment of violence that the less privileged stratum of the Romans expressed their collective opinion regarding the regime in charge of public affairs. The end of the Mouzalones, then, was brought about by their own inability to change the negative disposition of the people towards them, which, in turn, resulted in the people's bloody expression of their legitimate will.

5.4 Social Capital and Public Deliberations: Michael Palaiologos, Guardian of the Empire

With the Mouzalones and their associates out of the picture—some of whom following the Roman tradition fled to the Sultanate of Rum, while others found themselves imprisoned[77]—the management of state affairs fell completely into the hands of the senatorial elite. Of the senators, Michael Palaiologos was the swiftest to seize the role of Ioannes IV's protector. Granted, during the riot at Sosandra, Michael was best positioned among the senators to take control of the situation since most of the armed soldiers who instigated the coup d'état were Latin soldiers under his command. With the consensus of the soldiers present at the event by his side, Michael managed to offer protection to the young emperor, whose immediate retinue had no choice but to accept.

Being in control of the situation by relying on sheer force during the riot was one thing; maintaining the position of power in the long run was a completely different matter, as Michael was very well aware. With Ioannes IV under Palaiologan guard—Michael put his own two brothers, Ioannes and Konstantinos, in charge of the emperor's safety—the members of the *golden chain* started to quarrel over the issue of guardianship. According to Pachymeres, the senators gathered yet again to decide on the regent for the young emperor. All the leading *oikoi* were present promoting their own candidates

---

[77] Akropolites, *Chronike*, 77.14–34; Pachymeres, *Chronikon*, 89.29–91.9.

for the regency: Laskarides, Tornikioi, Strategopouloi, Philai, Batazai, Nostongoi, Kaballarioi, Kamytzai, Aprenoi, Anggeloi, Kantakouzinoi, Libadarioi, Tarchaneiotai, Philanthropenoi, and the Palaiologoi.[78] During the deliberation process which lasted for days, the senators sent for the patriarch at Nikaia, asking him to join them at Magnesia, as Pachymeres tells us, "not so much out of necessity, but to confirm more surely the action that was being taken."[79]

At the meeting of the senate, Georgios Nostongos put forward his own candidacy for the regency but was quickly shut down by other officials and dignitaries.[80] Other senators had their own prospective candidates; not before long, though, after a few speeches and arguments, Michael Palaiologos was elected regent for Ioannes IV. Pachymeres justifies this election by pointing out that:

> [Michael Palaiologos] is a most excellent general, his nobility is of old and sovereign, and thirdly, he is himself related to the emperor, both on his own and through his wife—[the emperor] was her second cousin and the son of his second cousin—thus it was normal for him, above the rest, to be given the guardianship over the emperor. These were the reasons he was preferred over others, and those who spoke in his favour promoted these. On the other hand, it is normal to think that he himself had orchestrated the affair, deceiving many men with good promises, especially those who happened to have lost positions of rank because of the harshness of the times.[81]

Thus, Michael prevailed thanks to his own accomplishments. The illustrious family background and sanguine connection to the emperor further helped his case of entrusting Ioannes IV in Michael Palaiologos' hands, as

---

[78] Pachymeres, *Chronikon*, 91.18–93.15.

[79] οὐ κατὰ χρείαν μᾶλλον, ἀλλ' ἵν' ἀσφαλέστερον τὸ γινόμενον καθιστῷτο. (ibid., 97.7–8).

[80] ibid., 95.1–12.

[81] Στρατηγικώτατον εἶναι τὸν ἄνδρα, καί οἱ ἐκ παλαιοῦ αὔταρκες εἶναι τὸ εὐγενές, καὶ τρίτον τὸ πρὸς τὸν κρατοῦντα συγγενές, ἅμα μὲν αὐτόθεν, ἅμα δὲ καὶ ἐκ τῆς συζύγου—τῆς μὲν γὰρ δεύτερος αὐτανέψιος ἦν, τοῦ δὲ δευτέρου αὐτανεψίου υἱός—, πολλὴν ἐμποιεῖν αὐτῷ τὴν εἰς τὸ κηδεμονικὸν τοῦ βασιλέως παρὰ τοὺς ἄλλους ἐκχώρησιν. Ἀλλὰ τὰ μὲν ἐκείνου πρὸς τὸ προτιμᾶσθαι τῶν ἄλλων δίκαια ταῦτ' ἦσαν, καὶ ὁ ὑπὲρ ἐκείνου λέγων ταῦτα προὐβάλλετο. Παρέχει δὲ καὶ τὸ εἰκὸς ἐννοεῖν ὡς κἀκεῖνος τὸ πρᾶγμα μετεχειρίζετο, οὐκ ὀλίγους κλέπτων ταῖς ἀγαθαῖς ὑποσχέσεσι, καὶ μᾶλλον οἷς ἐκπεσεῖν τῶν ἀξιωμάτων ξυνέβη ἐκ τῆς τοῦ καιροῦ δυσκολίας τὸ πρότερον. (ibid., 95.22–97.2).

his supporters emphasize. At a time when the Mongols were pushing the Turkic nomads to the Western borders of the Sultanate of Rum and an open Epeirote invasion west of Vardar was taking place, Michael Palaiologos, thanks to his military experience, became an obvious choice for the regency.[82] On top of his military prudence, Michael had experience in dealing with civil administration as confirmed by his tenure in Serres and Melenikon. All these accomplishments certainly made him a desirable candidate, but many other members of the *golden chain* families' careers followed a similar trajectory. What made Michael a particularly strong candidate, save his clear merit in public service, was the network of supporters he had carefully amassed over the course of his career among elites and commoners alike. Unlike Georgios Mouzalon, who relied solely on imperial favour in his career, Michael mobilized every possible social resource to gain support from socially diverse Romans: he used the well-known surname Palaiologos to boost his image; he connected himself to the imperial household through marriage; he strengthened the existing ties with the traditional allies of the Palaiologoi; he built new bridges with *novi homines* and intellectuals of the period; and finally, he successfully projected a positive image of his public persona to the public, thus swaying the social climate in his favour.

The only source of support Michael lacked was that of the church and its patriarch Arsenios Autoreianos. The incumbent patriarch was hand-picked by Theodoros II, to whom he had been a close associate.[83] Thus, winning over the patriarch in his power takeover was the last ingredient Michael needed to completely secure his position as the legitimate guardian of Ioannes IV. Much to the ecclesiastic circles' surprise, though, by the time the patriarch reached Magnesia, he found Michael Palaiologos not just a designated regent to Ioannes IV but a *megas doux*. In awaiting Arsenios' arrival, the senators had conferred, with the young emperor's politically unconscious consent, the dignity of *megas doux* to Michael Palaiologos, who held the office of *megas konostaulos* so that his title would befit the high position in the imperial service he now occupied.[84]

---

[82] Akropolites, 76.1–32.

[83] For the election of Arsenios Autoreianos see: Blemmydes, Akropolites, Pachymeres.

[84] For the dignity of *megas doux* see: Guilland, *Institutions* I, 542–551; Macrides, Munitiz, and Angelov, *Pseudo-Kodinos*, 276–278. Pachymeres (*Relations* II, 525.7–11) refers to the title of *megas doux* as dignity and not office; after the death of Michael VIII Palaiologos *megas doux* was demoted to an office (*Pseudo-Kodinos*, 276).

With the promotion from *megas konostaulos* to *megas doux*, Michael was elevated to a status similar to that of *protovestiarios* Georgios Mouzalon. In doing so, the senators supporting the Palaiologoi made Michael far less likely to answer for his deeds to the senate. As a *megas doux* and a regent, Michael was put above many other officials, even as his proximity to the emperor was now ceremonially justified. Other than nominal and ceremonial advantages the dignity of *megas doux* brought with it, Michael also gained access to the imperial treasurers. These he used judiciously, directing money from the treasury toward those who were in alleged need of it. Pachymeres simply states that "through these means [Palaiologos] created the foundations of his popularity amongst those who would not forget his goodwill."[85] The recipients of the coins from the treasury remain unknown. Since, however, the magnates were more concerned with tax exemptions and the turning of their *pronoiai*,[86] it is conceivable that the money taken from the treasury was used to buy the goodwill of the people in the streets through donations to charitable foundations and the organizing of public events around festivities for the masses. Save the public, the patriarch seems to have been no less susceptible to Michael's monetary charms. Upon the ecclesiastic delegation's arrival in Magnesia, Michael treated Arsenios and the leading metropolitans with the utmost respect and did not spare any money in making the church prelates' stay at the court comfortable. Furthermore, Michael made sure to show the archons of the church that he respected them by granting Arsenios uninterrupted access to the young emperor. The efforts paid off for the regent since the patriarch with other prelates accepted Michael's new position.[87] The one piece in the political puzzle Michael did not seem to control now appeared amenable to Palaiologan charm.

Once Michael had the leading churchmen on his side, yet another meeting followed, this time a joint session of the senators and the prelates. At the meeting, the magnates supporting Michael were quick to follow Michael's recent elevation to the dignity of *megas doux* with a rather bold suggestion of granting Michael further honours by naming him *basileopator* and promoting him to the rank of *despotes*, the highest dignity

---

[85] Κἀντεῦθεν ἀρχὰς ἑαυτῷ εὐμενείας προὐκατεβάλλετο, οἷς οὐκ ἦν τῆς εὐεργεσίας ἐπιλελῆσθαι. (Pachymeres, *Chronikon*, 101.25–103.1.

[86] ibid., 131.18–21; 139.6.

[87] ibid., 103.18–105.18.

available for any Roman save the emperor.[88] Michael and his supporters saw these further promotions as just compensation for the toils and labours Michael had undertaken on everybody's behalf. While these new honours were eventually bestowed on Michael, consensus was not reached immediately. Rather, Georgios Nestongos together with the Laskarides objected to the proposal.[89] The split among the senators was marked by an intense debate buttressed by rhetorical craftiness on both sides. In the end, the opposition to Michael's promotion was outvoted and the *megas doux* was elevated to the dignity of *despotes*.

In just a few months since Theodoros II's death and Michael's release from prison in August 1258, Palaiologos managed to mobilize enough support to occupy the highest positions in the Roman state.[90] Yet, as this episode reminds us, Michael's swift promotion within months was not applauded by everybody and there was significant opposition he had to deal with among the senatorial elites. The opposition, this time around, was expressed through political debate within the confines of the palace. Words were used instead of swords and, in the end, the pro-Palaiologan current prevailed thanks to their ability to keep the consensus on their side; needless to say, Michael's personal promises and the grants given to his allies surely aided the cause. Be that as it may, through coercion and promises, Michael was crowned *despotes* by Ioannes IV with the help of Arsenios, whose support demonstrated that the Palaiologoi had managed to win over the sympathies of the church as much as those of the state officials. Furthermore, Michael's title of *despotes* was universally acclaimed by the people; that is, those Romans and foreigners manning the empire's armies. Shortly after the meeting of the senate and the ecclesiastic heads, both Roman and non-Roman soldiers were asked whether they wished to see Michael on the throne and, according to Akropolites at least, everybody joyfully assented.[91] The public acclamation was the last thing

---

[88] For *despotes* see: Guilland, *Institutions* II, 1–24. For the title of *basileopator* in general and for its connection to tutelage and protection of a young emperor see: A. Leroy-Molinghen – P. Karlin-Hayter, "Basileopator," *Byzantion* 38 (1968), 278–281, especially 279; S. Tougher, *The Reign of Leo VI (886–912): Politics and People* (Leiden – New York: Brill 1997), 98–101.

[89] Pachymeres, *Chronikon*, 107.12–16.

[90] For the chronology of events from Theodoros II's death to Michael's elevation to *despotes* see: Macrides, *The History*, 348.n.1.

[91] Akropolites, 76.37–49.

necessary for Michael to fully legitimize his new position. By receiving no backlash from the public, a somewhat unpredictable judge, Michael could be proud of his endeavours in winning and maintaining public support despite the many fallouts he had with previous emperors and their dignitaries. With the soldiers' loud acclamation of him as *despotes*, the news of the latest elevation could spread smoothly around Magnesia and from there to other cities of the empire. It was in such circumstances that, after an initially bloody revolution, Michael Palaiologos succeeded in mobilizing enough public support—both lay and ecclesiastic, elite and common—in order to seize control of the imperial administration.

5.5 The Final Countdown: Michael Palaiologos Goes for the Throne

Even though his rise from *megas konostaulos* in disfavour to the *despotes* cum *basileopator* was swift, Michael was very cautious in crafting his public persona. In order to justify his rapid promotion, he had to rely on seemingly legal procedures that stemmed from reaching a public consensus in the senate, the church, and the armies.[92] Thus, from August to December 1258, Michael had to carefully negotiate with these three powerbrokers, who had different expectations from him in return for their support. An element that was particularly useful for Michael's maintenance of support was the wellbeing of the young emperor. Thus, Ioannes IV, offshoot of the line of Theodoros II and Ioannes III—two highly beloved monarchs among the people and the armies—served as a perfect shield for Palaiologos. Michael projected to the public the image of himself as a mere protector of the infant emperor, who needed capable guidance in order to grow up into an individual worthy of the imperial dignity and his ancestors' legacy.

While the young emperor's wellbeing kept the elites aligned with the public climate, Michael had to exercise far more caution with the senators, who, thanks to their own education, experience, and ambition were able to perfectly understand Palaiologos' political manoeuvres. The key to Michael's success in securing senatorial and ecclesiastic support for his cause rested with his incremental and careful political ascent.

---

[92] For the legality of the consensus in Byzantine political theory see: Kaldellis, *The Byzantine Republic*, 89–117.

During each step of his rise to power that involved senatorial discussion—from the murder of Mouzalones to his elevation to the dignity *despotes* and *basileopator*—Michael gained advantage over potential opponents by being able to discern in the debate that took place in the senate which senators were his allies and which were more reluctant to join the majority. Knowing who his opponents were, Michael, now a regent, could work on weakening their influence. In this endeavour, he had to be very cautious since most of his senatorial opponents were related to his supporters', or even his own, family.[93] For instance, Manouel Laskaris became an ardent opponent of Michael's rise, while his brother, Michael Laskaris, supported the Palaiologan agenda.[94] The tight familial links among the senators, to which Michael himself was not immune, ensured that the regent was not simply able to get rid of all his enemies. Rather, he had to find the least painful way to remove them from the court. In the case of the Laskarid brothers, then, he sent Manouel to Prousa where his proximity to the imperial centre ensured that any attempt at dissidence could not pass unnoticed.[95] Being sent to Prousa, on the other hand, meant that a loud opponent was far away from influencing the senate meetings with anti-Palaiologan speeches. While he managed to remove his opponents from the senate, many of whom willingly left the court in which they found themselves in the minority, Michael proceeded to the next step of strengthening his position in the senate: he promoted his allies to honours that would allow them access to the senate. Thus, Michael's brother Ioannes was honoured with the office of *megas domestikos* without having held any office or dignity in the past.[96] Upon being invested in his office, Ioannes Palaiologos was immediately dispatched together with Alexios Sarantopoulos and Ioannes Rhaoul—Michael's associates since his early days in the imperial service—to fight the Epeirote-led alliance against the empire.[97] By putting his brother in command of the armies, Michael ensured that the troops remained under his own men's command. In this fashion, any chance of instigating an open rebellion against the new

---

[93] For the prosopography and marriages of the Palaiologoi see: Cheynet et Vannier, *Études prosopographiques*, 129–183.

[94] For Manouel Laskaris see: *PLP* 14,551; for Michael Laskaris see: *PLP* 14,554.

[95] Pachymeres, *Chronikon*, 131.20–21.

[96] Akropolites, *Chronike*, 77.35–38.

[97] ibid., 77.38–43.

regime was reduced to a minimum. Furthermore, having a Palaiologos in charge of the armies meant Michael was able to continue promoting his *genos* in the Nikaian-dominated Balkans, in an effort to build a support base that would rival that of the Laskarides in Asia Minor.[98] Familial politics notwithstanding, other members of the Palaiologan alliance were also promoted to higher office, ensuring the *golden chain*'s loyalty to Michael.[99]

Having methodically and in stages cleansed the immediate senatorial elites of his opponents, Michael was left with his core supporters in the capital to deliberate on the affairs of the Roman state. It is at this point, as Pachymeres tells us, that Michael started lobbying for his elevation to the rank of co-emperor to Ioannes IV.[100] In the meetings of the senate, where the issue was first broached and approved before it would be taken for public approval by the army, pro-Palaiologan supporters made their case for Michael's elevation to the throne, using traditional political virtues associated with good emperors in their rhetoric:

> the best to rule is the one who comes through virtue and by proving that he is the best [to rule]. This benefits the populace since those who are appointed to rule accept the reason for which they have been elected. Just as we do not choose the doctor capable of rendering health from illness on the basis of fortune or birth, so too if we chose the one to govern on the basis of birth, then we have placed a pirate, rather than a captain, in charge of the ship. And the one who needs to be pure and well educated, so that he may rule well, is in danger of being very impure, since from his birth he is surrounded with imperial luxuries and soft living, and flattery settles in, while the truth is banished, and the worst things are presented as the best.[101]

---

[98] For the importance of generals consciously building their base of support with the armies and civilians see: Krallis, "Urbane Warriors," 154–168.

[99] Macrides, *The History*, 350.n.10.

[100] Pachymeres, *Chronikon*, 113.7–12.

[101] τὴν ἐξ ἀρετῆς καὶ δοκιμασίας ἀρίστης ὧν ἄρχειν μέλλει. Αὕτη γὰρ καὶ λυσιτελὴς τοῖς πλήθεσιν, ἐνδόντων τῶν εἰς ἀρχὴν καταστάντων ἐπὶ τίνι καὶ προσεκλήθησαν. Ἰατρὸν γὰρ οὔτε τὸν ἐκ τύχης οὔτε τὸν ἐκ γένους εἰς τὸ ποιεῖν ὑγείαν τοῖς νοσοῦσιν ἀξιόχρεων εἴποιμεν· καὶ εἰ ἐκ γένους τὸν κυβερνήσοντα ἐγκρινοῦμεν, καταποντιστὴν μᾶλλον ἢ κυβερνήτην ἐπιστήσομεν τῇ νηΐ. Κινδυνεύειν δ᾽ οὕτως καὶ τὸν μᾶλλον καθάρσεως, εἶτ᾽ οὖν παιδεύσεως, εἰς τὸ καλῶς βασιλεύειν δεόμενον ἀκάθαρτον εἶναι μάλιστα, ἅμα γεννηθέντα καὶ ἅμα τρυφαῖς καὶ σπατάλαις παραληφθέντα βασιλικαῖς, ἐφεδρευούσης τε κολακείας, ἐκποδῶν δ᾽ οὔσης ἀληθείας καὶ τῶν κακίστων ὡς καλλίστων ὑποκοριζομένων. (Pachymeres, *Chronikon*, 129.12–21).

By employing traditional Roman ideas of merit-based arguments to legally justify Michael's elevation to the imperial office, the pro-Palaiologan party in the senate managed to sway the remaining senators, who were all more or less prone to support the Palaiologan takeover.[102] Each of the virtues necessary for one to be justly elected emperor was promoted in antithesis to the alternative: merit vs. birth, education and experience vs. imperial luxury and softness of character. By pointing out the antithetic pairs of virtues and vices, the senatorial rhetoricians left only one possible path to benefitting the state: granting co-emperorship to Palaiologos. Anybody who voted against such a motion would be voting against the public good.

Pointing out the qualities required for proper rule, the senators supporting Palaiologos indirectly made an implicit comparison between Michael—the educated commendable state official—and young Ioannes IV—inexperienced *porphyrogennetos* who owed his position to his birth alone. By offering a veiled criticism of the incumbent emperor, the senators, speaking in support of Palaiologos, were further able to emphasize the necessity of Michael's imperial elevation since the reins of the state were in the hands of an inexperienced, even incapable, ruler. In the emerging rhetorical image, it appeared that the young emperor's faults could be rectified through Palaiologos' experienced guidance. Finally, such rhetoric of contrasting merit, embodied in Michael, and birth, represented by Ioannes IV, served another, more sinister, purpose. With the majority of the senators, both at home and in charge of the imperial troops in the Balkans, supporting Michael, the discreet juxtaposition of Michael and Ioannes IV could be easily understood as a threat to the young Laskaris' emperorship. Thus, to friends of Ioannes IV the message was clear: concede to Michael Palaiologos' demands, or the child-emperor would not be unharmed.

Having swayed the senators to support his election as co-emperor—through gifts, coercion, or removal from the court—Michael had to make his case before the church prelates if he wished to continue with the

---

[102] On traditional imperial virtues see: Menander Rhetor, *A Commentary*, D.A. Russel – N.G. Wilson (transl. and eds.) (Oxford: Oxford University Press 1981), 372.2–376.23; for imperial virtues in the Laskarid and early Palaiologan times that include piety, generosity, philanthropy, compassion, and gentleness see: Angelov, *Imperial Ideology*, 84–85. Also, see Leon VI's *Taktika*, in which the author makes a case for skill and personal worth in becoming a successful general: *The Taktika of Leo VI*, 16–36.

process. While neither the patriarch nor the metropolitans had to agree on his candidacy, Michael knew that he would need the patriarch to ceremonially crown him in front of the Roman citizens who would then publicly acclaim his elevation to the imperial office. Assuming imperial office with the blessings of the patriarch, a spiritual partisan of Theodoros II, Michael could be more certain to fully gain the needed public support even from the populace of Asia Minor whose sentiments were generally pro-Laskarid.[103] The Palaiologoi had managed to root their public support network in the Balkans, where the imperial imprint was smaller, if present at all. In Asia Minor, however, the Laskarid public imagery ruled supreme. While, however, senators could be convinced, bought, and, when necessary, removed and then replaced with Palaiologan men, Michael exercised no such power nor connections within the ecclesiastic circles.[104] If lack of public and senatorial support was the Achilles' heel of the Mouzalones, lack of ecclesiastic connections was Michael's weak spot. He therefore had to convince the church representatives and the patriarch himself to support him through less coercive methods, not least of all the patriarch himself. Arsenios Autoreianos was, alas, a particularly difficult nut to crack since, in public, he posed as the spiritual guardian of Ioannes IV and a close associate of the Laskarid *oikos*.[105] Thus, Michael's co-emperorship would infringe on Arsenios' own public image as protector of the young emperor. In order to keep the balance between his own position and that of the patriarch in the public eye, Michael opted to win over the church prelates by bribing them and making promises to grant a more elevated position to the church in state affairs. Entering negotiations with the patriarch, Michael was willing to renounce some of his own prerogatives in order to win over the prelates and the patriarch.[106] In his promises, Michael made sure to portray himself as an ideal pious Christian ruler who would obey his administrators and advisors, with special regard to the prelates. Other than respecting the decisions of the church above all, Michael also referred to actions that would benefit the masses—turning

---

[103] For pro-Laskarid sentiment in Asia Minor: Skoutariotes, *Synopsis Chronike*, 505.22–31, 506.19–507.6. 535.26–536.4; Pachymeres, *Chronikon*, 57.32–61.22.

[104] For more on Palaiologoi being notoriously absent from ecclesiastic offices: Cheynet et Vannier, *Études prosopographiques*, 129–183.

[105] Autoreianos, *Testament*, 952.36–953.9.

[106] Pachymeres, *Chronikon*, 131.10–133.1.

pronoiai of the fallen soldiers into the hereditary property, limiting taxation, and prohibiting non-Roman practices. Emphasizing his care for less privileged Romans, Michael left the representatives of the church rhetorically mute since he rooted his prospective imperial tenure in Christian virtue par excellence: *philanthropeia*.[107] Finally, by emphasizing his intention to support the intellectuals and the scholars of the empire, Michael sent a clear sign to the prelates—among whom many were active intellectuals—that they would find all the monetary support they desired from the emperor. Persuaded by Michael's promises, gifts, or eventual threats from the senators to whose families many prelates themselves belonged, the patriarch and the metropolitans capitulated and sanctioned Michael's elevation to imperial office.[108]

The support of the church came at a cost, though. First, in order to lift the curse hovering over Michael since he swore the oath to Ioannes III after the trial of 1253 never to attempt to usurp the throne, Arsenios demanded that Michael enter a new oath-binding relationship with Ioannes IV swearing to be a good guide to the young emperor, whose life and crown he himself would never attempt to take.[109] Michael could not but agree to these new terms that allowed him to legally obtain the throne without breaking the oath sworn to the previous emperor and tarnish his own carefully curated public image. In return, however, Michael "desired reciprocally a vow to be formulated, and oaths to be sworn, that if the youth [Ioannes IV] pursued to undertake any action against him [Michael], he would be under compulsion to be bound by the same conditions."[110] Thus, both emperors were bound by mutual oaths of co-emperorship sanctioned by the Church. Even though such oath-swearing practices were quite uncommon in the Roman Empire, they had existed in Roman political culture long before the empire was dressed in Christian clothes. Since the earliest days of the Roman Republic, a special vow—*sacramentum*—was put in place to curse the one who breached

---

[107] For *philanthropeia* in Byzantium see: D.J. Constantelos, *Byzantine Philanthropy and Social Welfare* (New Brunswick, NJ: Rutgers University Press 1968); for *philanthropeia* as imperial virtue see: Angelov, *Imperial Ideology*, 84; Skoutariotes, *Synopsis Chronike*, 505.22–26.

[108] Pachymeres, *Chronikon*, 133.26–135.4.

[109] ibid., 135.2–16.

[110] καὶ ἀντιστρόφως ἐζήτει τὴν ἀρὰν τίθεσθαι καὶ τοὺς ὅρκους γίνεσθαι, εἴ που καὶ ὁ νέος κατ' αὐτοῦ μελετήσας διαπράξοιτο, ὡς ἐξ ἀνάγκης τοῖς αὐτοῖς ἐνέχεσθαι. (ibid, 135.16–18).

the oath sworn under religious sanction.[111] It is, then, in a very Roman way that the cohabitation of the two emperors received both legal and religious sanction from everybody present.

The oath swearing did not end with the mutual exchange of oaths between the two emperors, however. Rather, during their traditional swearing of allegiance to the new emperor, the summoned magnates of the empire were made to add a special note to their oaths "for greater security of both [Ioannes IV and Michael Palaiologos], that the subjects be ready to raise their hands in vengeance against the one if he conspired against the other."[112] With such an addendum to the oath of faithful service the patriarch wished to make the conditions of joint rule public in order to protect the young emperor. By making the senators and other officials swear to take action against the potential plotter among the emperors, Arsenios also managed to turn all the officials into active agents in preserving the new status quo. Once all of the oaths were exchanged and written down, we can imagine that, not unlike the Mouzalones, Michael sent out new *prostagmata* around the lands of the polity notifying all the provincial magistrates of his accession and potentially the oaths taken to keep both him and Ioannes IV safely enthroned. Emphasizing Ioannes IV's imperial position was still the safest way for Michael to ascend to the imperial throne without any rebellions or divisions among the Roman public. In other words, by relying on Laskarid popularity as personified in Ioannes IV, Michael was able to retain the public consensus on his side without having to put in an effort to win over the populace for himself.

5.6 *Panem et Circenses*: Michael Palaiologos and the Public Consensus

Upon the exchange of oaths, Michael VIII took great care to make it clear to as many of his subjects as possible that he was now an emperor. While the *prostagmata* were on their way to reaching the hands of provincial governors and city councils, Michael's public acclamation in Magnesia took place. According to Akropolites, the senators and the soldiers, to

---

[111] J. Rüpke, *Domi Militiae: Die religiöse Konstruktion des Krieges in Rom* (Franz Steiner, 1990), 76–80.

[112] ἐπ' ἀσφαλείᾳ καὶ ἀμφοτέρων μείζονι, ἦ μὴν ἕτοιμον εἶναι τὸ ὑπήκοον ἐπ' ἐκεῖνον ὁρμᾶν φονώσῃ χειρὶ ὃς ἂν ἐπιβουλεύσοι θατέρῳ (Pachymeres, *Chronikon*, 135.25–26).

whom Pachymeres adds the prelates of the church as well, seated Michael VIII on a shield and lifted him up in order for the people to see him elevated and acclaim him emperor.[113] By employing one of the oldest ceremonial practices in the book, Palaiologos made it immediately clear in open public space that he had taken over Roman affairs.[114]

The moment Michael VIII was acclaimed emperor, he took on the task of repaying his supporters with great acts of generosity. At least according to Pachymeres the officials were further promoted and the most ardent supporters of the new emperor were connected to him through marital arrangements, the soldiers were granted their *pronoiai* in perpetuity, and the common folk of the empire was showered with gifts.[115] By effectively appeasing all the members of society, Michael was emptying the treasury but, in return, building up strong support for his imperial tenure among the rich and poor alike. Appeasing the magnates by promoting them in higher offices was a somewhat easier task than winning over the masses. The latter task demanded more effort and time. Yet, according to Pachymeres, in a rather ruthless public campaign: "[Michael VIII] also took out great sums from the public treasury and then, while making popular speeches to the gathered people for the purpose of [obtaining] their complete favour, he would draw out the money for them with both hands, throwing it abundantly to those people who collected it like dogs."[116] By making himself publicly seen, heard, and remembered for his emotional speeches and lavish donations, Michael VIII was steadily trying to shift the public climate to his favour. By slowly crafting the public persona of Michael Palaiologos the *Philanthropos* for the people of Magnesia, the new emperor was carefully taking over some of the main traits for which Ioannes III, the Almsgiver, and his son Theodoros II were loved for by the people. By assuming the traditional Laskarid epithets, well used in the public sphere, Michael VIII could hope to cast himself as the generous continuator of the previous emperor's policies. In crafting such an image for himself, though, Michael was also preparing to set Ioannes

---

[113] Akropolites, *Chronike*, 78.8–10; Pachymeres, *Chronikon*, 139.23–141.1.

[114] For imperial acclamations on shields see: Ch. Walter, "Raising on a Shield in Byzantine Iconography," *Revue des études byzantines* 33 (1975), 133–176.

[115] Pachymeres, *Chronikon*, 139.3–14.

[116] Τότε δὲ καὶ πόλλ' ἄττα τοῦ κοινοῦ ταμιείου ἐξεφόρει καί, δημηγορῶν τοῖς συνειλεγμένοις πρὸς χάριν ἅπασαν, εἶτ' ἀμφοτέραις ἐκείνοις ἐξήντλει τὰ χρήματα, χύδην ἐκρίπτων κυνηδὸν συλλέγουσιν. (ibid., 139.16–19).

IV aside, hoping that his co-emperor would not be missed by the people who would be too focused on Michael's splendour.

With the outbursts of personal generosity during public speeches, Palaiologos was able to go beyond the mere popular expectations of a good emperorship—to be a just and fair ruler who upholds the laws and keeps the Romans safe. By pouring money over those subjects gathered in front of him to hear him speak, Michael VIII was making the dreams of many commoners in Magnesia come to life. Such dreams are best encapsulated in the pamphlet found in the *Synopsis Chronike*, about a naïve citizen who was walking around Nikaia professing that "very soon a good emperor will show up."[117] Having heard about this man's wishful remarks, emperor Theodoros I Laskaris summoned the citizen and asked him:

> "And what of me? Do I not look like a good emperor to you?"
> the man said: "and what have you ever given to me so that I would think of you as good?"
> and the emperor said: "do I not give myself to you on a daily basis fighting to the death for you and your compatriots?"
> but the man responded back at him: "so does the sun shine and thus provides us with warmth and light, but we are not thankful to it; since it fulfills the job it is supposed to do. And you do what you are behoved to do, toiling and labouring, as you say, for the sake of your compatriots."
> the emperor then asked the man: "if I give you a gift, would I be good then?"
> "but of course," responded the simpleton.[118]

Thus, while "toiling and labouring" was part of his duties, Michael VIII also tried to differentiate himself from his predecessors occupying the

---

[117] ἀναφανήσεται γὰρ δι' ὀλίγου ὁ ἀγαθὸς βασιλεύς. (Skoutariotes, *Synopsis Chronike*: 463.7).

[118] καὶ ὁ βασιλεύς· 'τί δ' ἐγώ; οὔ σοι δοκῶ καλὸς βασιλεύς;'
καὶ αὐτός· 'καὶ τί μοί ποτε δέδωκας, ἵνα σὲ ἔχω καλόν;'
καὶ πάλιν ὁ βασιλεύς 'οὐ δίδομαί σοι καθ' ἑκάστην ὑπέρ σου καὶ τῶν ὁμοφύλων μέχρι θανάτου ἀγωνιζόμενος;'
ὁ δὲ ἀνὴρ ἀνθυπέφερε· 'καὶ ὁ ἥλιος ἐπιλάμπων θερμαίνει καὶ φωτίζει ἡμᾶς, ἀλλ' οὐκ ἔχομεν χάριν αὐτῷ· ὁ γὰρ προσετάχθη, ἀποπληροῖ· καὶ σὺ γοῦν ὃ ὀφείλεις ἐργάζῃ, ὑπὲρ τῶν ὁμογενῶν, ὡς εἴρηκας, κοπιῶν καὶ μοχθῶν.'
καὶ ἐπὶ τούτοις ὁ αὐτοκράτωρ ἐπέφερεν· 'ἀλλ' εἰ δώσω δῶρά σοι, ἔσομαι ἀγαθός;'
'καὶ μάλα γε' ἀντέφησεν ὁ ἁπλοϊκός. (ibid., 463.11–20).

imperial throne. By granting many personal gifts, however, the emperor caused the state to suffer since its treasury was being unreasonably emptied out, a fact that did not escape future Palaiologan critics.[119] At the time, though, Michael VIII's excessive generosity to the populace resonated well with the people of Magnesia and, in turn, the emperor received the immediate support he desperately needed in the capital city.

While being generous to Romans of all walks of life in order to gain their support, Michael, before his official coronation, visited the border fortresses in Asia Minor, including the city of Philadelphia in order to show the Roman *akritai*, as well as the Turkmens and the Saljuqs, that Roman affairs where in order.[120] What better way to demonstrate the might of the state than by conducting imperial processions around the border so that everybody could see Michael as the guarantor of stability in the realm? On the one hand, the local populace inhabiting the borders could rest assured that the state and its emperor were still there to take care of them. The soldiers stationed in the region would see an emperor ready to command the troops should the need arise.[121] Other than being an emperor, as many soldiers surely knew, Michael was a seasoned general with quite a few battles under his belt. On the other hand, the Turkmen chieftains were reminded that the emperor with his armies was close by, should they decide to raid Roman lands. Finally, the sultan and his magnates in Ikonion—many of whom were of Roman origins themselves—could see their ally and ex-official Michael Palaiologos in control of Roman affairs.

Not sparing a moment to consolidate the public image of himself as a capable and generous ruler, Michael and his senatorial allies were ready to take the final step in completing the imperial election: the coronation in Nikaia. Initially, the agreement between the patriarch and Michael was to crown Ioannes IV first as the senior emperor and then Michael as his junior colleague. Just before the coronation, however, the patriarch was sidelined by the senators and the vast number of prelates, who threatened to physically harm Ioannes IV should he be crowned at all.[122] This

---

[119] Anglelov, *Imperial Ideology*, 253–309.

[120] Pachymeres, *Chronikon*, 139.21–141.22.

[121] Theodoros II visited the region when he was proclaimed emperor: Akropolites, *Chronike*, 53.5–11.

[122] Autoreianos, *Testament*, 952.36–41; Pachymeres, *Chronikon*, 143.13–145.4.

time around, the senators did not place their threat under the veil of layered rhetoric. Rather the elite supporters of Michael VIII felt powerful enough to openly state that they would take whatever means necessary to see Michael and Michael alone crowned emperor. Arsenios, not wishing to lose the child, gave in under pressure and crowned Michael and his wife Theodora in a public ceremony, while the young emperor was given minor tokens remotely honouring his imperial status. Following the coronation in the church:

> While not noticing the child [Ioannes IV] who was engaged in childish games, the man who was now emperor delivered public speeches often on that day and afterwards, and to endear himself to the masses, he threw silver coins in the midst of them with both hands; those gathering them praised their alleged benefactor, forgetting about the child and his affairs, without knowing what level of evil they had reached: for the scheme of one [emperor] against the other had already begun.[123]

Thus, Michael continued to fortify his imperial position through displays of generosity and care for the people. This time, however, he was promoting the image of Michael VIII Palaiologos, the emperor of the Romans in his own right, and not a mere regent and guardian to young Ioannes IV.

The coronation of Michael VIII and Theodora represents a new beginning in Palaiologan public policies. In order to strengthen his own position, Michael, now having fully cleansed the senate of his opponents, opted to sideline the church in the same way he sidelined Ioannes IV on the day of the coronation. Arsenios, understanding what was happening, made Michael's job easier by going into self-imposed political isolation only to return to his duties after the reconquest of Constantinople in 1261.[124] The new emperor, on the other hand, used the patriarch to gain the public prestige he needed before the coronation. The fact that Arsenios was prevailed upon to crown Michael VIII as sole emperor by means of blatant threats remained a matter of private affairs. In the eyes

---

[123] Τότε δὲ ἀτημελήτως τὸ παιδίον διάγον πρὸς παιγνίοις ἦν παιδικοῖς, καὶ ὁ βασιλεύων ἐν δημηγορίαις τῆς ἡμέρας συχνάκις, εἶθ' ὕστερον καὶ προσφιλοτιμούμενος τοὺς πολλούς, κατὰ μέσον σφῶν ἐρρίπτει καὶ ἀμφοτέραις ἀργύρια· οἱ δὲ προσσυλλέγοντες ἀνύμνουν δῆθεν τὸν εὐεργέτην, παιδίον καὶ τὰ κατ' ἐκεῖνο χαίρειν ἐῶντες, μηδ' οἷ κακοῦ εἰδότες γεγόνασιν· ἡ γὰρ κατὰ θατέρου ἐπιβουλὴ τοῦ ἑτέρου ἐντεῦθεν ἤρχετο. (Pachymeres, *Chronikon*, 147.7–12).

[124] Autoreianos, *Testament*, 953.10–43.

of the public, the patriarch together with the high officials of the state and the church decided to solely crown Michael VIII because he was ready to rule while young Ioannes IV was not. Once the deed was done, Michael went as far as to privatize religious symbolism for his own public image.[125] In this aspect Michael outdid his predecessors by crafting an image of Michael Palaiologos, the protégé of Archangel Michael, whose accomplishments for the people of the empire were the result of divine grace alone.[126] The patriarch, on the other hand, could do nothing but watch from his self-imposed retirement how Michael mobilized diverse religious signifiers to boost the image of himself as a pious and divinely ordained emperor.

5.7 The Man Who Wrote the Book

In January 1259, Michael VIII Palaiologos sat on the imperial throne which he was to occupy until his death in 1282. He spent his life until 1259 serving in the imperial administration of Ioannes III and Theodoros II. His career had been a remarkable one: he obtained the best education possible under imperial tutelage; he served as a commander and governor of Serres and Melenikon under his own father Andronikos Palaiologos; he married an imperial niece; he commanded the Latin forces of the empire; and he became regent to Ioannes IV. On the flip side, for much of his career, Michael was suspected of plotting against the regimes of Ioannes III and Theodoros II: he had to undergo a trial, was incarcerated twice, and at one point committed high treason by running away to the Saljuq Sultanate of Rum, where he managed to build a solid career in exile. All these actions and events defining his career have one thing in

---

[125] For instance, in his treaty with the Genoese before the reconquest of Constantinople, Michael VIII sent a *peplos* to Genoa depicting himself entering the city's cathedral surrounded by his divine protector archangel Michael (C. Hilsdale, "The Imperial Image at the End of Exile," 151–199). For Michael VIII's depiction of himself in the mercy of divine agents in public spaces see: M.-A. Talbot, "The Restoration of Constantinople under Michael VIII," *DOP* 47 (1993), 243–261.

[126] For the role of divine grace in Michael VIII's propaganda see the autobiographical *typikon* (*De vita sua*). Also, otherwise religiously sparse in *The History*, Akropolites ascribes divine grace to Michael Palaiologos several times in the narrative (R.J. "The Thirteenth Century in Byzantine Historical Writing," in Ch. Dendrinos, J. Harris, E. Harvalia-Crook, J. Herrin, (eds.), *Porphyrogenita: Essays in Honour of Julian Chrysostomides* (London: King's College 2003), 76; Macrides, "Introduction," 54–55.

common: they were publicly witnessed episodes of his life. Thus, whether or not Michael plotted against the regime in private remains unknown and outside the scope of this project. What matters was how these snippets of Michael's public life were recorded and interpreted in the literary production of the people who were educated in the Roman Empire. In turn, this literary engagement with Michael's public life has allowed us to see the ways in which successful politicians of the period managed to navigate the political waters of the medieval Roman state.

The last months of Michael's service under other emperors are heavily blurred by the lack of a strong ruler. In this context the senate, the church, the army, and the people all played a crucial role in determining the future of the Roman Empire. In such circumstances, Michael's accumulated social capital allowed him to dominate the senate, while also winning over to his cause the soldiers and common civilians of Magnesia. The election of Michael VIII Palaiologos to imperial office was all but guaranteed. It was only through the careful curating of his public image, as he was dealing with a number of different socio-economic groups within the empire, that Palaiologos was able to climb all the way up to the imperial throne. Once elected emperor, Michael's public life underwent a transition from being a public servant under an emperor to being emperor of the Romans in charge of all the other magistrates. Yet, in his first months in office, we see Michael behaving as he had in the past. Much in the same vein as when he was able to employ his familial background to gain initial repute at the imperial school or in his first office, now too, Michael VIII, an emperor, used the young emperor Ioannes IV as a shield upon which to step as he launched his independent imperial career.

It was only after winning over a significant number of supporters in the wider public that Michael VIII decided to cast off all the anchors tying him to the previous regime. By removing from the public gaze the last obstacle to his own full control of the public sphere in the Roman Empire—the patriarch Arsenios—Michael VIII entered a new stage of his public life. He no longer needed anything or anybody as a buttress to his political prominence. There was nobody left in the high echelons of Roman society, lay or ecclesiastic, who could pose an immediate threat to him. Ioannes IV remained sidelined, since Michael VIII did not need the young Laskaris as a shield anymore. His public persona, that of a generous and capable emperor, was the shield upon which he now rested.

Having dominated the public sphere, Michael now needed to remain unchallenged by other Roman magnates. From the beginning of his career in the 1240s up until 1259, Michael had learned the art of crafting a public persona to win the support needed to prosper while avoiding imperial wrath. In 1259, Michael VIII became an emperor who now needed to rely on capable administrators and generals. The trick was to find suitable individuals who would not endanger his imperial prerogatives, nor, in any way, infringe on his public image. In other words, it was Michael VIII's turn to be vigilant over the alliances that were being forged among the *golden chain* households of the empire, most of whom were related to him to some degree. With this in mind, Michael VIII no longer had to worry about carving out a spot under the sun for himself in the empire's political arena; rather, he had to make sure that he kept his own public presence radiant enough to overshadow his own administrators and officials in order to preserve the public consensus on his side. Fortunately for Michael VIII Palaiologos, he had a considerable advantage over any potential rival: he was the one who "wrote the book" on how to, step by step, become an emperor. Anybody wishing to do the same would have to follow his blueprint.

CHAPTER 6

Conclusion

6.1 The Publics and Their Wants

Having followed Michael Palaiologos' career from his days at the imperial school in the later 1230s up until his imperial coronation in early 1259, we have encountered diverse publics with which Roman officials had to engage as they sought to promote their own careers or even maintain their position. The publics were numerous, and as has been argued here, their interests varied from one group to another. Other than having diverse interests, different publics expected to be communicated with in different ways. That is, not every public responded in the same way to a single message. As a consequence, Roman officials who mastered multiple registers of communication were the ones who could expect to gain public recognition for their service and, in turn, see themselves promoted to higher offices and even dignities. Depending on their place on the polity's social hierarchy, officials and other notables of the empire had to bear in mind that very position in order to effectively focus on the publics they specifically needed to court as they advanced through the ranks of the provincial and central administration. Thus, Michael Palaiologos had a very different starting position, as well as political aspirations, from Nikolaos Manglavites. The different agendas of the two men meant that they led distinctly different public lives and ensured that they strove to establish their social connections in different ways. The reason the two men clashed was that they shared the public sphere of Melenikon, where both state official and local notable wished to exercise undisputed control.

There was no one correct way of choosing which socio-economic faction one would engage with first. Rather, depending on a series of factors—one's own familial background, education, proximity to the institutions of power, local social networks, etc.—an ambitious politician would start forging alliances within his own interest group. Taking the needs of his career into consideration, a Roman official or notable would branch out to other targeted publics. Throughout this book we have followed Michael Palaiologos and his public life; in charting the publics of the Roman Empire, we follow the same man's order of engagement.

By sheer virtue of his birth and Andronikos Palaiologos' position in the imperial administration, from a young age, Michael had to engage with members of the *golden chain* of which the Palaiologan *oikos* was a significant link. Having benefited from an imperially sponsored education at court, the young Palaiologos was able to carve out a place for himself in the group of prospective officials-to-be. It is because of his education that Palaiologos was able to establish a firm network with other notables regardless of whether they originated from the empire's respected families or the emerging class of *novi homines*. The high state officials comprised a singular public defined by shared interests and cultural outlook. Most state officials wished to promote their careers and for this to happen they first had to rely on their peers. In their attempts to secure their positions, the senatorial elites were also there to help each other restrict the control that the emperor and his *oikos* exercised over them. This does not mean that there were no political factions within this public; rather, the ways in which they employed and mobilized the production of knowledge and memory in their discursive spaces constituted them as a singular public. After all, histories were written by and for the members of the senatorial elites.

From his early days all the way to his imperial proclamation, Michael had to rely on his peers, and he had to keep engaging with them in order to promote his career. The social network the Palaiologoi forged inevitably helped Michael during the trial for treason instigated by the emperor himself. Furthermore, the strong connection between the *golden chain* households led to Michael's marriage into the extended imperial *oikos*. Finally, it was with the support of the senatorial elites that Palaiologos was able to sway both public opinion and prominent ecclesiastics to place their trust in him and to leave the reins of the state in his hands.

Leaving the imperial centre to serve as governor of Melenikon and Serres under Andronikos Palaiologos' supervision, Michael had to learn how to make himself known to two intertwined yet clearly separate publics: the populace of the empire's cities as well as the city dwelling local notables. In making himself known to the wider populace of provincial cities, Michael relied on the help of local intellectual and spiritual figures such as Iakobos in Thessaloniki, who composed a whole programme to commemorate Andronikos as the caretaker and protector of the city and exalt Michael Palaiologos as his father's worthy heir. Next to public discourse, Michael also came to deploy material rewards in the form of provisions and grants for the commoners, as we see him doing in Magnesia and Nikaia during his rapid elevation from *megas konostaulos* to the imperial office. Even outside the Roman Empire, as we have seen from the example of the Saljuq Sultanate of Rum, governors and central administrators were aware of the importance of keeping the wider populace content. It is with this intention in mind that the Saljuq sultans in Ikonion were more than eager to host and employ Roman political refugees in their central administration. Having a Roman govern Romans was surely one of the most effective communicative actions a Persianate sultan could take. From speeches delivered in Thessaloniki to coins dispersed around Magnesia, Michael also learned that communicative actions taken in one city do not necessarily matter to the populace of another. Thus, while having similar interests, each city's dwellers comprised an almost self-regulating public on their own.

Obtaining the support of urban provincial potentates was a somewhat more challenging task. As we have seen, initially, Michael was not particularly successful in dealing with this group as he ended up being charged with treason once he had a fallout with Nikolaos Manglavites. Having learned his lesson, Michael VIII Palaiologos successfully kept on good terms with Thessalonian notables, such as the Spartenoi, with whom his father Andronikos had forged good ties. It is, unfortunately for us, impossible to know in what ways state officials like Andronikos and Michael Palaiologos cut deals with local notables in order to secure their support. The only clear and well-recorded action taken by imperial representatives to keep the local notables on their side was the grant of *pronoiai*, as was the case with the elites of Thessaloniki under Michael VIII's tenure. Be that as it may, local notables were not to be underestimated. They could easily affect wider public opinion in a given city and could prove useful allies and extremely dangerous adversaries to any imperial agent and member of the *golden chain*, given their privileged access to local discursive spaces. At the same time, these local actors often possessed the means and at times education with which to procure protection from officials at the imperial centre.

Being comprised of Romans of all walks of life, as well as non-Roman elements residing in the empire, soldiers represented both a public on their own as well as communicative catalysts for spreading ideas about specific persons or concepts, such as state unity. On the one hand, the support of the armed forces could forestall open rebellion against their favourite. On the other, being formed of Roman and non-Roman citizens the soldiers had homes in cities and villages away from the army camp. This meant that the soldiers also engaged with the distinctly local but still Roman public discourse as we have seen in the example of Michael Palaiologos' trial where the soldiers were asked to pass their own judgement. In his career promotion, Michael Palaiologos relied heavily on the soldiers who served under him, as we have seen by the example of the riots at Sosandra. Also, as communicative catalysts, Michael VIII as much as Ioannes III and Theodoros II made sure to keep the veterans on their side in the provinces by granting them extensive *pronoiai*, as we have seen in the cases covered in the first chapter.

The final public Michael Palaiologos needed to win over in order to advance to the highest dignities in the state was that of the leading ecclesiastics. The church prelates were a group closely connected to the senatorial elites of the *golden chain*; more often than not, the leading ecclesiastics originated from these reputable families, or were at least employed by senatorial households for educational purposes. Yet, the interests of the ecclesiastic public were closely connected to the institution of the patriarchate, to which the senators had no particular, unless ceremonial, affiliations. As we have seen, Michael Palaiologos employed ecclesiastics as intermediaries with the wider public in Thessaloniki: first with Iakobos and then with the unnamed designated metropolitan of Dyrrachion and the metropolitan of Thessaloniki, Manouel Disypatos. The ecclesiastics, while forming their own group, operated in the same discursive spaces as did local notables and city dwellers in general. For their ability to heavily influence the public discourse in provincial centres, the support the prelates could provide was of the utmost importance. We see the final instance of ecclesiastic support in the last chapter, where Michael Palaiologos seeks to win over the prelates who can then convince the patriarch to accept the new realities in the empire's political arena.

6.2 Concluding the Conclusion

Going back to the three questions asked in the "Introduction" to the present study—How did Michael Palaiologos and his associates come up with an effective plan for communicative action? Why would Michael care to forge an image of a divinely sanctioned New Constantine during his reign? Why was Michael elected emperor?—I believe that we can answer them by means of Iakobos' witty funerary Question and Answer format. The answer to the first question rests with the elite's training and education, which more than evidence of sclerotic classicism represented a veritable panoply of politically useful and frequently deployed rhetorical techniques. We saw Michael Palaiologos composing his autobiographical *typikon* with a specific agenda; we can tell that the content of Iakobos' speech and poems was not random, but very much audience oriented; we know how Georgios Akropolites wished to glorify Michael Palaiologos and why his namesake Pachymeres decided to take the opposite approach.

As for the second question: Michael VIII Palaiologos needed to find a common thread for his public persona that he could use to promote the image of a good ruler throughout the empire. During his days as a provincial governor and then *megas konostaulos*, Michael had learned about the complexities and the necessity of maintaining as wide a range of public support as possible. More often than not, Palaiologos had to work on gaining or maintaining the support of different interest groups simultaneously. For instance, this was the case in Thessaloniki when Iakobos composed such a funerary repertoire that every soul—be it members of the local elites, the literati, or the masses—in the city could engage with regardless of their social background. As much as he worked to maintain the good disposition of the publics towards him, at times, it was impossible to win over the needed support no matter the means employed, as Michael learned the hard way when dealing with Nikolaos Manglavites. Keeping the lessons learned in mind, Michael VIII Palaiologos embarked on a journey of spreading the word of his imperial abilities to every corner of the empire. In doing so he spared no expense, putting popularity above the treasury. Michael Palaiologos' actions, in the end, reinforce the idea of the indispensable role of public consensus in medieval Roman politics. The Roman Empire in the east never developed a dynastic system in the image of the Merovingians of Francia or the sultans of the Ottoman empire. Rather, the pathway to the imperial office was open to anybody who dared call themselves the best of the Romans.

Finally, why was Michael elected emperor in the first place? Simply put, because he developed a public persona that was appealing to a wide majority of the people and publics in the Roman Empire. Michael Palaiologos had the support of the urban populace and local notables in the big centres around the empire: Thessaloniki, Magnesia, Nikaia; he was able to cleanse the senate of his opponents and establish complete discourse dominance over the *golden chain* members; he swayed the church prelates to see things his way; and he was loved by his soldiers. Thus, in the end, Michael Palaiologos had become a public figure *par excellence*, employing all the available communicative actions at his disposal to gain the respect and support of the diverse publics constituting the empire of the Romans.

Bibliography

Primary Sources

Akropolites, George. *The History*. Macrides, R.J. transl. and comm. Oxford: Oxford University Press, 2007.

Bar Hebraeus. *The Chorography*. Budge, E.A.W. ed. and transl. London: Oxford University Press, 1932.

Barber, Charles and Papaioannou, Stratis, eds. *Michael Psellos on Literature and Art*. Notre Dame: Notre Dame University Press, 2017.

Barks, Coleman with Moyne, John, transl. *The Essential Rumi*. San Francisco: Penguin 1997.

Beihammer, Alexader Daniel, ed. *Griechische Briefe und Urkunden aus dem Zypern der Kreuzfahrerzeit*. Nicosia: Zyprisches Forschungszentrum, 2007.

Beneker, Jeffrey and Gibson, Craig A. eds. and transl. *The Rhetorical Exercises of Nikephoros Basilakes*. Washington, DC: Dumbarton Oaks Medieval Library, 2016.

Berbard, Floris and Livanos, Christopher, trans. and eds. *The Poems of Christopher of Mytilene and John Mauropous*. Washington, DC: Dumbarton Oaks Medieval Library, 2018.

Berger, Albrecht, ed. and transl. *Accounts of Medieval Constantinople: The Patria*. Washington: Dumbarton Oaks Medieval Library 2012.

Burgmann, Ludwig, ed. *Ecloga Basilicorum*. Frankfurt am Main: Löwenklau Gesellschaft, 1988.

Burguière, R. and Mantran, R. "Quelques vers grecs du XIIIe siècle en caractères árabes." *Byzantion* 22 (1952): 63–80.

Cameron, Averil and Herrin, Judith, eds., trans., and comm. *Constantinople in the Early Eight Century: The Parastaseis Syntomoi Chronikai.* Leiden: Brill, 1984.

Chatterjee, Paroma. *Between the Pagan Past and Christian Present in Byzantine Visual Culture: Statues in Constantinople, 4th-13th Centuries CE.* Cambridge: Cambridge University Press, 2021.

Delehaye, Hippolyte, ed. "Constantini Acropolitae hagiographi byzantini epistularum manipulus." *Analecta Bollandiana* 51 (1933): 263–284.

Dennis, George, ed., transl. and comm. *Maurice's Strategikon. Handbook of Byzantine Military Strategy*, G. Dennis ed. and trans. Philadelphia: University of Pennsylvania Press, 1984.

Dennis, George, ed., transl. and comm. *The Taktika of Leo VI.* Washington DC: Dumbarton Oaks, 2010.

Failler, Albert, éd. et intro., Laurent, Vitalien transl. *Georges Pachymérès Relations historiques*, I. Paris: Les Belles Lettres, 1984.

Festa, Nicola, ed. *Theodori Ducae Lascaris Epistulae CCXVII.* Firenza: Istituto di studi superiori pratici e di perfezionamento, 1898.

Forster, Edward Seymour, transl. *The Turkish Letters of Ogier Ghiselin de Busbecq.* Baton Rouge: Louisiana State University Press, 2005.

Grégoire, Henri, ed. *Recueil des inscriptions grecques chretiennes d'Asie Mineure.* Paris: Adolf M. Hakkert, 1922.

Grégoire, Henri. "Imperatoris Michaelis Palaeologi *De vita sua.*" *Byzantion* 29–30 (1959–1960): 447–474.

Heisenberg, Augustus, ed. et comm. *Aus der Geschichte und Literatur der Palaiologenzeit.* München: Verlag der Bayerischen Akademie der Wissenschaften, 1911.

Heisenberg, Augustus, ed. et comm. *Georgii Acropolitae Opera*, I. Lipsiae: B.G. Teubneri, 1903 (editionem anni MCMIII correctiorem curavit P. Wirth, Stuttgart, 1978).

Houtsma, Martijn Th., ed. *Histoire des seldjoucides d'Asie Mineure d'après l'abrégé du Seldouknāmeh d'ibn-Bībī.* Leiden: Brill, 1902.

Hörander, Wolfgang, ed. "Die Progymnasmata des Theodoros Hexapterygos." In W. Hörander et al. eds. Βυζάντιος. *Festschrift für Herbert Hunger zum 70. Geburtstag.* Wien: Österreichische Akademie der Wissenschaften, 1984: 147–162.

Hunger, Hunger. "Zum Epilog der Theogonie des Johannes Tzetzes." *BZ* 46 (1953): 302–307.

Kaldellis, Anthony and Krallis, Dimitris, eds. and transl. *Michael Attaleiates' the History.* Washington, DC: Dumbarton Oaks Medieval Library, 2012.

Lefort, Jacques, Oikonomidès, Nicolas; Papachryssanthou, Denise, et Kravari Vassiliki éds. *Actes d'Iviron III: de 1204 à 1328.* Paris: Peeters, 1994.

Macrides, Ruth J., Munitiz, J.A. and Angelov, Dimiter, eds., transl, and comm. *Pseudo-Kodinos and the Constantinopolitan Court: Offices and Ceremonies*. Aldershot, UK: Ashgate, 2013.
Menander, Rhetor. *A Commentary*, Russel, D.A. and Wilson, N.G. transl. and eds. Oxford: Oxford University Press, 1981.
Mercati, Silvio G. *Collectanea Byzantina I*. Bari: Edizioni Dedalo, 1970.
Meyer, Gustav. "Die griechischen Verse in Rabâbnâma." *BZ* 4 (1895): 401–411.
Migne, Jean-Paul, ed. *Patrologia Graeca* 142. Parisiis: Garnier Fratres, 1863.
Migne, Jean-Pail, ed. *Patrologia Graeca* 140. Parisiis: Garnier Fratres, 1865.
Miklosich, Fraz et Muller, Josef, eds. *Acta et diplomata medii aevi sacra et profana* VI vol. Vindobonae: C. Gerold, 1860–1890.
Mommsen, Theodor and Meyer, Pulus M. eds. *Theodosiani libri XVI cum constitutionibus Sirmondianis et leges novellae ad Theodosianum pertinentes* I. Berolini: Weidmann, 1905.
Munitiz, J.A. ed. *Nicephori Blemmydae Autobiographia sive Curriculum Vitae necnon Epistula Universalior*. Turhout: Brepols, 1984.
Prinzing, G. ed. *Demetrii Chomateni Ponemata Diaphora*. Berlin and New York: De Grutyer 2002.
Rabe, Hugo, ed. *Aphthonii progymnasmata*. Lipsiae: Teubner, 1926.
Rabe, Hugo, ed. *Hermogenis opera*. Lipsiae: Teubner, 1913 (reprinted 1969).
Russel, D.A. and Wilson, Nigel G. *Menander Rhetor: A* Commentary. Oxford: Oxford University Press, 1981.
Sathas, Konstantinos, ed. Μεσαιωνικὴ Βιβλιοθήκη VII. Venice: Phoenix, 1894.
Schopen, Ludwig, ed. and transl. *Nicephori Gregorae Byzantina historia: Graece et Latine*. Cambridge, UK: Cambridge University Press, 2012.
Schopen, Ludwig, ed. *Ioannis Cantacuzeni eximperatoris historiarum libri iv* III vols. Bonnae: Weber, 1828/1832.
Thomas, John and Constantinides Hero, Angela, eds. *Byzantine Monastic Foundation Documents* 1. Washington, DC: Dumbarton Oaks Research Library and Collections, 2000.
Volkman, Hans, ed. and transl. *Res gestae Divi Augusti das Monumentum Ancyranum*. Leipzig: Reisland 1942.
Δέδες, Δημήτριος. "Τα ελληνικά ποιήματα του Μαυλανά Ρουμή και του γιου του Βαλέντ κατά τον 13ον αιώνα." *Τα Ιστορικά* 10 (18/19) (1993): 3–22.
Τσουγκαράκης, Δημήτριος, εισ. και μετ. *Κεκαυμένου Στρατηγικόν*. Αθήνα: Κανάκη 1993.

Secondary Sources

Agapitos, Panagiotis. "Poets and Painters: Theodoros Prodromos' Dedicatory Verses of His Novel to an Anonymous Caesar." *JÖB* 50 (2000): 173–185.

Ahrweiler, Hélène. "Recherches sur l'administration de l'empire byzantin aux IX-XIème siècles." *Bulletin de Correspondance Hellénique* 84 (1960): 1–111.

Ahrweiler, Hélène. "L'histoire et la géographie de la région de Smyrne entre les deux occupations turques (1081–1317), particulièrement au XIIIe siècle." *TM* 1 (1965): 1–204 = *Byzance, les pays et les territoires*. Londres: Variorum Reprints, 1976.

Ahrweiler, Hélène. "Philadelphie et Thessalonique au début du xive siècle: à propos de Jean Monomaque." In Ahrweiler, H. ed. *Philadelphie et autres études*. Paris: Éditions de la Sorbonne, 1984: 9–16.

Alexiou, Margaret. "Of Longings and Loves: Seven Poems by Theodore Prodromos." *DOP* 69 (2015): 209–224.

Alexiou, Margaret. "The Poverty of Écriture and the Craft of Writing: Towards a Reappraisal of the Prodromic Poems." *BMGS* 10: 1–40.

Allsen, Thomas T. *Culture and Conquest in Mongol Eurasia*. Cambridge: Cambridge University Press, 2001.

Ando, Clifford. *Imperial Ideology and Provincial Loyalty in the Roman Empire*. Berkley, Los Angeles and London: University of California Press, 2000.

Ando, Clifford. *Law, Language, and Empire in the Roman Tradition*. Philadelphia: University of Pennsylvania Press, 2011.

Angelov, Alexander. "In Search of God's Only Emperor: *Basileus* in Byzantine and Modern Historiography." *Journal of Medieval History* 40 (2014): 123–141.

Angelov, Dimiter. *Imperial Ideology and Political Thought in Byzantium, 1204–1330*. Cambridge: Cambridge University Press, 2007.

Angelov, Dimiter. *The Byzantine Hellene: The Life of Theodore Laskaris and Byzantium in the Thirteenth Century*. Cambridge: Cambridge University Press, 2019.

Angold, Michael. *A Byzantine Government in Exile: Government and Society Under the Laskarids of Nicaea, 1204-1261*. Oxford: Oxford University Press, 1975.

Angold, Michael. *The Byzantine Empire 1025-1204: A Political History*. Cambridge and New York: Cambridge University Press, 1997^2.

Banarlı, Nihat Sami. *Resimli Türk Edebiyatı Tarihi*. Ankara: Türk Tarih Kurumu, 1984.

Bartusis, Mark C. *Land and Privilege in Byzantium: The Institution of Pronoia*. Cambridge, UK: Cambridge University Press, 2012.

Beck, Hans-Georg. *Senat und Volk von Konstantinopel: Probleme der byzantinischen Verfassungsgeschichte*. München: Verlag der Bayerischen Akademie der Wissenschaften, 1966.

Beck, Hans-Georg. *Res Publica Romana: Vom Staatsdenken der Byzantiner.* München: Verlag der Bayerischen Akademie der Wissenschaften, 1970.

Beihammer, Alexander D. "Defection Across the Border of Islam and Christianity: Apostasy and Cross-Cultural Interaction in Byzantine Seljuk Relations." *Speculum* 86 (2011): 597–651.

Beihammer, Alexander D. "Christian Views of Islam in Early Seljuq Anatolia: Perceptions and Reactions." In Peacock, A.S.C., de Nicola, B. and Yıldız, S.N. eds. *Christianity and Islam in Medieval Anatolia.* New York: Routledge, 2016: 51–76.

Beihammer, Alexander D. "The Formation of Muslim Principalities and Conversion to Islam During the Early Seljuk Expansion in Asia Minor." In Gellez, P. and Grivaud, G. eds. *Les Conversions a l'Islam en Asie Mineure, dans les Balakns et dance le monde Musulman: Comparaisons et perspectives.* Athenes: École française d'Athènes, 2016: 77–108.

Beihammer, Alexander Daniel. *Byzantium and the Emergence of Muslim-Turkish Anatolia.* New York: Routledge, 2017.

Belke, Klaus. *Tabula Imperii Byzantini 4, Galatien und Lykaonien.* Wien: Verlag der Österreichischen Akademie der Wissenschaften, 1984.

Belke, Klaus. "Transport and Communication." In Niewöhner, Ph. ed. *The Archaeology of Byzantine Anatolia: From the End of Late Antiquity Until the Coming of the Turks.* Oxford: Oxford University Press, 2017: 28–38.

Berger, Albrecht. "The Byzantine Court as a Physical Space." In *The Byzantine Court: Source of Power and Culture.* Istanbul: Koç University Press, 2013: 3–12.

Bernard, Floris. *Writing and Reading Byzantine Secular Poetry 1025–1081.* Oxford: Oxford University Press, 2014.

Brand, Charles M. "The Turkish Element in Byzantium, Eleventh-Twelfth Centuries." *DOP* 43 (1989): 1–25.

Bulliet, Richard W. *Conversion to Islam in the Medieval Period: An Essay in Quantitative History.* Cambridge, MA and London, England: Harvard University Press, 2013.

Bury, John B. *A History of the Later Roman Empire from Arcadius to Irene.* London: Macmillan, 1889.

Cahen, Claude. *Pre-Ottoman Turkey: A General Survey of the Material and Spiritual Culture and History (c.1071–1330).* Jones-Williams, J. transl. New York: Sidgwick & Jackson, 1968.

Cheynet, Jean-Claude, and Vannier, Jean-François. *Études Prosopographiques.* Paris: Éditions de la Sorbonne, 1986.

Cheynet, Jean-Claude. *Pouvoir et contestations à Byzance (963–1210).* Paris: Éditions de la Sorbonne, 1996.

Chitwood, Zachary. *Byzantine Legal Culture and the Roman Legal Tradition, 867–1056.* Cambridge, UK: Cambridge University Press, 2017.

Constantelos, Demetrios J. *Byzantine Philanthropy and Social Welfare.* New Brunswick, NJ: Rutgers University Press, 1968.
Constantinides, Constantine N. *Higher Education in Byzantium in 13th and Early 14th Centuries (1204–ca.1310).* Nicosia: Cyprus Research Centre, 1982.
Coureas, Nicholas. "The Latin and Greek Churches in Former Byzantine Lands Under Latin Rule." In Tsougarakis, N.I. and Lock, P. eds. *A Companion to Latin Greece.* Leiden and New York: Brill, 2015: 145–184.
Crow, Jim. "Alexios I Komnenos and Kastamon: Castles and Settlement in Middle Byzantine Paphlagonia." In Mullett, M. and Smythe, D. eds. *Alexios I Komnenos.* Belfast: The Queen's University of Belfast, 1996: 12–36.
Dagron, Gilles. *Constantinople imaginaire: étude sur le recueil des Patria.* Paris: Presses universitaires de France, 1984.
Delilbaşi, Melek. "Greekas a Diplomatic Language in the Turkish Chancery." In Moschonas, N.G. ed. *Η επικοινωνία στο Βυζάντιο.* Αθήνα: Κέντρο Βυζαντινών Ερευνών, 1993: 145–153.
Dölger, Franz. "Chronologisches und Prosopographisches zur byzantinischen Geschichte des 13. Jahrhunderts." *BZ* 27 (1927): 291–320.
Dölger, Franz and Karayannopolous, Johannes. *Byzantinische Urkundenlehre: Erster Abschnitt, Die Kaiserurkunden.* München: C.-H. Beck, 1968.
Drpić, Ivan. "Painter as Scribe: Artistic Identity and the Arts of graphē in Late Byzantium." *Word & Image* 29: 334–353.
Drpić, Ivan. *Epigram, Art, and Devotion in Later Byzantium.* Cambridge, UK: Cambridge University Press, 2016.
Drpić, Ivan, and Rhoby, Andreas. "Byzantine Verses as Inscriptions: The Interaction of Text, Object, and Beholder." In Hörandner, W., Rhody, A. and Zagklas, N. eds. *A Companion to Byzantine Poetry.* Leiden and Boston: Brill, 2019: 430–455.
Durak, Koray. "Defining the 'Turk': Mechanisms of Establishing Contemporary Meaning in the Archaizing Language of the Byzantines." *JÖB* (2009): 65–78.
El-Cheikh, Nadia M. *Women, Islam, and Abbasid Identity.* Cambridge, MA and London: Harvard University Press, 2015.
Estangüi Gómez, Raúl. *Byzance face aux Ottomans: Exercise du pouvoir et contrôle du territoire sous les derniers Paléologues (milieu XIVe – milieu XVe siècle).* Paris: Publications de la Sorbonne, 2014.
Failler, Albert. "Chronologie et composition dans l'Histoire de Georges Pachymérès." *REB* 44 (1980): 5–87.
Failler, Albert. "Chronologie et composition dans l'Histoire de Georges Pachymérès." *REB* 39 (1981): 145–249.
Failler, Albert. "La promotion du clerc et du moine à l'épiscopat et au patriarcat." *REB* 59 (2001): 125–146.

Featherstone, Michael. "The Everyday Palace in the 10th Century." In Featherstone, M. et al. eds. *The Emperor's House: Palaces from Augustus to the Age of Absolutism.* Berlin: De Gruyter 2015: 149–158.
Foskolou, Viky A. "In the Reign of the Emperor of Rome...": Donor Inscriptions and Political Ideology in the Time of Michael VIII Paleologos." *Δελτίον της Χριστιανικής Αρχαιολογικής Εταιρείας* 27 (2011): 455–462.
Foskolou, Viky A. "Ο Ῥώμης ἄναξ στην επιγραφή του Αγίου Δημητρίου Θεσσαλονίκης. Χορηγία, αυτοκρατορική πολιτική και ιδεολογία στα χρόνια του Μιχαήλ Η΄ Παλαιολόγου." *ByzSym* 23 (2013): 11–31.
Fryde, Edmund B. *The Early Palaeologan Renaissance (1261-c. 1360).* Leiden: Brill, 2000.
Gabriele, Matthew. *An Empire of Memory: Charlemagne, the Franks, and Jerusalem Before the First Crusade.* Oxford and New York: Oxford University Press, 2011.
Gaul, Niels. "Performative Reading in Late Byzantine Theatron." In Shawcross, T. and Toth I. eds. *Reading in the Byzantine Empire and Beyond.* Cambridge and New York: Cambridge University Press, 2018: 215–233.
Geanakoplos, Deno J. *Emperor Michael Palaeologus and the West (1258–1282).* Cambridge, MA: Harvard University Press, 1959.
Gerstel, S. *Rural Lives and Landscapes in Late Byzantium: Art, Archaeology and Ethnography.* Cambridge: Cambridge University Press, 2015.
Gökdemir, A., Demirel, C. et al. "Ankara Temple (Monumentum Ancyranum/Temple of Augustus and Rome) Restoration." *Case Studies in Construction Materials* 2 (2015): 55–65.
Golding, Paul R. "Han Law and the Regulation of Interpersonal Relations: 'The Confucianization of the Law' Revisited." *Asia Major* 25 (2012): 1–31.
Gorecki, Danuta Maria. "Books, Production of Books and Reading in Byzantium." *Libri* 14 (1984): 113–129.
Green, Katie. "Experiencing *Politiko*: New Methodologies for Analysing the Landscape of a Rural Byzantine Society." In Nesbitt, C. and Jackson, M. eds. *Experiencing Byzantium: Papers from the 44th Spring Symposium of Byzantine Studies, Newcastle and Durham, April 2011.* London and New York: Routledge, 2016: 133–152.
Guillad, Rodolphe. *Recherches sur les institutions byzantines* I. Berlin: Akademie Verlag, 1967.
Habermas, Jürgen. *Communication and the Evolution of Society*, T. McCarthy transl. Boston: Beacon Press, 1979.
Habermas, Jürgen. *The Theory of Communicative Action*, 2 vols., T. McCarthy transl. Boston: Beacon Press, 1984/1987.
Haldon, John. *Warfare, State, and Society in the Byzantine World.* London: UCL Press, 1999.

Haldon, John. *The Byzantine Wars*. Brimscombe: The History Press, reprint 2008.
Haldon, John. "Bureaucracies, Elites, and Clans: The Case of Byzantium, 600–1100." In Crooks, P. ed. *Empires and Bureaucracy in World History: From Late Antiquity to the Twentieth Century*. Cambridge, UK: Cambridge University Press, 2016: 147–169.
Hauser, Gerard. *Vernacular Voices: The Rhetoric of Publics and Public Spheres*. Columbia, SC: University of South Carolina Press, 1999.
Heather, Peter. *Empires and Barbarians: The Fall of Rome and the Birth of Europe*. Oxford and New York: Oxford University Press, 2012.
Hekster, Oliver. *Rome and Its Empire, AD 193–284*. Edinburgh: Edinburgh University Press, 2008.
Hendy, Michael F. *Catalogue of the Byzantine Coins in the Dumbarton Oaks Collection and the Whittemore Collection IV*. Washington, DC: Dumbarton Oaks Collections, 1999.
Herrin, Judith. "Realities of Byzantine Provincial Government: Hellas and Peloponnesos, 1180–1205." *DOP* 29 (1975): 253–284.
Herrin, Judith. *Margins and Metropolis: Authority Across the Byzantine Empire*. Princeton: Princeton University Press, 2013.
Hilsdale, Cecily J. "The Imperial Image at the End of Exile: The Byzantine Embroidered Silk in Genoa and the Treaty of Nymphaion (1261)." *DOP* 64 (2010): 151–199.
Hilsdale, Cecily J. *Byzantine Art and Diplomacy in an Age of Decline*. Cambridge, UK and New York: Cambridge University Press, 2014.
Hilsdale, Cecily J. "Worldliness in Byzantium and Beyond: Reassessing the Visual Networks of Barlaam and Ioasaph." *The Medieval Globe* 3 (2017): 57–96.
Ho, Ming-Sho. "Occupy Congress in Taiwan: Political Opportunity, Threat, and the Sunflower Movement." *Journal of East Asian Studies* 15 (2015): 69–97.
Ho, Ming-Sho. "From Mobilization to Improvisation: The Lessons from Taiwan's 2014 Sunflower Movement." *Social Movement Studies* 17 (2018): 189–202.
Ho, Ming-Sho. *Challenging Beijing's Mandate of Heaven: Taiwan's Sunflower Movement and Hong Kong's Umbrella Movement*. Philadelphia: Temple University Press, 2019.
Hock Ronald, F. et al. eds. *The Chreia in Ancient Rhetoric*. Atlanta: Society for Biblical Literature, 1986.
Hörander, Wolfgang. "Die Progymnasmata des Theodoros Hexapterygos." In Hörander, W. et al. eds. *Βυζάντιος. Festschrift für Herbert Hunger zum 70. Geburtstag*. Wien: Österreichische Akademie der Wissenschaften 1984: 147–162.
Horrocks, Geoffrey. *Greek: A History of the Language and Its Speakers*. Hoboken: Wiley Blackwell, 2010.

Jacoby, David. *La féodalité en Grèce médiévale: Les "Assises de Romanie"*, *sources, application et diffusion*. Paris and The Hague: De Gruyter, 1971.

Jovanović, Aleksandar. "Imagining the Communities of Others: The Case of the Seljuk Turks." *ByzSym* 28 (2018): 239–273.

Kaldellis, Anthony. *Hellenism in Byzantium: The Transformations of Greek Identity and the Reception of the Classical Tradition*. Cambridge, UK and New York et al: Cambridge University Press, 2007.

Kaldellis, Anthony. "How to Usurp the Throne in Byzantium: The Role of Public Opinion in Sedition and Rebellion." In Angelov, D.G. and Saxby M. eds. *Power and Subversion in Byzantium: Papers from the Forty-Third Spring Symposium of Byzantine Studies, University of Birmingham, March 2010*. Farnham, UK and Burglinton, VT: Ashgate, 2013: 43–56.

Kaldellis, Anthony. *Ethnography After Antiquity: Foreign Peoples and Lands in Byzantine Literature*. Philadelphia: University of Pennsylvania Press, 2013.

Kaldellis, Anthony. *The Byzantine Republic: People and Power in New Rome*. Cambridge, MA and London, UK: Harvard University Press, 2015.

Kaldellis, Anthony. "The Social Scope of Roman Identity in Byzantium: An Evidence-Based Approach." *ByzSym* 27 (2017): 173–210.

Kaldellis, Anthony. *Romanland: Ethnicity and Empire in Byzantium*. Cambridge, MA and London, UK: Harvard University Press, 2019.

Kalldelis, Anthony. *Byzantium Unbound*. Leeds: Arc Humanities Press, 2019.

Kauppinnen, Saara. *Dialogue Form in Greek Verse Inscriptions with Some Non-Inscriptional Parallels*, PhD dissertation. Helsinki, 2015.

Kazhdan, Alexander P. *Социальный состав господствующего класса Византии XI-XII вв*. Москва: Институт всеобщей истории, 1974.

Kazhdan, Alexander P. *Армяне в составе господствующего класса Византийской империи в XI—XII вв*. Ереван: Изд-во АН АрмССР, 1975.

Kazhdan, Alexander P. ed. *Oxford Dictionary of Byzantium*. Oxford: Oxford University Press, 1991.

Kennedy, George A. *A New History of Classical Rhetoric*. Princeton: Princeton University Press, 1994.

Kennedy, George A. *Progymnasmata: Greek Textbooks of Prose Composition and Rhetoric*. Atlanta: Society for Biblical Literature, 2003.

Kontogiannopoulou, Anastasia. "The Notion of and Its Role in Byzantium During the Last Centuries (13–15th c.)." *Byzantina Symmeikta* 22 (2012): 101–124.

Korobeinikov, Dimitri. "Orthodox Communities in Eastern Anatolia in the Thirteenth and Fourteenth Centuries, Part 1: The Two Patriarchates: Constantinople and Antioch." *Al-Masaq: Islam and the Medieval Mediterranean* 15 (2003): 197–214.

Korobeinikov, Dimitri. "Orthodox Communities in Eastern Anatolia in the Thirteenth to Fourteenth Centuries, Part 2: The Time of Troubles." *Al-Masaq: Islam and the Medieval Mediterranean* 17 (2005): 1–29

Korobeinikov, Dimitri. "Raiders and Neighbours: The Turks (1040–1304)." In Shepard, J. ed. *The Cambridge History of the Byzantine Empire*. Cambridge, UK: Cambridge University Press, 2008: 692–727.

Korobeinikov, Dimitri. "How 'Byzantine' Were the Early Ottomans? Bithynia in ca. 1290-1450." In Zaitsev, I.V. and Oreshkova, S.F. eds. *Османский мир и османистика: сборник статей к 100-летию со дня рождения А.С. Тверитиновой (1910-1973)*. Москва: Институт востоковедения РАН, 2010: 215–239.

Korobeinikov, Dimitri. "'The King of the East and the West': The Seljuk Dynastic Concept and Titles in the Muslim and Christian Sources." In Peacock, A.C.S. and Yıldız, S.N. eds. *The Seljuks of Anatolia: Court and Society in the Medieval Middle East*. London and New York: Routledge, 2013: 68–90.

Korobeinikov, Dimitri. *Byzantium and the Turks in the 13th Century*. Oxford: Oxford University Press, 2014.

Korobeinikov, Dimitri. "The Formation of the Turkish Principalities in the Boundary Zone: From the Emirate of Denizli to the Beylik of Menteshe (1256–1302)." In Çevik, A. and Keçiş, M. eds. *Uluslararasi Batı Anadolu Beylikleri Tarih, Kültür ve Medeniyeti Sempozyumu-II: Menteşeoğulları tarihi, 25-27 Nisan 2012 Muğla: bildiriler*. Ankara: Türk Tarih Kurumu, 2016: 65–76.

Krallis, Dimitris. *Michael Attaleiates and the Politics of Imperial Decline in Eleventh Century Byzantium*. Tempe: Arizona Center for Medieval and Renaissance Studies, 2012.

Krallis, Dimitris. "Urbane Warriors: Smoothing Out Tensions Between Soldiers and Civilians in Attaleiates' Encomium to Emperor Nikephoros III Botaneiates." In Lauxterman M. and Whittow M. eds. *Being in Between: Byzantium in the Eleventh Century*. London and New York: Routledge 2015: 154–168.

Krallis, Dimitris. "Historiography as Political Debate." In Kaldellis, A. and Siniossoglou, N. eds. *The Cambridge Intellectual History of Byzantium*. Cambridge: Cambridge University Press, 2017: 599–614.

Krallis, Dimitris. "Imagining Rome in Medieval Constantinople: Memory, Politics, and the Past in the Middle Byzantine Period." In Lambert, P. and Weiler, B. eds. *How the Past Was Used. Essays in Historical Culture*. London: British Academy, 2017: 49–69.

Krallis, Dimitris. "Popular Political Agency in Byzantium's Villages and Towns." *ByzSym* 28 (2018): 11–48.

Krallis, Dimitris. *Serving Byzantium's Emperors: The Courtly Life and Career of Michael Attaleiates*. Cham: Palgrave Macmillan, 2019.

Kyritses, Demetrios. "Political and Constitutional Crisis at the End of the Twelfth Century." In Simpson, A. ed. *Byzantium 1180–1204: 'The Sad Quarter of a Century'?*. Athens: National Hellenic Research Foundation, 2015: 97–111.

Kyritses, Dimitris. "The 'Common Chrysobulls' of Cities and the Notion of Property in Late Byzantium." *ByzSym* 13 (1999): 229–245.

Laiou, Angeliki E. "The Byzantine Aristocracy in the Palaeologan Perdiod." *Viator* 4 (1973): 131–151.

Lange, Christian and Mecit, Songül, eds. *Seljuqs: Politics, Society and Culture*. Edinburgh: Edinburgh University Press, 2011.

Latowsky, Anne A. *Emperor of the World: Charlemagne and Construction of Imperial Authority, 800-1229*. Ithaca and London: Cornell University Press, 2013.

Laurent, Vitalien. "La correspondance inédite de Georges Babouscomitès." In *Εἰς μνήμην Σπυρίδωνος Λάμπρου*. Ἀθῆναι: Ἐπιτροπὴ ἐκδόσεως τῶν καταλοίπων Σπυρίδωνος Λάμπρου, 1935.

Lauxterman, Marc D. *Byzantine Poetry from Pisides to Geometers, Texts and Contexts* I. Vienna: Verlag der Österreichischen Akademie der Wissenschaften, 2003.

Lemerle, Paul. "Le gouvernement des philosophes: notes et remarques sur l'enseignement, les ecoles, la culture." In *Cinq études sur le XIe siècle byzantin*. Paris: Centre National de la Recherche Scientifique, 1977: 195–248.

Lemerle, Paul. *The Agrarian History of Byzantium from the Origins to the Twelfth Century. The Sources and Problems*. Galway: Galway University Press, 1979.

Leroy-Molinghen, Alice and Karlin-Hayter, Patricia. "Basileopator." *Byzantion* 38 (1968): 278–281.

Lewis, Franklin. *Past and Present, East and West: The Life, Teachings, and Poetry of Jalal al-din Rumi*. New York: One World Publications, 2014.

Lock, Peter. *The Franks in the Aegean, 1204–1500*. New York and London: Routledge, 2013[2].

Macrides, Ruth J. "The New Constantine and the New Constantinople—1261." *BMGS* 6 (1980): 13–41.

Macrides, Ruth J. "Saints and Sainthood in the Early Palaeologan Period." In Hackel S. ed. *The Byzantine Saint: University of Birmingham Fourteenth Spring Symposium of Byzantine Studies, Volume 1980, Part 2*. London: Fellowship of St Alban and St Sergius, 1981: 67–87.

Macrides, Ruth J. "The Byzantine Godfather." *BMGS* 11 (1987): 139–162.

Macrides, Ruth J. "Kinship by Arrangement: The Case of Adoption." *DOP* 44 (1990): 109–118.

Macrides, Ruth J. "The Competent Court." In Laiou, A. ed. *Law and Society in Byzantium, Ninth-Twelfth Centuries*. Washington, DC: Dumbarton Oaks, 1992: 117–129.

Macrides, Ruth J. "George Akropolites' Rhetoric." In Jeffreys, E. ed. *Rhetoric Byzantium Papers from the Thirty-fifth Spring Symposium of Byzantine Studies, Exeter College, University of Oxford, March 2001*. Aldershot: Ashgate, 2003: 201–211.
Macrides, Ruth J. "The Thirteenth Century in Byzantine Historical Writing." In Dendrinos, Ch., Harris, J., Harvalia-Crook, E. and Herrin, J. eds. *Porphyrogenita: Essays in Honour of Julian Chrysostomides*. London: King's College, 2003: 63–76.
Macrides, Ruth J. "Introduction." In Georgios Akropolites, ed. *The History*. Oxford: Oxford University Press, 2007: 3–101.
Macrides, Ruth J. ed. *History as Literature in Byzantium: Papers from the Fortieth Spring Symposium of Byzantine Studies, University of Birmingham, April 2007*. Aldershot: Ashgate, 2010.
Macrides, Ruth J. "Trial by Ordeal on Whose Order?" In Armstrong, P. ed. *Authority in Byzantium*. Farnham: Ashgate, 2013: 31–46
Macrides, Ruth J. "The 'Other' Palace in Constantinople: The Blachernai." In Featherstone, M., Spieser, J-M., Tanman, G. and Wulf-Rheidt, U. eds. *The Emperor's House: Palaces from Augustus to the Age of Absolutism*. Berlin, München and Boston: De Gruyter, 2015: 159–168.
Magdalino, Paul. "Aspects of Twelfth-Century Byzantine Kaiserkritik." *Speculum* 58 (1983): 326–346.
Magdalino, Paul. "Byzantine Snobbery." In Angold, M. ed. *The Byzantine Aristocracy, IX to XIII Centuries*. Oxford: Oxford University Press, 1984: 58–78.
Magdalino, Paul. *The Empire of Manouel I Komnenos*. Cambridge, UK: Cambridge University Press, 2002.
Magdalino, Paul. "The Foundation of the Pantokrator Monastery and Its Urban Setting." In Kotzabassi, S. ed. *The Pantokrator Monastery in Constantinople*. Boston and Berlin: De Gruyter, 2013: 33–56
Magdalino, Paul and Macrides, Ruth J. "The Fourth Kingdom and the Rhetoric of Hellenism." In Magdalino, P. ed. *The Perception of the Past in Twelfth-Century Europe*. London and Rio Grande: Bloomsbury Academic, 1992: 117–156.
Mango, Cyril in collaboration with Efthymiadis, Stephanos. *The Correspondence of Ignatios the Deacon. Text, Translation, and Commentary (CFHB 39)*. Cambridge, MA: Harvard University Press, 1997.
Mango, Cyril in collaboration with Ethymiadis, Stephanos. *The Correspondence of Ignatios the Deacon. Text, Translation, and Commentary*. Cambridge, MA: Harvard University Press, 1997.
Marciniak, Przemysław. "Laughter on Display: Mimic Performances and the Danger of Laughing in Byzantium." In Alexiou, M. and Cairns, D. eds. *Greek*

Laughter and Tears: Antiquity and After. Edinburgh: Edinburgh University Press, 2017: 232–242.

Matschke, Klaus-Peter, and Tinnefeld, Franz. *Die Gesellschaft im späten Byzanz. Gruppen, Strukturen und Lebensformen*. Köln, Weimar and Wien: Böhlau Verlag, 2001.

Matthews, John F. "'Codex Theodosianus' 9.40.13 and Nicomachus Flavianus." *Historia: Zeitschrift für Alte Geschichte* 46 (1997): 196–213

May, Timothy. *The Mongol Empire*. Edinburgh: Edinburgh University Press, 2018.

McKitterick, Rosamond. *History and Memory in the Carolingian World*. Cambridge and New York: Cambridge University Press, 2004.

McKitterick, Rosamond. *Charlemagne: The Formation of a European Identity*. Cambridge and New York: Cambridge University Press, 2008.

Mecit, Songül. *The Rum Seljuqs: Evolution of a Dynasty*. London and New York: Routledge, 2014.

Messis, Charis and Papaioannou, Stratis. "Orality and Textuality (with an Appendix on the Byzantine Conceptions)." In Papaionnou, S. ed. *The Oxford Textbook of Byzantine Literature*. Oxford: Oxford University Press, 2021: 241–272.

Métivier, Sophie. "Les Maurozômai, Byzance et le sultanat de Rūm. Note sur le sceau de Jean Comnène Maurozômès." *REB* 67 (2009): 197–207.

Mullet, Margaret. "Aristocracy and Patronage in the Literary Circles of Comnenian Constantinople." In Angold M. ed. *The Byzantine Aristocracy, IX–XIII Centuries*. Oxford: Oxford University Press, 1984: 173–201

Mullett, Margaret. "Byzantium: A Friendly Society?" *Past and Present* 118 (1988): 3–24.

Mullett, Margaret. *Theophylact of Ochrid: Reading the Letters of a Byzantine Archbishop*. New York: Variorum, 2016; first published in 1997.

Mullett, Margaret. "Novelisation in Byzantium: Narrative After the Revival of Fiction." In Burke J. et al. eds. *Byzantine Narrative: Papers in Honour of Roger Scott*. Melbourne: Australian Association for Byzantine Studies, 2006: 1–28.

Neville, Leonora. *Authority in Byzantine Provincial Society, 950-1100*. Cambridge, UK and New York et al: Cambridge University Press, 2004.

Neville, Leonora. *Heroes and Romans in the Twelfth-Century Byzantium: The Material for History of Nikephoros Bryennios*. Cambridge, UK and New York et al: Cambridge University Press, 2012.

Neville, Leonora. *Guide to Byzantine Historical Writing*. Cambridge, UK and New York: Cambridge University Press, 2018.

Nicol, Donald. *The Reluctant Emperor: A Biography of John Cantacuzene, Byzantine Emperor and Monk, c.1295-1383*. Cambridge, UK and New York: Cambridge University Press, 1996.

Nicolaou-Konnari, Angel, and Schabel, Chris. *Cyprus: Society and Culture 1191–1374*. Leiden and New York: Brill, 2005.

Niewöhner, Philipp. "The Late Antique Origins of Byzantine Palace Architecture." In Featherstone, M. et al. eds. *The Emperor's House: Palaces from Augustus to the Age of Absolutism*. Berlin: De Gruyter, 2015: 31-52.

Niewöhner, Philipp. "Houses." In Niewöhner, Ph. ed. *The Archaeology of Byzantine Anatolia: From the End of Late Antiquity Until the Coming of the Turks*. Oxford: Oxford University Press, 2017.

Oikonomides, Nicolas. "The 'Peira' of Eustathios Rhomaios: An Abortive Attempt to Innovate in Byzantine Law." *FM* 7 (1986): 169–192.

Papadia-Lala, Anastasia. "Society, Administration and Identities in Latin Greece." In Tsougarakis, N.I.

Papadoyannakis, Yannis. "Instruction by Questions and Answer: The Case of Late Antique and Byzantine *Erotapokriseis*." In Johnson, S.D. ed. *Greek Literature in Late Antiquity*. Routledge, 2015: 91–105.

Papadoyannakis, Yannis. "Instruction by Questions and Answer: The Case of Late Antique and Byzantine *Erotapokriseis*." In Johnson, S.F. ed. *Greek Literature in Late Antiquity*. Routledge, 2015: 91–105.

Papaioannou, Stratis. "Encomium for the Monk Ioannes Kroustoulas Who Read Aloud at the Holy Soros." In Papaioannou S. and Barber C. eds. *Michael Psellos on Literature and Art: A Byzantine Perspective on Aesthetics*. Notre Dame, IN: University of Notre Dame Press, 2017: 218–244.

Papaioannou, Stratis. "The Aesthetics of Historiography: Theophanes to Eustathios." In Macrides, R.J. ed. *History as Literature in Byzantium: Papers from the Fortieth Spring Symposium of Byzantine Studies, University of Birmingham, April 2007*. Surrey: Ashgate, 2010: 3–24.

Papaioannou, Stratis. *Michael Psellos: Rhetoric and Authorship in Byzantium*. Cambridge, UK: Cambridge University Press, 2013.

Papaioannou, Stratis. "Readers and Their Pleasures." In Papaioannou, S. ed. *The Oxford Handbook of Byzantine Literature*. Oxford: Oxford University Press, 2021: 525–556.

Papazotos, Theodoros. "The Identification of the Church of 'Profitis Elias' in Thessaloniki." *DOP* 45 (1991): 121–129.

Peacock, A.C.S. *The Great Seljuk Empire*. Edinburgh: Edinburgh University Press, 2015.

Pizzone, Aglae. "Towards a Byzantine Theory of the Comic?" In Alexiou, M. and Cairns, D. eds. *Greek Laughter and Tears: Antiquity and After*. Edinburgh: Edinburgh University Press, 2017: 146–165.

Polemis, Demetios I. *The Doukai: A Contribution to Byzantine Prosopography*. London: Athlone Press, 1968.

Popović, Milan S. "Zur Topographie des spatbyzantinischen Melnik." *JÖB* 58 (2008): 107–119.

Popović, Milan S. "Die Sieldungstruktur der Region Melnik in Spatbyzantinischer und Osmanischen Zeit." *ZRVI* 50 (2010): 247–276.

Puech, Vicent. *L' aristocratie et le pouvoir à Byzance au XIIIe siècle (1204–1310).* I–II. Université de Versailles-Saint-Quentin-en-Yvelines, 2000 (PhD Thesis).

Puech, Vicent. "The Aristocracy and the Empire of Nicaea." in Herrin, J. and Saint-Guillain, G. eds. *Identities and Allegiances in the Eastern Mediterranean After 1204.* Farnham: Ashgate, 2011: 69–79.

Radić, Radivoj. "Georgije Akropolit i Srbi." In Živković, T.Z. ed. *Kralj Vladislav i Srbija XIII veka.* Beograd: SANU, 2003: 89–97.

Raffensperger, Christian. *Reimagining Europe: Kievan Rus' in the Medieval World, 988-1146.* Cambridge, MA and London: Harvard University Press, 2012.

Ransohoff, Jake. "'Consider the Future as Present': The Paranoid World of Kekaumenos." *Speculum* 93 (2018): 77–91

Redford, Scott. "Mavrozomês in Konya." In Ödekan, A., Akyürek, E. and Necipoğlu, N., eds. *1. Uluslararası Sevgi Gönül Bizans Araştırmaları Sempozyumu Bildiriler, İstanbul, 25-26 Haziran 2007=First International Byzantine studies symposium proceedings, Istanbul 25-26 June, 2007.* Istanbul: Vehbi Koc Vakfi, 2010: 48–50.

Redford, Scott. "The Alâeddin Mosque in Konya Reconsidered." *Artibus Asiae* 51 (1991): 54–74.

Rhody, Andreas. "Interactive Inscriptions: Byzantine Works of Art and Their Beholders." In Lidov, A.M. ed. *Spatial Icons. Performativity in Byzantium and Medieval Russia.* Moskau: Indrik, 2011: 317–333.

Rhody, Andreas. "Tower Established by God, God Is Protecting You: Inscriptions on Byzantine Fortifications—Their Function and Their Display." In Stavrakos, C. ed. *Inscriptions in the Byzantine and Post-Byzantine History and History of Art.* Wiesbaden: Harrassowitz Verlag, 2016: 341–370.

Rhoby, Andreas. "Text as Art? Byzantine Inscriptions and Their Display." In Berti, I., Bolle, K., Opdenhoff, F. and Stroth, F. eds. *Writing Matters Presenting and Perceiving Monumental Inscriptions in Antiquity and the Middle Ages.* Berlin and Boston: De Gruyter, 2017: 265–284.

Rhoby, Andreas. "Poetry on Commission in Late Byzantium (13th–15th Century)." In Hörandner, W., Rhoby, A. and Zagklas, N. eds. *A Companion to Byzantine Poetry.* Leiden: Brill, 2019: 264–304.

Richard, Jean. "Aspects du notariat public à Chypre sous les Lusignan." In Beihammer, A.D., Parani, M.G. and Schabel, C.J. eds. *Diplomatics in the Eastern Mediterranean 1000–1500: Aspects of Cross-Cultural Communication.* Leiden and New York: Brill, 2008: 207–221.

Riehle, Alexander. "Rhetorical Practice." In Papaioannou, S. ed. *The Oxford Handbook of Byzantine Literature.* Oxford: Oxford University Press, 2021: 294–315.

Roilos, Panagiotis. "Ancient Greek Rhetorical Theory and Byzantine Discursive Politics: John Sikeliotes on Hermogenes." In Shawcross, T. and Toth, I. eds. *Reading in the Byzantine Empire and Beyond*. Cambridge: Cambridge University Press, 2018: 159–184.
Rowen, Ian. "Inside Taiwan's Sunflower Movement: Twenty-Four Days in the Student Occupied Parliament, and the Future of the Region." *The Journal of Asian Studies* 74 (2015): 5–21.
Schimmel, Annemarie. *A Two-Colored Brocade: The Imagery of Persian Poetry*. Chapel Hill and London: The University of North Carolina Press, 2004.
Ševčenko, Ihor. "On the Preface to a Praktikon by Alyates." *JÖB* 17 (1968): 65–72
Shawcross, T. *The Chronicle of Morea: Historiography in Crusader Greece*. Oxford: Oxford University Press, 2008.
Shawcross, Teresa. "In the Name of the True Emperor: Politics of Resistance After the Palaiologan Usurpation." *Byzantinoslavica* 66 (2008): 203–227.
Shukurov, Rustam. "Christian Elements in the Identity of the Anatolia Turkmens (12th-13th Centuries)." In *Cristianità d'Occidente e Cristianità d'Oriente (secoli VI–XI): 24–30 aprile 2003*. Spoleto: Fondazione Centro italiano di studi sull'alto medioevo, 2004: 707–764.
Shukurov, Rustam. "Harem Christianity: The Byzantine Identity of Seljuk Princes." In Peacock, A.C.S. and Yıldız, S.N. eds. *The Seljuks of Anatolia: Court and Society in the Medieval Middle East*. London and New York: Routledge, 2013: 115–150.
Shukurov, Rustam. *The Byzantine Turks*. Leiden and New York: Brill, 2016.
Simpson, Alicia. *Niketas Choniates: A Historiographical Study*. Oxford: Oxford University Press, 2013.
Sode, Claudia. "The Formulation of Byzantine Urban Identity on Byzantine Seals." In Bedos-Rezak, B. ed. *Seals—Making and Marking Connections Across the Medieval World (The Medieval Globe)*. Leeds: Arc Humanities Press, 2019: 150–165.
Sönmez, Zeki. *Başlangıcından 16. Yüzyıla Kadar Anadolu-Türk İslam Mimarisinde Sanatçılar*. Ankara: Türk Tarih Kurumu Basımevi, 1995.
Speck, Paul. *Die Kaiserliche Universität von Konstantinopel*. München: Verlag der Bayerischen Akademie der Wissenschaften, 1974.
Stanković, Vlada. *Komnini u Carigradu (1057-1185) evolucija jedne vladarske porodice*. Beograd: Vizantološki institut SANU, 2006.
Steiris, Georgios. "Byzantine Philosophers of the 15th Century on Identity and Otherness." In Steiris, G., Mitralexis, S. and Arabatzis, G. eds. *The Problem of Modern Greek Identity: From the Ecumene to the Nation-State*. Newcastle upon Tyne: Cambridge Scholars Publishing, 2016: 173–199.

Stephenson, Paul. *Byzantium's Balkan Frontier: A Political Study of the Northern Balkans, 900-1204*. Cambridge and New York: Cambridge University Press, 2000.
Svoronos, Nicolas G. "Le serment de fidélité à l'Empereur Byzantin et sa signification constitutionnelle." *REB* 9 (1951): 106–142.
Talbot, Mary-Alice. "Empress Theodora Palaiogina, Wife of Michael VIII." *DOP* 46 (1992): 295–303.
Talbot, Mary-Alice. "The Restoration of Constantinople under Michael VIII." *DOP* 47 (1993): 243–261.
Tannous, Jack. *The Making of the Medieval Middle East: Religion, Society, and Simple Believers*. Princeton and Oxford: Princeton University Press, 2018.
Tekinalp, Macit V. "Palace Churches of the Anatolian Seljuks: Tolerance or Necessity?." *BMGS* 33 (2009): 148–167.
Tezcan, Baki. *The Second Ottoman Empire: Political and Social Transformation in the Early Modern World*. Cambridge and New York et al: Cambridge University Press, 2010.
Tinnefeld, Franz. "Intellectuals in Late Byzantine Thessalonike." *DOP* 57 (2003): 153–172.
Tougher, Shaun. *The Reign of Leo VI (886-912): Politics and People*. Leiden and New York: Brill, 1997.
Trapp, Erich, ed. *Prosopographisches Lexikon der Palaiologenzeit*. Wien: Verlag der Österreichischen Akademie der Wissenschaften, 1976.
Tsakmakis, Antonis. "Von der Rhetorik zur Geschichtsschreibung: Das 'Methodenkapitel' des Thukydides (1,22,1-3)." *Rheinisches Museum für Philologie* 141 (1998): 239–255.
Turan, Orhan, ed. *Müsâmeret ül-ahbâr. Moğollar zamanında Türkiye Selçukluları Tarihi*. Ankara: Türk Tarih Kurumu, 1944.
Turan, Orhan. "Les souverains seldjoukides et leurs sujets non-musulmans." *Studia Islamica* 1 (1953): 65–100.
Turner, Sam and Crow, Jim. "Unlocking Historic Landscapes in the Eastern Mediterranean: Two Pilot Studies Using Historic Landscape Characterisation." *Antiquity* 84 (2010): 216–229.
Uyar, Tolga B. "Thirteenth-Century 'Byzantine' Art in Cappadocia and the Question of Greek Painters at the Seljuq Court." In Peacock, A.S.C., de Nicola, B. and Yıldız, S.N. eds. *Islam and Christianity in Medieval Anatolia*. New York: Routledge 2016: 215–232.
Van Tricht, Filip. *The Latin Renovatio of Byzantium: The Empire of Constantinople (1204–1228)*, P. Longbottom, transl. Leiden and New York: Brill, 2011.
Vilimonović, Larisa. *Structure and Features of Anna Komnene's Alexiad: Emergence of a Personal History*. Amsterdam: Amsterdam University Press, 2018.

Vryonis, Speros Jr. *The Decline of Medieval Hellenism in Asia Minor*. Los Angeles: University of California Press, 1971.

Walter, Christopher. "Raising on a Shield in Byzantine Iconography." *REB* 33 (1975): 133–176.

Weiss, Günter. *Oströmische Beamte im Spiegel der Schriften des Michael Psellos*. München: Verlag der Bayerischen Akademie der Wissenschaften, 1973.

Whalin, Douglas. *Roman Identity from Arab Conquests to the Rise of Orthodoxy*. Cham: Palgrave Macmillan, 2021.

Wheeldon, M.J. "'True Stories': The Reception of Historiography in Antiquity." In Cameron, A. ed. *History as Text: The Writing of Ancient History*. Chapel Hill: University of North Carolina Press, 1989: 33–63.

Whickham, Chris. *Framing the Early Middle Ages: Europe and the Mediterranean, 400-800*. Oxford and New York: Oxford University Press, 2005.

Wilson, Nigel G. *Byzantine Books and Bookmen*. Dumbarton Oaks: Centre for Byzantine Studies, 1975.

Wittek, Paul. "Encore l'épitaphe d'un Comnène Konia." *Byzantion* 12 (1937): 207–211.

Wittek, Paul. "L'épitaphe d'un Comnène Konia." *Byzantion* 10 (1935): 505–515.

Woodman, John. *Rhetoric in Classical Historiography*. London: Croom Helm, 1988.

Yıldız, Sara Nur and Şahin, Haşim. "In the Proximity of Sultans: Majd al-Din Majd aI-Din Isqaq, Ibn 'Arabi and the Seljuk Court." In Peacock, A.C.S. and Yıldız, S.N. eds. *The Seljuks of Anatolia: Court and Society in the Medieval Middle East*. London and New York: Routledge, 2013: 173–205.

Yıldız, Sara Nur. "Manouel Komnenos Mavrozomes and His Descendants at the Seljuk Court: the Formation of a Christian Seljuk-Komnenian Elite." In Leder, S. ed. *Crossroads Between Latin Europe and the Near East: Corollaries of the Frankish Presence in the Eastern Mediterranean (12th–14th Centuries)*. Würzburg: Ergon Verlag, 2011: 55–77.

Zagklas, Nikolaos. "'How Many Verses Shall I Write and Say?': Poetry in the Komnenian Period (1081–1204)." In Hörandner, W., Rhoby, A. and Zagklas, N. eds. *A Companion to Byzantine Poetry*. Leiden: Brill, 2019: 237–263.

Zavagno, Luca. *The Byzantine City from Heraclius to the Fourth Crusade, 610-1204: Urban Life After Antiquity*. Cham: Palgrave Macmillan, 2021.

Άμαντος, Κωνστανίνος. "Σύμμεικτα: Πόθεν το όνομα Ταρχανειώτης." *Ελληνικά* 2 (1929): 435-436.

Βάρζος, Κωνστανίνος. *Ἡ Γενεαλογία τῶν Κομνηνῶν* Ι. Θεσσαλονίκη: Κέντρον Βυζαντινῶν Ἐρευνῶν, 1984.

Γκουτζιουκώστας, Ανδρέας. *Η απονομή δικαιοσύνης στο Βυζάντιο (9ος-12ος αιώνες): τα δικαιοδοτικά όργανα και τα δικαστήρια της πρωτεύουσας*.

Αριστοτέλειο Πανεπιστήμιο Θεσσαλονίκης: Σχολή Φιλοσοφική, 2004 (PhD Thesis).

Κιουσοπούλου, Τόνια "Το *βουλευτήριον* της Θεσσαλονίκης," Α. Κοντογιαννοπούλου (επιστημονική επιμέλεια). *Πόλεις και εξουσία στο Βυζάντιο κατά την εποχή των Παλαιολόγων (1261-1453)*. Αθήνα: Ακαδημία Αθηνών, 2018: 109-120.

Κολυβού, Φωτεινή. Μιχαήλ Χωνιάτης. *Συμβουλή στη μελετή του βίου και του έργου του το Corpus των Επιστολών*. Αθήνα: Ακαδημία Αθηνών, 1999.

Κοντογιαννοπούλου, Αναστασία. "Μεταξύ Κωνσταντινούπολης και Θεσσαλονίκης: Διοικητική και κοινωνική οργάνωση στις Σέρρες (1261-1383)." Α. Κοντογιαννοπούλου (επιστημονική επιμέλεια). *Πόλεις και εξουσία στο Βυζάντιο κατά την εποχή των Παλαιολόγων (1261-1453)*. Αθήνα: Ακαδημία Αθηνών, 2018: 121-160.

Κοντογιαννοπούλου, Αναστασία. *Τοπικά συμβούλια στις βυζαντινές πόλεις: Παράδοση και εξέλιξη (13ος-15ος αι.)*. Αθήνα: Ακαδημία Αθηνών, 2015.

Λάμπρος, Σπυρίδωνος. "Ἡ Ἑλληνική ὡς ἐπίσημος γλῶσσα τῶν Σουλτανῶν." *Νέος Ἑλληνομνήμων* 5 (1908): 40-78.

Μέκιος, Κωνσταντίνος Μ. *Ὁ μέγας δομέστικος τοῦ Βυζαντίου, Ἰωάννης Ἀξούχος καὶ πρωτοστράτωρ ὁ υἱὸς τοῦ Ἀλέξιος*. Ἀθῆναι: Ἀκαδημία Ἀθηνῶν, 1932.

Μέντζου-Μεϊμάρη, Κωνσταντίνα. "Χρονολογημέναι βυζαντιναί επιγραφαί του *Corpus Inscriptionum Graecarum* IV, 2." *Δελτίον Χριστιανικής Αρχαιολογικής Εταιρείας* 9 (1979): 77-132.

Жаворонков, Петр Иванович. "Состав и эволюция высшей знати Никейской империи: элита." Москва: ВО, 1991: 83-90.

Index

A

Akapniou, monastery in Thessaloniki, 188
Akropolites, Georgios, viii, xi, 8, 10, 18, 22–24, 28, 31–33, 43, 51, 53, 56–58, 63, 65, 66, 69, 72, 76, 77, 85–88, 91–109, 113–124, 126–128, 130, 131, 142, 143, 146, 147, 150, 152, 153, 160, 161, 163–165, 174, 175, 179, 181, 182, 184–187, 192–195, 200–202, 205, 207, 209, 211, 216, 217, 219, 221, 229
Aksaray, 130, 174, 176
Alexios I, Doukai, 38
Alexios I Komnenos, vii, 6, 35, 38, 40, 89, 92, 100, 111, 112, 121, 134, 135, 140–142, 175
Alexios III, 40
Alexios III Angelos, 110, 142–144
Andronikos I Komnenos, 112
Ankyra, 154–157, 159, 161, 163, 165, 166, 178
Antioch on Menander, 129
Aphthonios, xi, 54, 57
apographe, 59, 61
Apokaukos, Ioannes, 102, 103
Aqsarayi, 175
archontopouloi, 35
Aristotle, 22
Arsenios Autoreianos, xi, 180, 181, 207, 214, 219, 220
Asia Minor, 5, 9–11, 17, 27, 37, 64, 91, 108, 111, 123, 126, 131–141, 143, 147, 152, 154, 155, 159, 160, 165, 170, 176, 178, 185, 187, 191, 193, 194, 202, 212, 214, 219
Assizes of Romania, 148
Attaleia, 129, 130, 166
Attaleiates, Michael, 4, 15, 25, 89, 95, 96, 160
Augustus, Octavian, xi, 6–8, 49, 154–157, 159, 161, 162

© The Editor(s) (if applicable) and The Author(s), under exclusive license to Springer Nature Switzerland AG 2022
A. Jovanović, *Michael Palaiologos and the Publics of the Byzantine Empire in Exile, c.1223–1259*, New Approaches to Byzantine History and Culture, https://doi.org/10.1007/978-3-031-09278-7

INDEX

B
Babouskomites, Georgios, 45
Balkans, 5, 9–11, 18, 33, 64, 72, 84, 91, 94, 108, 114, 117, 121, 122, 127, 137, 142, 145, 146, 148, 154, 184, 185, 187, 212–214
Bar Hebraeus, 130
Basilakes, Nikephoros, 53
Bayju, 173, 175
Bekkos, Ioannes, 41, 45
Bithynia, 17, 34, 108, 109, 126, 127, 134, 135, 137, 149, 153, 154, 173, 175, 180, 184
Blemmydes, Nikephoros, xi, 8, 41–44, 53, 58, 70, 76, 115–117, 119, 122, 127, 128, 138, 161, 189, 207
Bulgaria, 9, 28, 72, 91–94, 109, 145, 201

C
Chadenos, Konstantinos, 188, 191
Chomatenos, Demetrios, 102–104
Choniates, Michael, 34
Christopher of Mytilene, 169, 170
Chronicle of Morea, 9, 137, 148–150, 167, 168
Constantinople, viii, 3–6, 9, 10, 17–19, 21, 23, 24, 26, 31, 34, 37, 47, 49, 57, 74, 91, 102, 111, 114, 126, 134, 136, 141, 144–147, 149, 150, 153, 158, 159, 161, 182, 192, 220, 221
Crusaders, 135
Cyprus, Kingdom of, 5, 32, 129, 145–150, 172

D
Demetrios Angelos, *despotes*, 66
Digenis Akritas, 8
Diocletian, 154

Disypatos, Manouel, 189–191, 228
Doukaina, Anna, wife of *sebastos* Georgios Palaiologos, 39, 82
Dyrrachion, vii, 184–190, 228

E
Eirene Doukaina Laskarina, daughter of Theodoros I Laskaris, 76, 77
Eirene Doukaina, wife of Alexios I Komnenos, 39
Ekloga Basilikon, 96
Empire of Nikaia, 5, 8–10, 150, 151
enkyklios paideia, 41
Epeiros, Despotate of, 5, 91, 94, 102, 122, 127, 147, 149, 186, 188
Ephesos, 8
exisosis, 59, 61, 74

F
Fourth Crusade, 4, 5, 8, 145
Franks, viii, 5–7, 9, 74, 75, 105, 108, 137, 142, 145–150, 153–155, 157, 168, 172, 184, 201, 205, 221
Frederick II of Hohenstaufen, 7

G
Gabalas, Leon, 63
Galerius, 154
Genoa, 148, 221
Germanos II, 41
Gregoras, Nikephoros, 8, 200
Guy de Lusignan, 145

H
Hermogenes, 197
Hexapterygos, Theodoros, 53
Holobolos, Manouel, 82, 83, 161
Homer, 78, 79, 81, 89, 123

INDEX 253

I
Iakobos, archbishop of Bulgaria, 28, 72–76, 78–84, 109, 115–117, 188, 227–229
Ibn Bibi, 130, 143
Ignatios the Deacon, 77
Ikonion, 29, 128, 130, 131, 135–137, 139, 140, 142, 143, 152–155, 159, 163, 164, 166–173, 175–177, 183, 219, 227
Iliad, 78
Ioannes II Komnenos, 4, 140–142, 202
Ioannes III Batatzes, 7, 10, 24, 27, 31–33, 35, 40, 53, 55, 58, 59, 69, 72, 75–78, 80, 86–92, 94–101, 105–110, 112, 114–121, 124, 127, 146, 150, 185, 187, 191, 194, 197, 204, 210, 215, 217, 221, 228
Ioannes IV Laskaris, 11, 18, 56, 181, 192–194, 199, 200, 204–207, 209, 210, 212–216, 218–222
Ioannes VI Kantakouzenos, 16
Isaakios I Komnenos, 36
Izzeddin Kaykaus II, 154

K
Kaballarios, Basileios, 124, 179, 180
Kaliman, 64
Kallikles, Nikolaos, 82
Kampanos, Nikolaos, 65–67, 69
Kastamon, 130, 153, 174, 175
Kaykaus I, 129
Kaykhusraw I, 129, 142, 143, 172
Kayqubad I, 143
Kilic Arslan I, 135
Kilic Arslan II, 141, 155
Konstantinos X Doukas, 36
Köse Dağ, 139, 151, 173
Kostomyres, Nikolaos, 45
Kotys, 127, 151

L
Laskaris, Manouel, 122, 211
Laskaris, Michael, 186, 211
Libanios, 53

M
Macedonia, 94, 106, 173, 186
Magnesia, 28, 42, 109, 182, 192, 193, 195, 198–200, 202, 206, 207, 210, 216–219, 222, 227, 230
Makrenos, Ioannes, 120
Makrotos, Ioannes, 105
Malikshah, 133–136
Manglavites, Nikolaos, 28, 88, 91, 92, 97, 98, 100, 185, 187, 225, 227, 229
Manouel I Komnenos, 34, 57, 74, 77, 141, 143
Manouel II, 107, 116
Manzikert, back of, 38
Manzikert, battle of, 133, 134, 139
Marmara, Sea of, 60
Masud I, 135, 136, 141
Mavrozomes, Ioannes, 144, 173
Mavrozomes, Manouel, 142, 143, 173
Mavrozomes, Michael, 144
Mehmed I of Karaman, 176
Melenikon, 27, 64, 76, 88, 90–95, 97, 98, 114, 120, 126, 188, 207, 221, 226, 227
Melissenos, Nikephoros, 134
Michael VII Doukas, 36, 38, 134
Michael (VIII) Palaiologos, v, vii, 3, 4, 8, 11, 16–30, 32, 33, 35, 40, 52, 59, 72, 78, 81–83, 85–90, 92–94, 97–101, 104, 105, 107, 108, 110, 113, 115, 116, 119, 120, 122, 124, 127, 129–132, 141, 144, 151, 153, 156, 157, 159, 161–164, 166, 172, 173,

175–177, 179–183, 185,
188–191, 194, 195, 197, 201,
205–207, 210, 213, 216–223,
225–230
Mongols, 51, 139, 151, 152,
173–175
Mouzalon, Georgios, 123, 125, 185,
192–195, 198, 207, 208

N
Nestongos, Andronikos, 95, 96, 110,
117, 118
Nikaia, 10, 28, 31, 33, 42, 46, 94,
109, 134, 135, 151, 153, 154,
180, 182, 183, 186, 195, 206,
218, 219, 227, 230
Nikephoros III Botaneiates, 25, 36,
38, 95, 134
Normans, 37, 144
Nymphaion, imperial palace at, 18,
33, 41, 42, 49, 83, 109, 188

O
Ogier Ghiselin de Busbecq, 155, 156

P
Pachymeres, Georgios, viii, xii, 23, 24,
32, 62, 86, 87, 89, 93, 94, 104,
106–108, 112, 113, 120, 121,
123–127, 130, 131, 153, 163,
175, 179–202, 204–209, 211,
212, 214–217, 219, 220, 229
paidopouloi, 123, 179, 201, 203
Palaiologina, Eirene, sister of Michael
VIII, 40
Palaiologina, Maria, sister of Michael
VIII, 40, 48, 119, 124, 179, 187
Palaiologina, Theodora, wife of *megas
domestikos* Andronikos
Palaiologos, 40

Palaiologos, Alexios *(despotes)*, 39
Palaiologos, Andronikos *(despotes)*, 39
Palaiologos, Andronikos *(megas
domestikos)*, 27, 40, 59, 62, 72,
75, 77, 80, 83, 89, 93, 94, 113,
115, 118, 119, 121, 184, 221,
226, 227
Palaiologos, Georgios *(sebastos* under
Alexios I Komnenos), 38, 39, 82,
111
Palaiologos, Georgios *(megas
hetaireiarches)*, 39
Palaiologos, Ioannes, brother of
Michael VIII, 211
Palaiologos, Konstantinos,
half-brother of Michael VIII, 179
Palaiologos, Nikephoros, 36–38
Palaiologs, Ioannes, brother of
Michael VIII, 40
Pantokrator, monastery in
Constantinople, 4
Partitio Romaniae, 145
Pergamon, 160, 161, 163
Philadelphia, 2, 42, 52, 101, 133, 219
Philes, Theodoros, 72, 121, 194, 195
philia, 112–114, 117
Phokas, metropolitan of Philadelphia,
101–104
Phrangopoulos, Andronikos, 46
Phrygia, 36
Prilep, 122, 127, 186, 187, 194
Principality of Achaea, 5, 145, 149
progymnasmata, xi, 52, 57, 73
pronoia, 60, 62, 208, 215, 217, 227,
228
Psellos, Michael, 33, 34, 53, 83
Ptochoprodromos, 169, 171

R
Res Gestae Divi Augusti, xii, 156, 159
Rhaoul, Alexios, 121, 122, 125
Rhaoul, Ioannes, 211

Rhodos, 63, 74, 179
Romanos IV Diogenes, 36, 37
Rumi, Jalal ad-Din Muhammad, 131, 166–170

S
Saljuq Sultanate of Rum, 5, 9, 29, 130–135, 139, 140, 144–151, 155, 159, 163, 173, 176–178, 182, 183, 203, 205, 207, 221, 227
Sangarios, river, 130, 153, 172, 176
Sarantopoulos, Alexios, 211
Senachereim, Michael, 46
Serres, 27, 69, 76, 90, 114, 120, 126, 185, 187, 188, 207, 221, 227
Skamander, 74
Smyrne, 42, 68, 121, 136
Sosandra, monastery around Magnesia, 200, 201, 204, 205, 228
St Demetrios, monastery in Constantinople, 23, 25, 26, 86, 114, 161
Strategopoulos, Alexios, 120, 121, 194, 195
Sulayman ibn Qutlumush, viii, 134, 135
Sultan Walad, 131, 166–170
Sunflower Movement, 1, 2
Synopsis Chronike, xii, 22, 45, 51, 61, 191, 194, 214, 215, 218
Syrgares, *kavalliarios*, 71

T
Taiwan, 1, 2, 4
Tarchaneiotes, Nikephoros, 118, 119, 179, 187
Tavtash, 174, 175
theatron, 23–25, 78
Theodora Palaiologina, wife of Michael VIII Palaiologos, 108, 220
Theodoros I Laskaris, 5, 10, 34, 40, 59, 90, 95, 110, 119, 142, 143, 194, 218
Theodoros II Doukas Laskaris, vii, 8, 24, 29, 32, 46, 47, 51, 70, 90, 99, 104, 112, 114–116, 120–128, 151, 153, 160, 161, 163, 175, 179–185, 187, 188, 191–197, 199–204, 207, 209, 210, 214, 217, 219, 221, 228
Theophilopoulos, Michael, 45
Thessaloniki, viii, 26–28, 34, 61, 65–67, 72–76, 78, 79, 81, 82, 84, 89, 90, 96, 106, 108, 114–116, 119, 122, 184, 186, 188–191, 203, 227–230
Turkmens, 133, 134, 136, 140, 152, 153, 159, 164, 172, 176, 219
Turks, 5, 9, 10, 37, 56, 60, 85, 86, 90, 91, 111, 119, 128–130, 132, 133, 135–142, 151–154, 164, 166, 173–176, 179, 184, 203
Tzetzes, Ioannes, 170, 171
Tzouroulos, 118
Tzyrithon, 66

V
Venice, xii, 145, 148, 150

Z
Zagarommates, Georgios, 121

Printed in the United States
by Baker & Taylor Publisher Services